For Gill and Cathy

KU-164-448

CONTENTS

PREFACE

Algorithms are central to computing; they are at the heart of all programs. Without them planes would not fly, bridges would collapse and nuclear power stations would explode. Even in less safety-critical systems where such dramatic events cannot occur, the correct choice of algorithm can make the difference between a response to a query coming, on the one hand, almost instantly and, on the other, long after any machine capable of doing the work has turned to dust.

For anyone intending to work in computing, it is essential to be able both to understand and to create algorithms. This book aims to give you exactly those skills—hence the title. The study of algorithms is fun, their discovery even more so. We hope to communicate the thrill of this exploration in these pages.

This book is aimed at people new to the subject. It has been written with students on the first and second years of computing courses especially in mind, and has been designed as an introductory textbook for modules concerned with algorithms and their design.

The content falls into two parts. Chapters 1 to 6 deal with the foundations of the subject. These chapters are concerned with demonstrating the algorithmic method in an elementary way for those who have no experience of such an approach: we mean by this, a systematic approach to problem formulation, problem solution, and subsequent program design. The understanding of some standard, fundamental algorithms, such as sorting methods, is also introduced here. As we teach the subject, this work forms the content of one first year module, forming 1/12 of that year's curriculum. In more detail, Chapter 1 sets the scene by describing a method of going from problem to solution and illustrating this with some simple examples. Chapter 2 deals with some elementary mathematics: this is not advanced, but it is important, so readers should ensure that they fully understand this material before progressing. Chapter 3 describes some classic sorting algorithms. These are included in their own right, because they are part of computing general knowledge, but also in order to get readers to start to think in terms of how there can be many different approaches to solving a problem and how these can affect the efficiency of the solution, the speed of the program. Chapter 4 deals with patterns and how their detection can be put to good use in writing programs. Chapter 5 is more technical and deals with the issue of algorithm complexity, a description of what happens to the time it takes to solve a problem as its size increases—a topic essential to an understanding of the subject. Chapter 6 deals with data structures and shows how the correct choice of data structure is crucial for designing efficient programs.

Chapters 7 to 12 deal with more advanced topics. They concentrate on techniques for writing algorithms. For us, this work forms the content of one second year module, forming 1/12 of that year's curriculum. In more detail, Chapter 7 deals with the issue of program correctness. This is important not just from the point of view of formality, but also because it is intimately related to how algorithms are designed. The remaining chapters form a toolbox of algorithm design techniques. Chapter 8 illustrates brute strength approaches to solving problems—these might not be elegant approaches, but they work (assuming we have time—sometimes more than the expected lifetime of the universe). The remaining chapters show approaches with increasingly more finesse. Chapter 9 illustrates the divide and conquer approach, Chapter 10 describes greedy algorithms and Chapters 11 and 12 give examples of the very powerful method of dynamic programming.

Although our book progresses as described above, it is not essential to sit down and read it from start to finish—indeed, we assume that few readers will do that. Many of the chapters, or even sections within chapters, are largely self-contained, so that readers who have the appropriate background knowledge may 'dip in'. However, because later parts of the book do assume such background knowledge, it is possible to 'signpost', to some extent, possible pathways through the text. The elementary mathematics of Chapter 2 are used again in Chapter 4, and the simple treatment of recurrence relations in Chapters 2 and 4 is addressed more rigorously in later chapters, particularly Chapter 9. The idea of correctness and the limitations of software testing are specifically identified in Chapters 1 and 4, and more formally treated in Chapter 7. Chapter 12, on multi-dimensional dynamic programming, most naturally follows from Chapter 11, though either stands alone for a suitably informed reader. Finally, the work in Chapter 5, on algorithm complexity, is crucial to the whole subject, and in that sense underpins all of it. The examples used in that chapter are primarily the sorting algorithms of Chapter 3.

One feature of this book is that the code is presented in both Ada and C. Given that most of the book is language independent, comprising English descriptions and diagrams, it seemed unfortunate to, at best, alienate and, at worst, lose much of our potential readership, by choosing a single language which might be unfamiliar to most. Consequently, we chose two languages. This should keep most people on board; even those preferring Pascal or Modula should be quite at home with Ada.

An unforeseen advantage of this approach is that the book provides a useful help in converting between these languages. This should be especially helpful for students, such as our own, who are taught either Ada or C initially and the other later.

Many of the algorithms described involve the use of arrays. A disadvantage of using Ada and C arises from the different ways that they number the positions in arrays. Although under the control of the programmer, the norm in Ada is to start with 1; with C it is to start with 0. So, if we are dealing with an array holding 5 values in Ada, we would typically number them from 1 to 5, whereas in C it would be 0 to 4. This is shown below:

Ada, typical numbering	1	2	3	4	5
Array, a					

C, typical numbering	0	1	2	3	4
Array, a					

We have dealt with this difference pragmatically. In Chapters 1 to 6, arrays in both cases are normally subscripted from 0 for consistency, even though this may be unnatural for Ada programmers. In the remainder of the book we use what is best for the algorithm. So, as suits the problem at hand, for one algorithm we might have Ada (and C) arrays starting at 0 and, in another, C (and Ada) arrays starting at 1. In the latter case, location 0 is left unused in the C implementation.

We are of the opinion that the only way truly to get to grips with any subject is to do it. Algorithms are no different, skill will come only by working at them. To this end we have given numerous exercises. These should be done! In case there is no tutor available, a full set of solutions is given. For those lecturers keen to set unseen exercises for their students, a set of additional exercises can be obtained from the publishers.

We have many thanks to give. We are indebted to Brian Burrows and Cathy French (both of Staffordshire University) and to the two anonymous referees used by the publishers for their comments about the manuscript. We are sure, though, that these people will accept that our main thanks must go to the 2000 plus students who have over the years worked through this subject with us and have in many ways influenced our views on how best to write about algorithms.

David Brunskill
John Turner
Stafford, UK

1

ALGORITHMS: ROUTE-PLANNERS FOR CREATING CORRECT PROGRAMS

OBJECTIVES

In this chapter you will learn

- that 'problems' are not textbook exercises, but situations taken from the real world in which some change is required
- that certain kinds of problems are 'algorithmic' though not all are
- that an algorithm is just a step-by-step approach to problem solving
- how to state an algorithm formally, and how to translate it into a working program

1.1 Finding the way

If you wanted to drive to a city you had never visited before from your home destination, you would probably use a road atlas. For example, in the UK, to get from Stafford to London (a distance of about 150 miles), you might plan: 'Get on the M6 at Junction 13, drive south, continue on the M5, then go on to the M42 at Junction 4A, then get onto the M40, then...'. You might have access to a software route planner, which will allow you to enter your starting point and destination, and then tell you which is the most direct route. In either case, the end result is a set of instructions, for instance:

1. Start: head for M6.
2. Join M6 at Junction 13, southbound.
3. At Junction 8 of the M6, take the M5 south.
4. Leave M5 at Junction 4A, join M42 eastbound.
5. Continue on M42 east until Junction 3A; join M40.
6. Continue on M40 until Junction 1A, which is Junction 16 of the M25.
7. Take the M25 south to Junction 15, which is Junction 4B of the M4.
8. Turn east on the M4 and continue into central London.
9. Stop.

Assume that the directions are correct. Most people, given such a set of directions, would arrive in London three hours or so after leaving Stafford, assuming the car did not break down. However, some might arrive very late, because they missed a junction, took a wrong turning, or misread a road sign.

Now, if we assume that the directions are accurate, that the driver *always* follows the directions faithfully, that the car keeps going, that there are no traffic holdups, that there are no diversions in operation, and no Acts of God (earthquakes, firestorms, etc.), how often will the driver arrive in London within four hours of leaving Stafford? Think about this for a moment.

The answer is—most of the time. Perhaps on one occasion, road signs are switched by night-time revellers; maybe on another, the driver dies at the wheel. You could think up other outlandish sets of circumstances. However, in theory, the driver will *always* arrive successfully at the destination. Indeed, if, instead of concentrating on real-life issues, we reconsider the original set of instructions, we can say that either they are *always* correct, or else they are incorrect.

EXERCISES 1.1

1. Think of a number. Add 3; multiply by 7; divide by 12. Write down the answer, or save it in your calculator's memory.

   Now take the answer you got above, and multiply it by 3; divide by 7; multiply by 4; subtract 3.

   What answer do you get? Why? Will it happen with any number? Why? Dream up a similar example, using different numbers and operations. Write down the general method for doing this trick as a set of simple instructions.

2. There is a famous sequence of numbers known as the *hailstone sequence*. This is the algorithm:

```
Read an integer value, x;
while x > 1 loop
   if x is even, replace x by x/2;
   else replace x by 3x + 1;
   end if;
   output x;
end loop;
end.
```

   Write down the output for: $x = 13$; $x = 9$; $x = 1$. What happens? Try other numbers. Will the algorithm always give the same final figure and then stop? Can you prove it?

Back to our driver problem: those real-life issues referred to above (traffic holdups, car breakdowns, etc.) are of importance. When we encounter, and deal with, problems in our lives, we make a lot of implicit assumptions and simplifications, and we are capable of very fast and very flexible responses. If we were planning on having beef stir-fry for dinner, and discover, as we reach for the oyster sauce, that there is none left, there are a number of things we might do: use soy sauce in place of the oyster sauce; have beans on toast instead; go out for a meal—such intelligent responsiveness is completely beyond computer systems. Computers must be given a precise set of instructions, and we have to think them out for them, first taking into account all the things that could go wrong, and telling the system what to do in each case. Of course, we cannot cover every possible event, and so sometimes the computer system will not have a set of instructions to follow. For this reason, we restrict the data that is allowed to be entered to a very small set, in order to reduce the number of things that could go wrong. These operations—stating what conditions are assumed, and what simplifications are being made—are the starting point for any algorithmic solution of a problem.

If computers are hopeless at dealing with the fuzziness of everyday life, they are excellent drudges. They never get their sums wrong, and they are happiest when doing hundreds or thousands of boring, similar, repetitive calculations. The only thing they ask of us is to be told exactly what to do, how to present the results, and when to stop doing it. Also, they expect no thanks!

1.2 Shampoo

Now consider a different kind of problem, but one which is also algorithmic in nature. Consumer products are usually available in a number of different size containers, each priced appropriately—it might be shampoo, though the product could equally well be cornflakes, or potatoes, or beer. We might, browsing the shelves, think about which is the 'best buy', purely on price per unit weight or volume.

For instance, perusing the shampoos, we might see prices displayed as shown in Table 1.1.

Table 1.1 Prices of shampoos

Brand	*Cost*	*Quantity*
Lank'n'Dry	£1.95	300 ml
Rotress	£1.30	275 ml
Glamlocks	£2.95	375 ml

Most supermarkets allow comparisons to be made directly, for example by displaying the cost per 100 ml; alternatively, we could make a comparison by use of a calculator, dividing the cost in pence by the quantity, in each case. Either way, we will get (to the nearest penny) the results shown in Table 1.2.

Table 1.2 Comparative cost of shampoos

Brand	*Cost/100ml*
Lank'n'Dry	65p
Rotress	47p
Glamlocks	79p

Real-life considerations affect the choices we make, in practice: the cheapest may be less effective, for instance, or we may simply have got used to a particular brand. However, considering for the moment simply the 'value-for-money' issue, it is clear that Rotress is the best buy.

Now, it may be that special offers are available. Suppose that Glamlocks is on offer on the basis of 'Buy 2 and get the third free'—how does this affect things? We will be paying twice the price, but getting a total quantity equivalent to three bottles, i.e.

$$\frac{2 \times £2.95}{3 \times 375} \equiv 52\,\text{p}/100\,\text{ml}$$

Now, Glamlocks looks like quite a good buy at the offer terms. Still not as cheap as Rotress, but cheaper than Lank'n'Dry.

The central algorithm in all the above deliberations may be stated:

```
1. For all shampoos
        Read product cost and volume
        Divide product cost by volume to get unit cost
        If less than previous unit cost, remember this as 'best_buy'
        Compare next brand
   Until no more products
2. Output 'best_buy'
3. Stop
```

The initial problem statement, however, has a number of deficiencies:

- It does not take into account special offers ('3 for the price of 2').
- The first evaluation will not have a 'previous unit cost' to compare against.
- The arithmetic is actually done on the basis of pence per 100ml.

The first of these deficiencies may be remedied by including a procedure such as the following:

```
If 3 for 2 offer
   Multiply cost by 2: this is new_cost
   Multiply volume by 3: this is new_vol
   Divide new_cost by new_vol to get current 'best_buy'
Endif
```

We also need some marker, or indicator, to show that a particular brand is, in fact, on offer. A simple binary method would be

```
offer_ind:  1  [3 for the price of 2]
            0  [No offer]
```

The second point could be addressed in a number of ways. The most immediately obvious way is to use the first unit value obtained as the current 'best_buy', and then compare the subsequent price against that.

The third point is simply a question of arithmetic conversion as appropriate: the price can be output as pence per ml, or pounds per 100 ml, or however we like. So the algorithm is now:

```
1. Read name, price, volume, offer_ind
2. If offer_ind = 1
      Calculate best_buy at 3 for the price of 2 items
   Else
      best_buy ← price/volume
   Endif
3. While more shampoos to read loop
      Read name, price, volume, offer_ind
      If offer_ind = 1
         Calculate current_price at 3 for the price of 2 terms
      Else
         Current_price ← price/volume
      Endif
      If current_price < best_buy
         best_buy ← current_ price
      Endif
   End loop
4. Print best_buy
```

This now translates almost immediately into a C or an Ada program (Fig.1.1). The Ada and C implementations of this and subsequent algorithms will frequently contain some small differences due to the different ways that the languages handle data types, and in terms of management of input-output facilities, but as far as possible they are parallel representations.

In C:

```
#include <stdio.h>
#include <string.h>
                    /* Shampoo */
void main()
{
  float price, current_price, new_cost, best_buy, vol, new_vol;
  int offer_ind;
  char more, *best_brand;        /* 'best_brand' is a pointer to a */
  char brand_name[25];   /* character string; array 'brand_name' */
       /* will hold the brand name currently under consideration */
  printf("Enter shampoo name:  ");
  scanf("%s", brand_name);
  printf("\nEnter price, and quantity in ml\n");
```

```
  scanf("%f%f", &price, &vol);
  price = price * 100.0;              /* Convert price to pence */
  printf("Enter 1 for a 3 for the price of 2 offer, 0 otherwise.");
  scanf("%d", &offer_ind);
  if (offer_ind)
  {                             /* Recalculate for special offer */
    new_cost = 2.0 * price;
    new_vol = 3.0 * vol;
    best_buy = new_cost / new_vol;  /* Cost per ml */
    strcpy(best_brand, brand_name); /* Save first brand examined */
  }                                 /*  as 'best_brand' */
  else
  {
    best_buy = price / vol;         /* Cost per ml */
    strcpy(best_brand, brand_name); /* Save first brand examined */
  }                                /*  as 'best_brand' */
  printf("\nMore shampoo? Enter y to continue:  ");
  getchar();                       /* Throw away lf from buffer */
  more = getchar();
  while(more == 'y')
  {
    printf("\nEnter shampoo name:  " );
    scanf("%s", brand_name);
    printf("\nEnter price in pounds, and quantity in ml\n");
    scanf("%f%f", &price, &vol);
    price = price * 100.0;            /* Convert price to pence */
    printf("\nEnter '1' to show a 3 for the price of 2");
    printf(" offer, '0' otherwise.\n\n");
    scanf("%d", &offer_ind);
    if (offer_ind)              /* Recalculate for special offer */
    {
      new_cost = 2.0 * price;
      new_vol = 3.0 * vol;
      current_price = new_cost / new_vol;   /* Cost per ml */
    }
    else
    {
      current_price = price / vol;          /* Cost per ml */
    }
    if ( current_price < best_buy ) /* Update 'cheapest so far' */
    {                               /* variables */
      best_buy = current_price;
      strcpy(best_brand, brand_name);
    }
    printf("\nMore shampoo? Enter y to continue:  ");
    getchar();       /* Throw away lf from buffer */
    more = getchar();
  }
  best_buy = best_buy * 100.0;    /* To get cost per 100 ml */
  printf("\nThe best value for money is %s ", best_brand);
  printf("which is %.2f pence per 100ml", best_buy);
}
```

In Ada:

```
with text_io; use text_io;
procedure shampoo is
```

```
package int_io is new text_io.integer_io(integer);
package flt_io is new text_io.float_io(float);
use int_io, flt_io;

price, current_price, new_cost, best_buy, vol, new_vol: float;
offer_ind, str_len: integer;
more: character;
brand_name, best_brand: string(1 .. 25);   -- String array 'best_brand' will hold the
begin                                      -- name of the shampoo currently
    put("Enter shampoo name: ");           -- under consideration
    get_line(brand_name, str_len);
    put("Enter price in pounds, and quantity in ml: ");
    get(price);
    get(vol);
    price := price * 100.0;                -- Convert price to pence
    put("Enter 1 to show a '3 for the price of 2' offer. Enter 0 otherwise.");
    new_line(2);
    get(offer_ind);
    if offer_ind = 1 then                  -- Recalculate for special offer
        new_cost := 2.0 * price;
        new_vol := 3.0 * vol;
        best_buy := new_cost / new_vol;    -- Cost per ml
        best_brand := brand_name;          -- Save first brand examined as
    else                                   -- 'best_brand'
        best_buy := price / vol;           -- Cost per ml
        best_brand := brand_name;          -- Save first brand examined as
    end if;                                -- 'best_brand'
    new_line;
    put_line("More shampoo?  Enter y to continue: ");
    get(more);
    while more = 'y' loop
        put("Enter shampoo name: ");
        get_line(brand_name, str_len);
        put("Enter price, and quantity in ml: ");
        get(price);
        get(vol);
        price := price * 100.0;            -- Convert price to pence
        put("Enter 1 to show a '3 for the price of 2' offer. Enter 0 otherwise.");
        new_line(2);
        get(offer_ind);
        if offer_ind = 1 then              -- Recalculate for special offer
            new_cost := 2.0 * price;
            new_vol := 3.0 * vol;
            current_price:= new_cost / new_vol;        -- Cost per ml
        else
            current_price:= price / vol;               -- Cost per ml
        end if;
        if current_price < best_buy then
            best_buy := current_price;          -- Update 'cheapest so far' variables
            best_brand := brand_name;
        end if;
        new_line;
        put_line("More shampoo? Enter y to continue: ");
```

```
        get(more);
        skip_line;
    end loop;
    best_buy := best_buy * 100.0;            -- To get cost per 100 ml
    put("The best value for money is ");
    put(best_brand(1 .. str_len));
    put(" which is");
    put(best_buy, fore => 3, aft => 2, exp => 0);
    put(" pence per 100 ml");
    new_line;
end shampoo;
```

Figure 1.1 'Best-buy' program

EXERCISES 1.2

1. Modify the above program so that it can handle special offers of other kinds, for example, 'Buy 2 and get the second half-price', or 'Buy 4 and pay for only 3'.

2. What changes to the program would be needed to allow it to deal in the same way with other kinds of goods?

3. Quality of goods is important for most of us. How could a 'quality indicator' be incorporated? For example, the user might enter a value between 1 (worse than useless) and 100 (excellent) along with brand name, price, and quantity. This number could then be used as a weighting factor, and provide output in terms of 'raw' and 'weighted' unit cost.

The solution, as it stands, appears to address the problem as originally stated. It is perhaps an appropriate response to the problem, but it contains implementation details—especially the `printf`/put and `scanf`/get statements—which are specific to a given product. The essence of the solution, however, may be stated, 'Given a number of items, which is the smallest?'. Answering this question allows a *general* solution, which may be modified for any number of different specific instances.

In fact, the task is to find the smallest value in a sequence of numbers (this could represent prices, for example). Perhaps the simplest way to do this is just to read and save the first value, and then to read in the second and compare with the first: if the second is smaller, save this instead as the new minimum. Repeat this process up to the end of the input list. For an example list of eight items whose prices have real values, and which are stored in an array (Fig.1.2):

In C:

```
#include <stdio.h>
#define prices 8
                    /* Minval program */
```

```
float items[prices]= {180.0,7.01,3.6,18.4,17.5,245.99,3.6,130.0};
     /* The list of prices from which the minimum is to be found */

float min_cost;
int i = 0;                /* Position marker for first array value */
void main()
{
  min_cost = items[i];       /* Set value of first item as minimum */
  for (i = 1; i < prices; ++i)
  {
    if (items[i] < min_cost) /* Compare first value with each of */
    {                        /* the rest, in turn, and overwrite */
      min_cost = items[i];   /* 'min_cost' if smaller */
    }
    printf("%d\n", min_cost); /* Output smallest */
  }
}
```

In Ada:

```
with text_io; use text_io;
procedure minima is
package int_io is new text_io.integer_io(integer);
package flt_io is new text_io.float_io(float);
use int_io, flt_io;

prices:constant := 8;
type price_type is array(1 .. prices) of float:
items: price_type := (180.0, 7.01, 3.6, 18.4, 17.5, 245.99, 3.6, 130.0);  -- The list of
min_cost: float;                    -- prices from which the minimum is to be found
i: integer := 1;                    -- Position marker for first array value

begin
  min_cost := items(i);             -- Save value of first item as minimum
  for i in 2 .. prices loop
    if items(i) < min_cost then     -- Compare first value with each of
      min_cost:= items(i);          -- the rest, in turn, and overwrite
    end if;                         -- 'min_cost' if smaller
  end loop;
  put(min_cost, fore => 3, aft => 3, exp => 0);      -- Output smallest
  new_line;
end minima;
```

Figure 1.2 Finding the minimum value in an array

1.3 Currency conversion

If you are going to another country, as a tourist or on business, you will need to convert some of your money into the currency used in the place you are going to. Exchange rates are published widely, and, of course, change slightly from day to day. However, prior to leaving, you want to know how many units of foreign currency you will get for each unit of your own currency, so that you can make judgements about costs on arrival. If your currency is the *belk*, and the country you are going to uses *gams*, you need to know how many *gams* you get for each of your *belks*. If the rate is 1000 *gams* to the *belk*, then you will be taking a lot of *gams*: however, prices on arrival will need to be divided by 1000 in order for you to see what any item 'really' costs (i.e. in your own currency). If, on the other hand, the rate is 0.15 *gams* to the *belk*, you will be taking far fewer *gams*, but prices on arrival will look cheap. You will need to divide by 0.15 to get the 'true' cost.

Enough of fantasy currencies: consider the situation in which someone travelling from the UK to the USA wants to change pounds sterling into US dollars. The agent will sell you dollars at, say, $1.48 to the pound. Clearly for £100 you will get $148: that is, the agent's selling price is £1 = $1.48. If, on your return, you want to change back $10 you did not spend, you may find that the same agent buys at, say, £1 = $1.51. This means that you get ($10/1.51) = £6.62, rather than ($10/1.48) = £6.76. Indeed, if you converted all the money initially into dollars, and then back to sterling, the transaction would be: £100 × 1.48 = $148; $148/1.51 = £98.01. That's an immediate loss of £1.99—and they charge commission!

The problem of losing out on currency conversion is just a fact of life: it certainly is not an algorithmic problem. However, the procedure for working out how much of a given foreign currency you will get, and how much of your own you will get back, is.

Suppose an (abbreviated) exchange rate table looks like Table 1.3, for sterling: the currency for each nationality represents what you get for £1.00.

Table 1.3 Exchange rates

Currency	*Agent sells at*	*Agent buys at*
Belgium	BF45.68	BF49.87
France	FF7.58	FF8.23
Germany	DM2.22	DM2.50
Hong Kong	HK$11.58	HK$12.50
Italy	L2350.00	L2460.00
Sweden	Kr10.50	Kr11.23
USA	$1.48	$1.51

Having some data to hand, the problem now has to be restated clearly. We want to know, given that we have a certain amount of sterling to start with, how much of any one of a number of foreign currencies we will get. Also, we may want to know how much sterling we will get back for the foreign money we still possess on return. So at present, we have a process which may be stated—provisionally—as:

1. Read amount of sterling
2. Read nationality indicator for currency conversion—this gives the selling price
3. Multiply the sterling quantity by the 'sell' value associated with the 'nationality indicator'
4. If conversion back is required

Read amount of foreign currency, and nationality indicator
Divide the amount of foreign currency by the 'buy' value associated with the nationality indicator

5. Print out results
6. If further conversions are required, repeat the process, i.e. steps 1–6
7. Stop

The procedure above is a 'first-cut' at the problem, but appears to specify what to do. Its development has highlighted the need to specify which country we are concerned with (the 'nationality indicator'), and the fact that we might want to do more than one conversion—either for different amounts of the same currency, or for a number of different currencies.

Stating the problem initially in this way suggests that the first question to be asked should in fact be rather more general, perhaps along the lines of, 'Do you want to convert sterling to a foreign currency, or vice versa?' Hence our input is just money—of some nationality—and our output is also money—of a different nationality. This in turn leads into the notion that the process should really accept *any* currency as input, plus a symbol for buying or selling, and provide its equivalent in any other currency. However, although such a generalisation is a good idea, the original problem is becoming increasingly complicated. For the moment, we keep it simple, and consider the conversion of sterling. The whole procedure might be expressed as:

1. Establish whether conversion is to or from foreign currency
2. Read amount of money
3. Read nationality indicator
4. While there is still a conversion to do
    If conversion is from sterling
        Multiply the sterling quantity by the 'sell' value associated with the nationality indicator
    Else if conversion back is required
        Divide the amount of foreign currency by the 'buy' value associated with the nationality indicator
    Print out the results
5. Stop

This problem restatement suggests that it is necessary to know initially whether conversion is to or from the home currency, and that since more than one conversion may be required—for different amounts, or for different countries—the process should be iterative, that is, following a 'sterling to dollars' operation, for instance, the user should be asked whether any more conversions are required, or whether to stop.

Further, only certain currencies can be dealt with, as things stand: those whose exchange rates we build into the algorithm's data bank. Nevertheless, bearing all this in mind, the algorithm may be again restated, as follows:

```
1. While data read is valid loop
   1.1  Establish if conversion is from sterling to foreign currency, or vice versa
   1.2  Read in money and nationality indicator
   1.3  If valid money type/nationality indicator
        1.3.1 If sterling_to_foreign
                 If data for this currency exists
                    Convert_to
                 Else error_message_1
                 Endif
              Else if foreign_to_sterling
                 If data for this currency exists
                    Convert_back
                 Else error_message_2
                 Endif
              Endif
        Else error_message_3
        Endif
   1.5  Print results
   1.6  Read next input
   End loop
2. Stop
```

Note that a number of instructions are included to take care of the fact that the computer is extremely stupid, and which prevent it from attempting to perform the arithmetic on obviously invalid data. Further, for a complete working program, messages and prompts to the user will need to be included, or else file-handling procedures. The algorithms for conversion are the heart of the process, and may be implemented as shown in Fig 1.3.

In C:

```
#include <stdio.h> /* Currency conversion */
int err_flag1 = 0, err_flag2 = 0, err_flag3 = 0;
float convert_to(float cash, char NatInd)
{
  /* This function converts to foreign currency */
  float curr_out;
  switch(NatInd)
  {
    case 'B':
      curr_out = cash * 45.68;
      break;
    case 'F':
      curr_out = cash * 7.58;
      break;
    case 'D':
      curr_out = cash * 2.22;
      break;
```

```
      /*
    ... Similar case statements for any other number of conversions
                                                                  */
    default:
      err_flag1 = 1;
      break;
  }
  return(curr_out);
}

float convert_from(float cash, char NatInd)
{
  /* This function converts from foreign currency */
  float curr_out;
  switch(NatInd)
  {
    case 'B':
      curr_out = cash / 49.87;
      break;
    case 'F':
      curr_out = cash / 8.23;
      break;
    case 'D':
      curr_out = cash / 2.50;
      break;
    /*
    ... Similar case statements for any other number of conversions
                                                                  */
    default:
      err_flag2 = 1;
      break;
  }
  return(curr_out);
}
```

In Ada:

```
with text_io; use text_io;
procedure currency is
err_flag1: integer := 0;
err_flag2: integer := 0;
err_flag3: integer := 0;
function convert_to(cash: float; NatInd: character) return float is
      -- This function converts to foreign currency
curr_out:float;
begin
  case NatInd is
    when 'B' =>
      curr_out := cash * 45.68;
    when 'F'=>
      curr_out := cash * 7.58;
    when 'D' =>
      curr_out := cash * 2.22;
              -- ... Similar case statements for any other number of conversion
    when others =>
```

```
            err_flag1 := 1;
    end case;
    return curr_out;
end convert_to;

function convert_from(cash: float; NatInd: character) return float is
        -- This function converts from foreign currency
curr_out:float;
begin
    case NatInd is
        when 'B' =>
            curr_out := cash / 49.87;
        when 'F'=>
            curr_out := cash / 8.23;
        when 'D' =>
            curr_out := cash / 2.50;
                        -- ... Similar case statements for any other number of conversions
        when others =>
            err_flag2 := 1;
    end case;
    return curr_out;
end convert_from;
end currency;
```

Figure 1.3 Currency conversion program

1.4 Other kinds of problems

What the above examples have illustrated is that there is an identifiable route from problem to program. In general, problems are stated very vaguely: 'How do I get to London?'; 'What's the best value for money?'; 'How many francs will I get for my dollars, and can I convert back all right?'.

In answering such questions in real life, we make dozens of assumptions, simplifications, and frequently we make use of estimation—when comparing two prices, or two distances, if one is clearly very much greater than the other, we can make a judgement without knowing the *exact* numbers involved. When using a computer for problem-solving, we humans have to do all the hard work first. The problem must be analysed and then stated as though you were explaining to a Martian. No prior knowledge is available to the computer. Once this essential idea is grasped, the next step is to state what kinds of things we are working with (the data) and then organise the solution as a sequence of instructions. Each instruction must clearly follow the next, each must be unambiguous, and it must at every step be clear what is to be done next. The process must also have some built-in condition that makes it stop.

The reason for analysing in detail the problems in Sections 1.2 and 1.3 and setting out possible solutions was twofold: first, to demonstrate that even (to us) trivial problems require careful, methodical analysis and precise statements for their solution; and secondly, to show the process of elaboration and refinement that takes place in problem-solving. Few real programmers address even simple problems and simply write down a program that works. The process of deriving a step-by-step, unambiguous, precisely specified and correct algorithm is always one which undergoes numerous iterations as we 'home in' on what appears to be a correct solution. The question of its correctness in reality is one that is considered later.

Not all problems are algorithmic in nature: building a flat-pack bookcase, cooking dinner, and moving house are all essentially algorithmic. However, playing tennis, raising a family, and driving a car are not algorithmic. One of the reasons that social scientists have such difficulty in clearly formulating their methods, and in creating repeatably correct solutions to problems of housing or welfare is that the problems they deal with are not algorithmic.

Some problems are clearly algorithmic, but are extremely difficult to solve. These fall into two categories: problems for which the amount of data is so huge it is practically unmanageable, such as economic theory, meteorology, and dynamical systems in general; and problems which seem simple, but for which no simple algorithm exists. An example of the latter kind is what is generally known as 'the travelling salesperson problem', where a salesperson has to make a number of visits, all at various distances from home base, and from each other. The question is, 'Given some number, *m* (miles, say), can the salesperson visit each location in such a way as to travel less than *m* miles?'. In any given instance, the answer is obviously either 'Yes' or 'No', but we know of no algorithm which will give us the answer to the question quickly. This problem is discussed further in Chapter 8.

1.5 Data structures

This subject is dealt with in detail in Chapter 6. However, some idea of the importance of selecting the best data structure for any problem is hinted at in Section 1.3. What currencies are we working with? Can the number be extended? How should it be stored in the computer? The allowable currencies may also need to be displayed at the start of the program, if the program operates interactively, rather than on files of known data.

In terms of the data actually being considered in this problem, the exchange rates might quite naturally be set out as shown in Table 1.4.

Table 1.4 Agents' buying and selling rates

Agent_sells:

B	F	D	L	K	U
45.68	7.58	2.22	2350	10.50	1.48

Agent_buys:

B	F	D	L	K	U
49.87	8.23	2.50	2460	11.23	1.51

This kind of layout for data is so common that most programming languages have a built-in data structure to reflect this organisation called an *array*. An array, at its simplest, may be thought of as a row of pigeon-holes into and from which items of data may be put and retrieved. The way in which an array is declared at the start of a program depends on the language—but that is a technicality of the programming, rather than a problem to do with algorithms.

The data types we actually worked with in the problems earlier were, for 'Shampoo': integers, floating-point values, single characters, and strings of characters. For 'Currency conversion', we dealt with integers, floating-point numbers, and single characters. It is essential when developing an algorithm to be clear about the kind of data that needs to be dealt with, and the way in which the data is most efficiently stored and manipulated. The input value types and the range of allowable values need also to be definitively stated. Finally, you must also be precise about the output expected in terms of data types and presentation—on paper, on screen, written to a file, or resulting in a change to a robot arm, or thermostat.

EXERCISES 1.3

1. Consider how to develop the 'currency conversion' program so that the user can interactively indicate whether conversion is to or from sterling, and input the currency to be bought or sold, together with a 'nationality indicator'. The program should then output the amount of money the user will get.

2. Check on how arrays are declared, accessed, and manipulated in both Ada and C. Think about some of the disadvantages associated with arrays—for instance, how large should it be? Can you have 4-dimensional arrays? What happens if the array fills up, but data is required to be entered?

1.6 Problem-solving and the algorithmic method

'Problems' are not features of nature: they exist only because we as human beings want to change something. If the present state is not the desired state then that situation is called 'a problem'. Getting to the desired state from the existing state is problem-solving. Assuming that the problem is, in fact, algorithmic, the steps to take in order to solve it are:

1. Clarify the problem: this is the most important part. Note carefully any assumptions and simplifications you make (e.g. 'I'll only deal with six different currencies'). Restate the problem so that it makes sense to you. Ask colleagues to read your problem restatement, and get them to tell you what *they* think it means: you can learn a lot this way.

2. Set out clearly what the allowable inputs are, and with what data types you are working. Write down some data for testing the final program, and note the output values you expect for this data.

3. State the output data types and format.

4. Write down, in natural language, your 'first-pass' algorithmic solution, that is, the set of instructions that will generate the output you want from some set of allowable input data. Try working it through with sample data: this will show errors, possibilities overlooked and ambiguities of language, and lead to an improved version. Write down the improved version, and repeat the process.

5. When you believe the algorithm is correct and complete, convert it to code. There may be technical difficulties in doing this, especially when manipulating complex data structures, but these are *programming* problems. If you get stuck at this stage, find a good programmer to help you.

6. When the program has compiled without error, check the results, using the data from step 2.

7. Devise a comprehensive test set to demonstrate that the program covers a number of different cases. Create test data that makes the program fail.

These steps will always give you a solution. Someone else may have a quite different solution which is also correct. The program may, however, be a correct solution to the wrong problem, i.e., not what was asked. The program may be used in ways that you never intended, and so give odd results. No program is ever completely correct, and no amount of testing will prove it so.

Summary

- 'Problems' represent the fact that the present situation needs to be changed in some way, or that information needs to be organised.
- An algorithm is the step-by-step recipe for a problem solution. There must be an input, an output, and a stopping condition.

2

NECESSARY MATHEMATICS

OBJECTIVES

In this chapter you will learn

- what is meant by a function
- what functions do, and how they can be represented graphically and algebraically
- how the logarithm of a number is related to a number raised to a power
- the value of graph-sketching when dealing with functions

2.1 What you need to know

The amount of mathematical knowledge necessary for successful problem-solving and algorithm development is not great, nor are the ideas and techniques difficult. This book is not about mathematical programming, which is a subject on its own. However, a certain mathematical foundation is required, for a number of reasons:

- to enable abstract ideas to be represented
- to allow a variety of calculations to be done on problems which require them
- so that symbols can be manipulated sensibly
- for the analysis of algorithmic efficiency.

An abstraction, of course, cannot by definition be visualised. The concept 'greater than', for example, is not easy to explain in words without reference to an implementation, and for this reason there are numerous examples and illustrations given throughout this book. Mathematics is the ultimate abstraction of events in the physical world. Symbol manipulation is inherent in the development of algorithms, and some knowledge of the meaning of a function and its graph is a definite requirement.

The last of the above points is addressed specifically in Chapter 5: the *efficiency* of an algorithm is of great importance—there are better and worse ways of doing things, and the analysis of algorithmic efficiency allows us to measure how well any solution we propose solves the problem, in terms of the time taken and storage space required.

Algorithm design is not just theory: it underpins all successful software, from word-processing packages to spacecraft operation.

2.2 Functions and mappings

A function, informally, relates two quantities in such a way that the way one of them behaves is dependent on the way the other behaves. So, for example, the seating capacity of a cinema is a function of the number of seats: increase the number of seats, and the number of people who can watch a film at any one time is increased. Less obviously, the capacity of a seagoing ferry is a function of a large number of maritime rules designed to ensure safety: one of these rules might be that there must be sufficient lifeboats to accommodate the maximum number of passengers.

In each case, an element of one set is related to others, and in fact is *dependent* on another. In the case of the ferry, the number of passengers allowed to board is dependent on (among other things) lifeboat capacity. In the case of the cinema, the number of filmgoers at any time is a function of the number of seats, and the number of seats is itself a function of the available floor space. And in general, floor space (area) is a function of length and breadth. Formally, we could write, $A = l \times b$: change either l or b, and A changes. Because of this, A is said to be the dependent variable in this instance, and l and b are the independent variables. In the equation $y = 2x$, the value of y is dependent on the value of x.

A *function*, or *mapping*, explicitly associates one or more members of a set (the *domain*) with one and only one member of another set (the *range*).

Functions may be shown pictorially, in a number of ways; e.g. see Fig. 2.1.

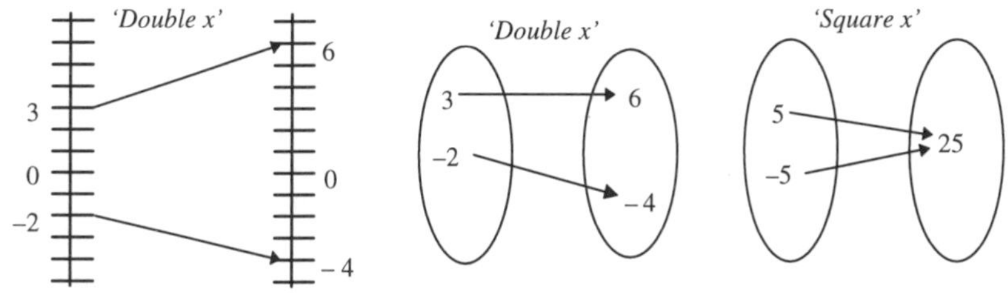

Figure 2.1 Pictorial representation of functions

2.2.1 Notation and techniques

A function, informally, may be something like 'square it', 'divide by 1.47', or 'treble it and subtract 5'. The effect of a function on a number may be seen by operating on some trial numbers, e.g.

$3^2 = 9$
$7^2 = 49$
$193.426/1.47 = 131.58$
$3 \times 7 - 5 = 16$
$3 \times 11.48 - 5 = 29.44$

We may write these, more generally, as:

$f\colon x \rightarrow x^2$
$g\colon p \rightarrow p/1.47$
$h\colon q \rightarrow 3q - 5$

Read these as 'f is a function such that it maps x to x^2', 'g is a function such that it maps p to $p/1.47$', and so on. The symbols are immaterial, though f and g will be used a lot to mean a function, and x, y, z are frequently used to stand for numbers. The words 'maps to' may be thought of as meaning 'converts to', so that, for example, f above converts 4 to 16 when $x = 4$, and it converts 5.70 to 32.490 when $x = 5.70$.

This understanding of variables and functions relates closely to what we do when we write a program; a function in Ada or C transforms an input to an output in an analogous way to the mathematical functions above. Equally, expressions such as the assignment InputVal := 5.70; or `inval = 5.70;` in a program are the same kinds of operations as setting a variable equal to a value, e.g. $x = 5.70$.

The effect of a function on a value may also be written directly as, for instance,

$f(7) = 49$ (f of 7 equals 49)
$g(193.426) = 131.58$
$h(7) = 16$

The values on which a function can operate (the domain of the function) are not unrestricted. For instance, the function $t\colon x \rightarrow (17/x)$ is not defined for $x = 0$, because division by zero is meaningless†. So the domain of t excludes zero.

Sketching the graph of a function for different values of x gives a visual impression of the way the function behaves in general. As well as asking the question, 'What is $f(9)$?' when f is 'square it', we can also ask, 'What number, when squared, makes 9?', i.e. what is $f^{-1}(9)$? Function notation is used frequently in algorithms, especially when considering efficiency.

The behaviour of any function—as mentioned above—is most easily investigated by taking a number of x values and then sketching a graph. For instance, $f{:}x \rightarrow 4x - 2$, or $g{:}x \rightarrow 4/x$ may be investigated for a number of different values of x as shown in Table 2.1 and Fig. 2.2.

Table 2.1 Values of $f{:}x \rightarrow 4x - 2$ and $g{:}x \rightarrow 4/x$

x	−3	−2	−1	0	1	2	3	4
$f(x)$	−14	−10	−6	−2	2	6	10	14
$g(x)$	−1.33	−2	−4	n.d.	4	2	1.33	1

† Division by zero does not equal 'infinity', as is sometimes suggested. First, because we do not know what infinity is; and secondly because if, for example, $(17/0) = \infty$, and, say, $(98/0) = \infty$, then $17 = 98$.

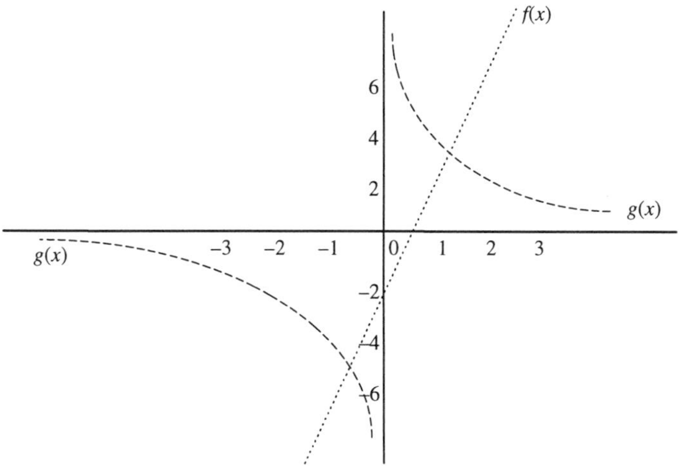

Figure 2.2 Graphs of $f:x \to 4x - 2$ and $g:x \to 4/x$

EXERCISES 2.1

1. Sketch and compare the graphs of:
   (i) $f\colon x \to 2x$
   (ii) $g\colon x \to (1/2)x$
   (iii) $h\colon x \to x^2$
   (iv) $j\colon x \to 1/x$
   (v) $m\colon x \to \sqrt{x}$
   (vi) $n\colon x \to 2^x$

2. Consider $f\colon x \to 1/(2 + x)$. Complete the table below, and sketch the graph.

x	−3	−2	−1	0	1	2	3
$f(x)$							

3. Sketch the graphs of $f\colon x \to (x + 1)/(x - 1)$, and $g\colon x \to x^x$.

2.3 Indices and logarithms

An *index*, or *exponent*, raises a number to a power. For instance, 2 raised to the power 3 (2^3) means three 2s multiplied together, and so $2^3 = 2 \times 2 \times 2 = 8$. In general, for any x we write $x \times x$ as x^2, $x \times x \times x \times x$ as x^4, and, more generally, $x \times x \times x \times x \times x \times \ldots \times x$ (the product of n xs) as x^n. The rules for dealing with indices are given here, without proofs. Readers should know these rules and be able to use the results.

(a) $x^3 \times x^2 = (x \times x \times x) \times (x \times x)$
$= x \times x \times x \times x \times x$
$= x^5$ (i.e. x^{3+2})

And more generally, $x^m \times x^n = x^{m+n}$.

(b) $x^m / x^n = x^{m-n}$

(c) $(x^m)^n = x^m \times x^m \times x^m \times x^m \times \ldots$ n times $= x^{m \times n}$

(d) $x^{-n} = 1/x^n$

(e) $x^0 = 1$

Logarithms (or just *logs*) are a way of representing numbers which is sometimes useful: in particular, logs are used a great deal in the analysis of algorithms. Logarithms are given to some *base*: there is nothing special about that—all numbers are defined in terms of a *base*. The base we use all the time in our everyday lives is the base 10—hence the number 173, for example, actually means

$(1 \times 10^2) + (7 \times 10^1) + (3 \times 10^0)$

which is

$(1 \times 100) + (7 \times 10) + (3 \times 1) = 100 + 70 + 3 = 173$

In base 2, which is common in computing, 173 = 10101101, or

$(1 \times 2^7) + (0 \times 2^6) + (1 \times 2^5) + (0 \times 2^4) + (1 \times 2^3) + (1 \times 2^2) + (0 \times 2^1) + (1 \times 2^0)$

Working this out, we get

$(1 \times 128) + (0 \times 64) + (1 \times 32) + (0 \times 16) + (1 \times 8) + (1 \times 4) + (0 \times 2) + (1 \times 1)$

$= 128 + 32 + 8 + 4 + 1 = 173$

A *logarithm* of a number is simply the power to which the base must be raised to give the number. So, for example, since $10^2 = 100$, we can write $\log_{10} 100 = 2$. Equally, $10^3 = 1000$, and so $\log_{10} 1000 = 3$. Of course, logs can be taken of any number, not just powers of 10; for instance $\log_{10} 500 = 2.699$ (to 3 d.p.), and so also $10^{2.699} = 500$.

Formally, $\log_a b = c \Leftrightarrow a^c = b$: the logarithm to base a of b is c if and only if a raised to the power c equals b. Logarithms to base 10 are most commonly used, but any base may be chosen. For instance, since $7^4 = 2401$, $\log_7 2401 = 4$.

In algorithmics, logarithms to base 2 are sometimes used (computers are binary machines, not denary). The same rules apply, so that, for instance,

$\log_2 8$	$= 3$	since	$2^3 = 8$
$\log_2 4096$	$= 12$	since	$2^{12} = 4096$
$\log_2 19.73$	$= 4.302$	since	$2^{4.302} = 19.73$

For many cases, and especially in considerations of algorithmic efficiency (see Chapters 5 and 6), the computations are relative, and so the base used is not significant, and frequently log is abbreviated to just 'lg'.

EXERCISES 2.2

1. Devise a method for finding the logarithm to any base of a number, and give an outline algorithm to do this (*Hint*: if $a^c = b$, $c \times \log(a) = \log(b)$).

2. Using a calculator, work out:

   (i) $(2^9)^2$
   (ii) $3^7 \times 3^2$
   (iii) $3^7/3^4$
   (iv) $2.61^4/2.61^3$
   (v) $5.62^3 \times 5.62^2 \times 5.62/5.62^6$
   (vi) 3^{-7}
   (vii) $-0.3^{-0.3}$
   (viii) $(1/4)^{-0.25}$
   (ix) 1^0

3. Using a calculator, work out:

   (i) $(\log_{10} 1000)^{-1}$
   (ii) $\log_2(1024)/\log_2(2)$
   (iii) $\log_2(2^5)$
   (iv) $2^{\log_2(8)}$
   (v) $\log_2(2)$
   (vi) $5 \times \log_2(2)$
   (vii) $\log_{10} 1.0$

2.4 Using a calculator to find roots

A square is a rectangle in which length and breadth are equal. Its area is the product of length and breadth: for example, a 6×6 square has area 36. The *square root* of a square is the length of a side—so the square root of 36 is 6. Similarly, a cube of dimensions length = 6, breadth = 6, height = 6 has volume = $6 \times 6 \times 6 = 216$, and the *cube root* of 216 is 6 (Fig.2.3).

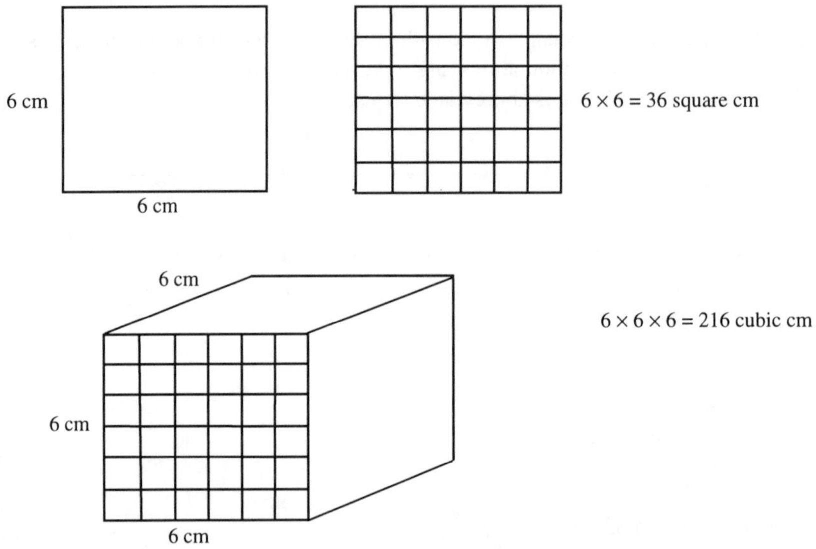

Figure 2.3 Relation of square roots and cube roots to area and volume

Your calculator may well have a key to find cube roots; however, if it does not, it is not obvious how to find, say, the cube root of 29 ($\sqrt[3]{29}$). Most calculators do have a square root key, though. Can that be used to help to find cube roots?

One approach is to take successive estimates, i.e. to guess, see how close the guess was, and then take a better guess. For example, we know that $216 = 6^3$; but suppose we had no idea what the cube root was, and our first guess at the root was, in fact, 5.5.

Divide the cubed number by the guess:

$216 \div 5.5 = 39.27$

Now take the square root of the answer:

$\sqrt{39.27} = 6.267$

Make this result the new guess, and do it again:

$216 \div 6.267 = 34.467$

$\sqrt{34.467} = 5.87$

Continuing,

Guess 3: $216 \div 5.87 = 36.79$

$\sqrt{36.79} = 6.066$

Guess 4: $216 \div 6.066 = 35.61$

$\sqrt{35.61} = 5.967$

Guess 5: $216 \div 5.967 = 36.196$

$\sqrt{36.196} = 6.016$

Guess 6: $216 \div 6.016 = 35.902$

$\sqrt{35.902} = 5.992$

Guess 7: $216 \div 5.992 = 36.05$

$\sqrt{36.05} = 6.004$

Guess 8: $216 \div 6.004 = 35.98$

$\sqrt{35.98} = 5.998$

Clearly, we are converging on the answer. Continuing the process will eventually yield two successive answers which are the same (i.e. 6). What is happening is that we are taking a guess, doing the arithmetic, and then making the answer the new guess; we continue this until two successive answers are the same (within the limits of the calculator display). That is,

New guess = Square root of (number/old guess)

If we denote 'number' by N, 'new guess' by x_{new}, and 'old guess' by x_{old}, then

$x_{new} = \sqrt{N/x_{old}}$

However, each time we get an answer (an x_{new}), we then divide that into the number again, i.e., we use that as the next x_{old}; so the equation is better expressed:

$$x_{r+1} = \sqrt{N/x_r}$$

This is an *iterative formula*: iterative formulae (or recurrence relations) are important in algorithm design, and will be encountered on several more occasions throughout this book.

It turns out that the following formula is more efficient for this particular task:

$$x_{r+1} = 1/3(N/x_r^2 + 2x_r)$$

Try the same values as earlier (216, 5.5) to check.

Clearly this kind of approach to the solution of mathematical problems is very amenable to computerisation. A sequence of simple steps is repeated until some condition is met—for example, repeat 25 times, or, repeat until the difference between successive answers is less than some figure (1 millionth, perhaps).

EXERCISES 2.3

1. Formalise these methods of working, and develop the algorithms for both approaches. Write a program to find cube roots in Ada or C.

2. Develop an algorithm which outputs the logarithm to base 2 of an input number.

Summary

- Relatively little mathematical knowledge is necessary in order to solve problems and design algorithms which represent generalised solutions.
- The idea of a function is of great importance, and it should be thoroughly understood.
- The ability to manipulate indices and deal with logarithms is a basic skill.

3

SORTING

OBJECTIVES

In this chapter you will learn

- the importance of sorting algorithms in computing
- some standard methods for sorting, in particular, selection sort, bubble sort, and insertion sort
- comparison methods, and an informal approach to the idea of efficiency

3.1 An impression of order

Sorting things out is a very natural human activity: we seem to like the impression of order we get as a result. Even very small children will sort out toys, or crayons, or pictures according to some (occasionally bizarre) criteria. When we play cards, we sort out our hand, and if we have a pocketful of small change, we frequently sort it out by denomination so that it is easier to count.

What we are doing, one could say, is allocating items to sets. When we play the card game solitaire (or 'patience'), the starting position is a random allocation of cards. The object of the game is to sort all the cards into four piles, by suit and in order, according to certain rules. There are a number of other games which operate on a similar principle, and most people find that the best way to learn how to play is to read the rules once, and then just start playing. We do not necessarily have to be able to state precisely what the rules are in order to play, and when we teach the game to a newcomer, the best approach is frequently to give an outline of the rules, and then to start playing: we 'learn by doing'.

Computers, of course, cannot learn by doing (though this is a very active research area), and so we have to spell out all the rules with painful precision, and prevent in advance, as far as possible, all the possible illegal moves that might be attempted.

When we are sorting, we are transforming a set of items in no particular order, into a sequence of ordered items (Fig.3.1).

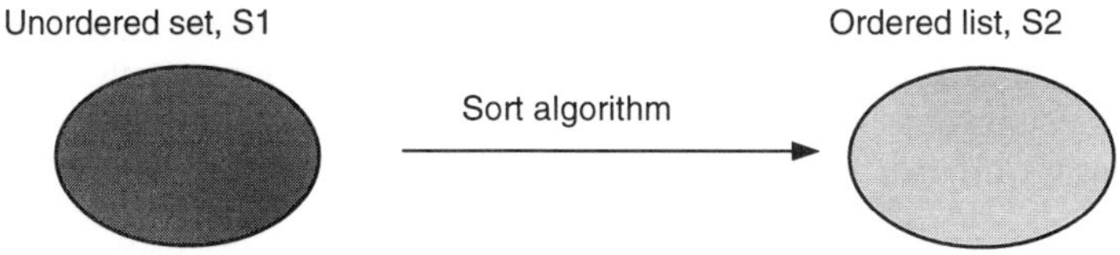

Figure 3.1 Sorting items by means of a rule

For instance, S1 = {11, 2, 48, 13, 9, 5, 6, 21}

Transform: S2 = {2, 5, 6, 9, 11, 13, 21, 48}

The above transformation results in the elements of S2 being in ascending order. This is the consequence of an unstated assumption: descending order could have been the requirement, or possibly odd numbers followed by even numbers, or other arrangements. As always, the allowable inputs and required output must be clearly stated at the beginning, together with a declaration of assumptions and simplifications made, and the data types or structures to be used.

3.2 Getting sorted

The idea of sorting items is fundamental in information systems and software engineering. This has nothing to do with any intrinsic value in the process of sorting itself, but rather because so many other procedures in computing rely on items having first been sorted.

Most information systems rely on files of data, in one form or another, being available to resolve customer queries, for example, to update customer accounts, and to amend details held about a customer. Every time we call our electricity company with a query, or our insurance company, or our bank, it is *our* records that must be consulted, and no other. We take this very much for granted, and get justifiably annoyed if our records cannot be found, or if the details held in them are incorrect. Yet banks and other large corporations hold data about literally millions of individual and corporate customers. In order for any particular file to be accessed quickly and easily, a method must be found for locating any given file among all those held as quickly as any other, and for accessing the appropriate record directly.

Real-time systems also need to store and retrieve data; maybe to locate a called party in a telephone switching system, or to access one of a number of sets of parameters in a ballistic missile system. The amount of data held is usually smaller in such systems, but the time taken for its retrieval must be much less than in data processing applications (often microseconds).

Any non-trivial real-world computer system, then, relies on being able to retrieve the data it needs to operate on quickly and efficiently. Whatever searching process is used, it must be measurable and repeatable: that is, some measure of the time taken, on average and in the worst case, is necessary so that the rest of the system operates in a reliable and predictable way. Algorithms for searching are considered in detail in Chapter 6; however, most practical searching techniques are based on the assumption that the data is first ordered†, that is, sorted, alphabetically or numerically, into ascending or descending order.

There are many different sorting algorithms: in this chapter, only three are

† Sometimes it is actually more efficient in practice to leave the data unsorted prior to searching; see Chapter 6 for an explanation.

considered, but the understanding of these is crucial to the idea of sorting in general, and for that reason, they are developed, step by step, from scratch.

The elementary algorithms considered are known as selection sort, bubble sort, and insertion sort. They are generally suitable for all small sets of data (of up to about 1000 items or so), and are sometimes good for larger arrays. The ideas incorporated are fundamental, and can be extended to handle extremely large quantities of data. The best variants are about equally efficient, that is, when coded in a standard procedural language:

- they take about the same amount of time to run
- they use about the same amount of memory

Although more sophisticated sorting methods exist, the algorithms developed here represent a thorough grounding in:

- real data sorting methods used in practice
- the application of the principles explained earlier to a specific problem, resulting in more than one correct solution
- an initial investigation into the relative efficiency of the methods

3.3 Selection sort

The first step in devising any algorithm is working out what the problem is. We need:

- a statement of the data types and/or data structures being operated on
- a formal problem statement
- a set of allowable inputs, and required outputs
- a clear explanation of the simplifications and assumptions used

Hence we have:

Data type: Integer

Problem specification: Given as input a sequence of unordered integers, produce as output a sequence of the same integers in ascending order.

Input data: A randomly ordered sequence of integers
Output data: The same integers in ascending order
Assumptions: All input data of correct type; input set finite

At this stage in any algorithmic problem, it is usually helpful to 'work things through' with sample data. We are treating this as a completely new problem, though as you gain experience in software development, you will discover that, frequently, you will be able to look at a problem statement, and say, 'Let's just use a selection sort', or 'There's a method called Bergowitz' algorithm which will solve that'. When a new problem is encountered, however, we need to work out a solution from scratch, and then work out how we worked out the solution.

Keeping the problem very simple, we might consider how to sort just three integers into ascending order, e.g.

Input	*Required output*
7, 4, 1	1, 4, 7
6, 2, 3	2, 3, 6
5, 8, 9	5, 8, 9
2, 9, 4	2, 4, 9
2, 0, –6	–6, 0, 2
4, –2, 5	–2, 4, 5

The process of transformation is so evident and intuitive that formalising it seems like stating the obvious. However, we can gain some useful insights into the processes we go through in converting the inputs to the outputs by such a formal statement. Think about what you do when you look at {6, 2, 8} and give {2, 6, 8} as 'the answer'. How did you do it?

Different people solve this problem different ways; when there are only three items, we can do it so fast we are hardly aware of the complex mental processes going on. However, when the input is {14, 1, 9, 23, –8, 102, 3, 41, 80, –3, 0, 55, 7}, we need to slow down a bit, and think about what we are doing. In order to sort this list, or a list of 200 items, we are going to have to be methodical, and hence be aware of the procedure. We need a set of instructions for how to do it. One way of articulating the procedure for ordering the three numbers might be stated:

1. Read the first number (x)
2. Remember x
3. Read the second number (y)
4. Compare x and y:
   If y is smaller than x
      Forget x and remember y instead
   Endif
5. Read the third number (z)
6. Compare z with the number currently remembered
   If z is smaller than the number currently remembered
      Forget the current number and remember z
   Endif
7. The currently remembered number is the smallest; take away the number in the first position, and place the currently remembered (the smallest) number first
8. Put the number that *was* in the first position into the place that the remembered number came from
9. Read the second number (p)

10. Remember *p*
11. Read the third number (*q*)
    If *q* is smaller than *p*
        Place *q* in the second position
        Place *p* in the third position
    Endif
12. Stop

This is obviously clumsy: it is perhaps a starting point, but a more elegant and general solution would be preferable. However, some points which might have occurred to you as you read through the algorithm above are: how is the input data set to be stored? What happens when more than one number is the same? And where does the computer 'remember' the current smallest? (We can do it 'in our heads'.) For the moment, the computer memory location for storing 'smallest_so_far' may be given the identifier *pos_val.*

At this point, it is a good idea to plug in some numbers: take S1 = {7, 4, 1} as input. The output, S2 = {1, 4, 7} does not in fact need to be a physically separate structure; since the numbers are being swapped about within S1 during the course of algorithm execution, S1 will contain the input prior to the transformation, and the output afterwards. Running through the algorithm with S1 = {7, 4, 1} step by step:

operation	***value***	***pos***	***pos_val***	***value < pos_val?***	**S1**
Start at first position: read no.	7	1	7		{7, 4, 1}
Read second no.	4				{7, 4, 1}
Compare last read with 'pos_val'				✓	{7, 4, 1}
Save pos'n and value of smaller		2	4		{7, 4, 1}
Read third no.	1				{7, 4, 1}
Compare last read with 'pos_val'				✓	{7, 4, 1}
Save pos'n and value of smaller		3	1		{7, 4, 1}
No more to read					{7, 4, 1}
If 'pos' has changed...					{7, 4, 1}
...swap 'pos_val' with no. in pos'n 1					{1, 4, 7}
Consider next position	4	2	4		{1, 4, 7}
Read third (last) no.	7				{1, 4, 7}
Compare last read with 'pos_val'				×	{1, 4, 7}
No more to read					{1, 4, 7}
Stop					{1, 4, 7}

As in previous chapters, the work above represents a 'first-pass' attempt at a solution. Only one set of test data has been used, but the method appears to be substantially correct. It has clarified a number of points, and provides a good platform for refining the algorithm and producing a more complete version, which will in turn need to be tested.

Some points which seem worth noting are given overleaf.

- The input data set will have to be held internally: this suggests an array declaration.
- When the smallest number in S1 has been selected, by the 'compare and remember smallest_so_far' process, its *position* must be remembered, so that the value that is to be swapped with the 'smallest_so_far' can be written there.
- Similarly, the *position* of the value currently read must be remembered.
- There is an implicit 'swap' routine involved in the exchange of data items.
- The need to stop when the last item is read is obvious, but a program will have to have the stop condition explicitly stated.

For the input set, there must be a test for whether, after all values have been examined, the position of the 'smallest_so_far' is different from the position we started with. If so, then an exchange is necessary.

Clearly, the process is iterative. Once an item is 'sorted', it stays put, and the same selection process operates on the remaining, unsorted items, until the last item is read. Consider how it would work on S3 = {10, 4, 14, –3, 12, 6}:

Sort array: S3	*Operation*
10 4 14 –3 12 6	Compare the value in position 1 (i.e. 10) with all remaining values. Swap the smallest into position 1.
–3 *4* 14 10 12 6	Compare the value in position 2 (i.e. 4) with all remaining values. Swap the smallest into position 2.
–3 4 *14* 10 12 6	Compare the value in position 3 (i.e. 14) with all remaining values. Swap the smallest into position 3.
–3 4 6 *10* 12 14	Compare the value in position 4 (i.e. 10) with all remaining values. Swap the smallest into position 4.
–3 4 6 10 *12* 14	Compare the value in position 5 (i.e. 12) with all remaining values. Swap the smallest into position 5.
–3 4 6 10 12 14	Resulting S3 for output.

Note that, for the six elements above, only five passes are required to sort the array completely. In general, for any number of elements, *n*, the number of passes required is $n - 1$. This is because—for the six items above—on the first pass, the first item is compared to the other five. Either it is already in the right place (the smallest), or else the remembered item will be swapped with it. Position 1 is then correct. On the second pass, since we know that position 1 is already correctly filled, we need only to compare the item in position 2 with those in positions 3 to 6: that is, we need to find the smallest among the *last five* elements. On the third pass, we only have to compare the item in position 3 with those in positions 4 to 6, i.e. we are considering the last four elements. And so on.

After the last two elements are checked, and sorted, we have finished: there is no point in checking the last item with itself!

> EXERCISES 3.1
>
> 1. Show how the selection sort algorithm would successively sort the following sequences into ascending order:
>
>   (i) {4, 8, 1}
>   (ii) {7, 7, 7, 7}
>   (iii) {2, 5, –1, 36, 5, 20, 8}

Much has become apparent about the way this algorithm operates, at this stage of development, and how the data should be structured:

- We begin with an array of *n* integers.
- There is iteration involved in the 'find the smallest' procedure at any one stage, as the item under consideration is compared successively with all the remaining ones and the smallest is selected.
- The loop which selects the smallest item must be contained within another loop: this outer loop must execute *n* – 1 times for an array of *n* items.
- The 'swap' procedure must be properly set out.

The last of the above points is easy to address: it is a classic mini-routine, used in many contexts. To swap two variables, `x` and `y`, we designate a third variable `temp`, which will be a temporary location for the swap procedure:

```
temp ← x;
x ← y;
y ← temp;
```

The reason we cannot simply write:

```
x ← y;
y ← x;
```

is that after the first of these operations (`x ← y;`), the value of `x` will be *overwritten* by the value of `y`. Hence, rather than swapping the values, we are making them both the same—equivalent to the assignment, `x = y;`. The refined algorithm now looks like this:

Declare integer array s1[*n*], where the array is s1[0 .. *n* – 1]
Declare any variables as integers

1. Loop from $i = 0$ to $n - 2$
2. Remember the *position* of the item under consideration: $a \leftarrow i$
3. Compare each item, in turn, with the current one
   Loop from $j = i + 1$ to $n - 1$
      If the next item is smaller than the saved one—if s1[j] < s1[a]
         Save this position instead: $a \leftarrow j$
      Endif
   End loop
4. If a is not the same as at the start (if $a \neq i$)
      Swap s1[a] with s1[i]
   Endif
5. End loop
6. Print out s1 (sorted items)

The algorithm appears slightly different when coded in Ada than it does when coded in C. The difference is in the *loop* statements: in order to loop through array items [0 .. n – 1] from 0 to n – 2 inclusive, we write `for(i = 0; i < n-1; ++i)` in C, but **for** i **in** 0 .. n-2 **loop** in Ada. The algorithms are shown in Fig 3.2.

In C:

```
#include <stdio.h>        /*   Selection sort    */
#define SORT_MAX  6
void sel_sort ( int s1[SORT_MAX] )
{          /* This function carries out the sort (ascending order) */
  int i, j, k, a, temp;
  for (i = 0; i < SORT_MAX - 1; ++i)
  {
    a = i;             /* Save position under consideration in 'a' */
    for (j = i + 1; j < SORT_MAX; ++j)
    {
      if (s1[j] < s1[a]) /* Compare the value of the item in */
      {                  /* each position in turn with ...*/
              a = j;     /* ..the one under consideration */
      }                  /* Save new position if value smaller */
    }
    if (a != i)          /* If saved position has changed after */
    {                    /* comparison with other elements */
      temp = s1[a];      /*.. swap contents of array positions */
      s1[a] = s1[i];
      s1[i] = temp;
    }
    printf ("\nThe array so far:\n");
    for (k = 0; k < SORT_MAX; ++k)
    {                                /* Display array contents */
      printf ("%d ", s1[k]);         /* after each pass */
    }
  }
}
```

```
void main()
{                       /* Main procedure to accept input data: */
   int i;               /* a list of integers in no special order */
   int inlist[SORT_MAX];
   void sel_sort ( int s1[SORT_MAX] );
   printf ("Enter %d integers: \n", SORT_MAX);/* User enters data */
   for (i = 0; i < SORT_MAX; ++i)
   {
     scanf("%d", &inlist[i]);          /* Read input data set... */
   }
   printf ("\n\nThe array before the sort:\n");
   for (i = 0; i < SORT_MAX; ++i)
   {
     printf ("%d ", inlist[i]);        /* Echo input data */
   }
   printf("\n\n");
   sel_sort(inlist);                   /* Do the sort */
   printf ("\n\n\nThe array after the sort:\n");
   for (i = 0; i < SORT_MAX; ++i)
   {
     printf ("%d ", inlist[i]);        /* Output sorted list */
   }
   printf("\n\n");
}
```

In Ada:

```
with text_io; use text_io;
procedure select_sort is
package int_io is new text_io.integer_io(integer);
use int_io;

SORT_MAX: integer := 6;
type sort_type is array (0 .. SORT_MAX - 1) of integer;
inlist: sort_type;

procedure sel_sort(s1: in out sort_type) is    -- This procedure carries out the sort
a, temp: integer;                              -- (ascending order)
begin
    for i in 0 .. SORT_MAX - 2 loop
        a := i;                                -- Save position under consideration
        for j in i+1 .. SORT_MAX - 1 loop      -- Compare the value of the item in
            if s1(j) < s1(a) then              -- each position in turn with...
                a := j;                        -- the one under consideration
            end if;                            -- Save new position if smaller
        end loop;
        if a /= i then                         -- If saved position has changed after
            temp := s1(a);                     -- comparison with other elements...
            s1(a) := s1(i);                    -- ...swap contents of array positions
            s1(i) := temp;
        end if;
        put("The array so far: ");
```

```
            new_line;
            for k in 0 .. SORT_MAX-1 loop
                  put(s1(k), width => 5);             -- Display array contents
            end loop;                                 -- after each pass
            new_line;
      end loop;
end sel_sort;

begin        -- Main procedure to accept input data: a list of integers in no special order
      put("Enter ");
      put(SORT_MAX);                                  -- User enters input data
      put(" integers:");
      new_line;
      for i in 0 .. SORT_MAX-1 loop
            get(inlist(i));                           -- Read input data set...
      end loop;
      put("The array before the sort: ");
      new_line;
      for i in 0 .. SORT_MAX-1 loop
            put(inlist(i), width => 5);               -- Echo input data
      end loop;
      new_line(2);
      sel_sort(inlist);                               -- Do the sort
      put("The array after the sort: ");
      new_line;
      for i in 0 ..SORT_MAX-1 loop
            put(inlist(i), width => 5);               -- Output sorted list
      end loop;
end select_sort;
```

Figure 3.2 Selection sort algorithm

When the program is compiled and executed, the result will be:

Enter 6 integers:

The array before the sort:
10 4 14 –3 12 6

The array so far:
–3 4 14 10 12 6

The array so far:
–3 4 14 10 12 6

The array so far:
–3 4 6 10 12 14

The array so far:
–3 4 6 10 12 14

The array so far:
–3 4 6 10 12 14

The array after the sort:
–3 4 6 10 12 14

As in the example on page 31, it is useful to 'walk through' the program, checking contents of variables at each stage.

Table 3.1 Contents of variables as the selection sort progresses

i	*a*	*j*	*s1[j]*	*s1[a]*	*s1[i]*	*Operation*	*s1[]*
0	0			10	10	Begin sort	10 4 14 –3 12 6
		1	4	10	10	s1[*j*] < s1[*a*]?	10 4 14 –3 12 6
	1					*a* = *j*	10 4 14 –3 12 6
		2	14	4	10	s1[*j*] < s1[*a*]?	10 4 14 –3 12 6
		3	–3	4	10	s1[*j*] < s1[*a*]?	10 4 14 –3 12 6
	3					*a* = *j*	10 4 14 –3 12 6
		4	12	–3	10	s1[*j*] < s1[*a*]?	10 4 14 –3 12 6
		5	6	–3	10	s1[*j*] < s1[*a*]?	10 4 14 –3 12 6
				10	–3	if(*a* ≠ *i*) s1[*a*] ↔s1[i]	–3 4 14 10 12 6
1	1	2	14	4	4	s1[*j*] < s1[*a*]?	–3 4 14 10 12 6
		3	10	4	4	s1[*j*] < s1[*a*]?	–3 4 14 10 12 6
		4	12	4	4	s1[*j*] < s1[*a*]?	–3 4 14 10 12 6
		5	6	4	4	s1[*j*] < s1[*a*]?	–3 4 14 10 12 6
						if(*a* ≠ i) s1[*a*] ↔s1[*i*]	–3 4 14 10 12 6
2	2	3	10	14	14	s1[*j*] < s1[a]?	–3 4 14 10 12 6
	3					*a* = *j*	–3 4 14 10 12 6
		4	12	10	14	s1[*j*] < s1[*a*]?	–3 4 14 10 12 6
		5	6	10	14	s1[*j*] < s1[*a*]?	–3 4 14 10 12 6
	5					*a* = *j*	–3 4 14 10 12 6
				6	14	if(*a*≠ *i*) s1[*a*] ↔s1[*i*]	–3 4 6 10 12 14
3	3	4	12	10	10	s1[*j*] < s1[*a*]?	–3 4 6 10 12 14
		5	14	10	10	s1[*j*] < s1[*a*]?	–3 4 6 10 12 14
				10	-3	if(*a* ≠ *i*) s1[*a*] ↔s1[*i*]	–3 4 6 10 12 14
4	4	5	14	12	12	s1[*j*] < s1[*a*]?	–3 4 6 10 12 14
							–3 4 6 10 12 14
						End sort: print s1[ ]	–3 4 6 10 12 14

This 'walk-through' is essential in the early stages of developing an algorithm. In particular, note that the *position* under consideration is remembered and updated if the contents of any subsequent position compared are smaller than the contents of the position currently remembered. We now have some confidence that the basic method works, though the program has not yet been tested.

EXERCISES 3.2

1. Modify the program in Fig 3.2 so that it outputs a count of comparisons, exchanges, and swaps after each pass. Print out s1[ ] after each completed pass of the outer loop.

2. The program always does $n - 1$ outer loops. Is it possible to include a test that ends the program when no more exchanges will be necessary?

3. Should the test `if (s1[j] < s1[a])` be `if (s1[j] ≤ s1[a])`? If so, why? If not, why not?

4. Devise appropriate test data for the program and test it. The aim of testing is to discover errors, so you should choose sets of data that you think are likely to cause problems (duplicated numbers, reversed sequences, large values, etc.).

3.4 Bubble sort

Probably the best-known method for sorting (but one of the least efficient) is the bubble sort. It gets its name from the fact that the smallest (or largest) element 'bubbles' to the end during sorting. The method is straightforward, and is as follows: consider two adjacent elements, and exchange them if necessary. Then move up one, and consider the next two, and exchange if necessary. Continue until there are no more elements in the list. For a list of n elements, repeat this process $n - 1$ times.

You can start at the beginning or the end of the list, and sort the elements into either ascending or descending order. An example, s1 = {6, 5, 4}, will illustrate the method. There are just three elements in s1. To bubble sort the elements of s1 into ascending order, and moving from left to right, we have:

6 5 4	6 and 5 are transposed: swap
5 6 4	6 and 4 are transposed: swap
5 4 6	End of first pass

The list is clearly not sorted at this point. We could have begun at the end of the list instead, and worked towards the left, resulting in:

6 5 4	Swap
6 4 5	Swap
4 6 5	End of first pass

This is different, but clearly no better. It is necessary to make a second pass in either case, in order to complete the sort. In the first case (sorting left to right), we have:

Begin second pass:	5 4 6	Swap
	4 5 6	OK: no swap
	4 5 6	End of second pass: s1 sorted

In the second case (right-to-left):

Begin second pass:	4 6 5	Swap
	4 5 6	OK: no swap
	4 5 6	End of second pass: s1 sorted

For the three elements of s1, two passes over the data were necessary to ensure that the data was correctly sorted. Obviously, no more than two passes will ever be necessary for any three elements, and sometimes one pass will suffice. For instance, s2 = {23, 12, 38} will be completely sorted after one pass:

23 12 38	Swap
12 23 38	OK: no swap
12 23 38	End of first pass: s2 sorted

For n items then, there must be $n - 1$ passes over all the data in order to ensure that the elements are correctly sorted in the worst case. Each pass over n data elements is itself $n - 1$ comparisons (and possible swaps), since for three elements there are two pairs to consider, for 13 elements there are 12 pairs to consider, etc.

The 'bubble' feature is evident in the examples above: for s1 and s2, working left to right, the larger elements appear in the rightmost positions. When s1 is sorted from right to left, the smallest elements appear in the leftmost position. In either case, for an input list of n elements that is reverse ordered (the worst case), one element at a time will become correctly positioned after each inner loop of comparisons, and so $n - 1$ such inner loops will be necessary to sort the list completely. What happens, in terms of the way that that the input list becomes organised, can be summarised as in Table 3.2.

Table 3.2 Operation of bubble sort algorithm for different output orders

Algorithm	*Left to right*	*Right to left*
Ascending order	Larger elements bubble to right	Smaller elements bubble to left
Descending order	Smaller elements bubble to right	Larger elements bubble to left

For an input set s1, comprising n elements, the algorithm for sorting from left to right into ascending order is:

Declare integer array s1[0 .. n–1]
1. Loop from $i = 0$ to $n - 1$

2. Loop from $j = 0$ to $n - 1$
3. Compare each pair of elements, in turn: if the second is smaller than the first swap them: $s1[j + 1] \leftrightarrow s1[j]$
4. End loop
5. End loop.

This translates into C or Ada as shown in Fig. 3.3.

In C:

```
#include <stdio.h>
#define LISTSIZE 6
void bubble_sort(int s1[LISTSIZE])
{         /* This function carries out the sort (ascending order) */
  int i, j, temp;
  for (i = 0; i < LISTSIZE - 1; ++i)      /* Outer loop */
  {
    for (j = 0; j < LISTSIZE - 1; ++j)   /* Inner loop: compare */
    {                                      /* adjacent values, and */
      if (s1[j + 1] < s1[j])               /* swap if transposed. */
      {                                    /* Do this to the end of */
        temp = s1[j];                      /* the list (one pass), */
        s1[j] = s1[j + 1];                 /* then return to the */
        s1[j + 1] = temp;                  /* outer loop, increment */
      }                                    /* and repeat the process*/
    }                                      /* up to LISTSIZE - 1 */
  }                                        /* pairs of elements */
}

void main()
{          /* Main procedure to accept input data: */
  int i;   /* a list of integers in no special order */
  int inlist[LISTSIZE];
  printf("\nEnter %d integers:  \n", LISTSIZE);
  for (i = 0; i < LISTSIZE; ++i)
  {
    scanf("%d", &inlist[i]);                /* Read input data */
  }
  printf("\n\n\nList s1 before the sort:\n");
  for (i = 0; i < LISTSIZE; ++i)
  {
    printf("%d", inlist[i]);  /* Display the list before sorting */
  }
  bubble_sort(inlist);                      /* Do the sort */
  printf("\n\nList s1 after the sort:\n\n");
  for (i = 0; i < LISTSIZE; ++i)
  {
    printf("%d", inlist[i]);                /* Output sorted list */
  }
  printf("\n\n");
}
```

In Ada:

```
with text_io;
use text_io;
procedure bubble1 is           -- This procedure carries out the sort (ascending order)
package int_io is new text_io.integer_io(integer);
use int_io;

LISTSIZE: integer := 6;
type sort_array is array(0 .. LISTSIZE - 1) of integer;
inlist: sort_array;

procedure bubble_sort1(s1: in out sort_array) is
temp: integer;
begin
    for i in 0 .. LISTSIZE - 2 loop              -- Outer loop
        for j in 0 .. LISTSIZE - 2 loop          -- Inner loop: compare adjacent values
            if s1(j+1) < s1(j) then              -- and swap if transposed. Do this to
                temp := s1(j);                   -- the end of the list (one pass),
                s1(j) := s1(j+1);                -- then return to the outer loop,
                s1(j+1) := temp;                 -- increment it, and repeat
            end if;                              -- the process up to LISTSIZE – 1
        end loop;                                -- pairs of elements
    end loop;
end bubble_sort1;

begin       -- Main procedure to accept input data: a list of integers in no special order
    put("Enter ");
    put(LISTSIZE);
    put(" integers:");
    new_line;
    for i in 0 .. LISTSIZE - 1 loop
        get(inlist(i));                          -- Read input data
    end loop;
    put("List s1 before the sort: ");
    new_line;
    for i in 0 .. LISTSIZE - 1 loop
        put(inlist(i));                          -- Display the list before sorting
    end loop;
    new_line(2);
    bubble_sort1(inlist);                        -- Do the sort
    put("List s1 after the sort: ");
    new_line;
    for i in 0 ..LISTSIZE - 1 loop
        put(inlist(i));                          -- Output sorted list
    end loop;
end bubble1;
```

Figure 3.3 Fundamental bubble sort algorithm

When executed on array s1 = {10, 4, 14, –3, 12, 6} the program output is as shown overleaf.

Enter 6 integers

List s1 before the sort:
10 4 14 –3 12 6

List s1 after the sort:
–3 4 6 10 12 14

EXERCISES 3.3

1. Include a piece of code which outputs the 'current state' of s1 after each complete pass.

2. Include variables which operate as counters for the number of comparisons, and the number of swaps. How do these values compare with those from Exercises 3.2, Q. 1? What conclusion do you draw?

3.5 Fewer bubbles

You should have discovered, if you completed Exercises 3.3, that the bubble sort takes rather more passes to sort the same data than the selection sort algorithm. In fact, bubble sort is one of the least efficient algorithms known for ordering data, and is little used in this form in practice.

The algorithm can be improved, however, in a number of ways. Think about the problems with it as it stands.

First, data which has already been sorted as the algorithm progresses is re-examined on each pass. For instance, given s1 = {10, 4, 14, –3, 12, 6} as input, then after the first pass the list will be s1 = {4, 10, –3, 12, 6, 14}. At this point, the last element (14) is in the correct place—the largest item has bubbled to the right. It does not need to be considered on the second pass, only the first five elements have to be tested. After the second pass, when s1 = {4, –3, 10, 6, 12, 14}, the last *two* elements are correctly positioned, and only the first four data items need to be checked, and so on, until just the first two need to be compared.

Hence what we want is to reduce the loop bound $j = n - 1$ by 1 after each pass over the data, that is, before the outer loop, ($i = 0$ to $n - 1$) increments, so that data already dealt with—which has 'bubbled' into the correct place—is not re-sorted unnecessarily. In terms of implementation, n is a constant, and so cannot be decreased: a more logical approach is to increase by 1 the value subtracted from the loop bound $j = n - 1$ each time that the loop completes. Hence we will loop from 0 to $n - 1$ the first time, from 0 to $n - 2$ the second time, and so on up to $n - (n - 1)$, for an algorithm which sorts items left to right in ascending order. After each inner loop iteration, the number of items to be sorted will decrease by one, and one more element will be in 'the right place'. For a 'worst case' (data reversed) sequence, e.g. {9, 8, 7, 6, 5, 4} the situation will be:

	0 1 2 3 4 5	
Start:	9 8 7 6 5 4	
$i = 0$ $j = 0 .. 5$:	8 9 7 6 5 4	Sort elements 0 .. 5
	8 7 9 6 5 4	
	8 7 6 9 5 4	
	8 7 6 5 9 4	
	8 7 6 5 4 9	'9' is now correctly positioned
$i = 1$ $j = 0 .. 4$:	7 8 6 5 4 9	Ignore element 5, sort elements 0 .. 4
	7 6 8 5 4 9	
	7 6 5 8 4 9	
	7 6 5 4 8 9	'8' is now correctly positioned
$i = 2$ $j = 0 .. 3$:	6 7 5 4 8 9	Ignore elements 4 and 5, sort elements 0 .. 3
	6 5 7 4 8 9	
	6 5 4 7 8 9	'7' is now correctly positioned
$i = 3$ $j = 0 .. 2$:	5 6 4 7 8 9	Ignore elements 3, 4 and 5, sort elements 0 .. 2
	5 4 6 7 8 9	'6' is now correctly positioned
$i = 4$ $j = 0 .. 1$:	4 5 6 7 8 9	Ignore elements 2 to 5, sort elements 0 .. 1

Clearly, the loop bound on j for n elements is $(n - 1) - i$. Hence the algorithm is as shown in Fig. 3.4.

In C:

```
#define LISTSIZE 6

void bubble_sort2(int s1[LISTSIZE])
{                /* This function does the sort (ascending order) */
   int i, j, temp;
   for (i = 0; i < LISTSIZE - 1; ++i)        /* Outer loop */
   {
      for (j = 0; j < (LISTSIZE - 1) - i; ++j)       /* Inner loop: */
      {                                      /* this time, on each pass */
         if (s1[j + 1] < s1[j])              /* sort one fewer items */
         {                                   /* than on the previous */
            temp = s1[j];                    /* pass, since the largest */
            s1[j] = s1[j + 1];               /* item among those being */
            s1[j + 1] = temp;                /* examined has 'bubbled' */
         }                                   /* to the end of the list */
      }                                      /* on each pass */
   }
}
```

In Ada:

```
LISTSIZE: integer := 6;
type sort_array is array(0 .. LISTSIZE - 1) of integer;

procedure bubble_sort2(s1: in out sort_array) is     -- This procedure does the sort
temp: integer;                                        -- (ascending order)
begin
    for i in 0 .. LISTSIZE - 2 loop                   -- Outer loop
        for j in 0 .. (LISTSIZE - 2) - i loop         -- Inner loop: this time, on each
            if s1(j+1) < s1(j) then                   -- pass, sort one fewer items
                temp := s1(j);                        -- than on the previous pass,
                s1(j) := s1(j+1);                     -- since the largest item among
                s1(j+1) := temp;                      -- those examined has 'bubbled'
            end if;                                   -- to the end of the list
        end loop;                                     -- on each pass
    end loop;
end bubble_sort2;
```

Figure 3.4 Improved bubble sort program—sorted items not re-sorted

A separate point concerning the original algorithm of Fig. 3.3 is that it keeps on sorting $n - 1$ lots $n - 1$ times, even after the data is correctly sorted. For example, if input data s2 = {1, 2, 3, 4, 5, 6, 7} is entered, there will be 36 comparisons of pairs of data even though no elements are ever exchanged, since the data is ordered to start with. Hence it would be a good idea to have a marker of some kind which ends the algorithm when no items are exchanged following execution of the inner loop which does the comparisons.

This is addressed fairly simply by declaring a marker value which is reset each time a swap occurs and tested prior to continuing. If this value has not changed since last time, then no swaps occurred on that inner loop. That means that each pair of data items has been compared on that pass, and none were found to be out of order: hence the data is now ordered, and the algorithm can stop. Call this marker variable `done`: the technique can be implemented as shown in Fig. 3.5.

In C:

```
#define LISTSIZE 6

void bubble_sort3(int s1[LISTSIZE])
{
            /* This function does the sort (ascending order) */
  int j, temp, done;
  do{             /* Begin 'do-loop': initialise 'done' to 1, */
    done = 1;       /* and re-initialise it on each pass through */

      for (j = 0; j < LISTSIZE - 1; ++j)
      {                         /* Check each pair of elements */
        if (s1[j + 1] < s1[j])  /* If transposed, exchange them */
```

```
            {
                  temp = s1[j];
                  s1[j] = s1[j + 1];
                  s1[j + 1] = temp;
                  done = 0;              /* and set 'done' to zero */
            }                            /* Continue comparing and */
        }                                /* exchanging until no elements */
     }while (!done);                     /* are exchanged on a pass: then*/
}                                        /* 'done' is not reset, and so */
                                         /* the loop is exited */
```

In Ada:

```
LISTSIZE: integer := 6;
type sort_array is array(0 .. LISTSIZE - 1) of integer;

procedure bubble_sort3(s1: in out sort_array) is   -- This procedure does the sort
temp, done: integer;                                -- (ascending order)
begin
    done := 0;
    while done = 0 loop                             -- Begin 'do-loop':
        done := 1;                                  -- initialise 'done' to 1, and
        for j in 0 .. LISTSIZE - 2 loop             -- re-initialise it on each pass
            if s1(j+1) < s1(j) then                 -- Check each pair of elements:
                temp := s1(j);                      -- if transposed, exchange them,
                s1(j) := s1(j+1);
                s1(j+1) := temp;
                done := 0;                          -- and set 'done' to zero
            end if;                                 -- Continue comparing and
        end loop;                                   -- exchanging until no elements
    end loop;                                       -- are exchanged: then 'done' is not
end bubble_sort3;                                   -- reset, and the procedure ends.
```

Figure 3.5 Improved bubble sort—program ends when no more exchanges occur

Clearly, this also represents an improvement; in fact, either of the two modified versions is a much more efficient version of the bubble sort than the original. However, the process has been rather tortuous: the initial idea appeared to be reasonable, and a perfectly good working algorithm resulted. Even on cursory examination, it turned out not to be the best way to do things, and so a couple of ways have been devised to 'tweak' it.

Such 'fine tuning' of algorithms is frequently a useful technique, but it also sets off warning bells among experienced program designers. Is more fine tuning possible? Do the 'improvements' made always improve things, or are they actually bad under certain conditions? Shouldn't we be looking for something intrinsically more elegant, rather that poking about at code that doesn't work very well? And what about maintenance?

In any event, the documentation will have to be very precise, so that any future changes (probably made by somebody else) take account of identifiers such as 'done', whose meaning is not immediately apparent.

EXERCISES 3.4

1. Incorporate the suggested modifications into either the C or Ada bubble sort programs, and retest them. Compare the numbers of comparisons and exchanges for the improved version.

2. Enter the following sequences of integers as input data for both the selection sort and the bubble sort programs, and execute them. Which algorithm is preferable in each case?

   (i) 2 5 –1 36 13 0 5 15 –11 20 8
   (ii) 4 4 4 4 4 4
   (iii) 1 2 3 4 5 6 7
   (iv) 81 60 59 53 38 4 –18 –36 –50
   (v) 38 47 50 56 63 86 90 49 114 120

3. How can the two modifications to the bubble sort be incorporated into one version? Does this represent the most efficient version? Try it with the data from Q.2, and compare the number of comparisons and exchanges with the original, and with the selection sort.

3.6 Insertion sort

A technique for sorting which is particularly good for part-ordered lists is *insertion sort*. The basis of the technique is similar to the way many people sort things naturally, especially playing cards. When a hand of cards is picked up after dealing, the cards are in no particular order: if we are sorting in ascending order, then a common method is to scan along from left to right, ordering the 'smallest so far' at each stage. So for example, given a hand as in Fig. 3.6, and ignoring suits—i.e. sorting on the basis of value only—the hand may change as it is sorted, as shown in Fig. 3.7.

K♣ 5♥ 2♥ 9♦ 6♠

Figure 3.6 Hand as dealt

→5♥ K♣ 2♥ 9♦ 6♠
→2♥ 5♥ K♣ 9♦ 6♠
→2♥ 5♥ 9♦ K♣ 6♠
→2♥ 5♥ 6♠ 9♦ K♣

Figure 3.7 Hand sorted

This method, although intuitive, is found by many people to be less easy to specify algorithmically than, for example, the bubble sort. So we proceed just as before, refining the solution until it appears to be ready for coding and testing. The data types, as before, we will take as integer, for simplicity.

Initially, it is often a good idea to 'talk through' the method (with a colleague, if possible), or to write it down in natural language. What is actually happening in Figs. 3.6 and 3.7? What we are doing is, first, considering the first and second elements, and moving over the second to accommodate the first if it is in the wrong relative order. In this example, the first step in Fig. 3.7 was to consider the king of clubs and the five of hearts: since the five is smaller, these were exchanged. The next card to consider was the two of hearts, which is smaller than both the five and the king; so the two went into the first position, and the five and the king had to 'shuffle up' to make room. The next card, the nine of diamonds, is smaller than the king of clubs, but larger than the five of hearts: so the king only moves, shuffling up to make way for the nine. Finally, the six of spades is smaller than the king and the nine, but bigger than the five, and so it moves into the place previously occupied by the nine, and the nine and the king shuffle up to make room for it.

That spells out what is happening in natural language, and so the next step is to write the first version of an algorithm which specifies the process unambiguously and precisely, in a step-by-step way.

Assume that n integers are under consideration: the 'compare and shuffle if necessary' process occurs, in the example, from the first two cards down to the last card. That is, there are $n - 1$ such comparisons to make—for example, in Fig. 3.7, there are four 'compare and shuffle if necessary' routines. When executing this process on a computer, we need to take into account the necessity for temporary storage of variables (what we humans do 'in our heads'), and the exact order in which actions are going to be done. For instance, we might think of the process as: compare any card with its neighbour to the left, and, if the card to the left is larger, compare with the one to the left of that, and so on, until we reach a card that is smaller, or we reach the start. Then put the card in its proper place: to do that, we have to 'shuffle up' all the cards from that place one step to the right. This reflects what happens usually when we sort a hand of cards, but it is probably not the best way to implement the process in software.

The reason that this intuitive approach is not necessarily the best in programming terms is that there is an implicit iterative process in the 'compare' activity. Since a loop will exist in which the item currently under consideration is compared successively with its neighbours, it would probably be simpler to execute the 'shuffle' within the same iteration. Hence on each pass, we compare with the item to the left, and move down that item one place right (where the current item came from) if it is larger. We then repeat those actions until the current item is in the correct place. This also means that the value of the current item will have to be saved separately, since it will be overwritten during the shuffle.

Notice also, that because of the way this algorithm works, the list *up to* the last item that was placed is always sorted up to that point. In Fig. 3.7, for example, when the nine of diamonds is placed (the third card), the first three cards are sorted. Hence we can initially specify the insertion sort algorithm for an array of integers s1(0 .. $n-1$) as:

Declare integer array s1[0 .. n–1]
1. Loop from $i = 0$ to $n - 1$
2.   If 'predecessor' is larger than current item
        Shuffle item up
    Endif
3.   Insert current item in the correct place
    End loop
4. Stop

Clearly, 'shuffle item up' and 'in the right place' must be clarified, and a temporary variable will need to be declared to hold the value of the current item. The 'shuffle up', as indicated above, is really no more than an overwriting if necessary of the array position to the right of the current one. The 'correct place' is the place prior to the one currently being evaluated. Consider the positioning of the seventh item in an array s1[0 .. 9], that is, s1[6]:

array s1:

0	1	2	3	4	5	6	7	8	9

If item 6 is under consideration, then s1[0 .. 5] are already sorted up to that point. Suppose we have, at this point,

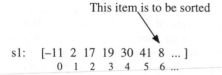

This item is to be sorted ↓

s1: [–11 2 17 19 30 41 8 ...]
0 1 2 3 4 5 6 ...

We need to save the contents of the current position, s1[6], in a variable, say `temp`; that is, `temp` ← `8`. We also need to save the current *position* itself, so that if it is necessary the item to the left can overwrite the contents of that position, e.g. s1[6] ← s1[5]. Then we need to decrement the current position so that the next value can overwrite, if necessary, which would be, in this case, the value 30 (s1[4]) overwriting the 41 in s1[5]. After three such 'comparisons and overwrites', the position would be:

temp = 8: compare with 17 ↓

[–11 2 17 19 19 30 41 ...]
0 1 2 3 4 5 6 ...

19 has overwritten 30 (s1[4]); it is itself (s1[3]) about to be overwritten by 17(s1[2]).

We need to continue in this fashion until either we reach an equal or smaller value than the one under consideration, or we reach the beginning, i.e. s1[0]. We then need to write the current value (8) into the proper position—in this case, s1[2]. Thus we need to begin by saving the *position* of the item under consideration, as well as its value, and then decrement that position number after each compare. This process at this stage (a kind of 'snapshot' of the whole sorting process) may be written:

```
i = 6                     /* this is the position currently being considered */
temp ← s1[i]              /* Save value of item being considered */
j ← i                     /* j holds the position of the neighbour to be compared */
Loop while (j > 0 AND temp < s1[j – 1]) /* Compare with every item in the list
                                           from the fifth down to the zeroth ... */
   s1[j] ← s1[j – 1]      /* ... and overwrite if s1[j] < s1[j – 1] */
   j ← j – 1              /* Decrement position counter */
End loop
s1[j] ← temp              /* Write current item into correct place */
```

Work through the above process to convince yourself that it works. Having done that, all that is necessary is to repeat the same process for the items in position 7, position 8, and position 9. For the whole input list, from s1[0] to s1[9], we need an outer loop from $i = 1$ to $i = 9$: this is so that the first comparison made between s1[j] (i.e. s1[1]) and s1[$j – 1$] (i.e. s1[0]) is valid.

The complete algorithm for an array s1[10, 4, 14, –3, 12, 6] is shown in Fig.3.8.

In C:

```
#include <stdio.h>
#define SORT_MAX 6
void main()
{
   int i, j, k, temp;
   int s1[SORT_MAX] = {10, 4, 14, -3, 12, 6};     /* Array to sort */
   for (k = 0; k < SORT_MAX; ++k)
   {
      printf("%3d", s1[k]);          /* Print out initial values */
   }
   printf("\n\n");
   for (i = 1; i < SORT_MAX; ++i)
   {          /* This is the position currently being considered  */
      temp = s1[i]; /*  Save value under consideration in 'temp' */
      j = i;    /* and save current position in 'j'. */
      while (j > 0 && temp < s1[j - 1])      /* Overwrite the item */
      {                               /* on the right with the value */
        s1[j] = s1[j - 1];            /* of the item on the left if the */
        j = j - 1;                    /* RH value is smaller, and */
      }                 /* decrement j, which thus identifies the */
      s1[j] = temp;   /* position on the left.  When no more */
   }                    /* exchanges, overwrite the 'next-smallest' */
```

```
  for (k = 0; k < SORT_MAX; ++k)
  {
    printf("%d ", s1[k]);            /* Print sorted list  */
  }
}
```

In Ada:

```
with text_io; use text_io;
package int_io is new text_io.integer_io(integer);
use int_io;

procedure insert is
SORT_MAX: integer := 6;
type sort_array is array(0 .. SORT_MAX - 1) of integer;
s1: sort_array := (10, 4, 14, –3, 12, 6);                    -- Array to sort
j, temp: integer;

begin
      for k in 0 .. SORT_MAX - 1 loop
            put(s1(k));                       -- Print out initial values
      end loop;
      new_line(2);
      for i in 1 .. SORT_MAX - 1 loop -- This is the position currently being considered
            temp := s1(i);                    -- Save value under consideration in 'temp'
            j := i;                           -- and save current position in 'j'
            while j > 0 and then temp < s1(j - 1) loop    -- Overwrite the item on the
                  s1(j) := s1(j - 1);         -- right with the value of the item on the left if
                  j := j - 1;                 -- the RH value is smaller, and decrement 'j',
            end loop;                         -- which thus identifies the position on the left.
            s1(j) := temp;        -- When no more exchanges, overwrite the 'next-smallest'
            for k in 0 .. SORT_MAX - 1 loop
               put(s1(k));                    -- Output sorted list
            end loop;
            new_line;
      end loop;
end insert;
```

Figure 3.8 Insertion sort

3.7 Other approaches to sorting

One suggestion which is sometimes made when dealing with sorting algorithms is that the input set should be sorted into a separate output set. So, for instance, we initially declare s1 and s2. Suppose the input is 7, 4, 11, 3, 2, 61. Then:

Input s1 = {7, 4, 11, 3, 2, 61}

s2 = {?, ?, ?, ?, ?, ?} {the '?' symbols indicate undefined values on declaration}

The idea is that we sort as shown in Fig. 3.9, giving output s2 = {2, 3, 4, 7, 11, 61}.

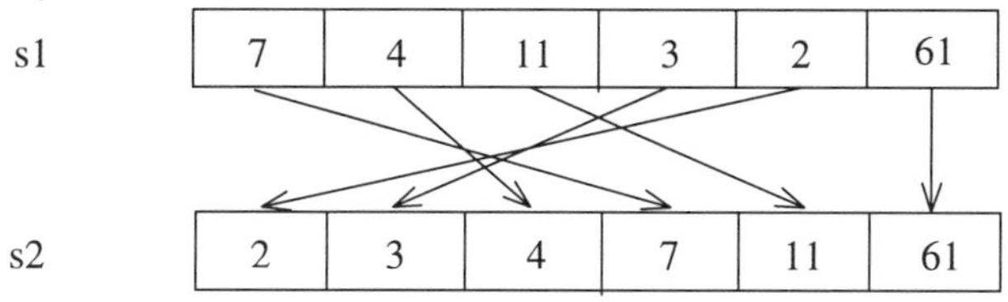

Figure 3.9 Conceptual representation of sorting by copying input array values to an output array

This might seem to be a sensible approach, since it avoids the need for swapping components within one array that acts both as input and output. However, in terms of the methods discussed in this chapter, the disadvantages far outweigh the advantages.

It is worth thinking the problem through: we may discover a simpler algorithm. How could the exchange of components between s1 and s2 be achieved? One possibility is to use the value of each item as an index into the output array. So, for Fig. 3.9, the first input value, s1[1] = 7; so write this into s2[7]. Write s1[2] = 4 into s2[4], and so on.

Several of the inadequacies of this approach in general are immediately obvious: except in the unusual and trivial case when the input data is known in advance, and comprises unordered integers differing by only 1 from each other, the resulting output array may be rather sparsely populated. Of course, it would be simple to write a small routine to compact the array—but then the algorithm is starting to elaborate in just the way we were trying to avoid.

Another unwanted side-effect is that s2 must be as large as the largest value in s1. Assuming that this value is not known prior to execution, s2 would have to be declared as 'large enough', say s2[1 .. 10 000]. However, there is no guarantee that 10 000, or any other value, is in fact big enough. Further, we are now starting to take up significant amounts of computer memory, and to no good purpose. A dynamic data structure would be a more logical approach (see Chapter 6), but the method is then quite different to that which we are investigating here.

It is also the case, of course, that although the method works for natural numbers, we have not thought about what to do with negative, or floating-point numbers. And what happens when the input data comprises characters or strings? There are other objections, but just from an initial consideration of what is involved, it is clear that writing the unordered input data into an ordered output array is not a viable proposition at this point.

It was pointed out in Chapter 1 that the most important part of providing a solution to any situation that is presented as 'a problem' lies in first understanding and articulating the problem. Consider what assumptions and simplifications you are implicitly making, and then think through your candidate solution with a small test data set. Only when you believe that your method appears promising should you set out the solution algorithmically: then retest with the same data—this will result in extension and refinement (or abandonment) of the algorithm.

Once the step-by-step solution is clear, correct and complete, it can be implemented as a program. The programming effort is minimal—especially as you become more familiar with your chosen language. Nine-tenths of the effort is in understanding, program design, and testing.

There are, in fact, many other sorting methods which are more efficient than the three discussed in this chapter. The idea of *efficiency* of algorithms has been alluded to several times in this chapter: efficiency is in fact a very precise notion, allowing us to compare methods directly in terms of the time (and/or space) taken for execution, in the worst case, and on average.

The analysis of the efficiency of algorithms in this way is the subject of Chapter 5, when we deal with time-complexity in particular; sorting methods will then be referred to again, as examples for such analysis.

Summary

- Sorting programs are fundamental in computing, and are widely used in very many different situations.
- In order to devise and code a sorting algorithm, considerable time must be taken in designing the method on paper first, and executing a 'walk through' or 'dry run' to check how the algorithm executes.
- There are many possible ways to sort. Three algorithms have been considered here: selection sort, insertion sort, and bubble sort.
- The primitive bubble sort is very inefficient. It can be much improved in a number of simple ways.
- Insertion sort is usually the best of the three ways considered here.

4

PATTERNS: SOLUTIONS WAITING TO BE FOUND

OBJECTIVES

In this chapter you will learn

- how *sequences* occur, both in nature and in society, and the importance of being able to manipulate data to do with sequences
- how sequences are formally represented
- examples of inferring a rule from data that appears to have some pattern, and then simulating real events
- the distinction between a sequence and a series

4.1 What happened next?

The chapter title indicates that in many cases, what is presented as 'a problem' is not a problem at all in the sense given earlier—that of creating a transformation process to get from an existing input state to a new output state. Often, the question—either directly or implicity—is concerned with prediction.

Government and private-enterprise agencies spend enormous amounts of time and money on trying to identify trends. These include such notions as: 'What proportion of the population will be aged over 65 in the year 2010?' 'What will be the rate of inflation over the next 12 months?' 'How many new homes will it be necessary to build over the next 5 years?'

City speculators try to spot trends for a living, and then make bets on them. Insurance companies attempt to project the likely total cost of claims over the coming year, so that premiums can be appropriately set. Manufacturers assess the market for their goods in order to be able to plan for the necessary investment in, or reduction of, plant and employee numbers.

Astronomers calculate where a comet is going to be three years hence by investigating its past behaviour. Mechanical engineers work out the required dimensions of a piston connecting-rod, and the tensile strength of its material for a given engine design, based on prior knowledge.

Classically, the search for pattern has been an integral part of the accepted scientific method. In physics, botany, chemistry, and many other disciplines, scientists and engineers spend much of their time repeating experiments with slightly different input conditions each time, in order to try to discern some general features of the situation. This has led to 'laws', such as Newton's laws of motion, the laws of heredity, and the laws of allowable chemical compounds based on valency.

Mathematicians are trained to find harmony in apparent dissonance, and sometimes wonder whether patterns are 'really there', or whether our minds impose them on the input from our sense data.

What has this to do with algorithms? The answer is that the above questions are mostly investigated by computers nowadays, which frequently provide models showing what may happen in the future. The computers, of course, are just the hardware on which the programs that actually do the forecasting run. And the programs are implementations of algorithms.

Algorithmic approaches to questions of the type above rely on data being present initially. For example, if we know that some event has occurred twice, five times, eight times, and eleven times over past consecutive years, how many times will it happen this year? Since we have the sequence 2, 5, 8, 11, ..., one possible answer is 14, though the likelihood of that being a correct forecast depends very much on the real-world context. If the event in question were air crashes, for example, one might hope that action was being taken to reduce the number. If the occurrence were thousands of job losses in a given industry, and the same conditions applied today as in the past, the forecast might be more accurate. If the incident were centimetres of rainfall over a given area, then the forecast of 14 is probably wrong (or else something very odd is happening).

It is when the event concerns the behaviour of physical systems that we can begin to have rather more confidence in our predictions. If we know *precisely* the force with which a football is kicked, for instance, and the angle at which it takes off, we can say, in theory, where it will land. In practice, it turns out to be extremely hard to make such a prediction with a high degree of accuracy repeatably, just because there are too many hard-to-measure variables. The force with which the ball is kicked, the actual ball geometry, variable wind and air resistance and so on, mean that real events are never exactly the same twice. Another example: if we observe that stopping distances for motor vehicles are 75 ft at 30 mph, 175 ft at 50 mph, and 315 ft at 70 mph, we can calculate the stopping distance for a vehicle travelling at 45 mph, or 120 mph, or any other speed within some acceptable margin of error, at least in theory. The reality may be different, so that any computer model should be considered as just that—a model. The extreme accuracy of the computer should not deceive you into thinking that this necessarily confers any great accuracy on the model.

Problems of this kind occur very frequently in reality, and so we explore the method for their solution in this and subsequent chapters. The method, for the most part, reflects common sense, though the formalisation of the approach may seem unfamiliar at first, especially if the notation is new to you. In particular, Sections 4.5 and 4.6 are detailed examinations of situations which may require some concentration to understand. If the details of the analysis seem difficult on first reading, skim over the maths, but follow the process that leads to the final algorithm. You can return to these sections later, when you have more confidence.

As mentioned earlier, the further the question is from the physical world, and the closer to sociological or psychological behaviour, the more tentative our response, and so the examples here are from 'hard' science and engineering, rather than from anthropology or psychology. Algorithms for solving problems in mechanics, for instance, are usually rather straightforward. Similar methods can be used for answering questions of astronomy (where will Jupiter be in three months' time?) or even subatomic physics (what happens when an electron hits a neutron at close to the speed of light?). The mathematics involved in the analysis of such problems may be straightforward, or extremely difficult, but, once some pattern has been discerned, devising an algorithm to give results for various different inputs, or to predict the situation under given circumstances, is usually not complicated.

4.2 Sequences

The process of distinguishing trends, in any of the suggested contexts, is frequently characterised by identifying sequences. In the example in Section 4.1, a sequence 2, 5, 8, 11, ... was suggested. When we look at such a sequence of numbers, we see immediately that

- it is increasing
- there is some regularity to the increase

It is not too difficult, in the example sequence, to spot that the rule for generating the next number could well be 'Add 3 to the previous one'. When the rule seems not to be obvious, it is often helpful to plot sequences on graph paper, as shown in Fig.4.1.

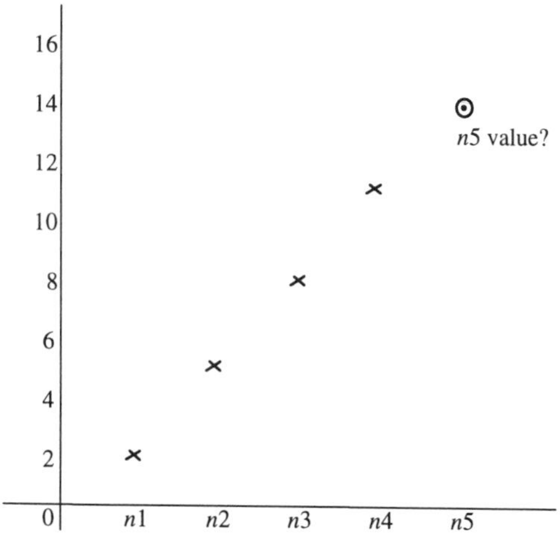

Figure 4.1 Linearly increasing sequence-members

This is not *necessarily* correct, because the real-life events the sequence refers to may not in fact be increasing in such a way, or action may be being taken to change the situation. The rule is also not necessarily correct in purely theoretical terms: more of this later.

Consider the following sequences:

(i) 2, 3, 4, 5, 6
(ii) 6, 11, 16, 21, 26
(iii) 2, 4, 8, 16, 32
(iv) 2, 5, 14, 41, 122

By playing around with numbers, or by graph-sketching, we might come up with the following informal rules for these sequences:

(i) 'Add 1 each time'
(ii) 'Add 5 to the previous one'
(iii) 'Powers of 2'
(iv) 'Multiply the previous one by 3, and then subtract 1'

Assume the rules are correct (they fit the existing data): what sort of function would generate such sequences? At this stage, we are dealing just with integers, and examples (i)–(iv) are based on the rule being applied to the numbers 1, 2, 3, 4, 5, 6, ...

Having made plain the assumptions and simplifications, an algorithm for any of them would be along the lines of:

1. Declare any data as necessary
2. Loop for $i = 1$ to 5
    Apply the rule to i
    Output i
   End loop
3. Stop

This algorithm can be made rather more precise for each case, of course, and an example of this is given on page 58. At this stage, however, the point that is illustrated is that the algorithm is trivial.

4.3 Notation for sequences

It is useful to have a shorthand for the rule which gives any particular sequence (this is the *generating function* for the sequence). We use the following notation:

$\{f_n\} = \{f_1, f_2, f_3, f_4, f_5, f_6, ...\}$

So, taking sequence (i) of Section 4.2 as an example, we could write

$f_n = n + 1, \; n = 1, 2, 3, 4, 5, ...$

So that $f_1 = 1 + 1 = 2$; $f_2 = 2 + 1 = 3$; $f_3 = 3 + 1 = 4$; $f_4 = 4 + 1 = 5$; $f_5 = 5 + 1 = 6$, etc. How far does this sequence extend? Can we say that $f_{-4} = -3$? There is in fact no reason why the sequence should not extend as far as you like, in either direction. If the sequence is being used in a model, however, then it is important to state at the outset what restrictions or limits are imposed by the reality.

The generating functions for the other examples are:

(ii) $f_n = 5n + 1, \quad n = 1, 2, 3, 4, 5$
(iii) $f_n = 2^n, \quad n = 1, 2, 3, 4, 5$
(iv) $f_n = (3^n + 1)/2, \quad n = 1, 2, 3, 4, 5$

EXERCISES 4.1

1. Write the first five terms of the sequences generated by the following functions:

(i) $f_n = n + 3$
(ii) $f_n = (n + 7)/2$
(iii) $f_n = 1/n$
(iv) $f_n = (n + 7)/2n$
(v) $f_n = (n - 3)/(n^2 + 1)$
(vi) $f_n = n/(n - 6)$
(vii) $f_n = (n - 1)2^n$
(viii) $f_n = n^n$

All the above functions are *direct formulae*: they give the value of any required term directly in terms of n. However, when we are looking for patterns, we tend to see a trend in terms of 'the way things are going': we look at past data and come up with a rule which seems to apply in terms of what has gone before. As a result, the rules are more often of the kind 'Add 5 to the previous one' than 'For the sequence of natural numbers, for each element multiply by 5 and add 1'—which is what the direct formula for (ii) is shorthand for. But we can just as easily use the same kind of shorthand to specify a sequence in terms of a 'starter value' and 'what happens next'. For example,

$$f_{n+1} = f_n + 3, f_1 = 1$$

says: 'The first term (f_1) is 1; the rule for what happens next is that you add 3 to the previous term'. This means that the resulting sequence is:

$f_1 = 1$
$f_2 = f_1 + 3 = 1 + 3 = 4$
$f_3 = f_2 + 3 = 4 + 3 = 7$
$f_4 = f_3 + 3 = 7 + 3 = 10$

and so on, i.e. the sequence 1, 4, 7, 10, 13, ...

This sequence also has a direct formula, of course: it is $f_n = 3n - 2$. Formulae expressed in terms of a 'what happens next' rule, such as $f_{n+1} = f_n + 3, f_1 = 1$ are often called *iterative* formulae, or *recurrence relations*, in which any f_n is expressed in terms of its predecessors. Recurrence relations are of considerable importance in the analysis of algorithmic efficiency, and we will be referring to them again in Chapter 5.

The iterative formulae corresponding to examples (i)–(iv) are:

(i) $f_{n+1} = f_n + 1, \quad f_1 = 2$
(ii) $f_{n+1} = f_n + 5, \quad f_1 = 6$
(iii) $f_{n+1} = 2f_n, \quad f_1 = 2$
(iv) $f_{n+1} = 3f_n - 1, \quad f_1 = 2$

So there are in fact two ways to specify the generating function for a sequence, depending on the information available. However, once one of them has been defined, the algorithm follows immediately. For instance, for (iv):

Initialise $x = 2$, $i = 1$
1. Loop while $i \leq 5$
        Print (x)
        $x \leftarrow (3x - 1)$
        $i \leftarrow i + 1$
    End loop
2. Stop

EXERCISES 4.2

1. Verify that the algorithm above gives the sequence 2, 5, 14, 41, 122 as output.

2. Write the first five terms of the sequences generated by the following iterative formulae:
    (i) $f_{n+1} = f_n - 5, \ f_1 = 1$
    (ii) $f_{n+1} = 3f_n - 2, \ f_1 = 3$
    (iii) $f_{n+1} = 2f_n - 3, \ f_1 = 5$

3. State the generating function for the following algorithm as an iterative formula and as a direct formula.

    Initialise $x = 3$, $i = 1$
    1. Loop while $i \leq 5$
            Print (x)
            $x \leftarrow (2x - 2)$
            $i \leftarrow i + 1$
        End loop
    2. Stop

4. Work out the output from the following algorithms, and state their generating functions as iterative formulae:

(i)
```
Initialise x = 1, i = 1
1. Loop while i ≤ 5
      Print (x)
      x ← (5x – 6)
      i ← i + 1
   End loop
2. Stop
```

(ii)
```
Initialise x = 6, i = 1
1. Loop while i ≤ 5
      Print (x)
      x ← ((x/3) + 2)
      i ← i + 1
   End loop
2. Stop
```

It is possible to define an iterative formula with more than one 'starter', for example,

$$f_n = f_{n-1} + f_{n-2},\ f_1 = 1,\ f_2 = 1$$

when we have

$$
\begin{aligned}
f_1 &= 1\\
f_2 &= 1\\
f_3 &= f_2 + f_1 = 1 + 1 = 2\\
f_4 &= f_3 + f_2 = 2 + 1 = 3\\
&\vdots
\end{aligned}
$$

This gives rise to the sequence 1, 1, 2, 3, 5, 8, 13, 21, ... which occurs surprisingly often in nature. This sequence was first investigated by a thirteenthth century Italian called Leonardo of Pisa, or Leonardo Fibonacci, and is thus known as the Fibonacci sequence. Pineapples have their features arranged according to a subset of this sequence, and so do many other plants. Fibonacci was apparently prompted to consider this pattern while studying rabbit populations, and wasps also breed according to this sequence (starting with a single drone, which has the queen as parent). Although the sequence is easy to formulate as a recurrence relation, its direct formula is less obvious. The Fibonacci sequence crops up fairly often in the study of algorithms, and it is important to be aware of it.

4.4 Unexpected successors

In Section 4.2 it was stated that any rule for the next term in a sequence is not necessarily correct, even theoretically: a single example will show why this is the case. Suppose we have the sequence

2, 4, 6, 8, t

The question is, 'What is the value of t?'. The most obvious answer is '10', which is very plausible, and may well be true. However, the values 34, or –131, or 11.136, or, indeed, any other number you care to think of, are also potentially correct. The reason is that a sequence may have any generating function. We may know that function in advance, in which case we can calculate the value of t. But when we do not know what the generating function for the sequence is, we can only *infer* it from the existing data and it then applies only to the data we have. Inferring that the next value is 10 is equivalent to proposing $f_n = 2n$ as the generator. But suppose that the generator is

$$f_n = 2n + (n - 1)(n - 2)(n - 3)(n - 4).$$

Then

$$\begin{aligned} f_1 &= 2 \times 1 + (1 - 1)(1 - 2)(1 - 3)(1 - 4) \\ &= 2 + (0 \times -1 \times -2 \times -3) = 2 + 0 = 2 \end{aligned}$$

Similarly,

$$\begin{aligned} f_2 &= 2 \times 2 + (2 - 1)(2 - 2)(2 - 3)(2 - 4) \\ &= 4 + (1 \times 0 \times -1 \times -2) = 4. \end{aligned}$$

In the same way, $f_3 = 2 \times 3 + (2 \times 1 \times 0 \times -1) = 6$
and $f_4 = 2 \times 4 + (3 \times 2 \times 1 \times 0) = 8$

However,

$$\begin{aligned} f_5 &= 2 \times 5 + (5 - 1)(5 - 2)(5 - 3)(5 - 4) \\ &= 10 + (4 \times 3 \times 2 \times 1) \\ &= 10 + 24 \\ &= 34 \end{aligned}$$

Hence, the first five terms of the sequence are: 2, 4, 6, 8, 34.

The generating function could have been $f_n = 2n + k(n - 1)(n - 2)(n - 3)(n - 4)$, where k is 3, or –11.44, or 17, or any other value at all. So the next term in a sequence, when we do not know its generating function in advance, may be *any* value.

4.5 Taking the temperature

Two examples of solving problems which are based on the idea of seeing a pattern are now presented. The first is fairly straightforward, while the second is a little more demanding, in terms of analysing the data and relating it to the real world. In both cases, however, the algorithm for the solution is not complicated.

Example 1: Consider weather forecasts: the temperatures to be expected in different parts of the country, and in different countries, may be given either in degrees Celsius or in degrees Fahrenheit. Some people naturally think of temperatures in one or other of these scales, depending on the system adopted nationally, and the scale they were taught at school. Normal body temperature is either 98.4 °F, or 37 °C. If we are in an environment in which temperatures are given in °C, and we want to know what that is in °F, we need to do a conversion (compare with the problem in Section 1.3). In order to convert temperatures in one scale to temperatures in the other, there must be some standard formula. Suppose we know some data in advance, e.g.

26 °C = 78.8 °F; 20 °C = 68 °F; 24 °C = 75.2 °F; 30 °C = 86 °F

Can we find a pattern? We have

°C	20	24	26	30
°F	68	75.2	78.8	86

Now, if the known data is plotted as points on a graph, a straight line will emerge. This graph can be used for direct conversion, in that a value on one scale can be read off against the other, or the gradient and intercept can be measured, and an approximate function obtained of the form F = *g* C + *k*, where *g* is the gradient, and *k* is the intercept, as in Fig. 4.2.

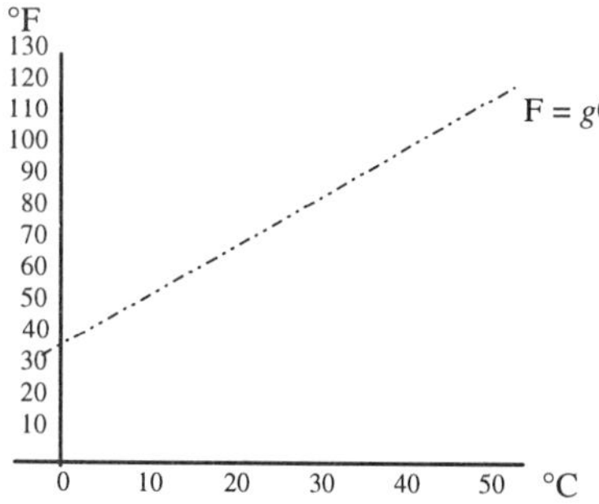

Figure 4.2 Temperature in degrees Fahrenheit against degrees Celsius

An alternative representation, before examining the data further, is to bear in mind that 0 °C, the freezing point of water, is 32 °F. The boiling point of water is 100 °C, or 212 °F. This gives us two equivalent scales: either 0–100 or 32–212. We could then represent this as shown in Fig. 4.3, in which the two scales are placed against each other, and the equivalent points are represented as mappings.

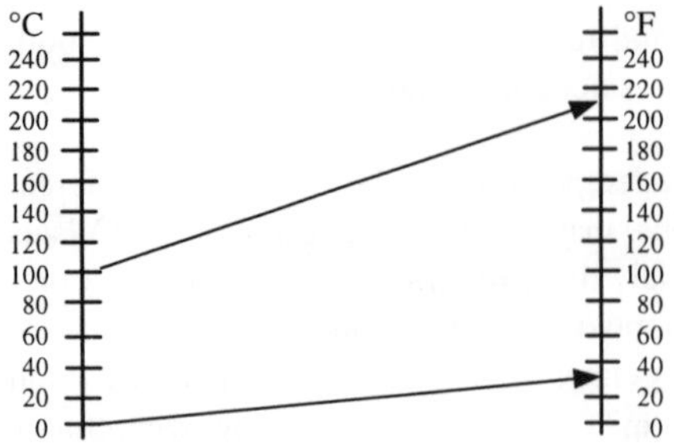

Figure 4.3 Temperature in degrees Celsius compared with temperature in degrees Fahrenheit

Clearly, an increase in temperature of 1 °C is equivalent to a 'bigger' rise in degrees Fahrenheit. In fact, an increase from 0 to 100 °C is equivalent to an increase from 32 to 212 °F. That is a change of 100 °C = a change of 180 °F, i.e. a 'scale factor' of (180/100), or 1.8, is applied to Celsius temperatures in order to get Fahrenheit. However, the other point to bear in mind is that the scales do not both start from the same point. 0 °C ≡ 32 °F, and so the process is:

For each Celsius value
    Multiply by 1.8
    Add 32

Thus, 0 °C = (0 × 1.8) + 32 = 0 + 32 = 32 °F
and 100 °C = (100 × 1.8) + 32 = 180 + 32 = 212 °F

We can check the method with the other data we know, namely:

°C	20	24	26	30
°F	68	75.2	78.8	86

$20 \times 1.8 + 32 = 36.0 + 32 = 68.0$
$24 \times 1.8 + 32 = 43.2 + 32 = 75.2$
$26 \times 1.8 + 32 = 46.8 + 32 = 78.8$
$30 \times 1.8 + 32 = 54.0 + 32 = 86.0.$

Although the investigation so far has been empirical, and the result has not been proved, the transformation that we have arrived at appears to be good for the known data. We have:

Input : Degrees Celsius
Output: Degrees Fahrenheit
Data type: Real numbers

Process:

Declare variables F and C as reals

1. Read C
2. Compute F = C × 1.8 + 32
3. Output F
4. Stop

The analysis of this problem has been painstaking, but methodical. The algorithm has been shown to be correct, though not formally proved so, and ultimately is trivial (see Fig. 4.4).

In C:

```
#include <stdio.h>
/* Temperature conversion */

void main()
{
   float cent, fahr;
   printf("Enter temperature in degrees Celsius: ");
   scanf("%f", &cent);
   fahr = cent * 1.8 + 32.0;
   printf("\n%.2f degrees Celsius is %.2f degrees", cent, fahr);
   printf(" Fahrenheit.");
}
```

In Ada:

```
with text_io; use text_io;
procedure CtoF is                    -- Temperature conversion
package int_io is new text_io.integer_io(integer);
package flt_io is new text_io.float_io(float);
use int_io, flt_io;
cent, fahr: float;
begin
   put("Enter temperature in degrees Celsius: ");
   get(cent);
   fahr := cent * 1.8 + 32.0;
   new_line(2);
   put(cent, fore => 3, aft => 2, exp => 0);
   put(" degrees Celsius is");
   put(fahr, fore => 3, aft => 2, exp => 0);
   put(" degrees Fahrenheit.");
end CtoF;
```

Figure 4.4 Temperature conversion algorithm

The second example examined in this section—a model of bacterial growth—also requires careful exploration, but again the central algorithm resulting from the analysis is neither lengthy nor complicated.

Example 2: Bacteria multiply quite rapidly. A single bacterium able to feed off its environment will grow for a short time, and then split into two bacteria. Each of these does the same thing, and so on, so that the propagation—in the absence of anything to stop it—is rapid, and resembles a cascade of bugs as shown in Fig. 4.5.

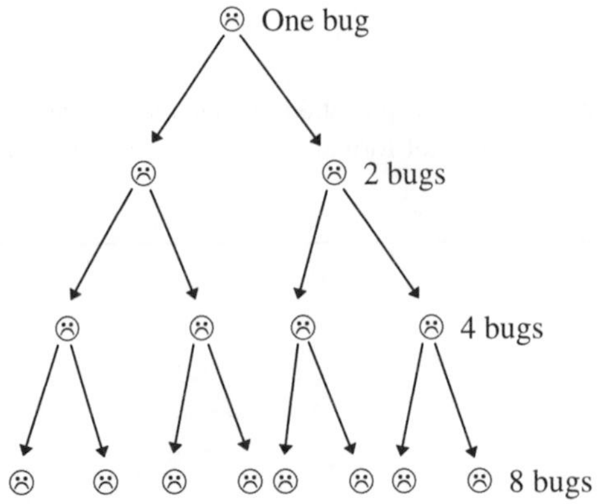

Figure 4.5 A cascade of bugs

Suppose the bacteria divide every 3 hours; how many will there be after a day? Clearly, the pattern is 1, 2, 4, 8, 16, ... , and so over the first 24 hours, assuming division every 3 hours, we have eight divisions:

Time:	00:00	03:00	06:00	09:00	12:00	15:00	18:00	21:00	24:00
No. of bugs	1	2	4	8	16	32	64	128	256
Term	f_0	f_1	f_2	f_3	f_4	f_5	f_6	f_7	f_8

The sequence begins with the 'zeroth term', f_0, at time zero, to make the arithmetic easier, and more easily related to what is actually happening: over 24 hours, there are (24/3) = 8 divisions. The generating function for the sequence is then clearly:

$f_n = 2^n$ (remember, $2^0 = 1$) or, equivalently, $f_{n+1} = 2f_n, f_0 = 1$

Using the direct formula, we have, after 2 days, $f_{16} = 2^{16} = 65\,536$. After 5 days, there are 2^{40}, or well over 1 000 000 000 000 bugs!

Having seen the pattern for bacteria multiplication, and deduced the generating function, the algorithm for calculating the number after any given period is extremely straightforward, being essentially just one calculation. We might improve its flexibility somewhat by allowing the time it takes the bacteria to divide to be variable, but the process is still an elementary one. In essence, we have:

Input: Number of days (d), hourly period of division (n)
Output: Number of bacteria (b)
Data type: Integer

Process:
Declare variables d, b, n as integers
Declare s (number of separations) as integer
1. Read d, n
2. Compute $s = (d \times 24)/n$
3. Compute $b = 2^s$
4. Output b
5. Stop

Obviously, in a real case of bacterial infection, the body's own resources rapidly mobilise and then kill harmful bacteria. However, when our natural defences are inadequate to some particularly virulent strain, we usually seek medical help, and get an antibiotic. How long does it take you to get better?

The essential factors involved here are the length of time prior to starting the antibiotic, and the rate at which the drug kills the bacteria. As usual, actual practice is much more complex than the situation we model, so we state our initial conditions clearly.

The first simplification we make here is that the drug alone does most of the work—we do not bring in any additional improvement due to the body's own defences until the number of infecting bacteria has dropped below some threshold level, which we consider acceptable. Second, we assume that the antibiotic has a constant effect—that is, it kills off a certain number of bugs per hour, on average, regardless of external conditions. These simplifications make the problem tractable, while the solution retains some usefulness as an estimator of recovery time.

Suppose that after 2 days the patient feels ill enough to see the doctor and start the drug. By that time there are 2^{16} = 65 536 bacteria present. If now the drug kills, say, 10 000 bacteria per hour, what happens?

Clearly, in the first 3 hours after taking the drug, 30 000 bacteria are killed, leaving 35 536 bugs. But at that point, they divide, so that there are 71 072 of them. After a further 3 hours, that number has been reduced to 41 072, but it immediately doubles to 82 144. Obviously, the numbers are not going to work: either the patient must go to the doctor earlier, or the drug needs to be more powerful.

What we want to know is how long it is going to take for you to recover, given the above details, and assuming you begin taking the drug at the start of day 3. We have most of the data we need to be able to answer this question, given the simplifications and assumptions stated:

- a known number of bacteria at the start (65 536)
- a known duplication rate for the organism
- the process by which the bacteria are reduced
- a minimal 'kill rate' for the antibiotic, to be determined
- a 'threshold level' of acceptable infection

Input : Kill rate for the antibiotic (k, integer)—number of bacteria killed/hr
Output: Time taken to reduce the number of bacteria to below the threshold

Given this information, the algorithm is, at its simplest:

```
Declare variables: h (hours for cure) and b (number of bugs) as integer;  t (threshold)
as integer; cured as boolean; k (kill rate) as integer
1. Initialise b = 65 536; t = /* to be determined */; h = 1
2. Initialise cured = false
3. Read (k)
4. Loop while not cured
      Loop from i = 1 to 3        -- The drug reduces b by 3 times...
         Compute b = b – k        -- ...the kill-rate before the organism...
      End loop                    -- ...duplicates again
      b ← 2*b                     -- bugs duplicate
      if b ≤ t                    -- If b has reached an 'acceptable' level...
         cured = true             -- ...we're OK.
         Compute h = 3*h          -- The level of infection is checked at
         Output h                 -- three-hourly intervals, and each time, h is
      Endif                       -- incremented. Hence the total time taken is 3 × h
      h ← h + 1
   End loop
5. Stop
```

Work through the above 'first-cut' algorithm: there are a number of ways it could be improved, and one major flaw.

The major error concerns the conditions for termination: it must be clear, for every algorithm, under what conditions it will stop, and this stopping condition must always be possible, for all legal input. For the algorithm above, if b doubles faster than it is decreased by the value of k on each pass, the loop will never end. If it were implemented and executed on a computer the system could 'hang' in an endless loop.

One way of correcting the algorithm is to allow some time period—say, 48 hours—for treatment, and output the value of b after this time, unless the threshold has first been reached. After the variable h has been declared and initialised as before, line 4 of the process would read,

```
4. Loop while (h ≤ 16) AND (not cured)

      -- Code for infection decrement and doubling

   End loop
```

There is another consideration here, which is of crucial importance in implementing the solution, but which is nowhere evident from the analysis: the magnitudes of the variables must be such that the machine can represent them correctly. Every computer system has some maximum and minimum size for different variable types (this point is expanded in Chapter 6), and the numbers involved must lie within this range. For this particular problem the numbers could easily get out of hand: the range for INTEGER types for instance, is –32 768 to +32 767 in many systems, so that even the initial value for 'bugs' could not be stored correctly as an integer: 65 536 would be represented as zero, while 35 000, for example, would be –30 536. The threshold value for infection must also be of an appropriate size.

There is a LONG INTEGER type in both C and Ada, which allows values for integers up to, typically, 470 974 463; for larger numbers than this, floating-point representation will be necessary, even though it is not really an appropriate type to model the variables we are dealing with. In order to get a feel for what sort of numbers are likely to be involved, we must return to the analysis of the process of infection. Recall that we had the sequence for the growth of bacteria given by the direct formula $f_n = 2^n$, and the indirect formula $f_{n+1} = 2f_n, f_0 = 1$. For a given number of bugs, b, which are *reduced* by a constant factor, k, every hour, and then duplicate every 3 hours, the sequence is:

No. of bugs:	b	$2(b - 3k)$	$2\{2(b - 3k) - 3k\}$	
Term:	f_1	f_2	f_3	..., or

No. of bugs:	b	$2b - 6k$	$4b - 18k$	$8b - 42k$	
Term:	f_1	f_2	f_3	f_4	... .

The recurrence relation, then, is $f_{n+1} = 2(f_n - 3k), f_1 = b$. We can check this by 'plugging in' some sample values: for instance, if $b = 24$, and $k = 2$, the sequence becomes

24, 22, 20, 18, **36**, 34, 32, 30, **60**, 58, 56, 54, **108**, 106, 104, 102, **204**, 202, ...
f_1 f_2 f_3 f_4 f_5

and note that, for instance, $f_4 = 2(f_3 - 3k) = 2(60 - 6) = 108$.

Now it is not easy to spot the direct formula simply by observing the pattern, although it can be deduced analytically; we will not pursue the analysis any further here, but simply state the equivalent direct formula, which is $f_n = 2^{n-1}\,b - (2^n - 2)3k$. Using the direct formula, we have for instance, $f_4 = 2^3 \times 24 - (2^4 - 2) \times 3 \times 2 = 108$.

The formulae above mean that we can predict how numbers are likely to grow in our model for various different initial values of b, t and k. We know that this number must be less than the maximum value the machine can deal with, which we take as 470 974 463 for long integers, so that:

$$\text{max\_val} > 2^{n-1}\,b - (2^n - 2)3k > 0$$

where max_val is the maximum value long integers can take. Further, if, as suggested earlier, we allow 48 hours as the period for treatment, then we have 16 reduction-and-duplication intervals to deal with, each of 3 hours, so that the maximum value for the bacterial population is $2^{15} \times b - (2^{16} - 2) \times 3k$. Taking b as 65 536 gives a maximum population size of $2^{15} \times 65\,536 - (2^{16} - 2) \times 3k = 2\,147\,483\,648 - 196\,602 \times k$. This is a tractable number, and it also implies that the kill rate for the antibiotic (k) will have to be in excess of 10 000 per hour for a cure to be effected.

Some suitable threshold levels can now be evaluated. For the patient to be cured, the number of bugs present must be below the threshold level, t. If we take k to be 10 000, we have:

$2^{15} \times 65\,536 - (2^{16} - 2) \times 3 \times k < t$

i.e., $2^{15} \times 65\,536 - (2^{16} - 2) \times 3 \times 10\,000 < t$

$\Rightarrow \quad 2\,147\,483\,648 - 1\,966\,020\,000 < t$

$\Rightarrow \quad t > 181\,463\,640$

which is perhaps a larger number than we would wish. A lower threshold can easily be achieved, by allowing a slightly larger value of k: if we would like t to be, say, 1000, we can do this by setting $t = 1000$ in the inequality above, and solving for k:

$1\,000 > 2\,147\,483\,648 - 196\,602 \times k$

$\Rightarrow k > 2\,147\,482\,648/196\,602$

$\Rightarrow k > 10\,922$

What all the above analysis does is enable us to determine some constants and a range of appropriate values for the input variable k for the program—which is, in the end, very simple—and allow the coding to proceed in the knowledge that the numbers that result from its execution will be dealt with accurately by the underlying machine. A little more tidying up and refinement gives the version shown in Fig. 4.6.

In C:

```
#include <stdio.h>
#include <stdlib.h>
#include <string.h>
                    /* Disease program */
void main()
{
  long int kill, bugs, thresh, max_val;
  int dupl_interval;/*Duplication interval represents 3-hr periods*/
  char again[4] = "yes";
  typedef enum boolean {FALSE, TRUE} boolean;
  boolean cured;
  thresh = 1000;  /* Threshold value: below this the patient is ok */
  max_val = 470974000;    /* The maximum size of INTEGER */
  while(strcmp(again, "yes" == 0))
  {
    printf("Enter kill rate/hr: ");
    scanf("%li", &kill);
    printf("\nThis drug will kill %li bugs per hour\n\n", kill);
    dupl_interval = 1;        /* Initialise time */
    cured = FALSE;
    bugs= 65536;          /* Number of bugs at start of treatment */
    while (dupl_interval <= 16 && !cured && bugs < max_val)
    {               /* Investigate for a period of up to 48 hours */
                    /* after treatment is started. */
      bugs = bugs - 3 * kill; /* bugs are killed in this period */
      if (bugs < 0)           /* If 'underflow' on subtraction... */
```

```
        {                        /* ...i.e. negative value for 'bugs'... */
          bugs = 0;                  /* set number of bugs equal to zero */
        }
        if (bugs >= 0)
        {
          printf("Bugs alive: %li\n", bugs);
        }                                   /* Keep track of population */
        if (bugs <= thresh)
        {                /* When the number of bugs has been reduced */
          cured = TRUE;      /* below the threshhold, end treatment */
          printf("\nTime to recover: %d hours\n", 3 * dupl_interval);
        }
        bugs = 2 * bugs; /* They breed after each three-hour period */
        ++dupl_interval;          /* Increment 'three_hour' variable */
      }
      if (!cured)
      {                                /* If not cured... */
        printf("Too little, too late: dead!\n");
      }                                /* ..output condolence message. */
      printf("\nAgain?  Enter yes to continue:  ");
      scanf("%s", again);
    }
}
```

In Ada:

```
with text_io; use text_io;
procedure disease is

package int_io is new text_io.integer_io(integer);
package flt_io is new text_io.float_io(float);
package long_int_io is new text_io.integer_io(long_integer);
use int_io, long_int_io, flt_io;

kill, bugs, thresh, max_val: long integer;
dupl_interval: integer;          -- The duplication interval represents 3-hour periods
str_len: integer := 3;
again:  string(1 .. str_len) := "yes";
cured: boolean;

begin
      thresh := 1000;
      max_val := 470974000;
      while again(1 .. str_len) = "yes" loop
            put("Enter kill rate/hr: ");
            get(kill);
            put("This antibiotic will kill ");
            put(kill, width => 3);
            put(" bugs per hour.");
            new_line(2);
            dupl_interval := 1;             -- Initialise time
            bugs := 65536;                  -- Number of bugs at start of treatment
            while dupl_interval <= 16 and  not cured and bugs < max_val loop
```

```
                                        -- Investigate for a period of up to 48 hours after
                                        -- treatment is started
          bugs := bugs - 3 * kill;      -- bugs are killed in this period
          if bugs < 0 then              -- If 'underflow' on subtraction, i.e. negative
               bugs := 0;               -- value for 'bugs', set number of bugs = 0
          end if;
          put("Bugs alive: ");          -- Keep track of population
          put(bugs, width => 3);
          new_line;
          if bugs <= thresh then
               cured := true;           -- When the number of bugs has been reduced
               put("Time to recover: ");     -- below the threshold, end treatment
               put(3 * dupl_interval, width => 3);
               put("hours.");
               new_line;
          end if;
          bugs := 2 * bugs;                  -- Bugs duplicate after each 3-hour period
          dupl_interval := dupl_interval + 1;  -- Increment 'three-hour' variable
     end loop;
     if not cured then                       -- If not cured...
          put("Too little, too late: dead!");  -- ..output condolence message
          new_line;
     end if;
     put("Again?  Enter yes to continue: ");
     skip_line;                              -- lose end-of-line from previous 'get'
     get_line(again, str_len);
  end loop;
end disease;
```

Figure 4.6 'Disease' program

The output from this program for some typical values of *k* is:

Enter kill rate/hr:
This antibiotic will kill 11250 bugs per hour

Bugs alive: 31786
Bugs alive: 29822
Bugs alive: 25894
Bugs alive: 18038
Bugs alive: 2326
Bugs alive: 0

Time to recover: 18 hours.

Again? Enter yes to continue: Enter kill rate/hr:

This antibiotic will kill 10925 bugs per hour

Bugs alive: 32761
Bugs alive: 32747
Bugs alive: 32719
Bugs alive: 32663
Bugs alive: 32551
Bugs alive: 32327
Bugs alive: 31879
Bugs alive: 30983
Bugs alive: 29191
Bugs alive: 25607
Bugs alive: 18439
Bugs alive: 4103
Bugs alive: 0

Time to recover: 39 hours.

Again? Enter yes to continue: Enter kill rate/hr:

This antibiotic will kill 10000 bugs per hour

Bugs alive: 35536
Bugs alive: 41072
Bugs alive: 52144
Bugs alive: 74288
Bugs alive: 118576
Bugs alive: 207152
Bugs alive: 384304
Bugs alive: 738608
Bugs alive: 1447216
Bugs alive: 2864432
Bugs alive: 5698864
Bugs alive: 11367728
Bugs alive: 22705456
Bugs alive: 45380912
Bugs alive: 90731824
Bugs alive: 181433648
Too little, too late: dead!

Again? Enter yes to continue: Enter kill rate/hr:

This antibiotic will kill 11050 bugs per hour

Bugs alive: 32386
Bugs alive: 31622

Bugs alive: 30094
Bugs alive: 27038
Bugs alive: 20926
Bugs alive: 8702
Bugs alive: 0

Time to recover: 21 hours.

Again? Enter yes to continue:

EXERCISES 4.3

1. What changes need to be made to the program of Fig. 4.6 to allow periods other than 48 hours for recovery?

2. The implementation of the algorithm in Fig. 4.6 has more complex conditions for the tests than are shown in the pseudo-code, and a variable max_val, which is set to 470 974 000. Why? What would happen if the initial value for bugs were much larger, for example, 16 000 000?

4.6 Stopping distances

In Section 4.1, it was stated that, given published figures for a vehicle's stopping distance at certain speeds, we could calculate the distance taken to come to a halt from any speed. We now explore that idea further: the pattern is not quite so obvious in this case as it was in the problem of Section 4.5, but the approach is the same, and the final algorithm is quite short and simple.

The Transport Research Laboratory in the UK publishes figures which represent the distance a family car takes to come to rest from the time that the driver first sees an obstacle ahead. As you would expect, the faster the car is travelling, the greater the stopping distance.

The distance required to come to a complete rest is made up of two components: reaction time, or 'thinking distance'; and braking distance. The thinking distance is a measure of how far the car has travelled at any given speed, given that there is a delay between a person identifying a hazard, and reacting to it. That reaction time will usually be very short (less than a second), but, at a speed of 100 mph for example, this represents a distance of about 100 feet (over 30 metres) travelled before the driver even hits the brake pedal.

The second component of the total stopping distance is the braking distance. This is a measure of how far the vehicle travels before coming to a complete rest once the driver has applied the brakes. There are, of course, numerous assumptions built in: brakes and shock absorbers in good condition, wheels not locked, dry road, etc. The data in Table 4.1 is given in the HMSO publication, The Highway Code:

Table 4.1 Stopping distances

Speed		*Distance in feet*			*Distance in metres*		
mph	*kph*	*think*	*brake*	*total*	*think*	*brake*	*total*
30	50	30	45	75	9	14	23
50	80	50	125	175	15	38	53
70	110	70	245	315	21	75	96

The first step in our analysis is just to study the data, to see whether the relationship between speed and stopping distance is immediately obvious. Here, it is not, and so we progress in a methodical way: we examine just the thinking distance component first, for both units (kph and mph), and then the braking distance component for both units.

Thinking distance, kph

kph	*Dist(m)*
50	9
80	15
110	21

There is obviously a pattern in the sequence of increasing distances: 9, 15, 21, ... This sequence could be rewritten: 3×3, 3×5, 3×7, ... , in which case the next term would be $3 \times 9 = 27$. If this idea is correct, we can construct a table for speeds other than those published, and extrapolate, that is, 'fill in the blanks', and decide whether the result looks plausible, as in Table 4.2.

Table 4.2 Extrapolated stopping distances for various speeds (thinking)

Speed, kph	*Dist (known)*	*Dist (proposed)*
20		$3 \times 1 = 3$
35		$3 \times 2 = 6$
50	$3 \times 3 = 9$	$3 \times 3 = 9$
65		$3 \times 4 = 12$
80	$3 \times 5 = 15$	$3 \times 5 = 15$
95		$3 \times 6 = 18$
110	$3 \times 7 = 21$	$3 \times 7 = 21$

It appears from this data that the thinking distance is calculated as $3 \times n$, where n increases by 1 for each 15 kph from 20 kph. Working this backwards, the implication is that at 5 kph, thinking distance is nil.

Saying that n increases by 1 for each increase of 15 kph from 5 kph is, of course, the same as saying that n increases by (1/15) for each 1 kph from 5 kph. Hence, in summary, the proposed method for calculating thinking distance in metres from some given speed in kph is:

- subtract 5 from the speed
- multiply the result by (1/15)
- multiply this result by a constant (3)

For example, thinking distance S_T for 80 kph is:

$$\begin{aligned} S_T &= [(80 - 5) \times (1/15)] \times 3 \\ &= (75/15) \times 3 \\ &= 5 \times 3 \\ &= 15 \text{ m} \end{aligned}$$

Try this with some of the other values to convince yourself that the function is correct for the data we have. When convinced (for now) we can say that for any speed v kph, the thinking distance S_T is given by:

$$\begin{aligned} S_T &= [(v - 5) \times (1/15)] \times 3 \\ &= (v - 5) \times (1/5) \\ &= (v/5) - 1 \text{ m} \end{aligned}$$

Thinking distance, mph

mph	*Dist(ft)*
30	30
50	50
70	70

Quite clearly, it appears that the thinking distance is simply the same as the speed in mph. So, in the absence of any other information, we can propose the simple function, for some speed v in mph, for thinking distance S_T:

$$S_T = v \text{ ft}$$

Braking distances, kph

kph	*Dist(m)*
50	14
80	38
110	75

There is no obvious pattern here. We might discover it, through trial and error, but it may be a better idea to leave this for the moment and look at the figures for mph, to see whether they are more tractable. We will return to this problem after that.

Braking distances, mph

mph	*Dist(ft)*
30	45
50	125
70	245

There is some kind of pattern here—the figures for distance are all multiples of 5. Pursuing this line of thought, we see that the sequence for distance is 5×9, 5×25, 5×49, ... Now 9, 25, 49, ... are square numbers: i.e. $9 = 3^2$, $25 = 5^2$, $49 = 7^2$, and so on. This is starting to look like the situation we analysed in (a), and so we take the same line, extrapolating as shown in Table 4.3.

Table 4.3: Extrapolated stopping distances for various speeds (braking)

Speed, mph	*Dist (known)*	*Dist (proposed)*
0		$5 \times 0^2 = 0$
10		$5 \times 1^2 = 5$
20		$5 \times 2^2 = 20$
30	$5 \times 3^2 = 45$	$5 \times 3^2 = 45$
40		$5 \times 4^2 = 80$
50	$5 \times 5^2 = 125$	$5 \times 5^2 = 125$
60		$5 \times 6^2 = 180$
70	$5 \times 7^2 = 245$	$5 \times 7^2 = 245$

Notice that in the 'proposed distance' column, the sequence of square numbers is one-tenth of the values for speed in mph, each time. So to get the braking distance in feet, for some given speed in mph, the proposed method is:

- Divide the speed by 10
- Square the result
- Multiply this result by 5

This gives us, at 50 mph, for instance, a braking distance S_B calculated as:

$S_B = (50/10)^2 \times 5 = 5^2 \times 5 = 25 \times 5 = 125$ ft, as required

Generalising, for some given speed v mph, the braking distance S_B in feet is

$$S_B = (v/10)^2 \times 5$$
$$= (v^2/100) \times 5$$
$$\Rightarrow S_B = v^2/20 \text{ ft}$$

We now return to the one unsolved part of the problem so far: part (c), which is the formula for calculating braking distance in metres for a given speed in kph.

A direct approach is to make use of the fact that we now have a formula for mph and feet; standard conversion factors are:

1 m = 3.3 ft; 1 km = 5/8 mile, or
1 ft = 0.303 m; 1 mile = 8/5 km

For example, 330 ft = 330/3.3 = 100 m

We need to work with speed in kph, rather than mph, and then we need to convert the result from feet to metres. The formula, $S_B = v^2/20$, assumes that v is expressed in mph, and gives the answer in feet. To make use of the formula for speeds expressed in kph, we need to multiply v by 5/8; we then need to divide by 3.3 to get an answer in metres.

Hence, if the input speed is in kph, and the braking distance is in metres,

$$S_B = ([\{(5/8)v\}^2]/20)/3.3$$

This looks rather nasty, and does not simplify well: the best fractional result after some manipulation is $(25/4224)v^2$.

Using a calculator gives

$$S_B = \{[(5/8)v]^2\} \times (1/20) \times (1/3.3)$$

$$= 0.390625\ v^2 \times 0.05 \times 0.303$$

$$\approx 0.006v^2 \text{ m}$$

which is less exact than the fraction, but good enough to work with here.

As a check, we have, for 80 kph, $S_B = 0.006 \times 80^2 = 0.006 \times 6400 = 38.4$ m. This is not perhaps so close as we would like to the original figure, which was 38 m. Why does the difference arise? There are two main reasons:

- The formula above is an approximation: the fractional expression gives 37.88 m.
- The original figures are from the UK Transport Research Laboratory, and so were almost certainly originally calculated for mph, and then converted, rounding. The published distances indicate this—245 ft, for instance, is actually 74.24 m, not 75 m as given.

So our formula is good enough for practical purposes. Also, it is important not to get too concerned in this instance with decimal places. In real life, many other factors are far more important. How alert is the driver? What is the road surface like? How good are the brakes? What kind of tyres are fitted? And even under identical circumstances, the same person would not stop in *exactly* the same distance each time. A reasonable margin of error is ±5 per cent, possibly ±10 per cent.

Finally we have, for stopping distance, $S_{STOP} = S_T + S_B$, and so, using miles per hour:

$$S_{STOP} = v + v^2/20 = 0.05v^2 + v \text{ ft}$$

and using kilometres per hour:

$$S_{STOP} = (v/5) - 1 + (25/4224)v^2 \approx 0.006v^2 + 0.2v - 1 \text{ m}$$

For verification, the original table is reproduced here, together with the figures obtained by the formulae.

Table 4.4 Calculated and published stopping distances

Speed		*Stopping distance (TRL)*		*Stopping distance (calc)*	
mph	*kph*	*ft*	*m*	*ft*	*m*
30	50	75	23	75	24
50	80	175	53	175	53
70	110	315	96	315	94

Following the analysis, the algorithm for calculating stopping distances can be specified. The various simplifications and assumptions have been identified already, and, given those, we have:

Input: Speed, units (mph or kph)
Output: Stopping distance in feet or metres
Data types: Speed (v), distance (s): real; units (u): character
Algorithm:
Declare s, v as floating-point
Declare u as character
1. Read (v)
2. Read (u)
3. If $u = m$ {mph}
    $s = 0.05v^2 + v$
   Else if $u = k$ {kph}
    $s = 0.006v^2 + 0.2v - 1$
   Else
    Output: 'Error in input units'
   Endif
4. Output s
5. Stop

This algorithm is given as a program in Fig. 4.7. Notice again that a relatively lengthy analysis has resulted in a very simple algorithm. This process, of examining the situation and formalising a sequence of steps which results in a solution that conforms to the already known data, is a fundamental one in engineering generally. This allows prediction and thus control over real events, although any such model is only as good as the analysis, and holds only within certain limits, which are stated at the outset.

The steps taken, as before, are:

- clarify the question
- make some simplifications, and state them
- decide what data types are allowed as input, and what the output should be
- analyse the data—look for patterns
- express the relationship between input and output as a formula
- check this with some sample data
- formalise the process of getting from input to output as a step-by-step approach
- work through the formalisation with test data.

In C:

```
#include <stdio.h>
#include <float.h>
#include <math.h>

        /* Program for calculation of vehicle stopping distances */

void main()
{
  int good_input = 1;
  float s, v;
  char u;
  printf("Enter speed:  ");
  scanf("%f", &v);
  printf("\nEnter units (m for mph, k for kph):  ");
  scanf("%c", &u);
  getchar();
  if (u == 'm')
  {
    s = 0.05 * pow(v, 2) + v;
  }
  else if (u == 'k')
  {
    s = 0.006 * pow(v, 2) + 0.2 * v - 1.0;
  }
  else
  {
    printf("Error in input units: m for mph, k for kph\n\n");
    good_input = 0;
  }
  if(good_input)
  {
    printf("\n\nStopping distance is %.1f", s);
    if(u == 'm')
    {
      printf(" feet.\n");
    }
    else
    {
      printf(" metres.\n");
    }
  }
}
```

In Ada:

```
with text_io; use text_io;
procedure stops is
package int_io is new text_io.integer_io(integer);
package flt_io is new text_io.float_io(float);
use int_io, flt_io;

good_input: integer := 1;
s, v: float;
u: character;
begin
     put("Enter speed: ");
     get(v);
     new_line;
     put("Enter units (m for mph, k for kph:  )");
     get(u);
     skip_line;
     if u = 'm' then
          s := 0.05 * v ** 2 + v;
     elsif u = 'k' then
          s := 0.006 * v ** 2 + 0.2 * v - 1.0;
     else
          put("Error in input units: m for mph, k for kph.");
          new_line(2);
          good_input := 0;
     end if;
     if good_input = 1 then
          new_line;
          put("Stopping distance is: ");
          put(s, fore => 3, aft => 2, exp => 0);
          if u = 'm' then
               put(" feet.");
          else
               put(" metres.");
          end if;
     end if;
end stops;
```

Figure 4.7 'Stopping distance' program

EXERCISES 4.4

1. Modify the program to produce speeds and stopping distances in the form of a table.

2. Investigate the process further. What happens when the object you are approaching is *not* stationary—e.g. a vehicle travelling at a constant speed less than yours?

4.7 Series

Often, in practice, we need to know the sum of a number of terms of a sequence, rather than the value of any given term. For instance, if, in Example 2 of Section 4.5, we had been dealing with animals, rather than bacteria, the situation would have been rather more complicated.

Suppose some creature called a 'tuggle' always produces exactly two males and two females on reproduction, and each pair reproduces every 13 weeks. Starting with a pair of tuggles, after 13 weeks there will be 6: the original pair, plus 4 more. After a further 13 weeks, each of the new pairs will have produced 2 more pairs each, and the original pair will have produced 4 more. Hence we now have a total of (2 + 4 + 8) tuggles from the original pair and their descendants, plus 4 more from the original pair of tuggles—their second litter. So the total number of tuggles is

$$2 + 4 + 4 + 8 = 18$$

Within a short time, there are going to be a lot of tuggles, and the sums could get quite tricky. Let us simplify matters at this point, and say that tuggles have a lifespan of a year and a day, but only ever produce one litter per pair. Then each pair will only ever produce 4 offspring, and the situation is simpler, as shown in Fig. 4.8.

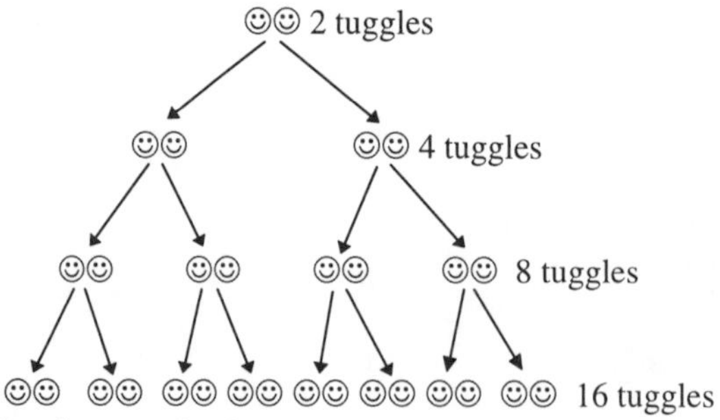

Figure 4.8 Tuggle reproduction

Now, how many tuggles will there be at the end of the year? In 52 weeks there will be 4 new sets of tuggles, at the rate of 1 new litter every 13 weeks. Hence we will have a total number of tuggles at the year's end:

$$tuggle_{TOT} = 2 + 4 + 8 + 16 + 32 = 62$$

This ought to look familiar: refer back to Example (iii) in Section 4.2, page 56. Then, we were concerned with the way in which the sequence grew: here, we are trying to find the total of the terms in the sequence.

The notation for series is not difficult. The series for $tuggle_{TOT}$ above has five terms, and sums to 62. We may write,

$S_5 = f_1 + f_2 + f_3 + f_4 + f_5 = 2 + 4 + 8 + 16 + 32 = 62$

More generally, for a series of N terms,

$S_N = f_1 + f_2 + f_3 + f_4 + f_5 + f_6 + ... + f_{N-1} + f_N$

The Greek symbol *sigma*, written Σ, is often used as a shorthand for the sum of a series. For instance,

$$\sum_{n=1}^{N} f_n$$

means the same as S_N above. In the same way, when $f_n = 3n - 1$, for example,

$$\sum_{n=1}^{5} f_n = 2 + 5 + 8 + 11 + 14 = 40$$

The 'sum to infinity' of a series, written

$$\sum_{n=1}^{\infty} f_n$$

is an important idea that crops up fairly often. It means 'keep going forever'. So, for example, when $f_n = 1/n$, we have

$$\sum_{n=1}^{\infty} f_n = (1/1) + (1/2) + (1/3) + (1/4) + (1/5) + (1/6) + ...$$

The sum of the first 10 terms is 2.93; the sum of the first 20 terms is 3.60. How big does this series get?

Now consider,

$$\sum_{n=1}^{\infty}(1/n^2) = (1/1) + (1/4) + (1/9) + (1/16) + (1/25) + (1/36) + ...$$

The sum of the first 10 terms is 1.55. Adding some more terms takes the sum to about 1.64. But then, adding in a lot more terms does not seem to increase this value significantly.

Series which tend towards a limiting value are called *convergent*. For example, the series

$$\sum_{n=1}^{\infty}(1/n^2)$$

will never reach the value 1.65. A related idea has been met before: compare this with the convergent *sequences* of Section 2.4 (p. 24). On the other hand, the series

$$\sum_{n=1}^{\infty}(1/n)$$

is *divergent*: it grows without limit as more terms are added, albeit very slowly.

4.8 Review: problem-solving and algorithm development

This is probably a good point at which to take stock of what we have done so far, and what happens next. The point that has been made repeatedly is that an algorithm is just a set of instructions for how to achieve some objective. Inasmuch as we make use of this kind of process all the time in our lives, algorithms have nothing to do with computing.

The other point that was made is that when an algorithm *is* to be executed by a computer, it must be 'bombproof'. Computers are just lifeless banks of switches: if these switches are thrown in the wrong sequence, the answer will be wrong. More programs are wrong on delivery because they are the right answer to the wrong problem, rather than for any other reason. So a set of instructions to be executed by a computer must be stated with great precision, and the machine must be told when to stop. For a computer, nothing is 'obvious'.

There is a technique for dealing with all this which can be summarised.

Summary

- Analyse the problem carefully. What exactly are you trying to achieve?
- Because computers cannot deal with the 'fuzziness' of real issues, the problem will have to be simplified by the programmer, and some assumptions made. State these clearly at the outset.
- Decide what kind of data you are working with, and how it is to be organised: these data structures will need to be declared at the start of the program.
- Make up some suitable test data. Note what the answers ought to be for your data.
- State what input types are allowed, and any range constraints (e.g. lower-case letters, integers in the range 1 to 100, etc.).
- Specify the output required.
- Write out the step-by-step process for getting from the input state to the output state. It is often best to do this in natural language first, and then code it, though if you are very experienced in a particular programming language, you may find it just as easy to write the algorithm directly in code.
- Test the program, using your original data and further test sets. Discover what data makes the program crash. Refine the program as necesssary.

5

EFFICIENCY AND COMPLEXITY

OBJECTIVES

In this chapter you will learn

- what is meant by the efficiency of an algorithm
- what is meant by the time-complexity of an algorithm
- the meaning of 'big *O*' notation
- how to compare one algorithm with another on the basis of efficiency, and make a judgement about which is 'better'
- how to evaluate different algorithms with the same big *O* efficiency but different performance in practice
- the relative efficiency of the sort algorithms introduced in Chapter 3

5.1 How is efficiency measured?

The idea of efficiency is intuitive. We know that there are better and worse ways of doing things, in general. Indeed, one of the supposed benefits of the computerisation of the workplace has been a massive increase in efficiency.

What exactly is meant by efficiency? As an example, suppose two cars, both with full tanks of petrol, set off at some time, and keep going until they run out of petrol. We then compare distances: say that car A has travelled 350 km, and car B 500 km. Which is more efficient?

Obviously we cannot make any kind of judgement about this situation until we have more information. Were the cars of the same make and type? Did both petrol tanks hold the same amount before starting? What kind of terrain was it? Was it the same for both? And so on. It would be possible to make a judgement if we were told that:

- initially, there are two cars, both standard family saloons of the same make and type, each with a tank full of petrol
- the cars are identical in all respects except that car A has Engine Management System Type A, and car B has Engine Management System Type B
- they are both driven at a steady 50 kph around a circular test track until they run out of petrol.

It might still be helpful to have some more information, but even with the scenario above, if it is the case that car A travels 350 km and car B 500 km, we would be inclined to say that Engine Management System B appears to make a big difference: that car B is more efficient.

In the office, increased efficiency might be claimed on a similar basis. If a new way of working results in a task that previously took three hours to do now taking only one hour to do, there is a clear saving of time. If a new computer database system results in records from five filing cabinets full of paper being transferred onto disk, there is a big space saving.

Algorithmic efficiency is no different. When algorithm B does the same task as algorithm A but in less time, then algorithm B is more time-efficient. When algorithm B does the same task as algorithm A but uses less space (computer memory), then algorithm B is more space-efficient. In this chapter, we deal with time-efficiency. The efficiency of an algorithm in terms of space is touched on in Chapter 6, since the choice of data structure is usually the critical factor in optimising space requirements.

When thinking about the cost-effectiveness of two or more competing systems or methods, we have to have a way to evaluate them: to measure one against the other in a meaningful way. In the original example of the two cars, it became possible to reach some kind of reasonable verdict once the problem was presented with some performance figures, and the conditions were standardised. So, although we were not told the capacity of the petrol tanks, the lack of this piece of information did not affect the evaluation, since we knew they were the same in each case. Whether they were both 40 litre tanks or 75 litre tanks, car B is still more efficient, in that it covers more kilometres to the litre than car A.

Similarly, when two algorithms are compared, they must be compared against the same data set, and under the same conditions. It is possible to time how long a program takes to run; alternatively, one could count how many program statements are executed—the more statements to execute for a given task, the more time taken. However, neither is a good indicator of how efficient an algorithm is in general. Any conclusion reached would be specific to that particular program operating on specific data at a given time. In general, the execution time for any given program will depend on, among other things:

- the CPU the program is running on
- the way the compiler works
- the programming language
- the way the program is constructed
- time for disk accesses and other I/O
- whether the system is single-user or multi-tasking.

For any measurement to be meaningful, there must be some standardisation. Suppose we want to compare the three sorting programs examined in Chapter 3, the bubble sort, selection sort, and insertion sort. To compare any two, we might require:

- both programs written in the same language
- the executable code in both cases produced by the same compiler
- the same hardware platform for each test
- identical data sets to test both programs.

Given the above conditions, suppose we discover that the bubble sort program takes 2.5 seconds to sort 1000 integers, and that the selection sort program takes 1.75 seconds to sort the same 1000 integers. Clearly, the selection sort program is more efficient. However, although the above conclusion may be true for the 1000 integers used in the test, how do we know it would be true for a different set of integers? Would it be true for characters, or strings? Would a second run give exactly the same time? Does the particular compiler or architecture favour one program over the other?

What is required is a method for describing an algorithm in terms of all data that might be encountered, and under any conditions.

5.2 Running time for a program

Consider the programs in Fig. 5.1: a double-precision floating-point operation is executed 1 million times: this allows execution time to be measured in a simple way. Suppose that, on a standard PC, the time it takes to run is about 7 seconds.

In C:

```
#include <stdio.h>
#include <stdlib.h>    /* Simple arithmetic program #1 */
void main()
{
   long int i;
   double x, y, z;
   x = 123.456;
   y = 234.567;
   for (i = 0; i < 1000000; ++i)
   {
      z = x * y;
   }
   printf("Done: z = %f\n", z);
}
```

In Ada:

```
with long_float_text_io, text_io; use long_float_text_io, text_io;
procedure arithprog_1 is                  -- Simple arithmetic program #1
x, y, z: long_float;
begin
   x := 123.456;
   y := 234.567;
   for i in 1 .. 1000000 loop
      z := x * y;
   end loop;
   put("Done: z =");
   put(z, fore => 6, aft => 7, exp => 0);
end arithprog_1;
```

Figure 5.1 Simple iterative computation

How long would it take to execute 10 million operations? If the loop bound is changed to 10 000 000, and nothing else changes, we would expect the program to take about 10 times as long to run, i.e. about 70 seconds. In general, when the time taken for a program to run is directly proportional to the amount of data it has to deal with, this relationship is said to be *linear*; this is explained in Section 5.3. However, at present, we still have no idea of whether this would be the case for other data, or under different circumstances. We have no general rule for how the time taken for output depends on the amount of input. Can the analysis of algorithms be done in a precise way? The answer is 'Yes'; the way this is done is shown here for a simple example, and then we consider the general case.

Any program actually contains a finite number of instructions to be executed. The time taken to execute any *one* instruction will vary from machine to machine, but will be constant for any given machine. So suppose we count the number of statements in a program written in Ada or C: this—ultimately—represents some number of binary instructions to be executed by the CPU. If one program contains 50 source code instructions, and another program contains 400 source code instructions of the same type, then the shorter program will take less time to run. The question is: 'What counts as an instruction?' Clearly, a statement such as

`x = 5;`/**x** := 5;

is fundamentally different to a statement such as

`for (x = 0; x < 1000; ++x)`/**for** x **in** 0 .. 1000 **loop**.

There obviously needs to be some standard for what counts as a single instruction, and one way to do this is to take an elementary operation (e.g. assignment, arithmetic, logical, etc.) as a single unit. The concept of certain source code operations being 'elementary' or 'atomic' in this sense, and not others, is of course open to debate; however, the units chosen here suffice to illustrate the point. The programs given in Fig. 5.2 are essentially the same as those of Fig. 5.1, but the loop bound is just 5, so that it is easier to see what is happening during execution.

In C:

```
#include <stdio.h>
#include <stdlib.h>
                      /* Simple arithmetic program #2 */
void main()
{
  long int i;
  double x, y, z;
  x = 123.456;                 /* one assignment operation */
  y = 234.567;                 /* one assignment operation */
  for (i = 0; i < 5; ++i)      /* initialize i = 0; execute */
  {                            /* following two statements, then...*/
                               /* ...increment: i = i + 1;... */
                               /* ...and test: if i < 5 continue. */
```

```
      printf("i = %d\n", i);
      z = x * y;                /* i = 0, 1, 2, 3, 4, 5.  When i = 5... */
   }                            /* ...we exit the loop, and go to... */
   printf("Done: z = %f\n", z); /* ...the final printf statement. */
}
```

In Ada:

```
with long_float_text_io, text_io; use long_float_text_io, text_io;
procedure arithprog_2 is
                                   -- Simple arithmetic program #2
package int_io is new text_io.integer_io(integer);
use int_io;
x, y, z: long_float;
begin
   x := 123.456;                   -- one assignment operation
   y := 234.567;                   -- one assignment operation
   for i in 0 .. 4 loop            -- initialise i = 0; execute following two statements,
                                   -- then increment: i = i + 1; and test: if i < 5 continue.
      put("i =");
      put(i);
      new_line;
      z := x * y;                  -- i = 0, 1, 2, 3, 4, 5.  When i = 5...
   end loop;                       -- ...we exit the loop, and go to...
   put("Done: z =");               -- ...the final 'put' statements.
   put(z, fore => 6, aft => 7, exp => 0);
   new_line;
end arithprog_2;
```

Figure 5.2 Simple arithmetic computation with fewer iterations

The output of these programs is as follows.

For the C version:

```
i = 0
i = 1
i = 2
i = 3
i = 4
Done: z = 28958.703552
```

For the Ada version:

```
i = 0
i = 1
i = 2
i = 3
i = 4
Done: z = 28958.7035220
```

Analysing the programs of Fig. 5.2, we see that:

- First there are two assignment operations (`x = 123.456, y = 234.567`)

- Next, in the **for** loop, there is an assignment (`i = 0`), a test (`i < 5`), and an increment (`++i`). This is explicit in C, and implied in the Ada **for** i in 0 .. 4 **loop** statement
- Within the loop,
  —there is an output statement, which we take as a number of primitive operations here for simplicity,
  —there is a multiplication and an assignment ($z = x * y$): two operations.
- Finally, there is a single output statement.

The loop is executed five times ($i = 0, 1, 2, 3, 4$); after assignment ($i = 0$), i is incremented five times altogether: after the fifth execution of the $z = x * y$ instruction, i is incremented to 5, which means that it fails the test (*if i < 5 continue*), and the next instruction executed is the final print of the value of z.

Clearly, within the loop, the print instructions and the assignment and arithmetic operations $z = x * y$ are executed five times altogether. Although, as mentioned above, I/O operations are susceptible to factors external to the computation, and so are not quite the same kind of primitive operations as the others, we will treat them as primitive for simplicity in this analysis. Hence the statements put("i = "); put(i); new_line; or `printf("i = %d\n", i);` count for three operations each time within the loop, and the final *print* counts as a further three operations.

So, in total, we have

Statement		*Number of instructions*
Initial assignment of values to x and y		2
for loop:	initialize i	1
	test i	6
	increment i	5
	print i (3×5 ops)	15
	computation: $z = x * y$ (2×5 ops)	10
Final print of the value of z		3
TOTAL		42

What would be the total if the loop had a bound of 10? The instructions to be executed more often would be: test i, increment i, print i, and $z = x * y$. There would be $10 + 1 = 11$ tests, 10 increments, $3 \times 10 = 30$ print operations, and $2 \times 10 = 20$ arithmetic operations. The initial assignments and the final print statement makes five more giving a total of: $2 + 1 + 11 + 10 + 30 + 20 + 3 = 77$. If the loop bound were 100, there would be $2 + 1 + 101 + 100 + 300 + 200 + 3 = 707$.

There is a pattern here, though it is not immediately obvious from the sequence 42, 77, 707. Looking back at the program in Fig. 5.2, we see that in general, for a loop bound of n, where n may be any positive integer value, the number of instructions executed follows the rule: $2 + (1 + (n + 1) + n) + 3n + 2n + 3$. So, for instance, when $n = 10$, we have a total number: $2 + (22) + 30 + 20 + 3 = 77$, as before. Hence the function that describes this program's execution time, symbolized as $T(n)$ here, is:

$$\begin{aligned} T(n) &= 2 + (1 + (n + 1) + n) + 3n + 2n + 3 \\ &= 2n + 3n + 2n + 2 + 2 + 3 \\ &= 7n + 7 \end{aligned}$$

The analysis has provided an extremely powerful way of predicting how long the program will take to run *in general* (e.g. when $n = 100$, $T(n) = (7 \times 100) + 7 = 707$) and the function $T(n)$ is often referred to as the *time-complexity* for a given problem. The time taken, in this case, turns out to depend almost entirely on the loop bound, n, and the time taken for any loop bound is given by the function $T(n) = 7n + 7$ in this case. This is a linear function: the time taken is proportional to the size of the input.

The actual running time (in microseconds, or minutes, or whatever), will depend on all the other factors referred to above; however, we now know that for some loop bound n, the program will take about kn time units to run, where k is a multiplicative constant (7, in this case).

As mentioned above, as the value of n increases, that is, as the amount of data that the algorithm has to deal with increases, the relative importance of the added constant (the '+7') decreases. When n is just 1, this constant represents 50 per cent of the value of $T(n)$; however, when n is 10 000, it represents less than 0.01 per cent of $T(n)$. As will be shown more clearly in Section 5.3, the recognition of which term in the expression for $T(n)$ contributes most to the way the function behaves allows a judgement to be made about the way the function behaves as n increases in general, and hence enables something meaningful to be said about the efficiency of the algorithm.

In terms of the real time taken for the execution of an algorithm, if, for example, we have a 1MIPS (1 million instructions per second) system, we would have the timings shown in Table 5.1 for different values of n. On a different system, or in a different environment, the time taken to complete one instruction might be 3 microseconds, or 0.3 microseconds; however, we know that, because of the result $T(n) = 7n + 7$, we can still work out the actual time taken.

Table 5.1 Running times for the program of Fig. 5.2 for various problem sizes

n	*T(n)*	*Actual time*
5	42	42 microseconds
10	77	77 microseconds
100	707	707 microseconds
1 000 000	7 000 007	7 seconds (approx)

EXERCISES 5.1

1. Investigate the programs of Figs 5.1 and 5.2 on a PC: what does this suggest about the CPU power in MIPS, and the time taken for I/O? Devise some other programs which will allow you to confirm or refute your hypothesis.

2. Determine $T(n)$ for the following program fragment—assume that the declarations have no cost:

In C:

```
#define length n
  /* As required for size of Num_List under consideration */
int Num_Array[length];
int ex_5_1(int Num_List[])
{
  int i, x = Num_List[0];
  for (i = 1; i < length; ++i)
  {
    if (Num_List[i] > x)
    {
          x = Num_List[i];
    }
  }
  return (x);
}
```

In Ada:

```
length: integer := n; -- As required for size of Num_List under consideration
type Numbers is array (0 .. length-1) of integer;
Num_List: Numbers;
function EX5_1(Num_List: Numbers) return integer is
x: integer;
begin
  x := Num_List(0);
  for i in 1 .. length - 1 loop
    if Num_List(i) > x then
      x := Num_List(i);
    end if;
  end loop;
  return x;
end;
```

5.3 Linear functions

The general form of a linear function is $f\colon x \to ax + b$, where a and b may be any numerical values. So, for example, if we have $f\colon x \to 7x - 19$, then $a = 7$ and $b = -19$. Similarly, for the function $g\colon x \to x/14 + 8.12$, $a = (1/14)$ and $b = 8.12$. We can 'plug in' different values of x, to find out $f(x)$ and $g(x)$ at those values; for example, when $x = 3$, then $f(x) = 7 \times 3 - 19 = 2$, and $g(x) = (3/14) + 8.12 = 8.33$. The function values when $x = 0$ are: $f(x) = -19$, and $g(x) = 8.12$. It is often useful to work out several such integer values around zero; then, tabulating such sample values, we have a table such as the one below (Table 5.2.)

Table 5.2 Functions f(x) and g(x) plotted for various values of x

variable	*–2*	*–1*	*0*	*1*	*2*	*3*
$f(x)$	–33	–26	–19	–12	–5	2
$g(x)$	7.98	8.04	8.12	8.19	8.26	8.33

If these values are plotted on a graph, the result is a straight line—the relationship between input (x) and output ($f(x)$ or $g(x)$) is linear (Fig. 5.3).

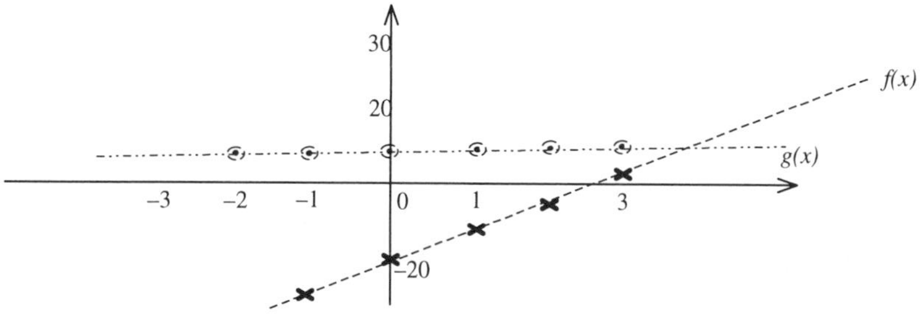

Figure 5.3 Graphs of linear functions

Recalling now the function $T(n) = 7n + 7$ from Section 5.2—see Fig. 5.4—it is clear that this is linear in just the same way as $f(x)$ and $g(x)$ in Fig. 5.3. Note also that as n increases, $T(n)$ increases in the same way: for example, as n increases from 200 to 400 (i.e. doubles), $T(n)$ also very nearly doubles (it increases from 1407 to 2807).

Similarly, when n increases from 100 to 300 (i.e. trebles), $T(n)$ also trebles (very nearly) from 707 to 2107. Hence if we can analyse a program and derive its time-complexity function $T(n)$, it is possible to say what will happen in terms of the time taken for small values of n, for large values, and how the time taken will increase as n increases.

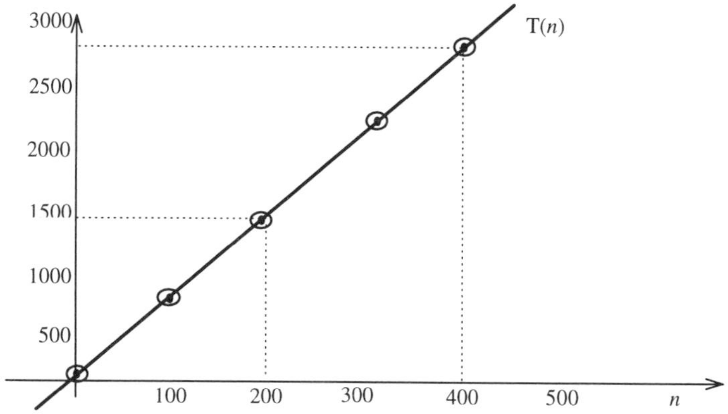

Figure 5.4 Graph of T(n) = 7n + 7

5.4 Big *O*

Although the procedure described in the previous sections provides a method for analysing an algorithm and getting a measure of its performance, such precision is actually not necessary for most applications. Table 5.1 from Section 5.2 is reproduced below, and illustrates the point:

n	$T(n)$	*Actual time*
5	42	42 microseconds
10	77	77 microseconds
100	707	707 microseconds
1 000 000	7 000 007	7 seconds (approx)

What we can say is that, if an algorithm's time-complexity is linear, then doubling the amount of data that has to be dealt with as input will result in (roughly) double the running time. And, in general, increasing the input data set by some factor t will result in execution taking t times as long.

For example, increasing n from 5 to 10 in Table 5.1 (i.e. doubling it) results in an increase of time taken from 42 to 77 microseconds, i.e. an increase of 83 per cent. The effect is more marked when n has large values: increasing n from 100 to 1 000 000 (i.e. by a factor of 10 000) results in an increase in time from 707 to 7 000 007 microseconds, which is a factor of 9900. For large n, it is obvious that the constant number added on ('+ 7' in this case) has very little effect, and that for some problem of size n, increasing the problem size by some factor I to $I \times n$ increases the time taken $T(n)$ to approximately $I \times T(n)$. This is the first important result:

- For a linear algorithm, an increase by some factor in input data size results in a increase in running time proportional to that increase in problem size.

To illustrate the point further, look at how three different functions behave for different values of n: they are all linear, and so although the actual time $T(n)$ is different in each case, they all behave, in general, in the same way.

$T(n) = 3n + 8$
$T(n) = 2n - 3$
$T(n) = (n/2) + 5$

For $T(n) = 3n + 8$, we have:

n	$T(n)$
5	23
10	38
1000	3008

For $T(n) = 2n - 3$, we have:

n	$T(n)$
5	7
10	17
1000	1997

Finally, for, $T(n) = (n/2) + 5$:

n	$T(n)$
5	7.5
10	10
1000	505

As these examples illustrate, saying that all linear algorithms behave the same way does not mean that the constants of proportionality, and the added constant, have no effect. An algorithm which has running time $T(n) = 1\ 235\ 000n + 27\ 988\ 224$ is linear, but it is obviously rather poor: we should look for a more efficient method. However, we now come to the second important result: no matter what the function for the algorithm's efficiency, we can say that it is *always* better than some other result. For example, $T(n) = 5n + 6$ is no worse than $f(n) = 6n$, when $n \geq 6$, since $T(6) = 5 \times 6 + 6 = 36$, and $f(6) = 6 \times 6 = 36$, while $T(7) = 5 \times 7 + 6 = 41$, and $f(7) = 6 \times 7 = 42$. Further, $T(n) = 5n + 6$ is *always* no worse than $f(n) = 12n$, for *all* positive values of n. Equally, $T(n) = 2n - 1$ will never take time greater than $2n$, and the algorithm with time-complexity $T(n) = (n/2) + 5$ is no worse than $f(n) = 6n$ for all positive n.

Table 5.3 Relations for a number of different time-complexity functions

n	$T(n) = 5n + 6$	$f(n) = 12n$
1	11	12
5	31	60
6	36	72
10	56	120
n	$T(n) = 2n - 1$	$f(n) = 2n$
1	1	2
5	9	10
6	11	12
10	19	20
n	$T(n) = (n/2) + 5$	$f(n) = 6n$
1	5.5	6
5	7.5	30
6	8	36
10	10	60

More formally, it is possible to state:

- For an algorithm dealing with problem size n, which has linear time-complexity, we can always find some value c such that the algorithm takes time no more than time $c \times n$ to execute for all $n \geq 1$.

In fact, we can go further than this: given some function $f(n)$ which represents the number of simple operations in an algorithm, we can always find a value of c such that the algorithm takes no more than time $c \times n$ to execute for all n greater than any number at all.

In all the discussion above, the language has sometimes had to become quite convoluted in order to express the meaning properly, and so a shorthand exists to make life easier: this is the 'big *O*' notation.

For a function whose time-complexity is linear, and which therefore follows all the rules for such functions given above, we simply say it is '$O(n)$' (read 'oh en', or 'of the order of n'). That is, in this case, and, in fact, in general for all functions, non-linear as well as linear:

> $f(n)$ is $O(g(n))$, means that it is always possible to find some k such that $f(n) \leq k \times g(n)$ for all values of $n > p$.

This definition refers to 'all values of $n > p$': so what is p? In a sense, we can take p to be anything we like: for instance, in the examples of Table 5.3, in which $g(n)$ was always just n, and one of the functions considered was $f(n) = 5n + 6$, we took $p = 1$. Then the value of k such that $f(n) \leq k \times n$ for all positive values of n was 12. And when $n = 3$, for instance, we have:

$$f(n) = 5n + 6$$

$$\Rightarrow f(n) = 5 \times 3 + 6 = 21, \text{ while } k \times n = 12 \times 3 = 36$$

Hence $f(n) \leq k \times n$ for $k = 12$.

However, the definition implies something rather more precise than is suggested by the above examples. In particular, we are saying that some specific function, $f(n)$, may be said to be $O(g(n))$ provided $f(n)$ is less than $k \times g(n)$ *eventually*. What is meant by 'eventually'? When $n > p$, *however big* p *may have to be*.

EXERCISES 5.2

1. For the following functions, which represent the number of statements executed by some linear algorithms for input data sets of size n, find the value of c such that the algorithm takes time no more than time $c \times n$ to execute, for all $n \geq 1$

(i) $f(n) = 2n + 3$
(ii) $f(n) = 3n - 2$
(iii) $f(n) = 7n + 15$
(iv) $f(n) = 1.5n + 32$
(v) $f(n) = (n/5) + 9$
(vi) $f(n) = 13n - 12$
(vii) $f(n) = 4n/3 + 128$
(viii) $f(n) = (n/2) + 3$

2. (i) In practice, what kind of values are realistic for time-complexity?
   (ii) How do the functions (i)–(viii) above behave as n gets very large indeed?

The reader may feel at this point that the definition is saying something circular. The following example, for an $O(n^3)$ algorithm, together with a graphical interpretation, should clarify things.

The piece of code in Fig. 5.5 represents a matrix-multiplication process, which calculates the products of the individual elements of two 2-dimensional arrays, resulting in an output 2-dimensional array. If X is a 4×5 matrix, say, and Y is a 5×6 matrix, then the resulting product, Z, is a 4×6 matrix.

In C:

```
#include <stdio.h>
#define u 4
#define v 5
#define w 6
       /* Matrix multiplication routine: X[u][v]*Y[v][w] = Z[u][w] */

void matrix_mult(float X[u][v], float Y[v][w], float Z[u][w])
{
     /* If u is 4, v is 5, and w is 6, then for input matrices */
     /* X[4][5], Y[5][6], the output matrix will be Z[4][6]   */

   int i, j, k;
   for (i = 0; i < u; ++i)       /* Count elements by columns for X */
   {
      for (j = 0; j < w; ++j)    /* Count elements by rows for Y */
      {
         Z[i][j] = 0.0;
         for (k = 0; k < v; ++k) /* Count by rows for X and... */
         {                       /* ...columns for Y for elements of Z */
            Z[i][j] += X[i][k] * Y[k][j];
         }
      }
   }
}
```

In Ada:

```
U: constant := 4;
V: constant := 5;
W: constant := 6;

type MATRIX is array (integer range <>, integer range <>) of float;

procedure matrix_mult(X, Y: in MATRIX; Z: in out MATRIX) is
begin
   for i in 1 .. U loop                          -- Count elements by columns for X
      for j in 1 .. W loop                       -- Count elements by rows for Y
         Z(i, j) := 0.0;
         for k in 1 .. V loop                    -- Count by rows for X, and by columns
            Z(i, j) := Z(i, j) + X(i, k) * Y(k, j);   -- for Y for elements of Z
         end loop;
      end loop;
   end loop;
end matrix_mult;
```

Figure 5.5 Matrix multiplication routine

This program might result in Z having the values shown in Table 5.4.

Table 5.4 Typical 4× 6 matrix cell values

Row/column	*0*	*1*	2	*3*	*4*	*5*
0	3.145	2.381	5.908	3.769	1.541	7.444
1	4.112	3.445	6.779	1.072	1.443	6.432
2	1.285	4.719	2.666	9.004	5.087	6.488
3	5.177	3.742	8.439	4.619	8.644	4.068

Since there are 4 rows and 6 columns, there are 24 cells whose values are to be entered. The statement `Z[i][j]+= X[i][k]*Y[k][j];`/Z(i, j) := Z(i, j) + X(i, k)*Y(k, j); which calculates the cell contents, is executed five times for every cell in this example. And since this has to be done for every cell, altogether there are $4 \times 6 \times 5$ such sets of calculations. The actual calculation of `Z[i][j]` for each matrix element involves an assignment, an addition, and a multiplication—three simple operations. Further, after each output matrix cell has been calculated and entered, `Z[i][j]` must be zeroed again—24 times in this case.

If the program were executed on input matrices `X[u][v]`, `Y[v][w]` with `u` defined as 10, and `w` defined as 25, then clearly there would be 250 executions of the `Z[i][j]` statement, which itself executes `v` times per cell. And in general, for `u` = n, `w` = n, `v` = n, there will be $n \times n \times n = n^3$ such operations.

A detailed count of the program statements, for `u` = n, `w` = n, `v` = n, bearing in mind that array accesses are being treated as simple operations at unit cost, reveals that the inner loop (`k`) executes its control statements $2n + 2$ times, as in Section 5.2; next, there is the `Z[i][j] += X[i][k]*Y[k][j];` statement within the loop, giving $3n$ such operations. So the total for the inner loop is $2n + 2 + 3n = 5n + 2$.

Now, this set of $5n + 2$ operations is executed n times, under the control of the second loop (`j`), which contains just one additional statement, `z[i][j] = 0.0`, giving $n(1 + 5n + 2)$ iterated statements. These operations in turn execute n times under the control of the outermost (`i`) loop. Hence the total number of operations for the whole program is:

`i = 0;`	1 op
`i < n`	$n + 1$ ops
`++i`	n ops

giving $2n + 2$ control operations for each of the loops `i`, `j`, `k`. Hence

$$
\begin{aligned}
\text{TOTAL} &= 2n + 2 + n[(2n + 2) + n(1 + (2n + 2) + 3n)] \\
&= 2n + 2 + n[(2n + 2) + n(5n + 3)] \\
&= 2n + 2 + 2n^2 + 2n + 5n^3 + 3n^2 \\
&= 5n^3 + 5n^2 + 4n + 2
\end{aligned}
$$

which is $O(n^3)$. Why?

Recall the definition given on p. 95:

> $f(n)$ is $O(g(n))$, means that it is always possible to find some k such that $f(n) \le k \times g(n)$ for all values of $n > p$.

We have, in this case, $f(n) = 5n^3 + 5n^2 + 4n + 2$, and $g(n) = n^3$. So the question is, is it possible to find some k such that $f(n) \le k \times g(n)$, where $g(n) = n^3$ for all values of n greater than some constant? Or, alternatively, is there some simple multiple of n^3 which is greater than $f(n) = 5n^3 + 5n^2 + 4n + 2$, once we reach a big enough value of n (when $n = p$)?

The answer is 'Yes': look at some typical results in Table 5.5.

Table 5.5 Effect of multiplicative constants on g(n) for various values of n compared with f(n)

n	$f(n)$	$k \times n^3, k = 3$	$k \times n^3, k = 8$	$k \times n^3, k = 12$
1	16	3	8	12
5	772	375	1 000	1 500
20	42 082	24 000	64 000	96 000

From this table, it can be seen, for instance, that $f(n) \le k \times n^3$ when $k = 8$, for $n = 5$. In fact, $f(n) \le k \times n^3$, $k = 8$ for all $n > 2$. The implication is that, given some problem size, n, and the algorithm which has a running time of $5n^3 + 5n^2 + 4n + 2$, we can *always* find a constant multiplier, k, for the n^3 term such that the algorithm will not take longer than $k \times n^3$ once n has reached some value, p. How big does n have to be before this is true? The answer depends on the particular function under consideration—p might have to be 100, or 1000, or larger before $f(n) \le k \times n^3$ for all

$n > p$. For this particular case, we have:

$$5n^3 + 5n^2 + 4n + 2 \leq k \times n^3$$

Now, k must be greater than 5, since the left-hand side of the inequality has terms in n^2 and less in addition to the n^3 term.

So if we take $k = 6$, then

$$5n^3 + 5n^2 + 4n + 2 \leq 6 \times n^3$$

At the point at which $f(n) = k \times g(n)$
$5n^3 + 5n^2 + 4n + 2 = 6 \times n^3$
—see Fig. 5.6.

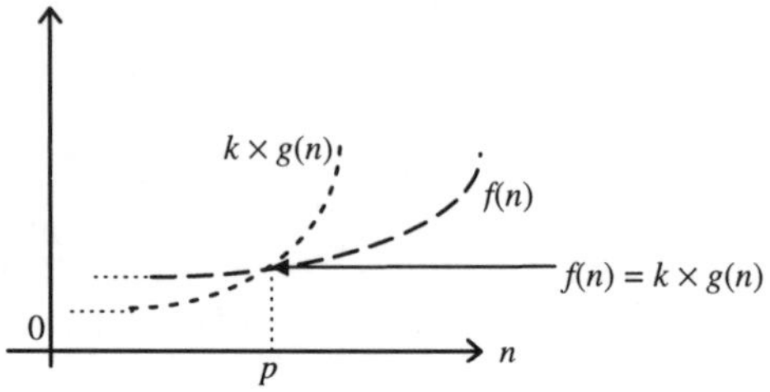

Figure 5.6 Intersection of the graphs of f(n) and k × g(n)

What value of n makes the equation balance? This problem can be solved analytically, but a graphical approach is perhaps more instructive: see Table 5.6 and Fig. 5.7.

Table 5.6 Values of f(n) = 5n³ + 5n² + 4n + 2 and 6n³ for increasing values of n

n	*0*	*1*	*2*	*3*	*4*	*5*	*6*	*7*	...	*20*
$6n^3$	0	6	48	162	384	750	1296	2058	...	48 000
$f(n)$	2	16	70	194	418	772	1286	1990	...	42 082

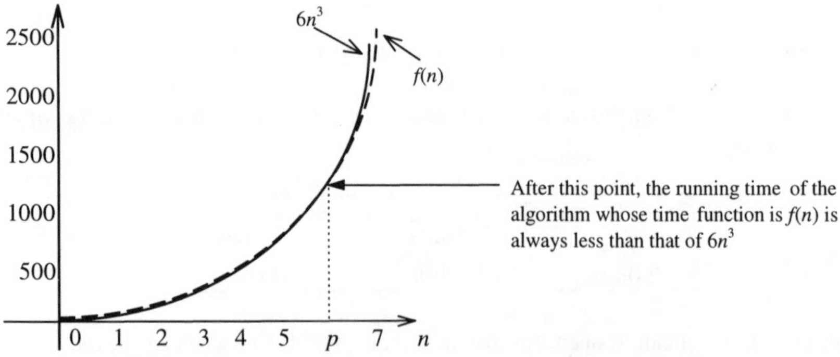

Figure 5.7 Graph of f(n) = 5n³ + 5n² + 4n + 2 and 6n³

For this example, then, we have $k = 6$ and $p = 6$, and we can say that $f(n)$ is $O(g(n))$ since $f(n) \leq 6 \times g(n)$ for all $n > 6$, where $g(n) = n^3$.

Hence we can say that the algorithm is $O(n^3)$.

The implication of this is that, in general, when we see an algorithm which has running time $5n^3 + 5n^2 + 4n + 2$, say, we can simply ignore the lower-order terms (those less than the highest power to which n is raised), because we know we can always find some k such that the running time is less than $k \times n^3$ when n is sufficiently large. Thus we can simply say, in this instance, that it is $O(n^3)$. Note that, although we can certainly say that $f(n)$ in this case is always eventually better than some $k \times g(n)$, where $g(n) = n^3$ we could not say the same thing for $g(n) = n^2$.

This is not to imply that lower-order terms are unimportant. An algorithm which has time-complexity $f(n) = 2n^2 + 3n + 8174$, for instance, is $O(n^2)$: but it takes a long time before $k \times g(n) = 3n^2$, for example, overtakes it, as Fig. 5.8 shows.

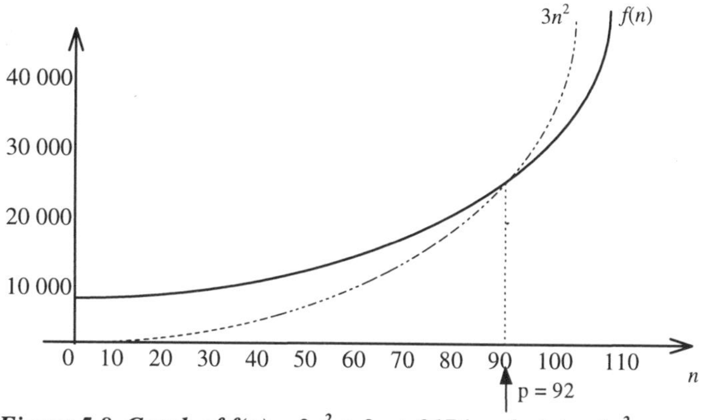

Figure 5.8 Graph of $f(n) = 2n^2 + 3n + 8174$ and $g(n) = 3n^2$

EXERCISES 5.3

1. State the time-complexity of the following functions, which represent the number of statements executed by some algorithms for input data sets of size n, and find the values of k and p for which $f(n) \leq k \times g(n)$, for all $n > p$, given that k is not larger than necessary.

   (i) $f(n) = 3n + 1$
   (ii) $f(n) = 3n^2 - 2$
   (iii) $f(n) = 2n^2 + 13n$
   (iv) $f(n) = n^3 + 52$
   (v) $f(n) = 4n^3 + 2n^2 + 7$

When a program has been analysed, and an expression such as $f(n) = 3n^2 + 4n + 3$ has been obtained, it is not strictly necessary, as indicated above, to do any arithmetic in order to obtain a big O term for the time-complexity. Consider how some example functions behave as n increases in size (Table 5.7).

Table 5.7 Behaviour of some functions for different values of n

Function	*n = 10*	*n = 1000*	*n = 1 000 000*	*O(g(n))*
$f(n) = 2n + 4$	24	2 004	2 000 004	$O(n)$
$f(n) = 3n^2 + 4n + 17$	357	3 004 017	3 000 004 000 017	$O(n^2)$
$f(n) = 5n^2 + 13n$	630	5 013 000	5 000 013 000 000	$O(n^2)$
$f(n) = n^3 + 4n - 91$	949	1 000 003 909	10^{18} – 3,999,909	$O(n^3)$
$f(n) = 2n^3 + n^2 + 4n - 3$	2137	2 001 003 997	$2 \times 10^{18} + ...$	$O(n^3)$

It is evident from Table 5.7 that each function value approximates increasingly closely to the value of its highest-order term (the highest power to which n is raised), multiplied by any coefficient of that term, as n gets larger. The definition for big O allows some coefficient—which we have called k—and so in determining the order of time-complexity for a function, we can simply ignore all terms lower than the highest.

For example, $f(n) = 2n + 4 \leq 3n$ ($k = 3$) for $n > 4$, and $f(n) = 2n^3 + n^2 + 4n - 3 \leq 3n^3$ ($k = 3$) for all $n > 2$. So $f(n) = 2n + 4$ is $O(n)$, and $f(n) = 2n^3 + n^2 + 4n - 3$ is $O(n^3)$. In general, when looking at any function value, we can simply ignore all coefficients, and all terms of lower order than the highest, in deciding its big O representation. Big O notation describes the *growth rate* for any particular algorithm—and here, the coefficients and additive constants for any given order are of little consequence: the *rate of increase* for $f(n) = n^3 - 3$, for example, is always greater than the rate of increase of $h(n) = 138n^2 + 99n + 20\ 173$, say.

However, for two algorithms of the same (big O) order, the coefficient and constants can be of considerable importance. For example, we might well find that one algorithm to perform some task has equation $f(n) = n^3 + 6$, while another algorithm, which produces the same output for some given input has equation $f(n) = 5n^3 + 2n^2 + 1$. Both algorithms are $O(n^3)$, but when $n = 10$, for instance, the first algorithm runs in 1006 time units, while the second takes 5201 time units. And for all n, the second algorithm will take around five times as long to execute as the first: this can be of considerable importance in practice, and so we seek not just the lowest-order algorithm that will do the job, but the most efficient algorithm of that order.

What forms might $g(n)$ take in practice? Theoretically, any form, but there are not, in fact, very many different expressions commonly encountered, and the more usual ones are listed below. A little practice and experience in examining algorithms enables rapid identification of the efficiency in big O terms to be determined quite quickly. Common forms are:

$O(1)$	(oh one—constant)
$O(n)$	(oh en—linear)
$O(n^2)$	(oh en squared—quadratic)
$O(n^3)$	(oh en cubed—cubic)
$O(n^x)$	(where x is a variable: e.g. $O(n^{1.54})$—oh en to the one point five four)
$O(x^n)$	(where x may be any value: e.g. $O(3.4^n)$— oh three point four to the en)
$O(\lg(n))$	(oh log en—logarithmic)
$O(n(\lg(n)))$	(oh en log en)

5.5 Efficiency in practical terms

What about real-world applications? Recall the example program given in Figure 5.2, and the results in Table 5.1. We had an $O(n)$ algorithm, whose actual running time was given by $T(n) = 7n + 7$. A different algorithm for achieving the same result might have $T(n) = 4n + 3$. However, both are linear: the coefficient and the constant do not change as n changes, and the value in either case increases only as n increases. In other words, the value of $T(n)$—that is, the time taken—is proportional to the value of n.

An $O(n^2)$ algorithm, on the other hand, behaves differently. Consider, for example, the function $T(n) = 3n^2 + 4n + 3$; the time taken for this algorithm to execute is proportional to the *square* of n. Hence if the problem size (n) trebles, the time taken increases by a factor of (about) 9, i.e. 3^2. For example, consider the time taken for this algorithm when $n = 10$ and when $n = 30$: the problem size has trebled. The time taken when $n = 10$ is $3 \times 10^2 + 4 \times 10 + 3 = 343$. When $n = 30$ the time taken is $3 \times 30^2 + 4 \times 30 + 3 = 2823$. Note that $9 \times 343 = 3087$, so that the time taken has increased by a factor of (about) 9. The reason that the increase in time taken is *approximately* the square of the increase in n is that the constants of proportionality, the lower-order terms and the additive constants all have an effect: we will return to this point later.

For now, in order to place the theory in reality, think again about the example program of Fig. 5.2, and the PC which was capable of 1 000 000 operations per second. How long will it take to execute an $O(n)$ algorithm, and how long for an $O(n^2)$ algorithm for various different problem sizes? Table 5.8 shows the figures for n from 1 to 1 000 000; this shows the calculations for the simplest cases, that is when $f(n) = n$, and when $h(n) = n^2$. *Particular* $O(n)$ and $O(n^2)$ algorithms may take very much longer or shorter times for specific values of n, depending on their constants, but Table 5.8 shows how we can expect the algorithms to perform in general.

Table 5.8 Numbers of operations for O(n) and O(n²) algorithms

n	$f(n)$		$h(n)$	
	No. of ops	*Time (seconds)*	*No. of ops*	*Time (seconds)*
1	1	0.000001	1	0.000 001
100	100	0.0001	10 000	0.01
1 000	1 000	0.001	1 000 000	1
100 000	100 000	0.1	10^{10}	10 000
1 000 000	1 000 000	1	10^{12}	1 000 000

The results in Table 5.8 are fairly clear, even obvious. But now think about actually performing a calculation making use of one of the algorithms above, on the PC which performs one million operations per second. When n = 100 000, an $O(n)$ algorithm requires about 100 000 operations,[†] and so its execution takes about one-tenth of a

[†] This is somewhat stylised: clearly, multiplicative and additive constants could have considerable impact on the actual running time of the $O(n)$ or $O(n^2)$ algorithms. However, the point about the relative performance in general is valid.

second. However, the $O(n^2)$ algorithm has to perform 10^{10} operations, which, at 1 000 000 operations per second, requires 10^4 = 10 000 seconds. How long is that? It is a simple matter to calculate: since there are 3600 seconds in an hour, the algorithm will take (10 000/3600) hours, which is just over two and three-quarter hours, to execute. If this surprises you, try it on a PC—but be prepared to wait!

A program with three nested loops is $O(n^3)$: it is left to the reader to calculate how long it would take to perform a calculation when n = 100 000 making use of such an algorithm. In general, any algorithm whose time complexity is $O(n^x)$, where x may be 2 or 3, or 7, or 3.79, etc., is said to be of *polynomial* time order. Polynomial algorithms are normally slower than linear ones. The way that the time taken increases in a general way for some polynomial and linear algorithms as n increases is shown graphically in Fig. 5.9.

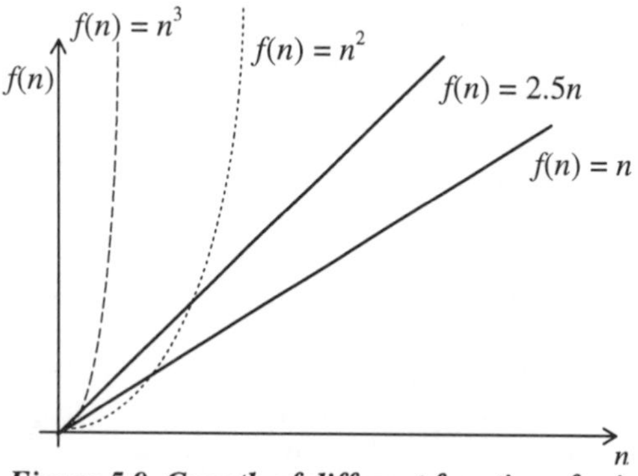

Figure 5.9 Growth of different functions for increasing n

Two important features should be noted from Fig. 5.9: first, the polynomial functions grow very rapidly. Regardless of the details of implementation, and the values of the constants and coefficients, an $O(n^3)$ algorithm is going to be much worse for all practical problems.

The second point is that the polynomial algorithms are actually 'better'—i.e. faster—than the linear algorithms when n is very small: why is that? The answer is that when, for example, $n = 2$, $n^2 = 4$, while $2.5n = 5$. So that, for very small problem sizes (when $n < 3$, in fact), the $O(n^2)$ algorithm will take less time. However, for all values of n greater than that, the linear algorithm is better.

This leads into a consideration of the importance of the coefficients and the additive constants in real cases. Suppose we have linear and polynomial algorithms which perform the same task. The linear algorithm will, in general, be preferable, and almost certainly so for cases when the amount of data to be dealt with is very large. However, suppose a detailed analysis of the algorithms yields the following results:

- for the linear algorithm, $T(n) = 17n + 1350$
- for the polynomial algorithm, $T(n) = n^2 + 1$

When $n = 10$, the linear algorithm takes 170 + 1350 = 1520 time units, while the polynomial algorithm takes $10^2 + 1 = 101$ time units: clearly, the $O(n^2)$ algorithm is better in this case. Even when $n = 25$, the linear algorithm takes 425 + 1350 = 1775 time units, while the polynomial algorithm takes only $25^2 + 1 = 626$ time units. It is only when n is greater than 46 that the linear algorithm becomes faster. When $n = 100$, the linear algorithm is much more efficient—3050 time units, against 10 001, or three times faster. As n increases still further, the advantages of the $O(n)$ algorithm against the $O(n^2)$ one become more obvious. However, if the two algorithms were possible approaches to solving a problem which *always* took somewhere between 1 and 50 values as input, the polynomial algorithm would probably be preferable.

The above discussion illustrates again the way the big O notation is used, and important details of implementation which may underly a simplistic interpretation. It does not detract from the fact that, in general, a linear algorithm is preferable to a polynomial one.

There is another aspect to consider: best- and worst-case performance. To give an example of what is meant by this, consider an algorithm which is designed to find a given number in an array. The *best* case is when the number is in the first position: the algorithm then has just one 'compare' operation to perform, and so takes constant time ($O(1)$), however long that may be: see Fig. 5.10. When the required number is in the last position, there are clearly n comparisons to do, plus the overhead due to loop variables, and so the algorithm is $O(n)$. This is the *worst* case: see Fig. 5.11.

What can we conclude from all this? First, to determine the precise perfomance for

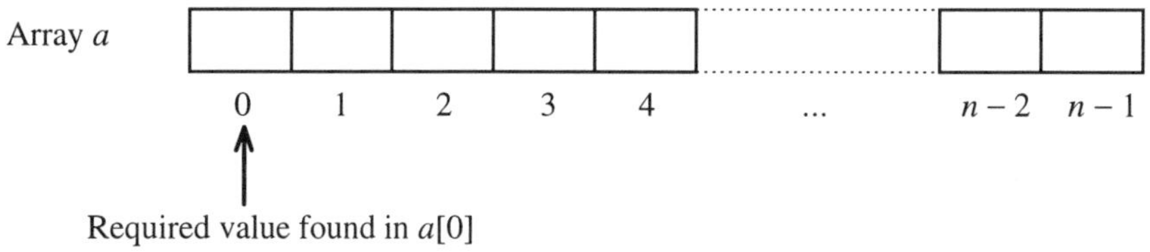

Figure 5.10 Finding a number in an array: best case

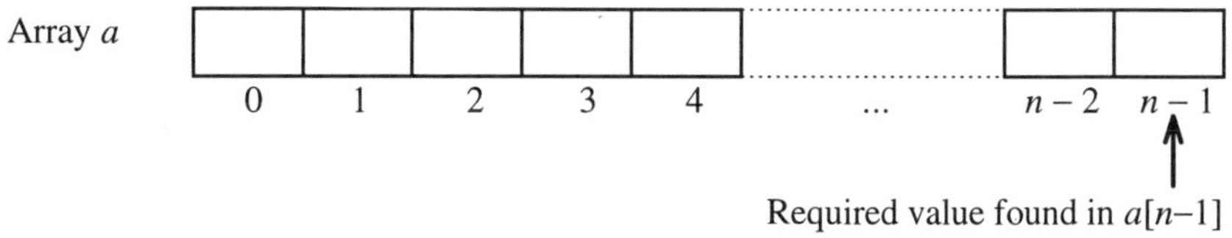

Figure 5.11 Finding a number in an array: worst case

any particular algorithm, a detailed analysis of the algorithm implemented in a programming language is necessary. This gives the time-complexity as a function of n: the complexity in big O notation can then be determined by considering how the function behaves for very large n. Alternatively, experience may allow a judgement to be made—it is possible, for instance, to look at an algorithm which has two nested loops, and simply say, 'That's $O(n^2)$'.

Second, the way that the algorithm behaves in practice may depend to some extent on the input data—for example, the insertion sort algorithm, which was considered in Chapter 3, is $O(n)$ for data that is already sorted, and $O(n^2)$ for random data. For these reasons, we use big O notation to mean the *worst case* efficiency. Saying that an algorithm is $O(n^2)$, for instance, does not mean that that it will always run in time that is some multiple of the square of the number of input data items, but that it will *never take more time* than some multiple of the square of the number of input data items, and may often be better.

This is a very useful result in practice: if we are dealing with such an algorithm, then we know what the worst that can happen is; and if we discover a method which has a better big O representation, then we know that it is a better algorithm. We are comparing like with like, just as in the example of the petrol efficiency of cars in Section 5.1.

5.6 Efficiency of sorting algorithms

Recall the sort programs of Chapter 3: the simple bubble sort algorithm appeared the least efficient, informally. In order to evaluate and compare the efficiencies of these programs rather more exactly, we need to consider the central algorithm in each case. The central algorithm for selection sort is reproduced in Fig. 5.12.

In C:

```
for (i = 0; i < SORT_MAX - 1; ++i)
{
   a = i;
   for (j = i + 1; j < SORT_MAX; ++j)
   {
      if (s1[j] < s1[a])
      {
         a = j;
      }
   }
   if (a != i)
   {
         temp = s1[a];
         s1[a] = s1[i];
         s1[i] = temp;
   }
}
```

In Ada:

```
for i in 0 .. SORT_MAX - 2 loop
   a := i;
   for j in i + 1 .. SORT_MAX - 1 loop
      if s1(j) < s1(a) then
         a := j;
      end if;
   end loop;
   if a /= i then
      temp := s1(a);
      s1(a) := s1(i);
      s1(i) := temp;
   end if;
end loop;
```

Figure 5.12 Selection sort algorithm

What can be said about the efficiency of this algorithm? Recall the way that the algorithm works for, say, four numbers:

↓

X: 7 $\underline{4}$ $\underline{3}$ $\underline{8}$ *Pass 1*: Compare 7 with 4, 4 with 3, and 3 with 8: 3 comparisons

↓

X: 3 4 $\underline{7}$ $\underline{8}$ *Pass 2*: Compare 4 with 7 and with 8: 2 comparisons

↓

X: 3 4 7 $\underline{8}$ *Pass 3*: Compare 7 with 8: 1 comparison. Sort completed

Here, there are four elements, and the selection sort method compares the first element with the second, then, if the second is smaller, it exchanges the stored position with the position of the second element, and compares with the third, and then the third (exchanged if necessary) with the last one. Swaps occur as necessary: in this example, only one swap of the items actually takes place, of 7 and 3 on the first pass. After that, the items are ordered, but the algorithm works through to the end, always, making passes two and three in this case, to examine the remainder.

Hence for four elements, there will be three passes to make comparisons: on the first pass there are three comparisons, on the second pass there are two, and on the third pass, there is just one (of the final pair). In general, for n elements, there will be $n - 1$ comparisons on the first pass, $n - 2$ on the second, $n - 3$ on the third, and so on, until there is just one comparison to make on the last pass.

It makes no difference how the elements are originally ordered, we still systematically compare elements as described, making, for 4 elements, a total of 3 passes, involving first 3 comparisons, then 2, then 1. The total number of comparisons for 4 elements is thus 3 + 2 + 1 = 6. For n elements, there will be a total of $n - 1$ passes, involving $(n-1) + (n-2) + (n-3) + (n-4) + \ldots + 3 + 2 + 1$ comparisons, where we are considering a 'comparison' as a unit operation.

Hence to find the total number of comparisons for any n elements we need to find the sum of the series $(n-1) + (n-2) + (n-3) + (n-4) + \ldots + 3 + 2 + 1$. A formula for such a sum exists, and its derivation can be demonstrated as follows. Suppose the series adds up to some value, X. Then:

$$X = (n-1) + (n-2) + (n-3) + (n-4) + \ldots + 3 + 2 + 1$$

We can write this series in reverse quite legally, so that also:

$$X = 1 + 2 + 3 + 4 + \ldots + (n-3) + (n-2) + (n-1)$$

Now, these two series can be added, term by term,[‡] giving:

$$\begin{array}{rcccccccccccccc} & X = & (n-1) & + & (n-2) & + & (n-3) & + & (n-4) & + \ldots + & 3 & + & 2 & + & 1 \\ + & X = & 1 & + & 2 & + & 3 & + & 4 & + \ldots + & (n-3) & + & (n-2) & + & (n-1) \\ \hline \Rightarrow & 2X = & n & + & n & + & n & + & n & + \ldots + & n & + & n & + & n \end{array}$$

this is because, $(n-1) + 1 = n$; $(n-2) + 2 = n$; ... $2 + (n-2) = n$; $1 + (n-1) = n$.

There are $n - 1$ terms in the series for X: hence the two series added together ($2X$) amount to $[(n-1)$ lots of $n]$. That is,

$2X = (n-1) \times n$ and hence,
$X = [(n-1)n]/2$

Hence the total number of comparisons for the selection sort is $n(n-1)/2 = (n^2 - n)/2$, always. For the specific example considered, we had $n = 4$, and so the total number of comparisons was $(4^2 - 4)/2 = (16 - 4)/2 = 12/2 = 6$. For the example in Chapter 3, there were 6 elements, and so the number of comparisons in total was $(6^2 - 6)/2 = 15$.

The number of comparisons, then, is fixed for this algorithm. The number of elements that are *exchanged* in total depends on the order of the input sequence. In the worst case (input reversed) whether the input sequence is an odd or an even number makes a difference (of one exchange).

We should also be clear about what is meant by the term 'exchange' in this context, and note that we should, for accuracy, distinguish 'exchange' and 'swap': an exchange occurs initially when the value of the first element, whose position is stored (in a in the algorithm) is larger than the second on comparison—if the second is smaller, the

---

‡ Compare, for instance:

$$\begin{array}{rrcl} & 9 & = & 1 + 3 + 5 \\ & + \; 9 & = & 5 + 3 + 1 \\ \hline \Rightarrow & 18 & = & 6 + 6 + 6 \end{array}$$

position of the second element overwrites the position stored as being that of the 'smallest-so-far' value. This 'smallest-so-far' value is then compared with the third term, and if the third is smaller, then the position of the third value is saved instead, overwriting the (previously updated) stored position, and so on. After all such comparison and exchange operations, the position term stored is that of the smallest number in the sequence. The value in this position is then swapped, using *temp*, with the value in the position currently under consideration (held in *i*), if the stored position is different from the position currently under consideration. For example, when four data items are input in reverse order, we have:

↓
4 3 2 1 *Pass 1*: exchange pos0 with pos1, pos1 with pos2, then pos2 with pos3:
0 1 2 3 3 exchanges, plus swap the contents of positions 0 and 3: 1 swap

  ↓
1 3 2 4 *Pass 2*: exchange pos1 with pos2: 1 exchange, plus a swap of the
0 1 2 3 contents of positions 1 and 2: 1 swap

    ↓
1 2 3 4 *Pass 3*: compare 3 with 4—no exchanges, no swaps
0 1 2 3

The reader is invited to confirm that, in general, for an even number n of data items input in reverse order, there are $n^2/4$ exchanges (and $n/2$ swaps). When there are an odd number of items input which are in reverse order, there are $(n^2 - 1)/4$ exchanges. For 4 items then, there is a total of $4^2/4 = 4$ exchanges. For 10 items, there would be $10^2/4 = 25$ exchanges.

Hence we have for the selection sort, in the worst case, a total number of operations due to comparison and exchange for an even number, n, of input items:

$$[(n^2 - n)/2] + [(n^2)/4 + (n/2)] = (3n^2)/4$$

Extra terms such as those due to loop initialisation and updating, and other sequential operations internal to the algorithm (such as 'swap', which is actually three operations, not one) will add to the expression, but will not change the power to which the highest-order term is raised. Hence, arguing as in Section 5.5, we can see that the selection sort is an $O(n^2)$ algorithm.

We now consider the other two sorting methods developed, to see whether they are any better than $O(n^2)$. An initial cursory examination suggests not, as both have nested loops, and hence it may appear on first inspection that there is no particular advantage to be gained by using any one sorting method over another. However, we will look at them in a similar way to the selection sort, to see what difference the constants and linear terms in these algorithms make.

The first version of bubble sort is the simplest. This, it may be recalled, was the easiest to understand and to code, involving simply the repeated comparison of pairs of adjacent elements, and their exchange if necessary. It was noted in Chapter 3 that, although this algorithm is very easy to write out, it is clearly not very efficient even in an informal sense, as it results in repetition of operations which have already been completed. Nevertheless, it will be useful to consider the simple version first (Fig. 5.13), operating on LISTSIZE elements, in order to determine the number of comparisons in the general case, and the number of exchanges, or swaps. The resulting complexity function can then be compared with that for selection sort.

We have:

In C:

```
void bubble_sort1(int s1[LISTSIZE])
{
  int i, j, temp;
  for (i = 0; i < LISTSIZE - 1; ++i)
  {
    for (j = 0; j < LISTSIZE - 1; ++j)
    {
      if (s1[j + 1] < s1[j])
      {
        temp = s1[j];
        s1[j] = s1[j + 1];
        s1[j + 1] = temp;
      }
    }
  }
}
```

In Ada:

```
procedure bubble_sort1 (s1: in out sort_array) is
temp: integer;
begin
  for i in 0 .. LISTSIZE - 2 loop
    for j in 0 .. LISTSIZE - 2 loop
      if s1(j + 1) < s1(j) then
        temp := s1(j);
        s1(j) := s1(j + 1);
        s1(j + 1) := temp;
      end if;
    end loop;
  end loop;
end bubble_sort1;
```

Figure 5.13 Simple bubble sort algorithm

This algorithm compares (LISTSIZE – 1) pairs of numbers (LISTSIZE – 1) times, swapping them if necessary. Taking the same four values as for the selection sort:

7 4 3 8	*Pass 1*:	Compare first pair
4 7 3 8		Compare second pair
4 3 7 8		Compare third pair
4 3 7 8	*Pass 2*:	Compare first pair
3 4 7 8		Compare second pair
3 4 7 8		Compare third pair
3 4 7 8	*Pass 3*:	Compare first pair
3 4 7 8		Compare second pair
3 4 7 8		Compare third pair

Clearly in this example there are three passes over all the data, and on each pass three pairs of items are compared, giving a total of nine comparison operations. And in general, for n items, there will be $(n - 1)(n - 1) = n^2 - 2n + 1$ comparisons. In the above case, there are 4 items, and so there are 9 comparisons. What about exchanges? Consider the worst case (items reversed), for four items:

Pass 1:	4 3 2 1	1 exchange
	3 4 2 1	1 exchange
	3 2 4 1	1 exchange
	3 2 1 4	TOTAL: 3 exchanges
Pass 2:	3 2 1 4	1 exchange
	2 3 1 4	1 exchange
	2 1 3 4	0 exchanges
	2 1 3 4	TOTAL: 2 exchanges
Pass 3:	2 1 3 4	1 exchange
	1 2 3 4	0 exchanges
	1 2 3 4	0 exchanges
	1 2 3 4	TOTAL: 1 exchange

Hence there are altogether 3 + 2 + 1 exchanges for 4 input items in reverse order. In general, for n input items in reverse order, there will be $(n - 1) + (n - 2) + (n - 3) + (n - 4) + \ldots + 3 + 2 + 1$ exchanges. As before, this series sums to $(n^2 - n)/2$. So altogether, for this version of the bubble sort, we have $(n - 1)(n - 1) = n^2 - 2n + 1$ comparisons, plus $(n^2 - n)/2$ exchanges in the worst case: this is $(3n^2 - 5n + 2)/2$, which—again ignoring terms other than those due to comparisons and exchanges, and treating the exchange as one operation—is $O(n^2)$.

How does this compare with the selection sort? Both take the same order of time (they are of quadratic time-complexity) but the key difference is the divisor: the quadratic expression is divided by 2 in this case, but it was divided by 4 for the selection sort. The difference this makes is not great, and may not matter when n is small. However, for increasing amounts of data, the effect is more marked.

For instance when $n = 1000$, we have:
Selection sort: $(3n^2)/4 = 750\,000$ comparisons and exchanges
Bubble sort: $(3n^2 - 5n + 2)/2 = 1\,497\,501$ comparisons and exchanges

For data that is already ordered, or very nearly so, neither algorithm, of course, makes any exchanges. However, the *relative* difference in time of execution is the same: the selection sort algorithm is very nearly twice as fast. We have $n^2 - 2n + 1$ comparisons for the bubble sort, against $(n^2 - n)/2$ for the selection sort. When $n = 1000$, there are 998 001 comparisons for the bubble sort, and 499 500 for the selection sort. Evidently, although both sorting algorithms are $O(n^2)$, the bubble sort (at least in this form) is a very poor choice. In Chapter 3, a number of improvements were suggested to the bubble sort, to make it more efficient. In particular, the fact that the simple version always makes $(n - 1)(n - 1)$ passes over the data, making often unnecessary comparisons, was addressed by:

(a) noting that, for unordered data, one more item is 'sorted'—i.e. in the correct place—after each pass, and so examining one fewer of the set of items each time;

(b) noting that, if no items have been exchanged on any one complete pass over the data, the data must be sorted, and so the algorithm should stop.

The improved versions are shown in Fig. 5.14.

In C:

(a)
```
void bubble_sort2(int s1[LISTSIZE])
{
   int i, j, temp;
   for (i = 0; i < LISTSIZE; ++i)
   {
      for (j = 0; j < (LISTSIZE - 1) - i; ++j)
      {
         if (s1[j + 1] < s1[j])
         {
            temp = s1[j];
            s1[j] = s1[j + 1];
            s1[j + 1] = temp;
         }
      }
   }
}
```

(b)
```
void bubble_sort3(int s1[LISTSIZE])
{
   int i, temp, done;
```

```
   do{
      done = 1;
      for (i = 0; i < LISTSIZE - 1; ++i)
      {
         if (s1[i + 1] < s1[i])
         {
            temp = s1[i];
            s1[i] = s1[i + 1];
            s1[i + 1] = temp;
            done = 0;
         }
      }
   }while (!done);
}
```

In Ada:

(a)

```
procedure bubble_sort2(s1: in out sort_array) is
temp: integer;
begin
   for i in 0 .. LISTSIZE - 1 loop
      for j in 0 .. ((LISTSIZE - 2) - i) loop
         if s1(j + 1) < s1(j) then
            temp := s1(j);
            s1(j) := s1(j + 1);
            s1(j + 1) := temp;
         end if;
      end loop;
   end loop;
end bubble_sort2;
```

(b)

```
procedure bubble_sort3(s1: in out sort_array) is
temp, done: integer;
begin
   done := 0;
   while done = 0 loop
      done := 1;
      for i in 0 .. LISTSIZE - 2 loop
         if s1(i + 1) < s1(i) then
            temp := s1(i);
            s1(i) := s1(i + 1);
            s1(i + 1) := temp;
            done := 0;
         end if;
      end loop;
   end loop;
end bubble_sort3;
```

Figure 5.14 Improved bubble sort algorithms

EXERCISES 5.4

1. Work out the efficiency of the algorithms for the improved bubble sorts in Fig. 5.14, in terms of the numbers of comparisons and exchanges each makes

   (i) in the best case—data initially ordered
   (ii) in the worst case—data reverse-ordered

2. Do these algorithms offer a measurable improvement over the simple version of the bubble sort? How much better, in relative terms?

3. Is either of the improved versions of the bubble sort preferable to the selection sort method, in the best and worst cases?

4. Calculate the number of exchanges and comparisons for the following sets of data using selection sort and the 'best' version of the bubble sort. Which is preferable?

   (i) 9 7 2 –4 6 19 –1 11 2 –3 0
   (ii) 3 3 3 3 5 3 3 3
   (iii) 8 7 6 5 4 3 9 2

5. Given the above methods, which algorithm would you choose to sort a list of 10, 1000, and 100 000 items? Why?

6. For both selection sort and the bubble sorts, what happens when there is more than one list item having the same value? Are unnecessary operations made? If so, how can this be addressed? If not, why not?

7. The above sorting algorithms have all been applied to integers. Write algorithms to sort floating-point numbers, and character strings.

The last sorting algorithm that was examined was *insertion sort*. This is also an $O(n^2)$ algorithm, but the way that it executes the process is different to the other two methods. The algorithm is shown in Fig. 5.15.

In C:

```
#include <stdio.h>
#define max 6

void main()
{
   int i, j, k, temp;
   int s1[SORT_MAX] = {10, 4, 14, -3, 12, 6};
```

```
   for (i = 1; i < max; ++i)
   {      /* this ('i')is the position currently being considered */
     temp = s1[i]; /*  Save value of item being considered  */
     j = i;  /* 'j' holds the current position, and will hold the */
            /* positions of the neighbour(s)to be compared */
     while (j > 0 && temp < s1[j - 1]) /* Compare with every item */
     {      /* in the list from the fifth down to the zeroth ...  */
        s1[j] = s1[j - 1];    /* Overwrite if s1[j] < s1[j - 1] */
        j = j - 1;            /*  decrement position counter  */
     }
     s1[j] = temp;            /* Put current item in correct place */
   }
   for (k = 0; k < SORT_MAX; ++k)
   {
     printf("%d ", s1[k]);    /* Print sorted list  */
   }
}
```

In Ada:

```
procedure insert is
SORT_MAX: integer := 6;
i, j, k, temp: integer;
type sort_array is array (0 .. SORT_MAX - 1) of integer;
s1: sort_array := (10, 4, 14, -3, 12, 6);
begin
   for i in 1 .. SORT_MAX - 1 loop        -- position currently being considered
      temp := s1(i);                      -- Save value of item being considered
      j := i;                             -- 'j' holds the current position, and will ...
                        -- ...hold the positions of the neighbour(s) to be compared
      while j > 0 and then temp < s1(j - 1) loop
                  -- Compare with every item in the list from the sixth down to the first ...
         s1(j) := s1(j - 1);              -- ... overwrite if s1[j] < s1[j - 1]
         j := j - 1;                      -- Decrement position counter
      end loop;
      s1(j) := temp;                      -- Put current item in correct place
      for k in 0 .. SORT_MAX - 1 loop     -- Print sorted list
         put(s1(k));
      end loop;
      new_line;
   end loop;
end insert;
```

Figure 5.15 Insertion sort algorithm

In working out the time-efficiency of the insertion sort algorithm, consider first the method operating on the same data that was used for the other methods:

↓

X: 7 4 3 8   *Pass 1*: Compare 4 with 7: 1 comparison

↓

X: 4 7 3 8   *Pass 2*: Compare 3 with 7 and with 4: 2 comparisons

$$\begin{array}{llll} & & \downarrow & \\ X\!: 3 & 4 & \underline{7} & 8 \end{array}$$ *Pass 3*: Compare 8 with 7: 1 comparison

X: 3 4 7 8 *Stop*: List sorted

The number of comparisons in this case is 1 + 2 + 1 = 4, which is noticeably better than either of the other two methods. What about the worst case? For instance:

$$\begin{array}{llll} \downarrow & & & \\ \underline{4} & 3 & 2 & 1 \end{array}$$ *Pass 1*: Compare 3 with 4: 1 comparison

$$\begin{array}{llll} & \downarrow & & \\ \underline{3} & \underline{4} & 2 & 1 \end{array}$$ *Pass 2*: Compare 2 with 4 and with 3: 2 comparisons

$$\begin{array}{llll} & & \downarrow & \\ \underline{2} & \underline{3} & \underline{4} & 1 \end{array}$$ *Pass 3*: Compare 1 with 4, with 3, and with 2: 3 comparisons

1 2 3 4 *Stop*: List sorted

For the worst case there are, for n elements, $1 + 2 + 3 + ... + (n-3) + (n-2) + (n-1)$ comparisons: that is, $(n^2 - n)/2$ comparisons. Note that this comparison count contrasts in the general case with the selection sort and bubble sort algorithms which *always* make $(n^2 - n)/2$ comparisons: insertion sort does indeed make exactly the same number of comparisons in the worst case, but will usually be better than that.

The number of items to be moved on each pass depends on the order of the input, but in the worst case, there is one more item to be moved each time than the number of comparisons on that pass: i.e. there are $2 + 3 + ... + (n-2) + (n-1) + n$ moves to be made for n items. This sums to $(n^2 + n - 2)/2$ moves, or exchanges (where an 'exchange' for this algorithm is really an overwrite, and so is properly one operation).

The total number of comparisons and exchanges in the worst case for n input data items is thus $(n^2 - n)/2 + (n^2 + n - 2)/2 = n^2 - 1$, and so insertion sort is $O(n^2)$. However, consider the best case:

$$\begin{array}{llll} \downarrow & & & \\ \underline{1} & 2 & 3 & 4 \end{array}$$ *Pass 1*: Compare 2 with 1: 1 comparison, no exchanges

$$\begin{array}{llll} & \downarrow & & \\ 1 & \underline{2} & 3 & 4 \end{array}$$ *Pass 2*: Compare 3 with 2: 1 comparison, no exchanges

$$\begin{array}{llll} & & \downarrow & \\ 1 & 2 & \underline{3} & 4 \end{array}$$ *Pass 3*: Compare 4 with 3: 1 comparison, no exchanges

For n ordered data items, the insertion sort makes just $n - 1$ comparisons, and no exchanges: i.e. it is $O(n)$. For example, when $n = 1000$, there are 999 comparisons. These are important results: insertion sort, although it is $O(n^2)$, will be faster on average than either of the other two methods, and much faster in certain cases. Even in the worst case, it is better than bubble sort and nearly as good as selection sort: the total number of comparison and exchange operations for n reversed input data items when $n = 1000$ is $n^2 - 1 = 1000^2 - 1 = 999\,999$. And, of course, the most important consideration is that input data will not usually be exactly reversed, and so in the great majority of cases, when evaluating the three methods considered here, the insertion sort is the algorithm of choice for sorting.

Summary

- The real-time duration of execution for any algorithm depends on the hardware.
- Big O notation gives the worst-case behaviour: it allows a judgement to be made about the relative efficiency of algorithms as a function of the input data size.
- The big O complexity is not an exact number: it describes how an algorithm treats n input items, and how it behaves as n increases.
- Constants and lesser terms in the expression for time-complexity can make a big difference in the running times of different algorithms with the same big O value.
- Selection sort, bubble sort, and insertion sort are all $O(n^2)$, but insertion sort is usually the best of the three in practice.

6

DATA STRUCTURES AND ABSTRACT DATA TYPES

OBJECTIVES

In this chapter you will learn

- different ways that real-world structures and events may be modelled by computer
- what is meant by a data structure and how data structures may have operations defined on them to create abstract data types (ADTs)
- ways of implementing the same ADTs with different data structures
- how the ADTs list, stack and queue may be realised as contiguous or as linked structures with appropriate operations defined

---

6.1 Representing data

In all the discussion so far, the data we have worked with has been of a very simple type. Mainly, we have worked with integers, though on some occasions characters or strings of text have been manipulated; reference has also been made to arrays, without any further explanation. This chapter is concerned with these and other ways in which data may be represented in terms of software, both from the point of view of what is convenient, or natural, and in terms of what is possible.

We, as human beings, go about problem-solving in a logical way (sometimes), and we solve problems that have to do with real things in the world. For example, when we shop, we have a list of items to buy; each of these has a price, and the bill at the end will be the total of those prices. So we think in terms of the cost of a loaf of bread, of a tin of beans, etc., and at the end we pay, either in cash or by means of credit transfer (cheque or credit card). Writing a program to calculate the cost of the shopping would not be difficult—something rather like this was done in Section 1.2. In designing the program, we move from a very generalised, abstract representation of the problem—'Work out the cost of the shopping'—to a specification that is increasingly detailed and specific. This general approach is often referred to as 'top-down programming', and it is not the only possible way to do it: however, it probably reflects the way many people tackle such problems.

How are ideas such as 'Five boxes of Crumblies at £2.13 each' to be modelled and manipulated by the computer? We use data types, and the data in the shopping bill will most probably be: real numbers, representing cost; integers, for the number of items; and character strings for item descriptions.

Digital computers, however, are not concerned with the cost of a box of Crumblies: they are simply very large banks of transistor switches. The task then, is to get from a problem statement that anyone can understand to a solution which exists as a program to run on a digital computer—that is, sequences of changes to bit patterns, which in turn means changes in voltage levels in order to turn certain transistors on or off. The compiler, linker, and other system utilities take care of this for us, of course, but we still need to know what is allowed and what is not. In C, Ada, and most other computer languages we can declare something to be an integer—the system 'knows' what that is. But we would not expect, in any standard third-generation language, to be able to declare 'shopping', and assume that the system could handle it as illustrated in Fig. 6.1.

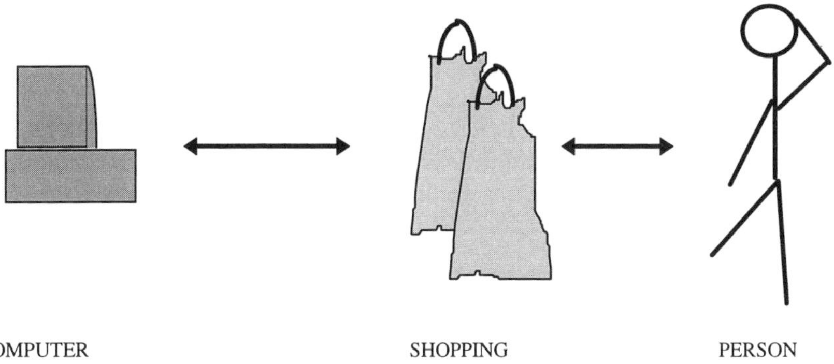

Figure 6.1 The concept 'shopping' is represented differently in human consciousness than it is in digital computers

The values which can be worked with will vary from machine to machine, according to the basic 'word' size (8 bit, 32 bit, 64 bit etc.), which is a feature of the hardware, and what is allowed by the system software. A positive integer in a 16-bit application will lie in the range 1 to 32 767: what happens if an integer computation results in a value larger than that? Normally, 'overflow' occurs: that is, although 32 767 + 1 = 32 768 in base 10, what the computer is dealing with, which is numbers in base 2, gives 32 767 + 1 = 0111 1111 1111 1111 + 1 = 1000 0000 0000 0000. Since the most significant bit is normally taken to indicate sign, in which '0' means positive, and '1' means negative, the binary value of 32 767 + 1 will be expressed in decimal as –32 768. Similarly, 'underflow' can occur, in which subtraction from a large negative number can result in a positive value being returned.

Both C and Ada allow a 'long integer' to be declared, the size of which is machine-dependent, but which may typically have values in the range –2 147 483 648 to + 2 147 483 647. Overflow and underflow can still occur, of course, but larger integer computations can be managed (however, any 'factorial' program, for example, will rapidly expose the limitations of this range).

An integer can certainly be declared, and used, much as we would use integers in our everyday lives: 7 is smaller than 11, 9 – 6 = 3, –2 × –8 = 16, 5 × 202 338 = 1 011 690. However, we must take care when doing this on a computer, since the range of numbers that exists is limited by the hardware and by the type of declaration ('long integer' or 'integer', for instance). On an 8-bit machine, we have only the range 0111 1111 to 1111 1111, or –128 to +127 in base 10, available as integers.

Real numbers—decimal fractions—often cannot be expressed exactly in binary. For example, although one-quarter can be, one-tenth cannot: 1/4 = 0.25 in base 10 ($2 \times 10^{-1} + 5 \times 10^{-2}$), and 0.01 in base 2 ($0 \times 2^{-1} + 1 \times 2^{-2}$); but 1/10 = 0.1 in base 10 and has no exact equivalent in base 2: 0.000110011001 comes close (equal to 0.0998535156), but no amount of precision will be exact. This is simply a general feature of our number system: for instance, 1/17 cannot be exactly represented as a decimal number.

When it comes to characters, the ASCII set is the accepted standard for representation: this allocates binary codes from 1 to 127 (or to 255 for the extended set) to specific character representations: 'A', for example has an ASCII value of 65 in base 10 (binary 0100 0001), and '6' has an ASCII value of 54.

The above preamble is in order to make the point that fundamentally, all data types are binary representations of abstractions such as '1' (the idea of oneness), or collections of symbols which stand for words conveying meaning.

So a computer is a machine whose output we are able to interpret as emulating real-world processes and activities if we give it the appropriate instructions. The *things* it has to use are nothing like the things it normally works with (voltage levels). So things have to be represented in:

- a way that makes sense to the computer
- a way that makes sense to the programmer and the user.

6.2 Concepts, symbols and operations

The abstraction referred to above is not something we have to think much about for programs dealing with simple data types. An integer is an abstraction, but each integer is modelled in the computer as a particular bit pattern, and any third-generation language will allow us to declare integers (to base 10) and use them as we would naturally. In principle, we can deal with integers as large or as small as we like. When collections of these simple types are dealt with as a unit—such as an array of integers—we refer to this as a data structure; when the data structure so formed also has a set of rules about what we are allowed to do, we have an abstract data type.

Formally, an abstract data type (ADT) is:

- a data structure
- the operations defined (allowed) on it

This definition appears to be saying little that is new: an integer is an abstraction modelled in the computer, on which certain operations are defined (and others are not). However, there is nothing to stop us from defining a new integer subtype, which has values and operations determined by us for some particular purpose: we could define a type `weird_int`, for instance, which had a range +1256 to +2117, and the operations 'add' and 'divide' only defined. An identical structure could be declared, on which different operations were defined (perhaps only 'greater than' and 'less than'): this would then be a different abstract type. A *data structure*, then, is composed of *data types*, which may all be the same type (as with arrays), or of different types (e.g. records). The composite data structures which can be constructed from the data types is a language-dependent feature.

Basic types available in one language may not be available in another: for example, Ada allows boolean as a basic type, but C does not. In order to have a boolean data type available in C, we must construct it as an enumerated type, for instance:

```
typedef enum boolean {FALSE, TRUE} boolean;
```

Now the function:

```
boolean testval (int a, int b)
{
   return ((boolean) (a == b));
}
```

returns `TRUE(1)` if `a = b`, and `FALSE(0)` otherwise.

The new boolean type can be used like any built-in type as shown in Fig. 6.2.

```
void main()
{
   int x, y;
   boolean equal;
   printf("Enter two numbers:  ");
   scanf("%d%d", &x, &y);
   equal = testval (x, y);
   if (equal)
   {
      printf("Same.");
   }
   else
   {
      printf("Different.");
   }
}
```

Figure 6.2 User-defined boolean type in C

Data structures constructed from the basic types available or created may then be manipulated in various different ways, in order to model different real-world behaviours. The rules for what operations are permissible define how the abstract type behaves.

There is no need to restrict ourselves to entities that are inherent in the nature of the computer, or which are simply mathematical: string handling, as mentioned above, is one example. Others which occur rather frequently are *stacks* and *queues*: we deal with these in Sections 6.6 and 6.7, but, very briefly, a stack is a representation of the abstract idea implicit in the natural language: one thing stacked on top of another, the last one placed on top being the first removed. A queue models the idea of a queue from everyday experience: the first person who arrives is the first to be served, and each newcomer tags on to the end. The data structures underlying the two different abstractions may be identical, or different. The sets of operations defined on the structures are chosen to enable the ADT to model the entity which occurs in the real world, or to allow its behaviour to reflect the abstraction we are trying to model.

6.3 Arrays and records

The discussion in Section 6.1 suggests that computer memory is composed of physically adjacent cells—so, simplistically, a computer with 16 Megabytes of memory can hold 16 million pieces of information, each a byte long. The number 13, for instance, is binary 0000 1101, and the character ‘A’ is 65, or 0100 0001. Each computer ‘word’ accommodates one such type, and so memory may be visualised as being an array (using the word ‘array’ in its natural language sense) of cells as shown in Fig. 6.3.

65	11	t	b	13	–14	......

Figure 6.3 Simple data types occupying complete memory units

All of computer memory may be visualised in this way, and an array as a data structure can be thought of similarly, as a subset of available (real) memory. So an array of integers, which might be declared as in Fig. 6.4 can be visualised as being a row of memory cells, each holding one data value of type integer as in Fig. 6.5.

In C:

```
int slots[50];
```

In Ada

```
type class is array(1..50) of integer;
slots: class;
```

Figure 6.4 Array declarations in C and in Ada

The ‘?’ symbols in the array locations of Fig. 6.5 indicate that the contents of the cells are *undefined* on declaration: since the contents of array components are equivalent to real memory address contents, they will usually contain whatever happened to be in that address prior to declaration (not zero, necessarily). Also, although we can visualise the array cells as being next to each other, they may very well not be physically adjacent in the computer's memory.

Clearly, since an array is a *data structure*, as opposed to a *data type*, we need to be able to access individual members of the structure. The subscripts 1, 2, 3, ... 49, 50 and 0, 1, 2, ... , 48, 49 in Fig.6.5 indicate two different schemes for identifying array members. In Ada, an array may have any subscript system, for instance –25 to +24, or 51 to 100; in C, arrays are subscripted from zero by default. Hence in Fig. 6.5, the fifth component is `slots[4]` or slots(5).

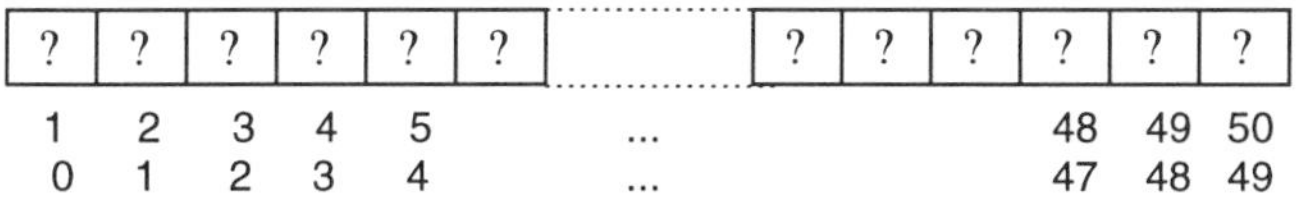

Figure 6.5 Conceptual structure for array of integers

We can assign values, e.g. slots(5) := 17;. More generally, we can assign values to any number of logically adjacent cells by means of a loop, as for example in Fig.6.6.

In C:

```
for (i = 12; i < 16; ++i)
{
   slots[i] = 0;
}
```

In Ada:

```
for i in 12 .. 15 loop
   slots(i) := 0;
end loop;
```

Figure 6.6 Array component assignment

Figure 6.6 illustrates the value zero being entered into locations 12, 13, 14 and 15 of the array 'slots'. Given the standard subscripting scheme for C and Ada, these would be physically different locations in the two instances: slots(12), for instance, would be equivalent to `slots[11]`, etc. To avoid this, we have frequently subscripted arrays from zero in both cases, even though this is not standard in Ada. Note that arrays are *static* structures—their dimensions must be stated on declaration, either explicitly, as above (50), or implicitly. In the latter case—an unconstrained array—the dimensions are determined at run-time. However, it must be made clear to the compiler (if it allows this) that this will happen, and once the dimensions are assigned on execution, they are fixed for that run of the program.

Many languages allow different types to be aggregated and treated as a single data structure. An Ada record or a C `struct` fulfils this purpose. A record is usually composed of a number of fields, which may have varying lengths and types. This is useful as it models the way data is traditionally held about human affairs, in files containing records which hold information about each individual item. Each entry has a number of fields associated with it, and a unique key, as, for example in Fig. 6.7.

Once an array of records is available, then an abstract file is produced, in which the time to access any one record is constant (O(1)). For instance, a file of electricity company customer data might be constructed as an array of records, as in Fig. 6.8.

Driver's licence:

Surname	type:string
Other names	type:string
Date of birth	type:integer
Address	type:string
Licence code	type:integer

Figure 6.7 Record structure for data

rec 1	rec 2	rec3	rec 4	rec 5	rec 6	
						Name
						Address
						Cust_id
						Amt_owing

Figure 6.8 Customer data records file

6.4 Lists

In Chapters 4 and 5, the importance of the idea of a *sequence* was referred to frequently. As an abstraction, a sequence may have any generating function, and may have as few or as many components as desired.

A sequence may also be considered a list of elements, and the ADT 'list' is fundamental in computing. The ADT list has all the properties of a sequence of elements: a rule, which implies that the elements have an order, and a length—the number of elements. Clearly, an array, which is often introduced as being like 'a row of pigeon-holes', is a natural data structure for representing the ADT 'list'. Although array components must all be of the same type, that type can be a *record*, as mentioned above, and so if the real-world entity to be modelled is, for example, electricity company accounts, or a club membership list, then an array of records would seem to be a data structure which will do the job. What operations should be defined on it?

As a minimum, one would expect to be able to:

- add new members
- delete members
- update entries
- search for a specific member.

Other operations, such as 'Check number of list members' might be required—but in the first instance, of course, the list will have to be created.

Consider the simplest kind of list, a list of integers (which might be unique keys for a real list). If an array is used, then insertion will require the creation of a 'space', and deletion will result in a 'hole'. Insertion will cause elements to be shifted, and so will deletion if space is to be efficiently managed, and so provision must be made for this when the size of the array is first declared. Further, given that an array is a static structure, it is necessary to know the limit, or end-point, so that an appropriate message can be output if an attempt to add a member to a full list is made, or to delete from an empty list. Assuming that we might also want to know the actual size of the list at any time, an 'end-marker' can be declared, which will address both of these points. This end-marker may be a separate variable, or the value may be placed in the last position in the array (i.e. the first unoccupied position).

Putting this together results in a data structure which may be visualised rather like Fig. 6.9. The value of 'lim' in Fig. 6.9 is just 6. If 'lim' = 'max' then the list is full.

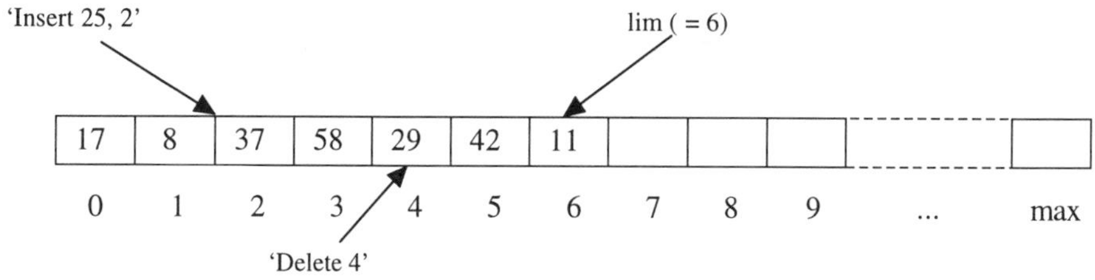

Figure 6.9 Array data structure and operations

Because of the nature of an array, the operations 'delete' and 'search for' can take array indices as their parameters, e.g. 'delete 4' to remove the element with 4 as its subscript and 'search for 9' to find the component whose subscript is 9. In practice, however, it is more likely that we would wish to delete the component whose *value* is for instance 39, and search for a particular key value.

The insert operation, then, would normally require two parameters: the value to be inserted, and the position in which to place it. Consider the task of inserting the value 25 in position 2, as in Fig. 6.9. In this particular case, we know that the array has sufficient free space to make the insertion, but in general we would need to check. Hence we have:

Input: List
Output: List
Operations
1. Check that the list is not full
2. Check that the requested position exists
3. Shift items up to make room for the new item
4. Make the insertion
5. Update list size value

In the algorithm of Fig. 6.11, we use a temporary integer marker, 'mark' set to the value of 'lim' prior to the operation. By then shifting elements by [(mark + 1) – new_pos] places, we make room for the new element e.g. [(mark + 1) – new_pos] = 7 – 2 = 5, and so we move [6] (the contents of position 6) to position 7, then [5] to [6], [4] to [5], [3] to [4], and [2] to [3]. Finally, we need to insert the new element, and update the end marker, 'lim', as shown in Fig. 6.10. To insert the value x into the list 'slots' in the position with index *k*, see Fig. 6.11.

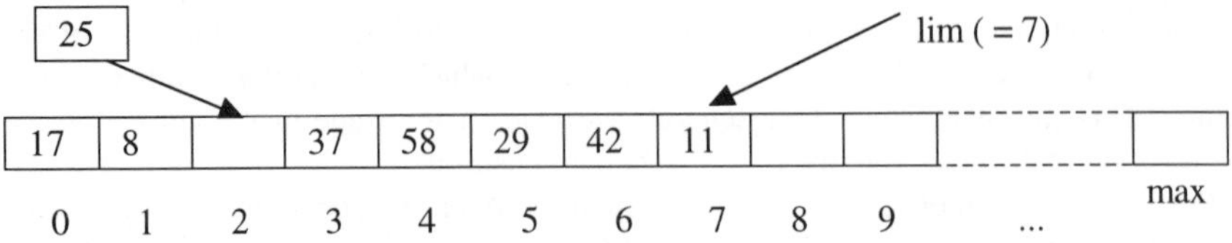

Figure 6.10 Array 'slots' immediately before insertion of value 25 in slots[2]

In C:

```
if (lim == max)      /* Assume array declared as int slots[max+1] */
{
   printf("FULL");
}
else if (k < 0 || k > lim)
{
   printf("Invalid position.");
}
else
{
   for(mark = lim; mark >= k; --mark)
   {
      slots[mark + 1] = slots[mark];
   }
   slots[k] = x;
   ++lim;
}
```

In Ada:

```
if lim = max then                    -- Assume declaration of array slots(0 .. max)
   put("FULL");
elsif k < 0 or k > lim then
   put("Invalid position");
else
   for mark in reverse k .. lim loop
      slots(mark + 1) := slots(mark);
   end loop;
   slots(k) := x;
   lim := lim + 1;
end if;
```

Figure 6.11 Inserting an element x, into an array in position k

Note that, in Fig. 6.11, although both arrays are subscripted from zero, there is a difference in the meaning of the associated declarations. In the C version, we will need to declare `slots[max + 1]`, since this will allocate slots[0, 1, 2, .. max – 1, max]. The one extra position is required since we shift up by one to make room for each new element: when the final element is inserted, whatever (garbage) is in the rightmost position in the array must shift right. The Ada declaration automatically provides one extra place, as it starts from zero.

To delete the element whose index is *k*, we need to follow a similar procedure, except that after deletion, all the elements must be shifted back one. If this is not done, then not only are we wasting space, but the value of lim is not correct any more as an indicator of the size of the list. See Figs 6.12 and 6.13.

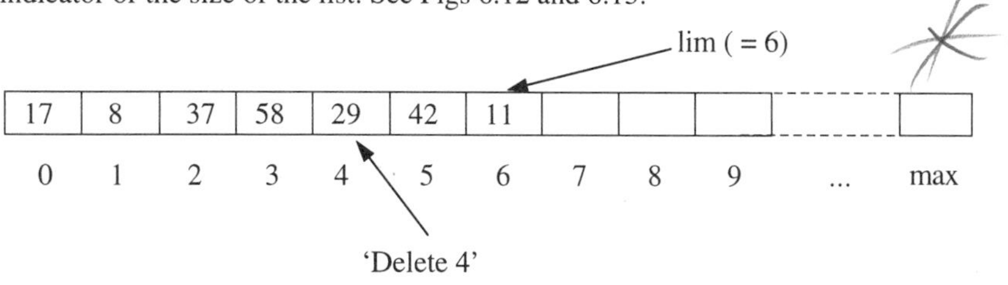

Figure 6.12 ***Array 'slots' immediately before deletion of value in slots[4]***

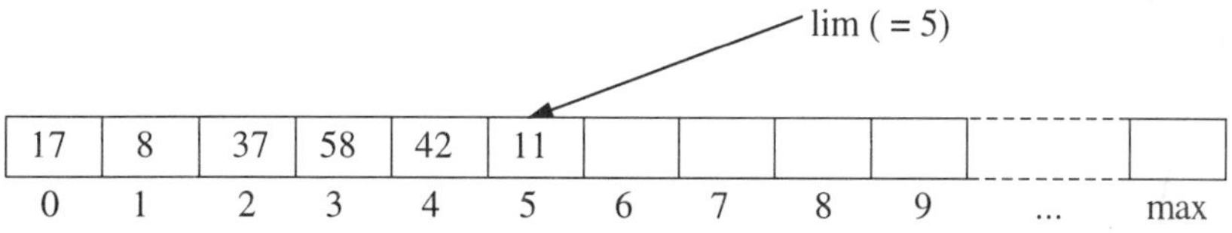

Figure 6.13 ***Array 'slots' after deletion***

The procedure is simply to check that the requested delete is legal (i.e. the array position exists), then shift all elements left one from $(k + 1)$, overwriting. Finally, the value of lim must be updated (Fig. 6.14).

In C:

```
if (lim < 0)
{
   printf("EMPTY LIST");
}
else if (k < 0 || k > lim)
{
   printf("Invalid position.");
}
else
{
   for (mark = k; mark <= lim; ++mark)
   {
      slots[mark] = slots[mark + 1];
   }
   --lim;
}
```

In Ada:

```
if lim < 0 then
   put("EMPTY LIST");
elsif k < 0 or k > lim then
   put("Invalid position.");
else
   for mark in k .. lim loop
      slots(mark) := slots(mark + 1);
   end loop;
   lim := lim - 1;
end if;
```

Figure 6.14 Deletion of array item

The search procedure works along similar lines. To find a value *x* and output its position, *k*, in the array if it exists, or else to output an appropriate message if the value is not found, we have the algorithm of Fig. 6.15. Note that the test for an empty list is true when lim is less than zero, since the arrays in both cases are subscripted to include zero.

In C:

```
found = 0;
k = 0;

if (lim < 0)
{
   printf("EMPTY LIST");
}
else
{
   while (found == 0 && k <= lim)
   {
      if (slots[k] == x)
      {
         found = 1;
      }
      else
      {
         ++k;
      }
   }
   if (found)
   {
      printf("%d", k);
   }
   else
   {
      printf("Value not found");
   }
}
```

In Ada:

```
found := 0;  -- Boolean would be better, but using 1/0 here for simplicity and consistency
k := 0;

if lim < 0 then
   put("EMPTY LIST");
else
   while (found = 0 and k <= lim) loop
      if slots(k) = x then
         found := 1;
      else
         k := k + 1;
      end if;
   end loop;
   if found = 1 then
      put(k);
   else
      put("Value not found");
   end if;
end if;
```

Figure 6.15 Linear search for an array value

It should be evident that all these algorithms are $O(n)$ in terms of execution time, and that the number of operations in any particular case of insertion or deletion is proportional to (lim – k). If we wish to delete a particular *value* in the list, as opposed to specifying its position, then obviously we will require a search followed by a delete.

It may have occurred to the reader that working with a presorted list would be more efficient. Then the operation search, for instance, can cease searching as soon as it encounters a value greater than the one being searched for (for a list sorted into ascending order). This should improve matters, since we can expect on average to have to inspect only half the components in the list. In the worst case, when the required element is in the last position, clearly every element will have to be checked, but this is better than simple sequential search, when every element will always have to be checked: however, it is still $O(n)$. Is there a more efficient way to search for a value in a presorted list?

The answer is 'Yes', and the algorithm is based on the way many people search a list in reality. To find a given value in a list of values sorted into ascending order, we do not examine the first element, then the second, then the third, and so on, until either the required item is found, or we know it is not in the list. A more sensible approach is to pick the middle value, and then, based on whether that is greater than the required item or not, search just one-half of the list. This is called 'binary search' and is rather like a game which goes:

A: 'I'm thinking of a number between 1 and 100. Guess what it is.'
B: 'Is is less than 50?'

If now *A* answers ‘Yes’, *B* knows that the number is in the range 1 to 49. *B* can next say, ‘Is it less than 25?’ If the answer is ‘No’, then *B* now knows that the number lies between 25 and 49, and might make the next guess based on the partition $(25 + 49)/2 = 37$. Equally, if *A* answers ‘No’ initially, then this provides just as much information, since *B* now knows that the number lies between 50 and 100.

For any upper limit on the list, n, the first step reduces the search space to $n/2$. The next time it is $n/4$, then $n/8$, and so on. This is a highly efficient searching algorithm: for 250 items, just 8 steps reduce the search space successively to 125, 64, 32, 16, 8, 4, 2, 1. Halving the space to be searched each time in this way means we are reducing it by 2^n, where n is the number of guesses. And since $2^8 = 256$, there will be no more than 8 steps required to find any given value in the list, or 9 steps to show it is not present.

More generally, since $2^n = L \Leftrightarrow \log_2 L = n$ (refer to Chapter 2), any value in a list L can be identified in at most $\log_2 L + 1$ steps. So searching for a given value in a sorted list of one million values will not take more than 21 guesses. Algorithms such as this, which have logarithmic efficiency—i.e. are $O(\lg(n))$—are of considerable practical value, so long as the overhead associated with having to sort the list prior to searching is acceptable. When a list is updated frequently, it may not be acceptable, but for one which does not change very often, and so does not frequently have to be re-sorted, it is usually the search algorithm of choice.

To find an element k in an array ‘bin’, the algorithmic process is:

```
Loop: calculate the middle position as [bin(first) + bin(last)]/2
   If the value in the middle position is greater than k
      Calculate the mid-position of the lower half
   Else if the middle position is less than k
      Calculate the mid-position of the upper half
   Else return the found value
End loop
Stop
```

The algorithm as stated above has a major deficiency: it is fine so long as the element to be found is present, but what happens when it is not? The stopping condition for the algorithm should include the condition,‘no more search space’. Thus the algorithm can be restated, for an array bin of integers in which k is the item to be found, in which ‘lo’ and ‘hi’ are the array limits:

```
while lo <= hi loop
   mid ← (lo + hi)/2;
   if bin(mid) < k
      lo ← mid + 1;
   else if bin(mid) > k
      hi ← mid – 1;
   else return (mid)      {found}
```

```
    end if;
end loop;
return (NOVAL)        {not found}
```

The algorithm is best seen diagrammatically. Consider a binary search for a value which is not present—the worst case—in the array of 10 integers shown in Fig. 6.16. Suppose we wish to search for the value 35:

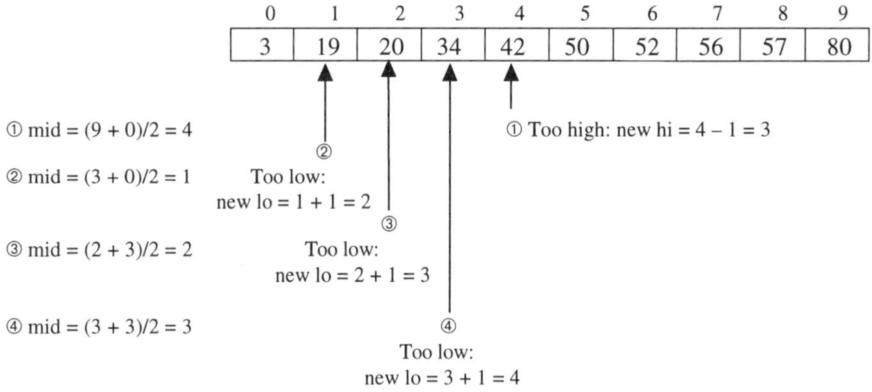

Now lo = 4, hi = 3: it is not true that lo <= hi, and so exit loop and return (NOT FOUND).

Figure 6.16 Binary search process

The process represents the worst case for searching—item not in list. What happens is that first, the mid-point is calculated: this is position 4. Since the value of the 4th element is too high, the middle is recalculated as (hi – lo)/2, but with hi updated as one less than the previous mid-point. That is, ['new hi' (= old middle – 1) plus lo]/2, = [(4 – 1) + 0]/2 = 1, since we are using integer arithmetic.

This time, the search fails again, but with too low a value in position 1. So now the middle is recalculated as [new lo (= old middle + 1) plus hi]/2, i.e. (2 + 3)/2 = 2. Since the value in position 2 is too low, the middle is again recalculated as position 3, which is also too low. The next recalculation results in a new lo = 4, and it is no longer the case that lo <= hi, since hi = 3. Hence the value is not found.

The full algorithm is shown in Fig. 6.17.

In C:

```
int bin_sch(int k, int n)  /* Search array bin[0 .. n]. Value */
{                          /* of k is got from the user, n is */
  int lo, hi, mid;         /* passed in */
  lo = 0; hi = n;
  while (lo <= hi)
  {
```

```
      mid = (lo + hi)/2;
      if (bin[mid] < k)
      {
         lo = mid + 1;
      }
      else if (bin[mid] > k)
      {
         hi = mid - 1;
      }
      else
      {
         return mid;          /* ..to calling routine.  */
      }
   }
   return -1;         /* Calling routine should test return value... */
}                     /* ...if -1 is returned then value not found.  */
```

In Ada:

```
function bin_sch(k: integer; n: integer) return integer is
                                --Search array bin(0 .. n). Value of k is got
lo, hi, mid: integer;           -- from the user; n is passed in
begin
   lo := 0;
   hi := n;
   while lo <= hi loop
      mid := (lo + hi)/2;
      if bin(mid) < k then
         lo := mid + 1;
      elsif bin(mid) > k then
         hi := mid - 1;
      else
         return mid;            -- ...to calling routine.
      end if;
   end loop;
   return - 1;                  -- Calling routine should test return value...
end bin_sch;                    -- ...if -1 is returned, then value not found.
```

Figure 6.17 Binary search algorithm

This, as mentioned, is an extremely efficient method of searching. For the example in Fig. 6.17, there were 10 elements, and steps:

1. mid = 4
2. mid = 1
3. mid = 2
4. mid = 3
5. exit

Now $2^4 = 16$, and since $10 < 2^4$, we know that at worst there will be 5 steps involved in exhaustively searching the list.

For a list implemented as an array, and which is rarely updated, binary search is by far the most efficient way to search for data items. However, it was pointed out earlier that when deletions and insertions are common, an unsorted list is usually at least as efficient, as the overhead of re-sorting after each operation, or else searching for the correct place to insert initially is avoided. Further, since the insert and delete operations are themselves $O(n)$ without consideration of the efficiency of the search method, the whole process can only be at best $O(n)$.

6.5 Linked lists

The limitations of an array as a data structure for representing lists have been mentioned in Section 6.4. Specifically, for insertions and deletions, the remaining items must be shuffled up—which is particularly expensive when the item to be inserted or deleted is the first. Further, the maximum size of the array may not change once it has been determined, either by declaration, or at run-time. A much more efficient structure for managing such operations would be a dynamic one, which can shrink or grow as necessary at run-time: such a structure is a *linked list.*

When dealing with an array, the idea of sequential ordering is implicit in the structure: the elements of the sequence are logically contiguous items. A linked list models each data item as a 'node' which contains a 'link' to the next node. This may be visualised for, say, a list of club members as in Fig. 6.18.

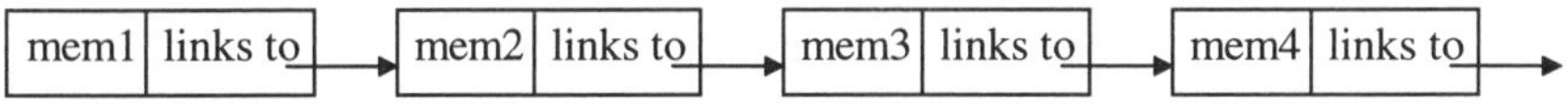

Figure 6.18 Linked list—conceptual structure

In order to access any list element, we can search for the relevant data by a simple sequential search. Because the conceptual model is like a chain, a deletion is achieved by simply 'unlinking' a member, and a new member can just be tagged on to the end of the list—or, with a little more effort, linked in somewhere in the middle of the chain. The great advantage of this structure is that it is dynamic: the amount of storage is never more than is needed, and it is not necessary to know beforehand how big the structure will need to be.

Given the advantages of such a dynamic structure, it is not surprising that linked lists have many applications in all branches of computing. Fig. 6.18 suggests a single data item (mem n) plus a link, for simplicity, but a list node may typically have a number of members which may be made up of different types, each such record being in a linked list of such structs/records—for example, a vehicle-owner registration list as shown in Fig. 6.19.

Clearly, this is a more space-efficient method of dealing with lists when the maximum list length is not known in advance. But what are the nodes, what are the links, and how are they to be implemented? The code in Fig. 6.20 gives the type declarations for a node containing just one integer data item together with a pointer,

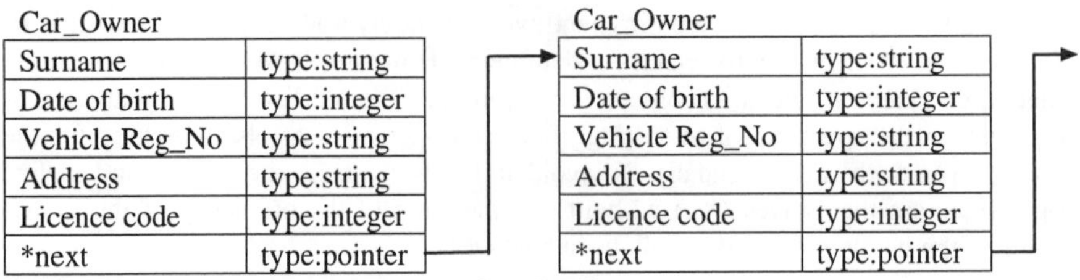
Car_Owner
Surname | type:string
Date of birth | type:integer
Vehicle Reg_No | type:string
Address | type:string
Licence code | type:integer
*next | type:pointer
Car_Owner
Surname | type:string
Date of birth | type:integer
Vehicle Reg_No | type:string
Address | type:string
Licence code | type:integer
*next | type:pointer

Figure 6.19 Linked list of car ownership details

plus the operation for inserting a new item somewhere in the middle of a list which already exists.

The 'insert' procedure makes use of the `malloc`/new operator to allocate a new memory location to be used as a node, together with a temporary pointer which accesses this new node. This new node can then be linked into a list after a node pointed to by 'prev_elt_ptr': where *this* comes from is explained subsequently.

In C:

```
struct item
{
  int item_val;    /* Single integer value for each record*/
  struct item *next;  /* pointer to next struct item   */
};
typedef struct item *link;   /* link is pointer to struct item  */

void insert (int new_elt, link prev_elt_ptr)
{
                        /* Insert procedure */
  link temp;  /* Going to create temporary pointer pointing... */
                        /* ...to new struct about to be created... */
  temp = malloc(sizeof(struct item));     /* ...here */
  temp->item_val = new_elt;      /* Assign value to item_val... */
  temp->next = prev_elt_ptr->next;        /* ...and link it in */
  prev_elt_ptr->next = temp;
}
```

In Ada:

```
type item;
type link is access item;
type item is
  record
   item_val: integer;
   next: link;
  end record;

procedure insert(new_elt: in integer; prev_elt_ptr: in out link) is
temp: link;                         -- Temporary pointer pointing to new
begin                               -- record about to be created ...
```

```
    temp := new item;                      -- ...here
    temp.item_val := new_elt;              -- Assign value to item_val ...
    temp.next := prev_elt_ptr.next;        -- ...and link it in.
    prev_elt_ptr.next := temp;
        -- Note—the line: prev_elt_ptr.next := new item'(new_elt, prev_elt_ptr.next);
        -- achieves the same result as this code.
end insert;
```

Figure 6.20 Algorithm for insertion of a node into a linked list

What the code is doing is illustrated in Fig. 6.21: new item 'memX' is inserted into the list in position 3—actually 'insert after mem2'.

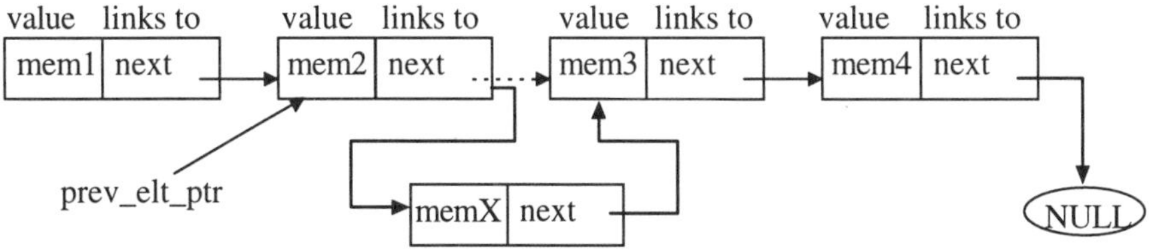

Figure 6.21 Insertion of a node into a linked list: conceptual scheme

It is important to realise that the meaning assigned to operations is very much at the discretion of the person who implements the structure, and the implementer is responsible for ensuring that pointers, in particular, are passed in the correct way and point to the required structure: this is explained further following the 'insert' analysis. First, however, consider the code again which is central to the 'insert' operation (Fig. 6.22). Suppose a linked list of integers includes the subsequence ... 6, 17, 4, 11 and we want to insert the integer 9 after the value 17. Fig 6.23 shows what happens.

In C:

```
① temp = malloc(sizeof(struct item)); /* Create item */
② temp->item_val = new_elt;          /* Assign value to item_val   */
③ temp->next = prev_elt_ptr->next; /* temp->next points to where */
   /* prev_elt_ptr->next was pointing, and then prev_elt_ptr->next */
④ prev_elt_ptr->next = temp;                       /* points to temp   */
```

In Ada:

```
① temp := new item;                 -- Create item here
② temp.item_val := new_elt;         -- Assign value to item_val
③ temp.next := prev_elt_ptr.next;   -- temp.next points to where prev_elt_ptr
④ prev_elt_ptr.next := temp;        -- was pointing, & prev_elt_ptr.next points to temp
```

Figure 6.22 Linking in a node somewhere in a linked list

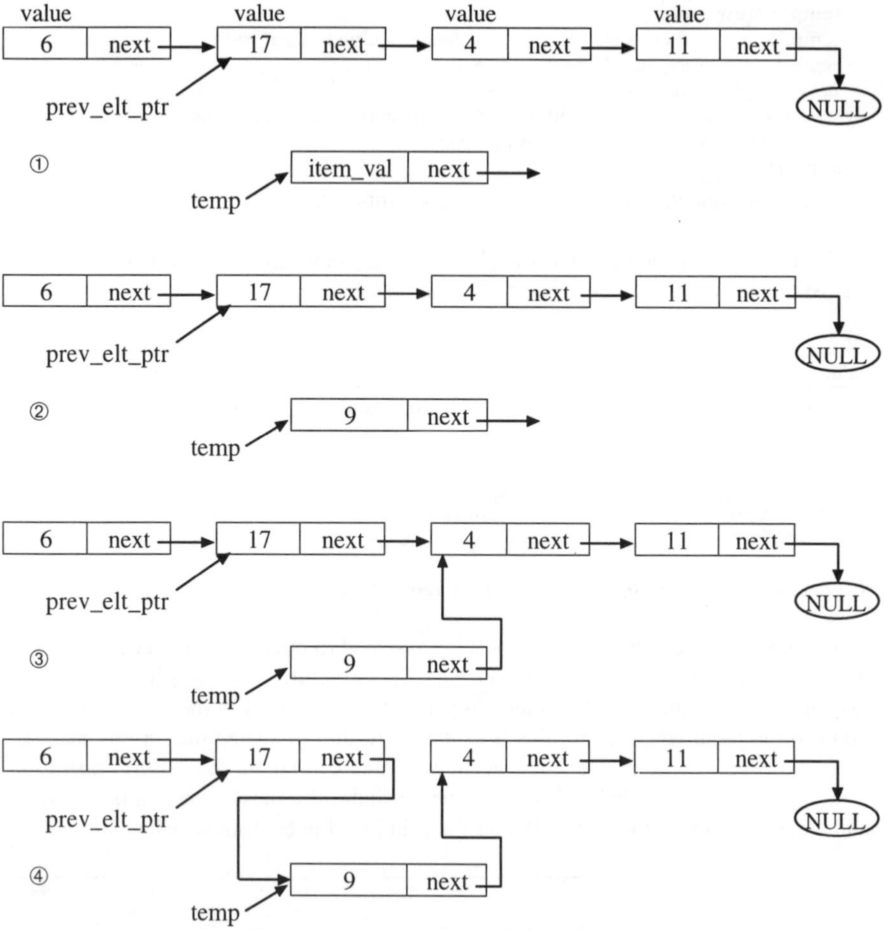

Figure 6.23 Insertion of a node into a linked list: line-by-line process

The subsequence is now ... 6, 17, 9, 4, 11. Note that in order to achieve the 'insert after' facility, the insert code has a pointer to the previous item passed to it, plus the item value (9). Where does the pointer to the previous item come from? One approach is to define a search function (which is a list operation we would like to have anyway), and search for the previous item, returning the pointer to it (Fig. 6.24).

In C:

```
link search(int x, link p1)
{
   if (p1 == NULL)
   {
      printf("Empty list.");
```

```
    }
    else
    {
        while((p1 != NULL) && (p1->item_val != x))
        {
            p1 = p1->next;
        }
    }
    return p1;    /* Calling routine must check p1: if p1 = NULL... */
}                 /* ...item was not in the list */
```

In Ada:

```
function search(x: integer; p: link) return link is
p1: link := p;                          -- The temporary access variable 'p1' is necessary
begin                                   -- in Ada, as access variable 'p' is a mode 'in' variable
   if p1 = NULL then                    -- and may not be updated directly.
      put("Empty list.");
   else
      while ((p1 /= NULL) and then (p1.item_val /= x)) loop
         p1 := p1.next;
      end loop;
   end if;
   return p1;                           -- Calling routine must check p1: if p1 = NULL...
end search;                             -- ...item was not in the list
```

Figure 6.24 Search procedure for a node in a linked list

The search function needs a value passed to it, which will subsequently be the value to be inserted after, plus a *header* pointer, which marks the start of the list. The pointer returned, which points to the value to be inserted after, can then be passed to the insert function, together with the new value to be inserted, i.e. 9. But where does the header that the search function needs come from? For this, we can simply declare an access or pointer variable which is initialized to NULL, and then update it after each list operation. For example, if the list is initially empty, and the first operation just allocates a node, the situation looks like Fig. 6.25.

Note also that the next pointer of the last cell in the list is always shown as pointing to NULL: this is defined in both C and Ada, and marks the end of the list. Use of a header makes for easier list management in general: for instance, when is a linked list defined, but empty? It is when head = NULL

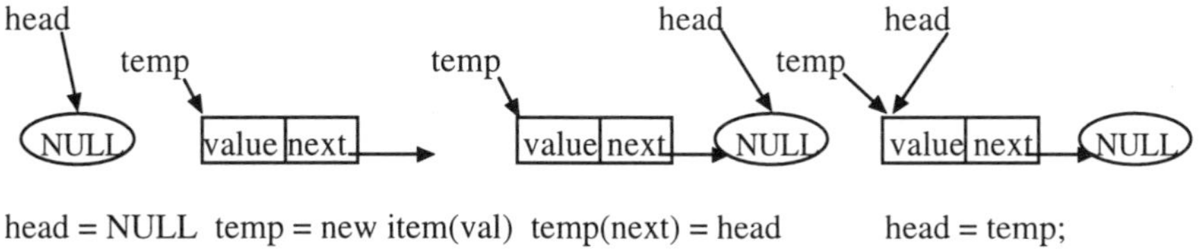

Figure 6.25 Linking in the first node in a linked list

Since a linked list is a dynamic structure, new nodes must be conjured up when required, and disposed of when no longer needed. As mentioned earlier, in C the `malloc` function passes a pointer (which may need to be typecast) to `temp` of the appropriate size of storage needed, and `free` releases that storage for use again. In Ada, the new function creates a new record accessed by the temp pointer. The Ada temporary access type can also be freed by instantiating the standard package unchecked_deallocation, but this is not essential for small programs, and the Ada environment will reclaim dynamically allocated space anyway.

The delete operation is illustrated in Fig. 6.26, with the algorithm in Fig. 6.27. Note that, like insert, this is actually 'delete after'.

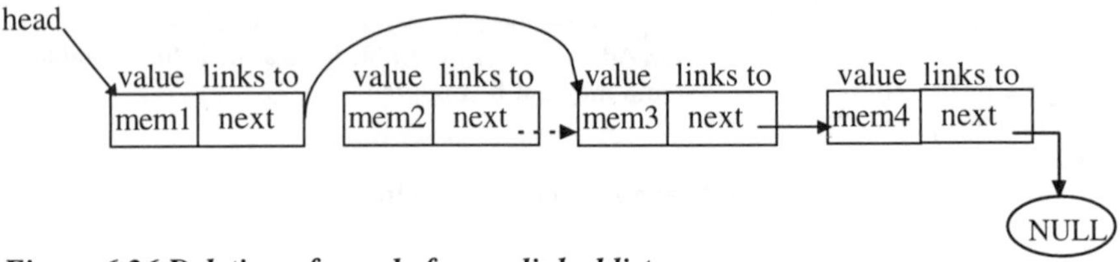

Figure 6.26 Deletion of a node from a linked list

In C:

```
        /* Delete function for linked list operations (disposal of
                                        redundant data not shown) */

void del(int elt)
{
  link p1, p2;
  if (head == NULL)
  {
    printf("No value to delete: list empty.\n");
  }
  else
  {
    p1 = head->next;            /* p1 points to the second element */
    p2 = head;                  /* p2 points to the first element */
    if (p2->item_val == elt)    /* If first item is to be deleted... */
    {
      head = p1;                /* ...move head pointer along one */
    }
    else
    {
      while ((p1 != NULL) && (p1->item_val != elt))
      {
        p2 = p1;                /* Step p2 and p1 along the chain... */
        p1 = p1->next;          /* ...with p2 one step behind p1... */
      }
      if(p1->item_val == elt)  /* ...until the item is found... */
      {
        p2->next = p1->next;      /* ...so link round it... */
      }
```

```
      else    /* ...or else we reach the end without finding elt */
      {
        printf("\nThe value %d is not in the list.\n", elt);
      }
    }
  }
}
```

In Ada:

```
procedure del(elt: in integer) is        -- Delete function for linked lists (disposal
p1, p2: link;                            -- of redundant data not shown)
begin
  if head = NULL then
    put("No value to delete: Empty list.");
  else
    p1 := head.next;                     -- p1 points to the second element
    p2 := head;                          -- p2 points to the first element
    if p2.item_val = elt then            -- If first item is to be deleted...
      head := p1;                        -- ...move head pointer along one.
    else                                 -- Else step along the list...
      while p1 /= NULL and then p1.item_val /= elt loop
          p2 := p1;                      -- ...so step p2 and p1 along the chain...
          p1 := p1.next;                 -- ...with p2 one step behind p1, until...
      end loop;
      if p1 = NULL then                  -- ...we reach the end without finding elt...
        put("Item");
        put(elt, width => 4);
        put(" is not in the list.");
      else
        p2.next := p1.next;              -- ...or we find it, in which case, we link round it
        put("Item");
        put(elt, width => 4);
        put(" has been deleted.");
      end if;
    end if;
  end if;
end del;
```

Figure 6.27 Deleting a node from a linked list

In order to display all the items in the list, we might use the code in Fig. 6.28.

In C:

```
void display_all (link h)    /* header passed in */
{
  if(h == NULL)
  {
    printf("\nEmpty list.");
  }
  else
  {
```

```
      printf("List is: ");
      while (h != NULL)
      {
        printf("%4d ", h->item_val);
        h = h->next;
      }
   }
}
```

In Ada:

```
procedure display_all(start: in link) is          -- header passed in
h: link;
begin
      h := start;
      if h = NULL then
            put("Empty List.");
            new_line;
      else
            put("List is: ");
            while h /= NULL loop
                  put(h.item_val);
                  h := h.next;
            end loop;
            new_line;
      end if;
end display_all;
```

Figure 6.28 Output linked list values

6.6 The stack ADT

It was mentioned earlier that stacks and queues are commonly encountered ADTs in computing, and that their underlying structures may be whatever is convenient in terms of the application, the machine, the system, and the language with which we are working. In terms of program implementation (C or Ada), one way to realise the ADTs would be by means of arrays. However, the stack or the queue itself is *abstract*—a concept, not a data type. Hence, we could equally well use a linear linked list of structs/records, each representing the individual items, and using pointers/access types in the usual way.

The point is that the same abstraction—for example, a process for the issuing of railway tickets, or one for the creation of an address book—may be represented in the computer by different operations defined by the programmer on the same data structures. Equally, the same process may be modelled in two different ways by similar operations defined on different data structures. In each case, however, users of the process have no knowledge of the implementation details, nor do they need to. Thus, a sequence of data types *S*, may be represented as shown diagrammatically in Fig. 6.29.

The idea behind an abstract data type is that it is the representation in the computer of a principle commonly used in everyday life. For example, a pile of plates, or a deck

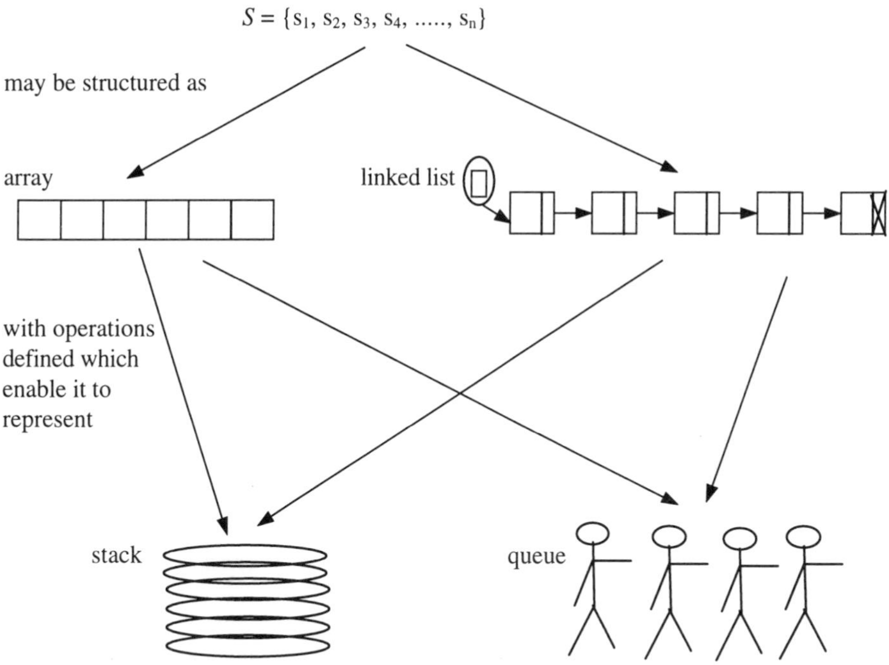

Figure 6.29 Data structures used to represent abstractions stack and queue

of cards is a stack. The pile is added to at the top (an item is *pushed* onto the stack), and the first one removed is taken from the top (*popped* from the stack).

The simplest composite data structure which might be used to develop an ADT is an array; the fundamental operations which need to be defined for a stack are push and pop, and these clearly involve simply adding an element to the start of the array, or removing it from the start, i.e.

Push:

Data structure: array stack
Input: element *new_elt*, stack_array
Output: modified stack_array
Operation: stack[0]←new_elt

Pop:

Data structure: array stack
Input: stack_array
Output: element *new_elt*
Operation: return stack[0]

One question which might occur to the reader is, 'How big does the array have to be?' In principle, the array is infinite, as we do not know how large the stack will grow as the program using it executes, but in practice its size must be known in advance, since it must be defined in the program prior to execution. In Fig. 6.30, item *new_elt* is about to be pushed onto the stack which is implemented as an array: in order for this action to occur, elements *a* to *g* must all be shuffled down one.

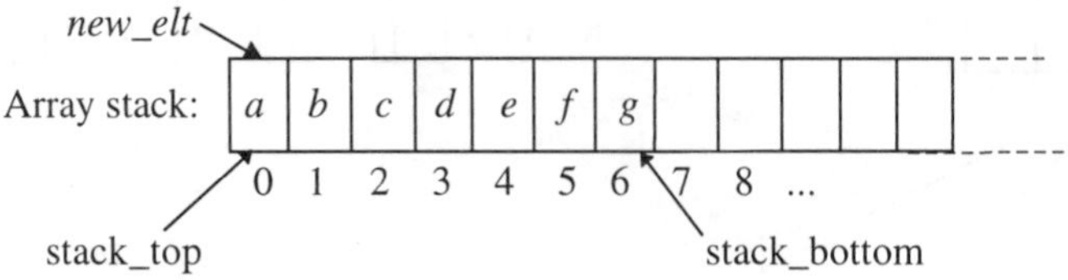

Figure 6.30 Stack ADT implemented as an array: initial representation

What the foregoing discussion implies is that the push and pop operations are not quite so straightforward as at first suggested. The push operation must somehow take account of the array limits, and output an appropriate error condition when the array is full; when there is room for the new element to be added, all the other elements must first be moved down. The pop operation must also do some checks—for instance, we may not remove an item from an empty stack.

There is a more efficient way of managing the push operation: instead of shuffling items down from the top each time a new item is pushed onto the stack, it is much simpler to add to the stack from the bottom. As an abstraction, this is the same thing—top and bottom are relative in this context—but it perhaps reflects the way things often happen in reality (think about a stack of plates again—the stack is built up from the bottom). However, its implementation is now much easier: we define an array index `free_loc`, initialised to zero, as the first free stack location, and then either increment it after a push, or decrement it before a pop, as shown in Fig. 6.31. The outline algorithms to implement the stack operations required are also given in Fig. 6.32.

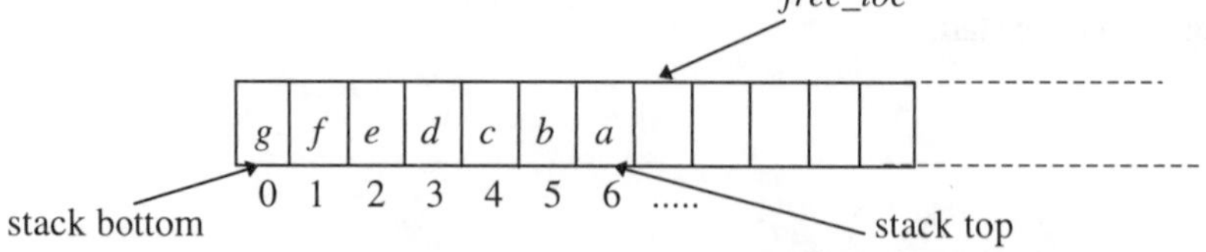

Figure 6.31 Stack ADT implemented as an array: final representation

In C:

```
#define n 10                  /* Maximum size of stack */

int stack[n], free_loc = 0;

void push(int new_elt)        /* Passed in by calling program */
{
   if(free_loc == n)
```

```
    {
      printf("Error: stack full.\n");
    }
    else
    {
      stack[free_loc++] = new_elt; /*Place new_elt in array position*/
                 /* held in free_loc, and then increment free_loc   */
    }
}


int pop(void)
{
    if(free_loc == 0)
    {
      printf("Error: stack underflow.\n");
      return (0);
    }
    else
    {
      return stack[--free_loc];      /* Update stack:decrement */
                              /* free_loc and then return value */
                          /* in array position held in free_loc */
    }
}
```

In Ada:

```
n: integer := 10;
type stack_type is array(0 .. n-1) of integer;
stack: stack_type;
free_loc: integer = 0;
procedure push(new_elt: in integer) is
begin
   if free_loc = n then
      put("Error: stack full.");
      new_line;
   else
      stack(free_loc) := new_elt;       -- Update stack: place new_eltt in array position
      free_loc := free_loc + 1;         -- held in free_loc, and then increment free_loc
   end if;
end push;

procedure pop(free_loc: in out integer; popped: out integer) is
begin
   if free_loc = 0 then
      put("Error: stack underflow.");
   else
      free_loc := free_loc - 1;         -- Update stack: decrement free_loc
      popped := stack(free_loc);        -- and then return value held in array position
                                        -- given by free_loc
   end if;
end pop;
```

Figure 6.32 Elementary stack operations for contiguous data structure

Although the array representation of a stack is easy to comprehend and to program, it has a serious disadvantage, this being the limitation on size: either we declare a very large structure, which may be wasteful of space, or we declare a structure which will be large enough most of the time, but may give rise to overflow. Either option is a poor choice in software engineering terms. A better solution in most cases is to use a dynamic structure, such as a linked list.

The linked structure has already been examined in Section 6.5, and all that it is necessary to do to create a stack is to define push and pop as operating on the first component of the list. We use the same fundamental structure as previously (Fig. 6.33).

In C:

```
struct stack_item
{
   int item_val;
   struct stack_item *next;
};
typdef struct stack_item *st_link;
st_link head = NULL;
```

In Ada:

```
type stack_item;
type st_link is access stack item;
type stack_item is
   record
     item_val: integer;
     next: st_link;
   end record;
head: st_link;                        -- 'head' is NULL on declaration
```

Figure 6.33 Declarations for a stack as a linked structure

The header points to the top of the stack, and other operations, such as `display_all`, may be used as required. The `insert` and `delete` operations can be used as the basis for push (which is just 'insert first') and pop, so that we have Fig. 6.34

In C:

```
void push(int new_elt)  /* Pass in new value to place */
{                       /* on top of the stack */
   st_link temp;
   temp = malloc(sizeof(struct stack_item));        /* Get a node */
   temp->item_val = new_elt;    /* Make new node's value equal to */
   temp->next = head;           /* new item value, set new node */
   head = temp;                 /* pointer to head and head pointer */
}                               /* to new item */
```

```
void pop(int *top_val)
{
   if(head == NULL)
   {
      printf("Empty stack.\n");
   }
   else
   {
      *top_val = head->item_val;    /* Get 'top-of-stack' value */
      head = head->next;     /* Move head pointer down one item*/
   }
}
```

In Ada:

```
procedure push(new_elt: in integer) is
begin
   head := new stack_item'(new_elt, head);   -- See comment for linked list 'insert'
end;                                         -- operation, Section 6.5

procedure pop(top_elt: out integer) is
begin
   if head = NULL then
      put("Empty stack");
   else
      top_elt := head.item_val;              -- Get 'top-of-stack' value
      head := head.next;                     -- Move head pointer down one item
   end if;
end pop;
```

Figure 6.34 Push and pop operations for stack as a linked structure

6.7 The queue ADT

A queue is perhaps an even more familiar concept than a stack: new queue members join at the rear, and are served from the front. In terms of data structures for implementation of the queue ADT, an array is inherently a poor mechanism for representation, since, as items are added and removed, the queue 'travels backwards' until it hits the array limit—see Fig. 6.35.

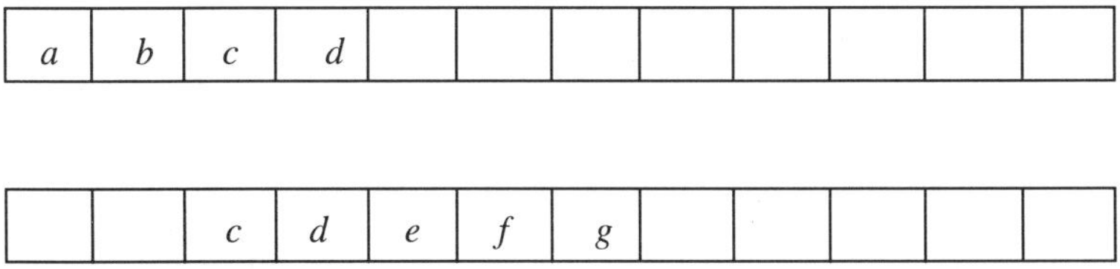

Figure 6.35 Queue with four members (top); queue with two members removed and three added (bottom). Notice how the queue data 'travels backwards'

The diagrams illustrate the major problem with simple array representation for a queue: not only may it be wasteful of space, but, considering the situation in Fig. 6.36 (bottom), after a further five items have been queued and then nine serviced, it will not be possible to queue any more items, even though the structure is eleven-twelfths empty, and this situation may occur in practice quite often. Further, the management of the array size turns out to be inefficient in practice, and so the simple array implementation is not normally used for a queue. It is possible to overcome most of these problems by making the queue circular, but at the cost of a slightly more complicated algorithm.

The method depends on modular arithmetic, which is similar to 'clock arithmetic', in which 17:00 hours is read as 5 o'clock: once we get to 12, we start again from one o'clock, and to convert from 24-hour time to 12-hour time, we subtract 12. This value (12) is known as the modulus.

It is more common to include zero in any number system, so that we count from 0 to 11. In Fig. 6.36, there are 12 components, which we may consider as numbered from 0 to 11. *Front* and *Rear* are markers which we will initialise to zero, and increment or decrement as items are added to and removed from the queue, but using modulus 12. Why does this work? Consider the situation in which items are just being added to the queue: *Front* stays at zero, but *Rear* is incremented each time an item joins the queue. Thus we have:

Rear:		0
First item: *Rear* ←(*Rear* +1)mod12	= 1 mod 12 =	1
Second item: *Rear* ←(*Rear* +1)mod12	= 2 mod 12 =	2
Third item: *Rear* ←(*Rear* +1)mod12	= 3 mod 12 =	3
⋮		
Eleventh item: *Rear* ←(*Rear* +1)mod12	= 11 mod 12 =	11
Twelfth item: *Rear* ←(*Rear* +1)mod12	= 12 mod 12 =	0
Thirteenth item: *Rear* ←(*Rear* +1)mod12	= 13 mod 12 =	1
⋮		

Thus the queue is confined to a specific area of memory, and the only other decision to be made is whether to allow new queue arrivals to overwrite existing members when *Rear* = *Front*, or whether to institute a count to keep track of the size of the queue, and signal when it is full or empty. In practice, a count is usually used. The scheme is shown opposite in Fig. 6.36.

The queue is implemented as a linear array, but the use of modular arithmetic allows it to be conceptualised as a circular track. Queuing theory is an important branch of computing. It has many applications, including task scheduling in operating systems generally. The linked representation is more common for queues, but a circular array can be preferable on occasions.

The basic algorithms for this implementation are given in Fig. 6.37, making use of a count to keep track of queue length, but, as with all ADTs, the precise way in which any program making use of a queue operates is dependent on decisions made by the

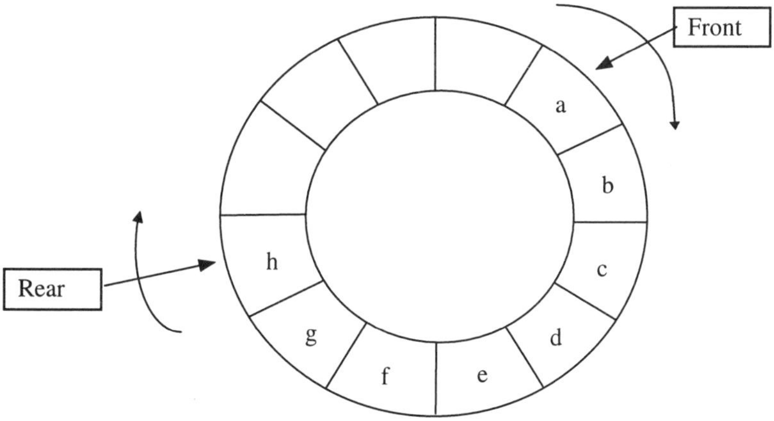

Figure 6.36 Queue implemented as a circular array

individual programmer. However, the implementation details are transparent to any user of the ADT queue: the user has to know only what function names to use to add a member to the end of a queue, or to service the customer at the head of the queue. How the queue works is not apparent or necessary to know in order to use it.

In C:

```
#define MAXQ 100
struct item
{
  int len, front, rear; /* 'len' = number of queue members */
  int members[MAXQ];    /*  The queue of members */
};
typedef struct item q_item;

void initq(q_item *q) /* Initialise: set variables to zero */
{
  q->len = 0;
  q->front = 0;
  q->rear = 0;
}

void add_to_q(int new_mem, q_item *q) /* Pass in value of... */
{            /* ...new member, and pointer to queue */
  if(q->len == MAXQ)
  {
    printf("Queue full.\n");
  }
  else
  {
    q->members[q->rear] = new_mem;     /* Queue new member */
    q->rear = (q->rear + 1) % MAXQ;    /* Update rear marker */
    ++q->len;                          /* Increment count */
  }
}
```

```
void serv(q_item *q, int *cust)  /* Pass in pointer to... */
{              /*...queue and pass out pointer to item ('customer  */
                                                   /* awaiting service') */
  if(q->len == 0)
  {
    printf("No-one awaiting service: queue empty.\n");
  }
  else
  {                        /* Locate customer at front of queue */
    *cust = q->members[q->front];
    q->front = (q->front + 1) % MAXQ;           /* Increment...*/
                          /*...front marker ('Front' and 'Rear'... */
                         /* ...travel in same direction)*/
    --q->len;            /* Decrement queue length */
  }
}
```

In Ada:

```
MAXQ: integer := 100;
type queue_type is array (0 .. MAXQ - 1) of integer;

type q_item is
   record
      front: integer;
      rear: integer;
      len: integer;                  -- 'len' is number of queue members
      members: queue_type;           -- The queue of members
   end record;

procedure init_q (q: out q_item) is
begin                                -- Initialise: set variables to zero
   q.front := 0;
   q.rear := 0;
   q.len := 0;
end init_q;

procedure add_to_q(new_mem: in integer; q: in out q_item) is
begin                                -- Pass in new member, and pointer to queue
   if q.len = MAXQ then
      put("Queue full");
      new_line;
   else
      q.members(q.rear) := new_mem;     -- Queue new member
      q.rear := (q.rear + 1) mod MAXQ;  -- Update rear marker
      q.len := q.len + 1;               -- Increment count
   end if;
end add_to_q;

procedure serv(q: in out q_item; cust: out integer) is -- Pass in pointer to
begin                          -- queue, and pass out item ('customer awaiting service')
   if q.len = 0 then
      put("No-one awaiting service: queue empty.");
```

```
        new_line;
    else                                      -- Locate customer at front of queue
        cust := q.members(q.front);
        q .front := (q.front + 1) mod MAXQ;   -- Increment front marker
        q.len := q.len – 1;                   -- Decrement queue length
    end if;
end serv;
```

Figure 6.37 Queue implemented as a contiguous structure

The use of a dynamic data structure to implement a queue is fairly straightforward. The version given here is based on the linked list ADT given in Section 6.5, since the operations required for the data structure to represent a queue are not difficult. Essentially, we need the insert and del operations, but with the proviso that we always insert at the end, and remove from the front. Hence we need pointers to the head of the list and to the tail of the list: then join_q may be the operation which makes use of the tail pointer to indicate where to link in the new item, and serv is the operation which returns the item at the head of the queue (just as for the stack). The situation is shown in Fig. 6.38, which illustrates first the initial situation, when both the head and tail pointers are NULL, and then the position for a queue of three items.

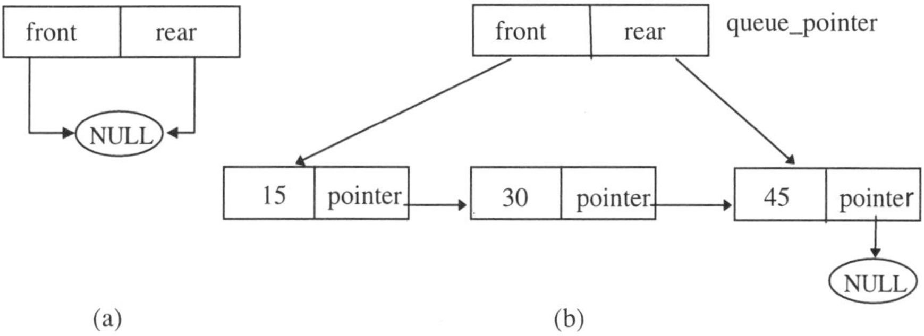

Figure 6.38 Linked implementation of (a) empty queue; (b) queue with three members

The diagram shows that we start with a declaration of a structure containing just two pointers, both of which are initially NULL. When the first member is added to the queue, both the head and tail pointers point to that item, and the item's pointer is NULL.

Subsequent additions always link in after the member currently pointed to by the tail pointer, and the tail pointer is moved along to point to the latest addition. Members at the head of the queue are removed by reference to the front pointer, which is then moved down to point to the first remaining member. The code for these operations is given below in Fig. 6.39.

In C:

```
struct item
{
  int member;
  struct item *next;
};
typedef struct item q_item;

struct queue_limits
{
  q_item *front;
  q_item *rear;
};
typedef struct queue_limits q_type;
void init_q(q_type *q_ptr)
{
  q_ptr->front = NULL;              /* 'Front' and 'Rear' markers */
  q_ptr->rear = NULL;               /* are set to NULL */
}

void join_q(int new_mem, q_type *q_ptr)
{
  q_item *q;
  q = (q_item *)malloc(sizeof(q_item));
  q->member = new_mem;            /* Allocate the new item value */
  q->next = NULL;
  if(q_ptr->rear == NULL)
  {
    q_ptr->front = q;             /* Only queue item */
    q_ptr->rear = q;
  }
  else
  {
    q_ptr->rear->next = q;        /* Link in new node at rear */
    q->rear = q;
  }
}

void serv(q_type *q_ptr, int *cust)
{
  q_item *q;                        /* Temporary pointer */
  if(q_ptr->front == NULL)
  {
    printf("No customers awaiting service: queue empty.\n");
  }
  else
  {
    *cust = q_ptr->front->member;  /* Find the first queued value */
    q = q_ptr->front;            /* and pass back a pointer to it. */
    q_ptr->front = q->next; /* Move back the 'Front' pointer */
    free(q);           /* to point to the next item, and free q */
    if(q_ptr->front == NULL)
    {
      q_ptr->rear = NULL;   /* Set 'Rear' = NULL if the last item */
    }                       /* was removed */
  }
}
```

In Ada:

```
type q_item;
type q_item_link is access q_item;
type q_item is
   record
      member: integer;
      next: q_item_link;
   end record;
type q_limits;
type lim_link is access q_limits;
type q_limits is
   record
      front: q_item_link;
      rear: q_item_link;
   end record;
subtype q_type is q_limits;

procedure init_q(q_ptr: in out q_type) is
begin                          -- Initialise: 'Front' and 'Rear' markers are set to NULL
   q_ptr.front := NULL;
   q_ptr.rear := NULL;
end init_q;

procedure join_q(new_mem: in integer; q_ptr: in out q_type) is
q: q_item_link := new q_item'(new_mem, NULL);     -- Create new node, with value
begin                                    -- 'new_mem' passed in, and accessed by q
   if q_ptr.rear = NULL then
      q_ptr.front := q;                  -- Only queue item
      q_ptr.rear := q;
   else
      q_ptr.rear.next := q;              -- Link in new node at rear
      q_ptr.rear := q;
   end if;
end join_q;

procedure serv(cust: out integer; q_ptr: in out q_type) is
begin
   if q_ptr.front := NULL then
      put("No-one waiting: queue empty");
      new_line;
   else
      cust := q_ptr.front.member;        -- Get value associated with first node
      q_ptr.front := q_ptr.front.next;   -- Move back the 'Front' marker
      if q_ptr.front = NULL then         -- Set 'Rear' = NULL if the last item
         q_ptr.rear := NULL;             -- was removed
      end if;
   end if;
end serv;
```

Figure 6.39 Queue implemented as a linked structure

Which representation is chosen for a queue depends on the programmer and the situation: accesses to arrays operate in constant ($O(1)$) time, since no one access takes in principle any more time than any other, while for a linked representation, we have the time to access the ith item in a linked list of n items on average equal to $(1 + 2 + ... + (n - 2) + (n - 1) + n)/n = [n(n + 1)]/2n = (n + 1)/2$: i.e. it is $O(n)$.

EXERCISES 6.1

1. Write a program making use of a linked list which links user-input integers in ascending order, and prints out the sorted list after each allocation.

2. Modify the program of Q.1 so that any integer can be searched for in the list created.

3. Write a program which accepts an input string from the user and outputs the string in reverse order (use a stack).

Summary

- The ADTs list, stack and queue are of fundamental importance in computing. Users are not concerned with how they work, just with what they do.
- The choice of ADT to model a real-world situation should be based on how well the abstraction models the reality.
- The entity represented by any ADT is determined by its components and the operations defined on them by the implementer.
- The underlying data structure which is operated upon may be a composite contiguous or linked structure. The same ADT may be created by the use of more than one data structure.
- Stacks are widely used in system programming, for parsing languages and for holding return addresses in function calls.
- Queues are used widely: for scheduling tasks by operating systems, and for print spoolers; for simulations of many situations from supermarket checkouts and allocation of automated teller machines to airport management.
- The use of ADTs allows a realistic, modular approach to software design, in which the implementation details are hidden at design stage.

7

PROGRAM CORRECTNESS

OBJECTIVES

In this chapter you will learn:

- why testing is an inadequate means of ensuring that programs are correct
- how to prove that programs are correct
- the connection between designing programs and proving their correctness
- algorithms for the following problems:
  —swapping
  —minimum
  —summing the elements of an array
  —finding the number of occurrences of a value in an array

In this chapter we introduce the subject of program correctness. In it we deal with the problem of how to prove that a program is correct. By 'prove' we do not mean running enough test cases to be fairly sure that a program does what it should. No, we aim for something much stronger: a mathematical proof of the program's correctness. However, before anyone's 'mathsphobia' turns them off, rest assured of two things.

First, this is not a book on formal methods. It is true that the authors have written on that subject, but the intent here is only to skim across that ground: the authors are most decidedly wearing their programmers' hats here. Consequently, most of what we do in this chapter could be labelled as programming. So, in fact, when it comes to the crunch, very little (overt) mathematics will be used, and what little there is will be introduced as we go along. (Of course the case could be made that programming is a mathematical activity, in that programmers and mathematicians alike create models that describe systems using equations, though programmers usually call these program statements. But in that case, good programmers are much better at mathematics than they think, and there is no need to be afraid of mathematics anyway.) Moreover, it is not the case that the techniques explained here can only be used in a totally formal, rigorously mathematical way or not at all. They can be used informally to advantage.

Second, the techniques of program correctness described here are intimately linked to the issue of how algorithms are designed in the first place. It would be wrong to think of an analysis of program correctness as having to come *after* an algorithm has been designed. This could be done, but it would not be the most efficient way to use these techniques. Instead, they should be used *as* an algorithm is being designed. Viewed in this light, they represent an algorithm design technique, rather than a formal method. In passing, it is worth mentioning that, even before they were introduced to the theory of program correctness, both authors used its techniques in an informal way when they worked as programmers. What we offer then is a useful and natural programming technique. The cost, some mathematics, is well worth paying.

7.1 The limitations of testing

Consider a man playing Russian roulette. He has a revolver with six chambers. A bullet is put in one of these, the rest are left empty. The casing is spun around. Then the man holds the gun to his head and pulls the trigger. Not just once or twice, but three, four and five times. Even then he *might* be alive.

It is the same with testing. (You may find the analogy is offensive. However, it probably does not go far enough: a computer program may risk the lives of others, not just that of the 'player', the programmer.) Consider some programmers. They have written a program, and have tested it once, twice, thrice, four and five times. Each time it has given the correct answer. Should they be content to accept its accuracy? No. There is always the possibility that the next test case might expose a bug in the program.

To illustrate the point we will consider the small piece of code shown in Fig. 7.1.

In C:

```
lowest = a[1];
i = 2;
while (i<10)
{
   if (a[i]<lowest)
   {
      lowest = a[i];
   }
   i = i + 1;
}
```

In Ada:

```
lowest := a(1);
i := 2;
while i<10 loop
  if a(i)<lowest
    then
      lowest := a(i);
  end if;
  i := i + 1;
end loop;
```

Figure 7.1 Does this progam fragment find the lowest number in locations 1–10 of a?

This aims to find the 'lowest' number in the first ten locations (that is, from 1 to 10) of an array, a.

Does it work? Clearly, given the unnatural context in which the problem is presented, our first thoughts are likely to be that it does not, that it is flawed. (Of course, in real life, the context is reversed, programmers are likely to assume supernatural accuracy of their code. They want to believe in their 'baby's' perfection. And only as a last resort might they be prepared to accept that it is flawed.) For the time being we will put aside trying to understand the code, and set out to test it. To be fair to testing, although there are far better testing techniques, we will adopt the particularly naive approach of pure black box testing using data created 'randomly' to see if it gives the correct results.

Consider the five test cases shown in Fig. 7.2, where the tables show the value of the array, a. For each of the inputs the code gives the correct answer. Perhaps our hopes that the program is correct would be high at this stage. But, as it happens, these are bad test cases: there is a bug, but they do not show it.

11	3	2	56	32	69	81	90	222	2

2	444	1	65	51	51	99	98	1	1

90	11	333	38	2234	61	73	80	7	59

622	11	134	367	555	31	20	6	79	8

65	21	89	80	995	290	81	98	59	38

Figure 7.2 Five 'bad' test cases

The test case in Fig. 7.3 is a good one, it does show the presence of the bug.

6	8	3	4	3	7	8	9	5	2

Figure 7.3 A 'good' test case

Given this data, the program returns the answer 3, which is clearly wrong. It should be 2. Were we unlucky to have to wait until now, the sixth test case, to find the problem? No, as we shall see below, we were fortunate to find it so soon.

We have found a problem. What is the 'bug'? An analysis of the code shows that the problem arises because the looping ends too early: the tenth location is never considered. The error in the code is as textually minor, an equal sign missing, as it is semantically serious. The loop condition should read:

In C:

```
while (i<=10)
```

In Ada:

```
while i<=10 loop
```

The interesting point is this: how many random test cases are needed before we are guaranteed to find the bug? The answer is that however many test cases we run this is never guaranteed. Certainly, with more test cases comes a higher chance of detecting the problem; but it is never certain.

Perhaps we will settle for a weaker condition: how many test cases are required before there is a 50 per cent chance of finding the error? To calculate this, we note that the error becomes apparent only if the following condition is satisfied:

- the lowest value is in the last array location and only there.

There are ten array locations, so the probability that the lowest value is stored in the last one is 1/10. However, it may be that the same value has appeared earlier in the array, in which case the program would have picked up the value there, and so give the correct answer anyhow, leaving the error to go undetected. The probability of this happening will depend on the range from which the numbers are chosen. Clearly, as this increases, the probability of repeated values decreases and the likelihood of this misleading effect occurring is reduced. To simplify things, we will ignore this effect and assume that the probability of detecting the error with each test case is 1/10, but remember this is an overestimate. The mathematics behind the analysis is not essential to understand the argument. However, it is straightforward.

With just one test case the error is found with a probability of 0.1; consequently, it follows (since the probabilities of all the possible eventualities must add up to one) that the probability that the error is not found is 0.9. In two test cases, since the tests are randomly chosen (independent) the probability of neither test case detecting the error is 0.9×0.9, which equals 0.81. This means that the probability of detecting the error has now increased to 0.19. (This is found by subtracting the probability of not finding the error in either case from 1. That is, $1 - 0.81$.) From this, the generalisation should be clear: the probability of detecting the error using n test cases is given by:

$$1.0 - 0.9^n$$

Using this formula we can complete Table 7.1.

Table 7.1 Probability of error detection as the number of test cases increases

Number of test cases	*Probability of detecting error*	*Probability of not detecting error*
1	0.1	0.9
2	0.19	0.81
3	0.271	0.729
4	0.344	0.656
5	0.410	0.590
6	0.469	0.531
7	0.522	0.478

We can see, therefore, that it takes seven random test cases before the probability of detecting the error is at least half.

In practice, we may settle for a system that is not certain to be totally correct, that does not guarantee complete safety. After all that is the way we live. For instance, anyone who travels in a car must be prepared to accept a risk of being involved in an accident. (It is worth saying in passing that the word 'accident' can be as much a euphemism for error, as the word 'bug'.) But, we are unlikely to accept a 50–50 chance, or even a 1 in 50 chance of being killed. However, even for our simple minimum problem, to get a reasonable degree of confidence requires a very large number of test cases. The probability analysis has been continued to show how many test cases are required before a given level of 'safety' is reached. (See Table 7.2.)

Table 7.2 Number of test cases required to get a given level of confidence that the error will be detected

Chance of not detecting the error is less than	*Number of test cases required*
1 in 1	0
1 in 10	22
1 in 100	44
1 in 1 000	66
1 in 10 000	88
1 in 100 000	110
1 in 1 000 000	132
1 in 10 000 000	153
1 in 100 000 000	175
1 in 1 000 000 000	197

It is left to readers to decide how much testing they would require before they were happy to travel in an aircraft which relied on our piece of code for its airworthiness.

If the above analysis of testing makes you worried, remember that it is concerned with a very short and very simple piece of code. Reality is worse: a realistic program, taken from an aircraft or nuclear power station control system, for instance, is much longer and far more complex. Unless the very best system development techniques are adopted, it must, therefore, have far less chance of being correct.

To conclude our justification for adopting the ideas of program correctness, we suggest the following as the acid test as to whether you are truly content with the accuracy of a piece of code: would you risk your life on it? It is actually rather rare for programmers to be confronted with such a stark decision, at worst it is usually their jobs which are on the line. However, in other areas it is all too common. For instance, the mountaineer who wants to descend a mountain by abseiling down a rope has to risk everything on the strength of the rope's anchor point. If it gives way, the mountaineer will be killed. Life's contract is not satisfied by 'I tested it'.

Finally, it is perhaps only fair to give the other side of the story. The problem with trying to prove something is that it is not an easy job; errors are always possible, and we can easily make a mistake in the proof. Therefore, it would be wrong to rely entirely on proofs of correctness for the verification of a program. Consequently, we certainly do not argue for less testing. Our position is to advocate both: belt and braces, testing and proof.

7.2 The proof process

With the motivation complete we are almost ready to describe how to prove programs are correct. However, there is one question which needs to be answered: exactly what do we mean by saying that a program is correct? We are not interested here with issues such as user-friendliness and speed of execution. We require only two things.

The first requirement is that if we input valid data then if an output is returned it is acceptable. Note that we do not demand anything of the program if the input is invalid. (At least that is the case from the program correctness point of view—from a wider software engineering perspective things are different.) So, for instance, if we have a program which calculates the factorial of a number and which, therefore, is designed to work on natural numbers (non-negative, whole numbers), we have no concern as to how it deals with an input of −1. Furthermore, note that we do not require that there is a unique answer, only that the result we have is acceptable (see Fig. 7.4). To illustrate this point, consider a program to find the position of the minimum number in an array. It is possible that the minimum value is replicated in a number of different positions, and we may be prepared to accept any one of these.

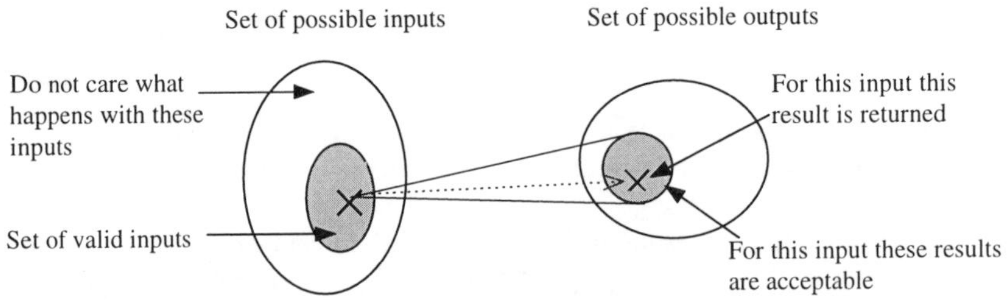

Figure 7.4 The relationship between input and output for a correct program

If the program behaves like this, we say it is conditionally correct.

Notice that we only demanded in the description above that *if* an output is given it is correct. It is not unreasonable to demand in addition that an answer *is* given. This gives us our second requirement: the program is guaranteed to give an output. That is, the program terminates. If, in addition to being conditionally correct the program terminates, then it is said to be totally correct.

Thus, our proof technique is in two parts:

PROOF OF PROGRAM CORRECTNESS
To prove a program correct:
1. Prove that whenever it terminates it gives an acceptable answer.
2. Prove that it terminates.

7.3 Straight-line code segments

Our first attempt at proving a program's correctness will involve a very simple piece of code consisting just of assignment statements. That is, there will be no conditionals (ifs) and no loops. Although very simple, such straight-line sections of code are the basic building block of programs. Whatever else we do, we ought to be able to get them right.

7.3.1 Swap

We will illustrate what to do using as an example the swap problem. This is dealt with in most introductory programming courses. It involves two variables and requires us to write code which after its execution causes the value of one variable to equal what the other started as, and vice versa. For instance, to illustrate what is required, and it is interesting to note how in spite of our formality, we lapse into example, if the two variables start like this:

Before	1	2

Then following the code's execution, the situation is like this:

After	2	1

We will call the two variables x and y. Then, a naive and compelling, though *incorrect*, solution would be this:

In C:

```
x = y;
y = x;
```

In Ada:

```
x := y;
y := x;
```

At first sight this does what is required: it makes $x = y$ and $y = x$, but it is flawed. The problem is that once the assignment to x is made, its value is lost; being replaced by the value of y. Thus, when the assignment to y is made we are picking up the original value of y, not x. To see this we dry-run the code with example data, as shown in Fig. 7.5.

In C:	In Ada:	x	y
Initial values:		1	2
`x = y;`	`x := y;`	2	2
`y = x;`	`y := x;`	2	2

Figure 7.5 Program trace

To overcome this problem we can use an additional variable which throughout stores the original value of x.

We use a variable t to store the original value of x. The code, then, is simply:

In C:

```
t = x;
x = y;
y = t;
```

In Ada:

```
t := x;
x := y;
y := t;
```

Does it work? Yes. (Assuming that the language used supports assignment between values of the types used.) Are we sure? Would we be prepared to risk our lives on its correctness? Would we abseil from it?

A dry run (Fig. 7.6) shows that it certainly gives the correct result for our example data (test data). The numbers show the value of the variables after each statement has been executed.

In C:	In Ada:	x	y	t
Initial values:		1	2	?
`t = x;`	`t := x;`	1	2	1
`x = y;`	`x := y;`	2	2	1
`y = t;`	`y := t;`	2	1	1

Figure 7.6 Program trace

We have seen that we cannot trust testing in general. But surely for a problem as simple as this it would be adequate? No. At the very least, this follows because anyone who knows what the correct program is can easily write an incorrect piece of code that, if treated as a black box, gives any level of testing performance.

EXERCISES 7.1

1. Write a version of the above program which for numbers between 0 and 99 'works' on 99 per cent of randomly chosen test cases.

We will not rely on testing; we will prove the program correct. Our proof starts by showing the conditional correctness of the code. First, we need to formalise the specification of swap. With variables x and y, we require that the following two facts be true:

1. The final value of x equals the original value of y.
2. The final value of y equals the original value of x.

If we carry on like this, we will have a problem: we will confuse the names of the variables, the names of the pigeon-holes if you like, with the values they store. To clarify what is going on, we will introduce some notation. We leave the basic (undecorated) variable names to denote locations. So x, y and t denote the locations of the variables. We let a subscript of 0 represent a variable's original value. So, at the start the values stored in x and y are x_0 and y_0, respectively. We let a decoration of $'$ represent later values. So, during the execution the values stored in x and y are x' and y', respectively.

Our specification must link the input to the output. As far as the input is concerned, we want the code to work for any values (assuming they are of the same type and the assignment operator is defined for them); we place no preconditions on x and y. Alternatively, we can say that the precondition is always satisfied, it is always true. As far as the output, the final state, is concerned, we can 'translate' the above requirements into the postcondition:

$x' = y_0$ and $y' = x_0$

Now we must show that executing the code from the precondition leads to the postcondition. In school algebra we use symbols because we know that, since they represent arbitrary values, any equation shown to be true using them is true for all values. Whereas if we had used specific numbers, we would never know if we were just lucky and that for other values the statement might be false. We adopt a similar approach here: rather than use specific test data, as we did in the dry runs above, we work with symbols. With this exception, all we do is to dry-run the code. (Of course, ordinarily a program cannot work using symbols as input, it needs values. So we will have to 'execute' the program ourselves.) The technique is called symbolic execution.

SYMBOLIC EXECUTION

- the dry running of a program using symbolic rather than actual values

The results of a symbolic execution of the present code are shown in the Fig. 7.7.

In C:	In Ada:	x	y	t
Initial values:		x_0	y_0	?
`t = x;`	t := x;	x_0	y_0	x_0
`x = y;`	x := y;	y_0	y_0	x_0
`y = t;`	y := t;	y_0	x_0	x_0

Figure 7.7 Symbolic execution of a code fragment to swap two values

We notice that after the execution of the final line, $x' = y_0$ and $y' = x_0$. This is exactly what was required by the specification. We have proved the conditional correctness of the code.

The next, final step is to prove that the code terminates. This is easy. It follows because there are no loops. We now have proved the total correctness of the code.

To reinforce the point and as an excuse to show a nice algorithm, we will look at another method to swap two values. This time one designed to work with numbers (or to be more precise values of a type that supports addition and subtraction, and is closed in the sense that neither of these operations lead to results that are out of bounds for the numbers used). The nice thing about the following algorithm is that it does not need an additional variable to store intermediate results.

The algorithm is constructed as follows. We start with the two values, x and y. We visualise the situation as shown below:

The distance from x to y is $y - x$.

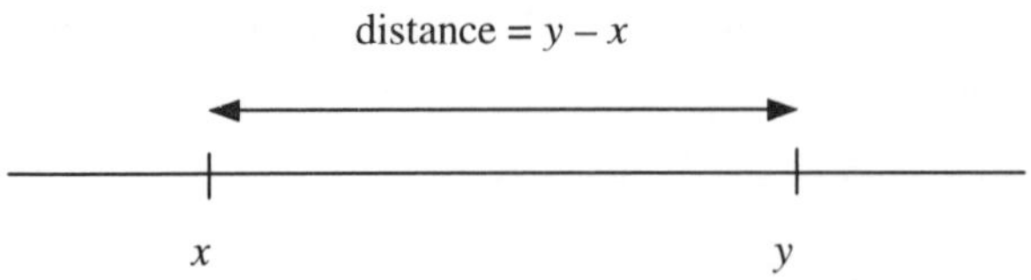

We note that if we know both the original value of x and the distance between it and y's original value, then there is no need to keep track of y. This follows because we can always reclaim y's value by adding the distance to x. To avoid using another variable to store the distance, and since we do not need y's value any more, we will use y to store the distance.

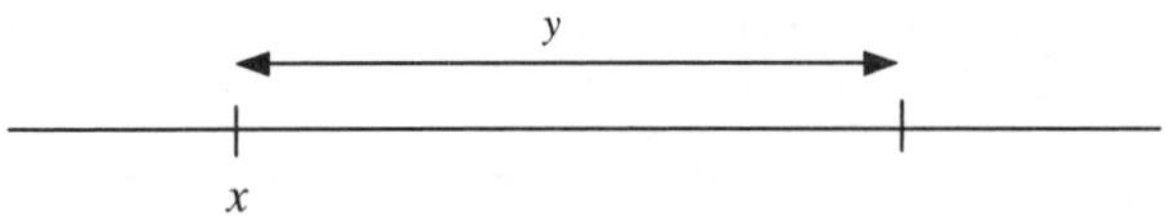

Of course, we could also construct x's value if we knew y's value and the distance between them. Consequently, without fear of losing information, we can set x to the original value of y. This is done by adding the distance (stored in y) to x.

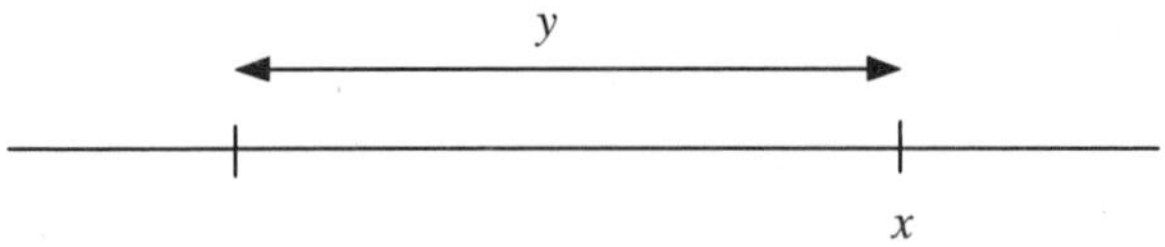

Finally, we can reclaim x's original value by subtracting the distance (stored in y) from the original value of y (stored in x).

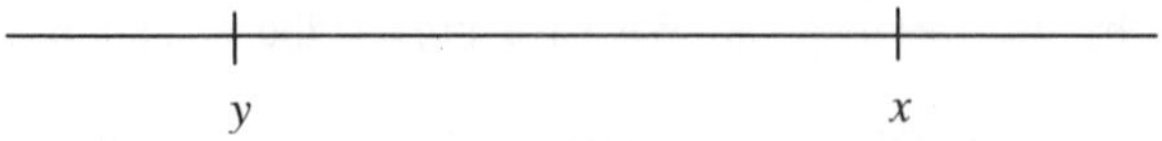

We assign this value to y, and the swap is complete. The code for this is shown in Fig. 7.8.

In C:

```
y = y - x;
x = x + y;
y = x - y;
```

In Ada:

```
y := y – x;
x := x + y;
y := x – y;
```

Figure 7.8 Program fragment to swap two numbers

To prove the code's correctness we will use symbolic execution again. We need the following piece of algebra:

REVISION: MINUS A MINUS IS A PLUS:	$-(-x) = x$

Thereafter the proof is simple, as Fig. 7.9 shows.

In C:	In Ada:	x	y
Initial values		x_0	y_0
`y = y - x;`	y := y - x;	x_0	$y_0 - x_0$
`x = x + y;`	x := x + y;	$x_0 + (y_0 - x_0) = y_0$	$y_0 - x_0$
`y = x - y;`	y := x - y;	y_0	$y_0 - (y_0 - x_0) = x_0$

Figure 7.9 Symbolic execution of a code fragment to swap two numbers

Notice that after the execution of the final statement the new value of x is the original value of y and the new value of y is the original value of x. This is as required. Again, termination is guaranteed because there are no loops.

EXERCISES 7.2

For each code fragment below:

(i) describe its effect
(ii) prove it has this effect

1. In C:

```
a = c - a;
c = c - a;
a = b - a - c;
b = b - a;
a = a + b;
```

In Ada:

```
a := c – a;
c := c – a;
a := b – a – c;
b := b – a;
a := a + b;
```

2. In C:

```
a = c - b;
b = a + b;
a = c;
c = c - b;
a = b - a;
b = a;
```

In Ada:

```
a := c – b;
b := a + b;
a := c;
c := c – b;
a := b – a;
b := a;
```

7.4 Conditionals

We now extend our bag of proof techniques to include a treatment of how to deal with conditionals (ifs). Again the technique is simple:

CORRECTNESS OF CONDITIONALS

- Analyse each possible route through the conditional, treating each as a straight-line segment and using symbolic execution.
- Ensure that the combined consequences of the routes satisfy the specification.

To illustrate the technique, we will prove the correctness of a code fragment to find the lower of two values. We place no preconditions on the values. (We are not even concerned about their type. However, we do need an ordering on them. In other words, the less-than operator must be defined.)

What do we expect of the answer? What is the specification of the problem? Naively we might say simply that the answer must be less than or equal to both the values. This is certainly true, but it does not go far enough. (If the values are 4 and 5, an answer of 2 would satisfy that condition.) In addition, we need to specify that the answer must be one of the values. Therefore, if the two values are x and y and the result is stored in a variable lowest then, using the notation described earlier, our required postcondition is:

$$(\text{lowest}' \leq x_0 \text{ and lowest}' \leq y_0) \text{ and } (\text{lowest}' = x_0 \text{ or lowest}' = y_0) \quad (1)$$

The algorithm to achieve this is just a formalisation of the English: if x is less than y set lowest to x, otherwise set it to y. This is shown in Fig.7.10.

In C:

```
if (x<y)
{
    lowest = x;
}
else
{
    lowest = y;
}
```

In Ada:

```
if x<y
  then
    lowest := x;
  else
    lowest := y;
end if;
```

Figure 7.10 Program fragment to find the lowest of two numbers

To prove the conditional correctness of the algorithm, we need to show that executing the code leads to (1). We begin by analysing the effect of the two routes separately.

First, the **then** route. This segment is executed if the condition is satisfied. That is, if:

$$x_0 < y_0$$

If this route is followed, the statement assigning lowest the value of x is executed, giving:

$$\text{lowest}' = x_0$$

Combining these two results gives:

$$x_0 < y_0 \text{ and lowest}' = x_0$$

Second, the **else** route. This segment is executed if the condition is not satisfied.

That is, if:

not ($x_0 < y_0$)   i.e. $x_0 \geq y_0$

Then, after lowest is assigned the value of y, we know:

$x_0 \geq y_0$ and lowest′ = y_0

We now combine the results from each segment. Since there are no alternatives to the **if** or the **else**, one route or the other must have been followed. Consequently, we know:

($x_0 < y_0$ and lowest′ = x_0) or ($x_0 \geq y_0$ and lowest′ = y_0)   (2)

The question now is how to deduce the problem's specification, equation (1), from equation (2). (Normally in school mathematics we make proofs in which one line equals the next. The proof can flow in both directions. Here we use a different approach: we show that one statement implies another because the latter statement is weaker in the sense that it is always true whenever the first statement is. The flow is in only one direction. As an example of this type of reasoning, we can say that if $x > 5$ then it follows that $x > 2$. The converse is not true.) We take the proof step by step.

If lowest′ = x_0 then, since it is a weaker condition, it is certainly also true that lowest′ $\leq x_0$ and, similarly, if lowest′ = y_0 then lowest′ $\leq y_0$. Therefore, it follows from (2) that:

($x_0 < y_0$ and lowest′ = x_0 and lowest′ $\leq x_0$) or
($x_0 \geq y_0$ and lowest′ = y_0 and lowest′ $\leq y_0$)   (3)

We note now that if $x_0 < y_0$ and lowest′ = x_0 then it follows that lowest′ $\leq y_0$. Similarly, if $x_0 \geq y_0$ and lowest′ = y_0 then lowest′ $\leq x_0$. Consequently, it follows from (3) that:

(lowest′ = x_0 and lowest′ $\leq y_0$ and lowest′ $\leq x_0$)   or
(lowest′ = y_0 and lowest′ $\leq x_0$ and lowest′ $\leq y_0$)   (4)

Finally, we notice that there is a common factor in each bracket in (4), taking this out (distributing) gives:

(lowest′ $\leq x_0$ and lowest′ $\leq y_0$) and (lowest′ = x_0 or lowest′ = y_0)

Which is what was required (phew!). The proof of conditional correctness is now complete. Termination is again obvious.

EXERCISES 7.3

In C:

```
if (x<y)
{
  if (y<z)
        t = y;
  else
        t = z;
}
else
{
  if (x<z)
        t = x;
  else
        t = z;
}
```

In Ada

```
if x<y
   then
      if y<z
         then
            t := y;
         else
            t := z;
      end if;
   else
      if x<z
         then
            t := x;
         else
            t := z;
      end if;
   end if;
```

1. If $x = 3$, $y = 5$ and $z = 4$ what is the value of t?

2. What do you think the code does?

3. Either prove the code does what it should, or show why it is incorrect.

7.5 Iterations

We conclude our discussion of program correctness by showing how to deal with loops. Again the technique is easy. Stripped of its formality, it is analogous to this: given a number of dominoes standing on their sides and placed in a line in such a way that whenever one falls over it knocks over the next, then if the first domino falls over they all do (Fig. 7.11).

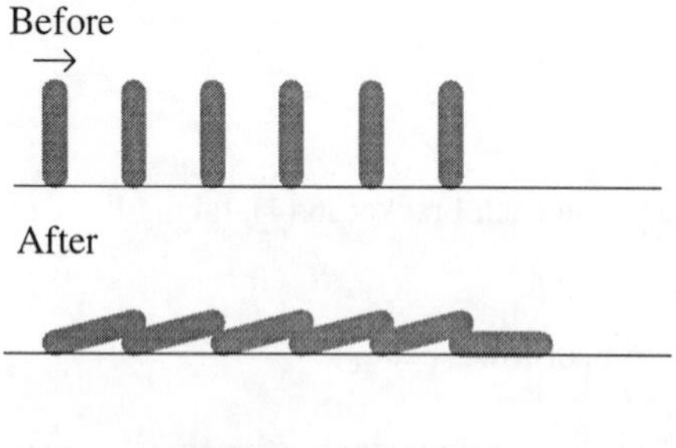

Figure 7.11 When correctly positioned, if the first domino falls over they all do

We relate this to proving that a loop is correct through the idea of an *invariant*. This is something which is true when we first enter the loop and after each iteration, and which, provided we iterate the right number of times, guarantees that we get the correct solution.

PROOF OF CORRECTNESS: LOOPS
If the following conditions are satisfied, then a loop is correct:
1. The loop is entered with the invariant true.
2. If at the start of an iteration the invariant is true, then it is true at the end.
3. The loop is exited correctly.

We illustrate the technique using two examples.

7.5.1 Sum

The problem is this: sum the values in an integer array.

As an example, if the array holds:

1	2	3	4	5

then the answer required is 15.

We can solve this problem by gradually building up to the answer by taking into account one element at a time. That is, starting with no elements considered, we have a sum so far of 0.

Considered sum so far = 0

We then add in the first element.

Considered	1					sum so far = 1

Then the second, the third, the fourth, and finally the fifth, giving:

Considered	1	2				sum so far = 3
Considered	1	2	3			sum so far = 6
Considered	1	2	3	4		sum so far = 10
Considered	1	2	3	4	5	sum so far = 15

This leaves us with 15. The correct answer.

Generalising, if the array is called a and the number of elements is n, then the algorithm can be coded as:

In C:

```
sum_so_far = 0;
for (i=1; i<=n; i++)
{
    sum_so_far = sum_so_far + a[i];
}
sum = sum_so_far;
```

In Ada:

```
sum_so_far := 0;
for i in 1..n loop
  sum_so_far := sum_so_far + a(i);
end loop;
sum := sum_so_far;
```

Figure 7.12 Program fragment to sum the numbers in an array

(We note that if we knew that n was more than zero we could have initialised sum_so_far to a(1). Also, that it would be more normal to call sum_so_far sum, and that would avoid the need for the final assignment. However, in the technique we show here the names mean exactly what they say; calling the running total 'sum' in the middle of the loop would be misleading.)

Although we have said nothing yet about proving the correctness of this algorithm, by developing it in a natural, ordinary way, we have already set up the key to the proof: the invariant. Before reading further, try to identify it.

Again we are faced with the acid test: would we 'abseil' from this piece of code? Before we decide, we had better prove that it is correct.

First, we prove the algorithm's conditional correctness. We begin by specifying the problem. Using the same variable names as above, we want:

$$\text{sum} = a(1) + a(2) + \ldots + a(n)$$

For the proof we need to identify a loop invariant. Rather than working from the code, it is easier to think about what we had in mind when we developed the program. This is because our design strategy must have included an invariant, even if we did not call it that. We just need to identify what it was. Well, we wanted sum_so_far to be exactly that: the sum of the numbers considered so far. And this gives us part of our invariant: whatever the value of the loop counter i, sum_so_far is the sum of the first i elements in the array. We note that if i is zero there are no elements. We will write the segment of the array from 1 to i as a(1..i). With this notation we can write this part of the invariant as:

$$\text{sum\_so\_far} = \text{sum } a(1..i)$$

The other thing we require is that we do not go too far, we need to ensure that:

$$i \le n$$

To make the proof simpler we will annotate the program in Fig. 7.13 to show the invariant and where we have things to prove.

In C:

```
sum_so_far = 0;
/* A: sum_so_far = sum a(1..0) and i≤n */
for (i=1; i<=n; i++)
{
   sum_so_far = sum_so_far + a[i];
   /* B: invariant, sum_so_far= sum a(1..i) and i≤n */
}
/* C: sum_so_far = sum a(1..n) */
sum = sum_so_far;
```

In Ada:

```
sum_so_far := 0;
-- A: sum_so_far = sum a(1..0) and i≤n
for i in 1..n loop
  sum_so_far := sum_so_far + a(i);
  -- B: invariant, sum_so_far = sum a(1..i) and i≤n
end loop;
-- C: sum_so_far = sum a(1..n)
sum := sum_so_far;
```

Figure 7.13 Program fragment annotated for proof of program correctness

The first thing to prove is that the loop is entered with the invariant holding. Well, at A sum_so_far is 0 and that is certainly the sum of the first zero elements. So we are off to a good start.

We need to prove that if we start the loop with the invariant correct, then we leave it with the invariant correct. That is, the invariant still holds at B. Suppose the invariant was correct at the end of the ith iteration, then:

sum_so_far = sum a(1..i) and $i \le n$

Then, when we iterate again i is incremented by 1, so:

$i' = i + 1$

and by B this array location, $i + 1$, has been added to sum_so_far, giving:

sum_so_far′ = sum_so_far + a($i + 1$)

But the hypothesis was that sum_so_far = sum a(1..i). Consequently,

sum_so_far′ = sum a(1..i) + a($i + 1$)
= a(1) + a(2) + + a(i) + a($i + 1$)
= sum a(1..$i + 1$)
= sum a(1..i')

Although not part of the proof it may help to visualise the process as in Fig. 7.14.

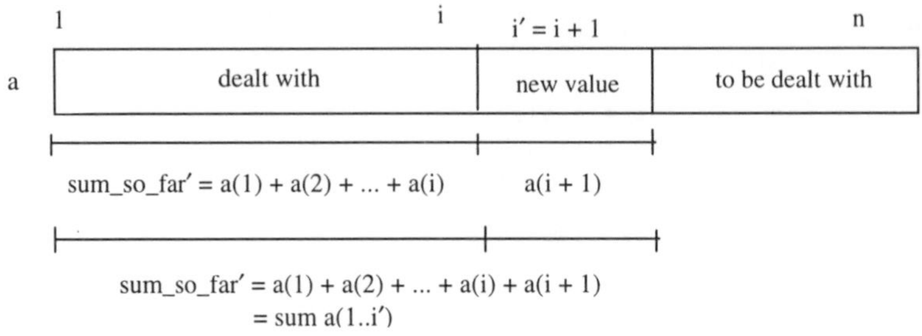

Figure 7.14 The effect on sum_so_far of adding in the next value of a

Additionally, we comment that, because of the working of a **for** loop, $i' \leq n$. Thus, the loop invariant still holds.

Finally, we need to show that we leave the loop at the correct time. That is, when we reach C we have added in all the elements. To get to C the loop must have finished. So we know two things: the final value of i was n and, since the invariant was true at B, that sum_so_far = sum a(1..i). Taken together this means that at C:

sum_so_far = sum a(1..n)

which is what was required.

To complete the proof we need to show that the program terminates. This time we do have a loop but, being a **for** loop, the termination is certain.

7.5.2 Occurrences

Our second example of a proof of loop correctness deals with the problem of finding the number of occurrences of a value x in an array a.

More formally the specification of the problem is this. If there are n elements in a, and the variable occurrences gives the answer, then we require:

occurrences = number of x in a(1..n)

For instance, if $x = 1$, $n = 6$ and a is as follows:

5	3	1	1	9	1

the answer required is 3.

Once again we use the natural technique which is to use a variable x_so_far to hold the number of occurrences of x found so far. Initially this is set to 0. Then we work through the array element by element incrementing x_so_far whenever an x is met. This time, although we could use a **for** loop, we illustrate the technique using a **while** loop. A counter i, initially set to 0, will show where we are in the search. The invariant is:

x_so_far= number of x in a(1..i) and $i \leq n$ (see Fig. 7.15)

In C:

```
x_so_far = 0;
i = 0;
/* A: x_so_far = number of x in a(1..0) and i≤n  */
while (i<n)
{
   i = i + 1;
   if (a[i]==x)
   {
      x_so_far = x_so_far + 1;
   }
   /* B: invariant x_so_far = number of x in a(1..i)and i≤n */
}
/* C:x_so_far = number of x in a(1..n) */
occurrences = x_so_far;
```

In Ada:

```
x_so_far := 0;
i := 0;
-- A: x_so_far = number of x in a(1..0) and i≤n
while i<n loop
  i := i + 1;
  if a(i) = x
    then
      x_so_far := x_so_far + 1;
  end if;
  -- B: invariant x_so_far = number of x in a(1..i) and i≤n
end loop;
-- C:x_so_far = number of x in a(1..n)
occurrences := x_so_far;
```

Figure 7.15 Program fragment to find the number of occurrences of a value in an array

First, we prove the conditional correctness of the algorithm. At A, $i = 0$, therefore $i \leq n$. Moreover, a(1..i) equals a(1..0) which is empty and so the number of occurrences of x must be 0, which is what x_so_far equals. We are off to a good start.

Now for B. We assume the invariant holds after i iterations. That is:

x_so_far = number of x in a(1..i) and $i \leq n$

On the next iteration, we know i is incremented, so $i' = i + 1$. Since the loop condition is satisfied, $i < n$. Therefore, it follows that $i' \leq n$. For x_so_far there are two cases to consider, according to whether or not the condition on the **if** is satisfied:

Case 1: $a(i') = x$. In this case the **then** is executed and so:

x_so_far′= x_so_far + 1
  = number of x in a(1..i) + 1
  = number of x in a(1..i + 1)   since element $i + 1$ is an x
  = number of x in a(1..i')
and the invariant holds.

Case 2. $a(i') \neq x$. In this case the **then** is not executed, and so

x_so_far′ = x_so_far
  = number of x in a(1..i)
  = number of x in a(1..i + 1)   since element $i + 1$ is not an x
  = number of x in a(1..i')
and the invariant holds.

In both cases the invariant holds at B.

Now for C. To get to C means that the loop condition is not satisfied, otherwise we would not have left the loop, so $i \geq n$. But we know from the invariant that $i \leq n$. Therefore, $i = n$. Moreover, we know from the invariant that:

x_so_far = number of x in a(1..i)

Substituting for i gives x_so_far = number of x in a(1..n), and C is true. Finally, the assignment to occurrences ensures that the specification is satisfied

This time we do have to do some work to prove that the program terminates: with a **while** loop this cannot be taken for granted. (Why?) However, in this case termination is simple to show. Each time through the loop we add 1 to i so eventually i must cease to be less than the array size n (n is finite), thus terminating the loop. This completes the proof.

EXERCISES 7.4

1. A cup competition involves 10 teams. How many matches need to be played before the cup is won?

2. Given the grid below, is it possible to cover it with rectangles of the type shown without them overlapping each other or overhanging the sides?

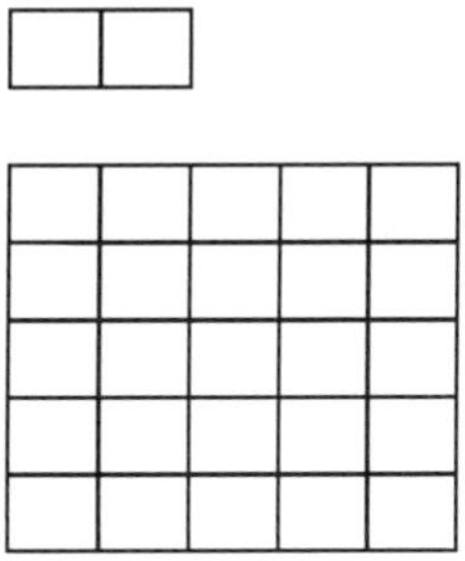

3. Write a program which calculates whether an integer array is sorted into ascending order. Prove the program is correct.

7.6 The incremental approach

As mentioned at the start of the chapter, in the present context we are really interested in proof because of its links with algorithm design. In this section we spell these out, and present a useful design technique: the incremental approach.

Each of the proofs we have looked at has involved code which does not suddenly and mysteriously, as if by some sleight of hand, extract the answer from nowhere. Rather, the proofs build up to it progressively. They work by finding, at each step, an 'answer_so_far' (Fig. 7.16), and using this to find the answer to the next bigger problem; and so on, until an answer to the whole problem has been found.

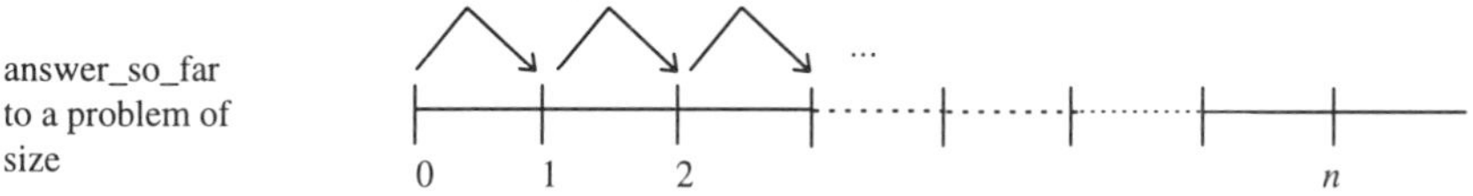

Figure 7.16 Incrementally building towards a solution

The approach is particularly useful for problems involving arrays. The incremental approach involves working along the array keeping track of the 'answer_so_far', continuing until all the elements have been looked at. This is explained overleaf.

INCREMENTAL APPROACH FOR ARRAY PROBLEMS
To solve for a problem of size n:

Consider a problem of size 0, the empty array, find the 'answer_so_far'.
Consider the first element, update the 'answer_so_far'.
Consider the second element, update the 'answer_so_far'.
⋮
Consider the nth element, update the 'answer_so_far'.

The final update represents the solution to the whole problem.

As we would expect, given its roots, an advantage of this method is that it lends itself to proof much more readily than poorly designed code. In practice, the 'proof' may not be rigorous, possibly just being carried out in the mind. However, that is better than nothing. Moreover, since algorithms of this type do their work in a clear way, people are happy to believe in them and there is naturally a higher degree of confidence about their correctness. (*But note*—a majority view does not constitute a proof: a majority of people once thought the earth was flat.) Usually being able to explain an algorithm is more than half the battle in being able to prove it correct.

We notice that the approach is bottom-up; working from smaller to larger problems. It is essentially a special case of dynamic programming, which is the subject of two later chapters.

EXERCISES 7.5

1. Write a program which takes an array a and copies it in reverse order to an array b.

Summary

- Testing programs is necessary, but not sufficient, to show that they are correct.
- Code can be mathematically proved to be correct, using:
  —symbolic execution
  —loop invariants.
- Errors can be made in proofs, so testing and proof should be combined.
- It is better to design with proof in mind, than to try to prove poorly designed code is correct.
- The incremental approach builds up to a solution methodically.
- Algorithms described
  —swapping
  —minimum
  —summing
  —occurrences.

8

BRUTE STRENGTH METHOD

OBJECTIVES

In this chapter you will learn
- the brute strength method
- algorithms for the following problems
  - —shops
  - —selection enumeration
  - —permutations
  - —travelling salesperson

As its name suggests, the brute strength method is not a clever method, relying on some subtle technique to ensure an efficient algorithm. Rather, it gets the correct answer by analysing all possible options and choosing the best of these.

> BRUTE STRENGTH METHOD
> - Enumerate all possible answers.
> - Choose the best of these.

Since brute strength algorithms require no insight, they tend to be easy to identify. Of course, there is a downside to this. First, for many problems that can be solved by brute strength alone, the time required for their solution grows exponentially as the size of the data increases. For such problems, even modest data sizes make the solution impractical in a reasonable time, however fast the processor on which the program runs. Second, as one would expect, brute strength algorithms can be much less efficient than purpose-built, 'clever' algorithms. However, when faced with a new problem which we cannot solve efficiently, it is better to have some solution rather than none, and the brute strength approach can give us that. Moreover, once a brute strength algorithm has been written it can give both a check on and a starting point for more efficient approaches. As a last general point, we note that it is often possible to improve the efficiency (if not the complexity) of a brute strength algorithm by stopping once we have found an answer or, the *branch and bound method*, by looking no further down a route once we know it cannot lead to an answer.

For a simple example to illustrate the technique, consider the problem of finding the lowest number in an unordered array. Clearly, the lowest value could be in any position. A brute strength approach to this problem would postulate that each element in turn was the lowest and, by checking its value against all the others, ascertain whether or not this was so. For instance, consider the following three element array:

3	1	2

We start by postulating that the first element, 3, is the lowest. We check this against the other elements and see that it is not the lowest (1 is less than 3, for instance). We then postulate that the second element, 1, is the lowest. By checking this against all the other elements, we see that there are no lower ones. Consequently, it must be the lowest. We could carry on to complete the full enumeration of the possibilities, but at this stage we know we have the correct answer so we can save time by stopping now. The algorithm's complexity is $O(n^2)$. This follows because we may need to consider each element for the role of lowest, and this, in turn, requires comparing it with each of the other elements (see Chapter 1, Fig. 1.2). Of course this is not the best way to solve the problem; it compares unfavourably with the $O(n)$ algorithm seen in the previous chapter.

8.1 Shops problem

For our first serious example of the brute strength approach we will look at the shops problem. Its starting point is a row of shops; a company which wishes to purchase a *single continuous segment* of neighbouring shops in the row. It takes as its input the profits expected from each shop; some of which may be negative. The problem is to find the maximum profit that can be made by the company.

Before we investigate algorithms to solve this problem, we will look at a number of examples. In each case we will show the best option by shading the shops concerned. Consider the following data which shows the profits from each of the three shops in a row:

	Shop 1	Shop 2	Shop 3
Profit (£1000s)	10	2	5

Clearly, the maximum profit is £17 000, which comes from buying all three shops. However, there may be occasions when buying all the shops is not best. For instance, when we have the following figures:

	Shop 1	Shop 2	Shop 3
Profit (£1000s)	10	–2	–5

Here the best we can do is £10 000, which comes from buying the first shop and ignoring the others. The problem is made harder because sometimes we will want to buy a shop to make up a continuous row, even though its individual contribution to the profit is negative. As an example of this consider the following:

	Shop 1	Shop 2	Shop 3
Profit (£1000s)	6	–2	5

We could choose Shop 1 on its own for a profit of 6. However, Shop 3 makes a good profit and we would like to take that on as well, but we cannot do this directly because Shops 1 and 3 would not make up a continuous group. As it happens in this case, it is worth taking on Shop 2 as well, even though it makes a loss. This is so because taken all together the three shops give a profit of 9, with the loss from the one shop being more than made up for by the profit from the extra shop that can be brought in. Finally, we note that there may be occasions, where all three shops are losing money, when we wish to buy none and leave with a profit of 0.

The brute strength approach is simple: we list each possible group of shops, calculate the profit from each group and take the highest. Fig. 8.1 shows all possible groups when we have four shops in the row.

Figure 8.1 All possible continuous groups in a row of four shops

We note that each group, apart from the empty one, is defined by its starting shop and its finishing shop. For instance, in the situation in Fig. 8.1 we can list these methodically as shown in Table 8.1.

We will call the number of shops n. This approach leads to the code shown in Fig. 8.2.

Table 8.1 Start and finish points for continuous shop groups

Start shop	*Finish shop*
empty	
1	1
1	2
1	3
1	4
2	2
2	3
2	4
3	3
3	4
4	4

In C:

```
for (start=1; start<=n; start++)
{
   for (finish=start; finish<=n; finish++)
   {
      /* calculate the profit from start to finish */
      :
      :
   }
}
```

In Ada:

```
for start in 1..n loop
  for finish in start..n loop
    -- calculate the profit from start to finish
    :
    :
  end loop;
end loop;
```

Figure 8.2 Program fragment to enumerate all starting and finishing points

There is still the problem of calculating the profit in each segment but this simply involves summing each of the individual profits, see Fig. 8.3.

In C:

```
this_profit = 0;
for (i=start; i<=finish; i++)
{
   this_profit = this_profit + profit[i];
}
```

In Ada:

```
this_profit := 0;
for i in start..finish loop
  this_profit := this_profit + profit(i);
end loop;
```

Figure 8.3 Program fragment to calculate the profit from a group

Finally, we need to keep track of the maximum found so far, and update this whenever we find anything better. Putting all these points together gives Fig. 8.4.

In C:

```
max_profit = 0;
/* list all possible segments */
for (start=1; start<=n; start++)
{
   for (finish=start; finish<=n; finish++)
   {
      /* calculate the profit from start to finish */
      this_profit = 0;
      for (i=start; i<=finish; i++)
      {
         this_profit = this_profit + profit[i];
      }
      /* update max if better */
      if (this_profit>max_profit)
      {
         max_profit = this_profit;
      }
   }
}
```

In Ada:

```
max_profit := 0;
-- list all possible segments
for start in 1..n loop
  for finish in start..n loop

    -- calculate the profit from start to finish
    this_profit := 0;
    for i in start..finish loop
      this_profit := this_profit + profit(i);
    end loop;
    -- update max if better
    if this_profit>max_profit
      then
        max_profit := this_profit;
    end if;
  end loop;
end loop;
```

Figure 8.4 Program fragment to calculate the profit from a group

From the code we can see that we have three nested loops, giving a complexity of $O(n^3)$. Can we do any better? Yes, we can. As we said, the brute strength approach is often very inefficient. More efficient approaches are investigated in the exercises.

EXERCISES 8.1

1. In each of the following situations, where the numbers show the profits from the shops, calculate the maximum profit that can be gained from a contiguous group.

   (i) 2, 1, 3, 1
   (ii) 2, 1, 3, –1
   (iii) 2, 1, –3, 2
   (iv) 2, 3, –1, 2

2. Find an $O(n^2)$ algorithm to solve the shops problem.

3. (*Hard*) Find an $O(n)$ algorithm.

8.2 Selection enumeration

One way of applying the brute strength method, and a common requirement for many programs, is to enumerate all possible selections from a number of options. In this section we will look at situations where:

- it does not matter in what order the options are chosen
- the only choices to make are whether an option is chosen or not.

A situation in which this type of selection is needed is where a company has the opportunity to invest in a number of different projects and may want to decide which selections form the best portfolio. Or, again, and a common computing problem, we may want to complete a truth table, which involves listing all possible inputs. We note that in both these cases the problem is equivalent to the generation of a power set, the set of all subsets of a set.

We will start by working through the selections open to a company constructing a portfolio. Suppose it has no projects to invest in. Then, it has only one possible portfolio, the empty one containing no projects. Suppose now it has one potential project. In this case there are two possible portfolios: the empty one, and the one including this project. If we call the project A, and denote a selection by a 1 and a non-selection by a 0, then we can enumerate the possible selections as in Table 8.2.

With two projects, A and B, to choose from, the possible portfolios are shown in Table 8.3.

Table 8.2 Portfolios constructable with one project to choose from

Portfolio	*Project A*
1	0
2	1

Table 8.3 Portfolios constructable with two projects to choose from

Portfolio	*Project A*	*Project B*
1	0	0
2	0	1
3	1	0
4	1	1

We notice that now the number of possible portfolios has doubled to four. Finally, we will look at the situation where there are three projects, A, B and C, to choose from. This gives Table 8.4.

Table 8.4 Portfolios constructable with three projects to choose from

Portfolio	*Project A*	*Project B*	*Project C*
1	0	0	0
2	0	0	1
3	0	1	0
4	0	1	1
5	1	0	0
6	1	0	1
7	1	1	0
8	1	1	1

We note that once again the number of portfolios has doubled.

We will look at portfolio selection again in Chapter 12, but for now we make the following general points. First, as the number of choices increases so does the number of possible selections. We can see this more clearly by using the previous results to complete Table 8.5, showing the number of selections possible as a function of the number of options.

Table 8.5 Number of portfolios available as a function of the number of options

Number of options	*Number of selections*
0	1
1	2
2	4
3	8

At this stage, from observation, we may postulate that the number of selections doubles each time we add an option. This is in fact always the case because each option gives rise to two possibilities: we choose it or we do not, and this doubles the number of possibilities. It follows, therefore, that the number of selections is 2^n.

Second, we note that there are clearly two parts to each portfolio table. For each, in the top half the first option is not selected and in the bottom half it is. However, apart from this, the two halves are the same. If we look at earlier tables, tables with fewer options, we see that this pattern is repeated.

Before looking at the algorithm to generate all these selections, we need to know how to store the information about what is selected and what is not. We will do this in an array, a. A 0 in location *i*, say, will show that option *i* is not selected, and a 1 will show it is. (Alternatively, and, perhaps more elegantly, we could use true and false to show this.) We will call the number of options *n*. Now we need to think about how to enumerate all the selections. One way to do this is recursively: the first selection is either 0 or 1, leaving us to make the next selection, for the second option, in the same way, and so on. With print_a being a procedure to print the array, this leads to the code in Fig. 8.5.

In C:

```
void selection(int option)
{
    int i;
    for (i=0; i<=1; i++)
    {
        a[option] = i;
        if (option==n)
        {
            /* finished, print selection */
            print_a();
        }
        else
        {
            /* not finished, make next selection */
            selection(option+1);
        }
    }
}
```

In Ada:

```
procedure selection(option: in NATURAL) is
begin
  for i in 0..1 loop
    a(option) := i;
    if option=n
      then
        -- finished, print selection
        print_a;
      else
        -- not finished, make next selection
        selection(option+1);
```

```
    end if;
  end loop;
end;
```

Figure 8.5 Program fragment to enumerate all selections

From the main body of the program we call this with:

In C:

```
selection(1);
```

In Ada:

```
selection(1);
```

We can see how this works by drawing the recursive tree showing what calls are made. See Fig. 8.6.

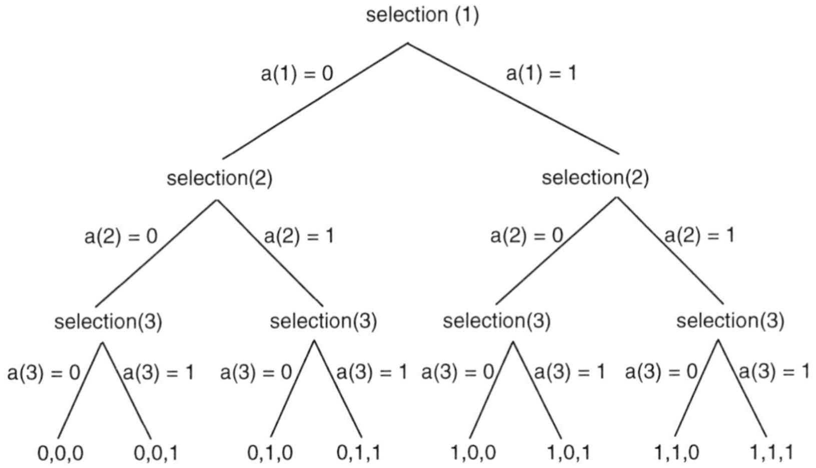

Figure 8.6 Recursive tree for three options

Each selection call leads to two routes, one with the present option being selected (1) and one with it not (0), and, until we have finished, recursive calls to make a selection for the next option. We see that each route through the tree leads to a different selection.

The complexity of the algorithm is $O(2^n)$, which, it should be noted, cannot be improved upon because of the very nature of the problem, which requires us to enumerate all 2^n possibilities.

EXERCISES 8.2

1. Enumerate all possible selections where there are four options to choose from.

2. Describe an iterative algorithm to solve this problem.

8.3 Permutations

A common use of the brute strength method is to list all possible orderings of a sequence of options. For instance, we may need to find the shortest route around a group of cities, and we can clearly do this by looking at all possible routes, measuring the length of each, and selecting the best. We will look at this specific problem in the next section. For now we will look at the more general problem, which in terms of the jargon is to enumerate all *permutations* of a group of values. By permutations we mean selections in which:

- the order of the choices matters
- each option must be used exactly once.

We note here that there are two differences between this and what we did in the previous section. First, here each option must be used; previously an option might or might not have been used. Second, here the order matters; before it did not.

To reinforce our understanding of the problem, we will look at some examples. With no options there is a single permutation, the empty ordering. With one option, a, say, there is again a single permutation; it must be chosen. With two items, a and b, there are two permutations:

a b
b a

The two are different permutations because the order does matter. With three items, a, b and c, there are six permutations:

a b c
a c b
b a c
b c a
c a b
c b a

We notice that as the number of options increases so does the number of permutations. To see this more clearly, it is once again worth completing a table, this time showing the number of permutations as a function of the number of options. See Table 8.6.

Table 8.6 Number of permutations as a function of the number of options

Number of options	*Number of permutations*
0	1
1	1
2	2
3	6

It is, perhaps, too early to see a trend, but there is one: the number of permutations equals the factorial of the number of options. For instance, where the number of options is 3, 3 factorial gives us $1 \times 2 \times 3$ which equals 6, which is just what is required. This result is true in the general case:

- there are $n!$ permutations of n options.

We can justify this result as follows. To begin with we can choose any one of the n options; but for our second choice we are limited to $n - 1$ items from which to choose, since we cannot re-use the one already chosen; and our third choice must be made from $n - 2$ options; carrying on like this, when we make the final choice (the nth) there is only one option from which to choose. Each time a choice is made the number of possible routes is multiplied by the number of choices available here. Hence, we get the sequence $n \times (n - 1) \times \ldots \times 1$, which is $n!$. We can see this better by illustrating the process in terms of a decision tree. Figure 8.7 shows the situation where there are three options, a, b and c.

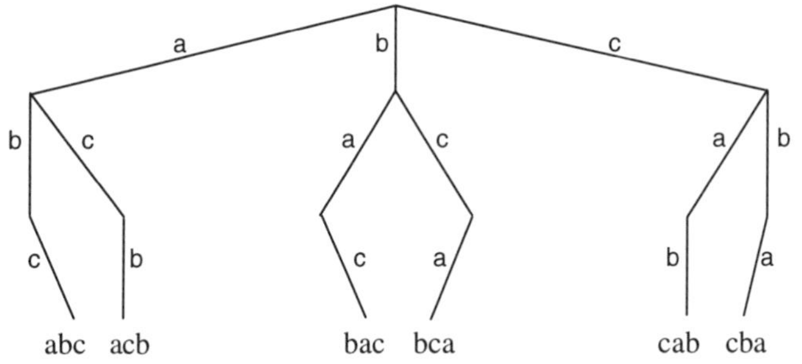

Figure 8.7 Permutation decision tree

Notice that the tree has six leaves and these enumerate all permutations of the three options.

We must now get down to the non-trivial problem of writing an algorithm to generate these permutations. A good starting point is the selection problem that we solved in the previous section. There are clear similarities between that problem and this. In both cases n choices have to be made. In both there is a decision tree. In both the choices need to be printed out. It is reasonable to think, therefore, that we can re-use the same general approach. But we will have to make modifications to account for two crucial differences.

First, for the selection problem there were only two possibilities at each stage, select or do not select (1 or 0). Here there are potentially any one of the n options. We can deal with this simply by looping through the n options, rather than the two choices.

Second, in the selection problem it did not matter what had already been chosen; here it does (once an option has been chosen it cannot be re-used), and so we will have to remember what options have already been used. We will do this by using an array (used) to keep track of what has been used; whenever we use an option, *i,* we will set used (*i*) to true. We must be careful, though, because as the recursion unfolds we will 'unuse' options, and so we must set their used value to false. These ideas lead to the code in Fig. 8.8.

In C:

```
void perm(int option)
{
   int i;
   for (i=1; i<=n; i++)
   {
      if (used[i]==0)
      {
         a[option] = i;
         used[i] = 1;
         if (option==n)
         {
            print_a();
         }
         else
         {
            perm(option+1);
         }
         /* unuse i */
         used[i] = 0;
      }
   }
}
```

In Ada:

```
procedure perm(option: in NATURAL) is
begin
  for i in 1..n loop
    if not used(i)
      then
        a(option) := i;
        used(i) := TRUE;
        if option=n
          then
            print_a;
          else
            perm(option+1);
        end if;
        -- unuse i
        used(i) := FALSE;
    end if;
  end loop;
end;
```

Figure 8.8 Program fragment to enumerate all permutations of n values

Before we can use this we have some work to do in the main body of the program. Since to begin with we have used none of the options, we need to initialise all of used to false. We do this as shown in Fig. 8.9.

In C:

```
for (i=1; i<=n; i++)
{
      used[i] = 0;
}
```

In Ada:

```
for i in 1..n loop
   used(i) := FALSE;
end loop;
```

Figure 8.9 Initialising the permutation process

We can then begin the recursion with:

In C:

```
perm(1);
```

In Ada:

```
perm(1);
```

To see what happens we will dry-run the algorithm for *n* equal to 3. The results are shown in Fig. 8.10.

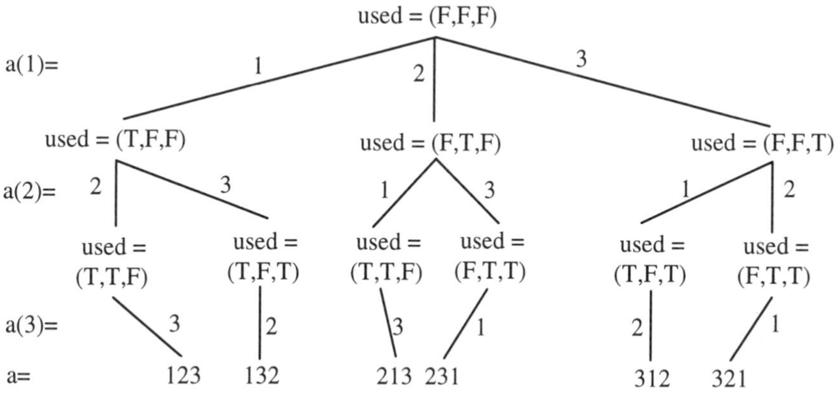

Figure 8.10 Dry-run of the permutation code

EXERCISES 8.3

1. Enumerate all possible permutations of four options.

   Sometimes, rather than selecting all the items from a group, we want to choose fewer items. For instance, we may want to choose 2 items from 3, this gives rise to the following permutations:

   (1,2), (1,3), (2,1), (2,3), (3,1), (3,2)

2. Enumerate all possible permutations of 2 items chosen from 4.

3. Alter the perm procedure to enumerate the permutations of m items chosen from n.

8.4 The travelling salesperson problem

The travelling salesperson problem is one of the great problems of computer science. Its specification is easy, its efficient solution is hard, perhaps impossible. However, here, we will content ourselves with just finding a solution, and not worrying too much about its complexity. The problem is this: given a set of cities and, where present, the length of the road between each pair, find the distance of the shortest tour which visits all the cities exactly once and gets you back to your starting point.

Consider the 'map' in Fig.8. 11. (The numbers show the length of the roads.)

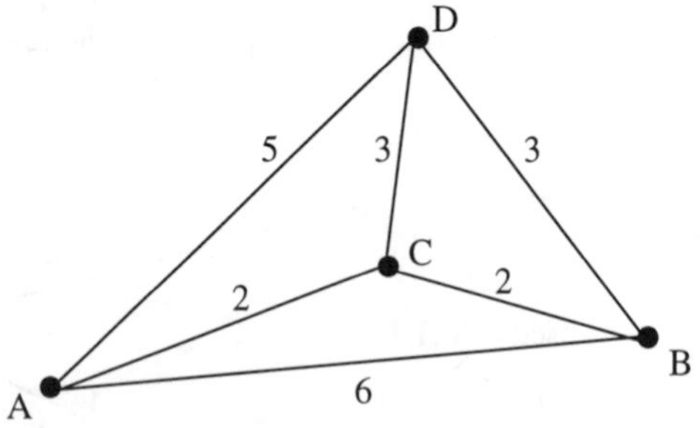

Figure 8.11 An example road network

We can try a trial and error approach to finding the answer. Let us try going from A t B to C to D and back to A again (we will write this as ABCD, and note that the link fro D to A is included in this). This is shown in Fig. 8.12.

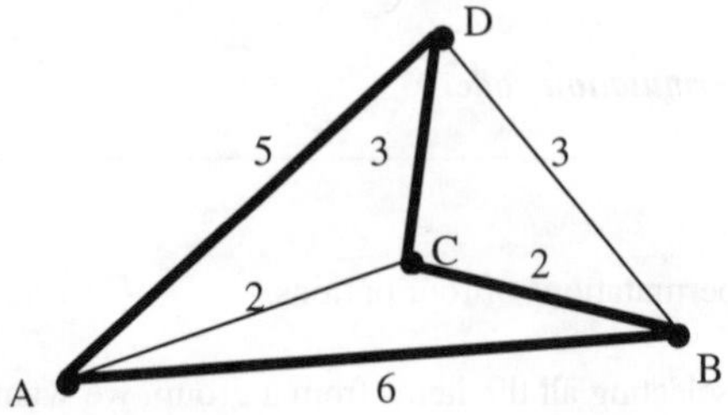

Figure 8.12 A tour of length 16

Its length is 16. Can we do better? Yes, with a length of 12, ACBD is shorter (Fig. 8.13).

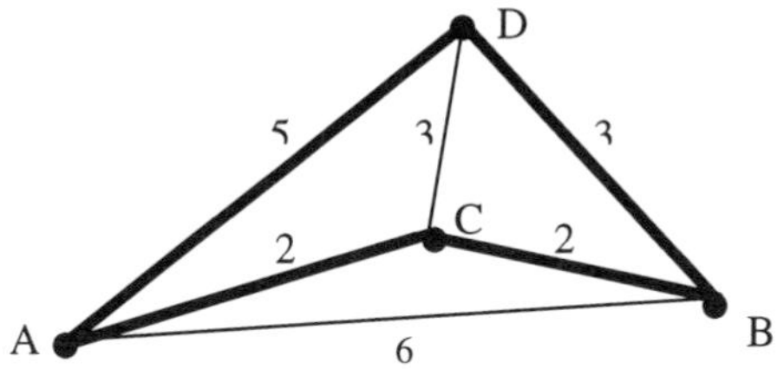

Figure 8.13 A tour of length 12

But is this the best? If we are to be convinced that it is, we need to be methodical in our approach and ensure that we do not miss any possibilities; we can do this by enumerating all possible routes and finding the length of each. We can think of a permutation of the cities as specifying a route. Thus, what we need to do requires enumerating all the permutations. We show these in Table 8.7. As we can see, the best we can do is indeed 12.

Table 8.7 All possible tours and their lengths

Route	*Length*	*Route*	*Length*
ABCD	16	CABD	14
ABDC	14	CADB	12
ACBD	12	CBAD	16
ACDB	14	CBDA	12
ADBC	12	CDAB	16
ADCB	16	CDBA	14
BACD	14	DABC	16
BADC	16	DACB	12
BCAD	12	DBAC	14
BCDA	16	DBCA	12
BDAC	12	DCAB	14
BDCA	14	DCBA	16

Using the work from the previous section the solution is now simple. We can use that work to enumerate the permutations, which we think of as describing routes. Then, rather than print out a permutation, we calculate the length of the route it denotes. This is done quite simply as follows. If we store the length of each road in a two-dimensional array d, where d(*i,j*) represents the distance from *i* to *j* and, as before, we use an array a to store the present permutation/route, then the length of the route is given by summing the lengths of each 'road'. This is done as shown in Fig. 8.14.

In C:

```
length = 0;
for(i=1; i<n; i++)
{
   length = length + d[a[i]][a[i+1]];
}
length = length + d[a[n]][a[1]];
```

In Ada:

```
length := 0;
for i in 1..n–1 loop
   length := length + d(a(i),a(i+1));
end loop;
length := length + d(a(n) ,a(1));
```

Figure 8.14 Program fragment to find the length of a tour

Note that we need to remember to loop back from the final place to the starting point. In the code this is 'done' in the statement outside the loop. All we need to do then is to keep track of the best result found so far, which once we have enumerated all the possible routes must be the shortest.

As always, once we have an algorithm we need to see if we can make improvements. One obvious way to do this comes from the realisation that it does not matter from which point we start a cycle. This follows because wherever we start from, by the time that we get back to our starting point we have used exactly the same roads and, therefore, covered the same distance. For instance, if we have a cycle ABCD (remember this means A to B to C to D to A), say, then its length is equal to that of BCDA, CDAB and DABC. We can make use of this as follows. If we can start from anywhere then we can, without loss of generality, start at node 1. With this determined, to list all possible cycles we need only to enumerate all the permutations of the other $n - 1$ nodes. Thus, we need only to consider $(n - 1)!$ routes, rather than $n!$. That is, we have an algorithm which is n times faster than that which we started with. Not a bad saving for such little effort. We will look at other ways of 'tweaking' the algorithm in the exercises.

Before we finish this chapter it is worth asking this question: is there a better way to solve the travelling salesperson problem than by using the brute strength approach? Since this gives us an exponential time algorithm, this comes down to asking whether there is a polynomial time algorithm (one of the form n to the power something, however large). In spite of considerable research effort around the world, the answer is, we do not know. Certainly we can find, through branch and bound techniques for instance, ways of reducing the cost, but these do not change the complexity. Certainly we can find heuristic approaches which very quickly get the answer right most of the time, but these methods are not guaranteed to be accurate. But no one has been able to find a better way which is guaranteed to give the optimal answer. Of course, that does not mean that a better way does not exist; it is always possible that by a spark of genius one will be found. After all this effort, though, the suspicion must be that a better way does not exist. However, we cannot be happy with just a suspicion, we would like to be able to prove that it is the case. But no one has managed that either.

Not only is the travelling salesperson problem important in its own right, but many other problems such as Hamiltonian cycles and satisfiability are similar. Indeed, their similarity is such that it has been shown that if a better solution exists for the travelling salesperson problem then one exists for them too, or, alternatively, if it can be proved that one does not exist then the same would apply to them as well. Fame and fortune awaits the person who cracks it one way or the other.

EXERCISES 8.4

1. For each of the following maps find the length of the shortest tour.

(i)

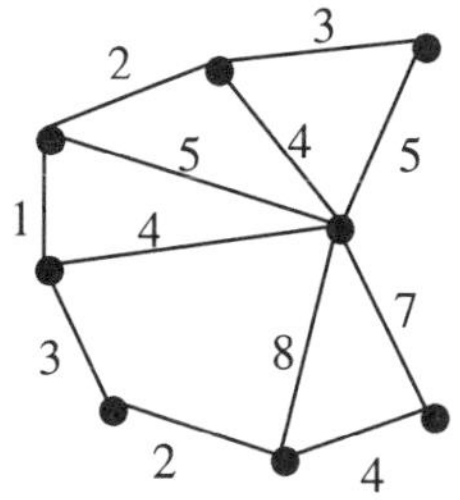

(ii)

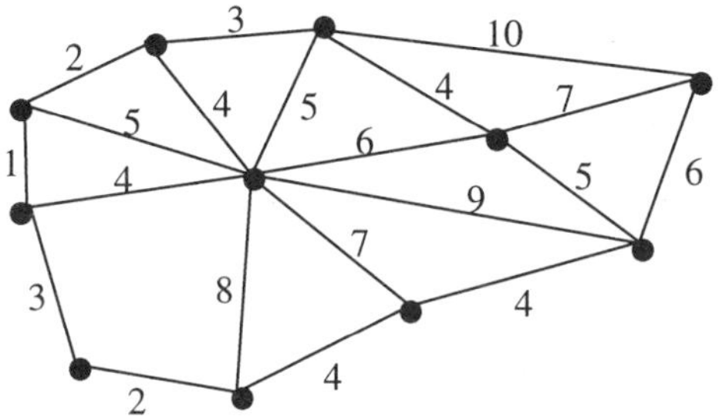

2. Describe ways in which the algorithm shown in the text could be improved to make it more efficient.

Summary

- The brute strength method enumerates all possible answers and chooses the best.
- 2^n different portfolios can be selected from n items.
- There are $n!$ different permutations of n items.
- Algorithms described:
  —shops problem
  —portfolio enumeration
  —permutation enumeration
  —travelling salesperson.

9

DIVIDE AND CONQUER

OBJECTIVES

In this chapter you will learn:

- the divide and conquer method
- algorithms for the following problems
  —Quicksort
  —lowest two numbers in an array

The divide and conquer method is one of the best algorithmic approaches. It so often leads to solutions that, when confronted with a new problem, it is usually worth considering immediately after the most direct approaches have failed. When it works it can lead to elegant, often recursive, algorithms.

> DIVIDE AND CONQUER
> The divide and conquer approach solves a problem by:
> - dividing the data into parts
> - finding subsolutions for each of the parts
> - constructing the final answer from the subsolutions.

In fact, we have already used the divide and conquer approach: it was the method used for the binary search algorithm as described in Chapter 6 (See Fig. 6.17). Readers may find it useful at this stage to read through that material again.

Before looking at some cxamples, it is worth noting the distinction between the divide and conquer method and the top-down approach. Superficially they look the same in that both divide a larger problem into smaller ones. However, there is a difference: in the divide and conquer approach the data is broken into pieces; whereas in the top-down approach the function is broken into parts. So, for example, consider the problem of painting a room. The divide and conquer approach would break the problem into parts, with, for instance, each part representing the whole job, from beginning to end, of painting a single wall. On the other hand, the top-down approach would split the task into a number of subjobs, stripping, filling, sanding, cleaning, undercoating, etc., and each of these would be completed for the whole room before the next was started. In fact, this difference can be useful: for more complicated problems it is often worth using both methods. Finally, a distinction should also be drawn between divide and conquer and divide and rule, the latter being a political concept.

9.1 Quicksort

As our first illustration of the divide and conquer method we will look at yet another algorithm to sort an array of values. (We do not apologise for this: the sorting problem is a very fruitful source of interesting algorithms.) The algorithm described in this section is called Quicksort. It is due to Hoare. As we will see later, it is quick in only some cases, in others its performance is no better than more simple sorts. Even so, it is worth looking at because it is a particularly elegant algorithm, in that it is easy to understand (we hope) and, once understood, its correctness is clear. In spite of this, it is interesting to note that it was not found until 1960, even though its domain is an area which had been particularly well researched beforehand. As such, it gives hope to all of us that even now there may be other simple, elegant and important algorithms waiting to be found.

As would be expected within the context of this chapter Quicksort involves both a divide and a conquer phase. These are described below.

QUICKSORT

- If the array has size zero or one, it is sorted and there is nothing to do.
  Otherwise:
- Divide the problem by using the first element as a pivot; putting it in the 'middle', and comparing all the other elements with it, putting them:
  —in a 'left batch' when they are less than it
  —in a 'right batch' when not.
- Recursively Quicksort the left and right batches
- Conquer the problem by appending
  —the sorted left batch
  —the pivot
  —the sorted right batch.

At this stage it might not be obvious what is happening, but a simple example should make it clear. We start with the following array:

5	8	3	2	6

We take out the first element, the pivot, and put it in the 'middle':

pivot
5

We compare each of the other numbers in turn with the 5. When they are less we put them to the left, when more than or equal to the right. The next element is 8. This goes to the right, to give:

pivot	right batch
5	8

This is followed by a 3 which, because it is less than 5, goes to the left. This gives:

left batch	pivot	right batch
3	5	8

The remaining elements are 2, which goes to the left, and 6, which goes to the right. Thus, at the end of the divide phase we are left with:

left batch		pivot	right batch	
3	2	5	8	6

We can see that even at this stage we have made some useful progress: all those elements in the left batch are less than 5 and all those to the right are at least equal to 5. This means that once these batches are themselves sorted, the conquer phase is easy (we simply append the parts). We are now left with the left and right batches to sort. We deal with these recursively, treating them in the same way as the whole array. Dividing the left batch gives:

new left batch	new pivot
2	3

Since the left batch is of size one this must already be sorted, so we can conquer this subproblem by appending the parts, to get:

2	3

Similarly, dividing the right batch gives:

new left batch	new pivot
6	8

Again we get to a base case, so we can merge to get a sorted right batch:

6	8

Now that we have solved all subproblems, we are finally ready for the conquer phase for the original problem. This is simple: since the left and right batches are now sorted we just append them with the pivot in-between to give, as required:

2	3	5	6	8

Is this method efficient? We will start by counting the number of comparisons required in the example. In the divide phase we made 4 comparisons with the pivot. We then had to sort the left and right batches; each of these processes taking an extra comparison. Thus, the whole sort required 6 comparisons. This compares well with the 10 comparisons required by the selection sort (4 to find the lowest element, 3 for the next lowest, then 2, then 1). So it appears to be a good method. But, to be sure of this we need to generalise, to see if it is still efficient for other, especially larger, problems.

We let the number of items to sort be n. Clearly, the number of comparisons required to sort an array is a function of n. That is, everything else being equal, the larger n is the more comparisons are required. We will call this function $T(n)$ (rather less rigorously, we can think of $T(n)$ as representing the time needed to sort n items). Then, we ask: what are the costs and the results of each pass through?

To compare each of the other elements against the pivot 'costs' $n - 1$ comparisons. But since we are mainly concerned with what happens for large problems, that is for large values of n, we can reasonably approximate this to n (it is in any case a conservative approximation). The result of this divide phase is that we have both left and right batches to sort. These are, *if we are lucky* (we will come back to this later) each of size $n/2$ (actually $(n - 1)/2$, but again we are conservative in our approximation) and each, therefore, requires $T(n/2)$ comparisons to sort. We are left, then, with:

$$T(n) = n + 2T(n/2) \qquad (1)$$

we also know that $T(1) = 0$.

To solve this recurrence relation we will work like this. First, notice that if the equation works for n, it works for anything else. In particular, it holds for $n/2$. Therefore, replacing n by $n/2$ everywhere gives:

$$T(n/2) = n/2 + 2T(n/4) \qquad (2)$$

We can substitute (2) in (1) to give:

$$T(n) = n + n + 4T(n/4) \qquad (3)$$

Similarly:

$$T(n/4) = n + 2T(n/8)$$

and we can substitute this into (3) to get

$$T(n) = n + n + n + 8T(n/8)$$

We should now see a trend developing: at each step we use another n comparisons and have twice as many subproblems, each of half the previous size, to sort. We can write this as:

$$T(n) = xn + 2^x T(n/2^x) \qquad (4)$$

The question is: when can we stop? Well we know exactly how many comparisons are required to solve a problem of size 1, it is 0. So we can stop when the subproblem size reduces to 1. That is,

$$n/2^x = 1$$

$$\therefore \; 2^x = n$$

And this is where logarithms come in useful, because it follows from the definition of log base 2 that:

$$x = \log n$$

In general, x is not an integer. Yet, of course, any algorithm must use an integral number of steps. However, we can afford to approximate, and x is good enough. We substitute for x into (4), and noting that $T(1) = 0$, get the result:

$$\begin{aligned} T(n) &= n \log n + 2^{\log n} T(1) \\ &= n \log n \end{aligned}$$

So, *if we are lucky*, Quicksort has complexity $O(n \log n)$. This is an enormous improvement on the simple sorts, such as selection sort, which were $O(n^2)$.

Perhaps we should now explain what we meant by saying, *if we are lucky*. Well, it is this: the whole analysis thus far has been based on the assumption that the divide phase partitions the problem into two batches of equal size. Unfortunately, this is not necessarily the case. For instance, consider the following array:

5	4	3	2	1

Now, when we compare the other values against the pivot, since they are all less, they all go into the left batch, and the right batch remains empty. Giving:

left batch

4	3	2	1

pivot

5

right batch

Thus, rather than ending up with two problems each half the original size, we have one problem whose size is only one less than what we started with. Thus, what we have, in effect, is a selection sort. That is, we have an algorithm with complexity $O(n^2)$, not $O(n \log n)$ as in the best case.

We are now left with the problem of implementing this algorithm. The main problem we will encounter is one of space: we really do not want to keep creating new lists of elements every time we do a divide; we would much rather use just the space that the array takes up and no more. We can do this, but we must be careful. We start with an input array, a. Our aim is to sort a from the first to the *n*th element. If the procedure to do this is quicksort, our call is:

In C:	In Ada:
`quicksort(a, 1, n);`	**quicksort**(a, 1, n);

To avoid using any extra space, we will do the division step within the array. That is, the left and right batches will be stored within the array. We start with the pivot in the first position, and compare the remaining elements with it. We use a counter *i* to show our current position in the array. There are two possibilities:

1. a(*i*) is not less than the pivot's value, in which case there is nothing to do
2. a(*i*) is less than the pivot's value and space must be made to the left of the pivot.

The space making is done by moving the pivot to the right, and the new value to the vacated space. In detail, the steps are:

1. Move the value after the pivot to a(*i*).
2. Move the pivot value to a(pivot+1).
3. Move a(*i*) to a(pivot).
4. Increment pivot.

Thus, at the end of every step the following is true:

		pivot	*i*	
a	less than a(pivot)	a(pivot)	not less than a(pivot)	not looked at

An example will illustrate how this works. We start with the following array:

a	5	8	3	2	6

We choose the first element as a pivot. So to begin with we have:

	pivot				
a	5	8	3	2	6

We use *i* to point to the remaining elements in turn; we start with *i* equal to 2.

	pivot	*i*			
a	5	8	3	2	6

In this case a(*i*) is not less than 5, so it is in the correct position. We increment *i*, to get:

	pivot		*i*		
a	5	8	3	2	6

This time a(*i*) is 3, which is less than the pivot, so we want to move it to the left. However, there is no space available; we have to make it. We do that as described above, to get:

		pivot	*i*		
a	3	5	8	2	6

We increment *i* and repeat the operations to get:

			pivot	*i*	
a	3	2	5	8	6

We make a final increment to *i*, but this time a(*i*) does not need moving. This leaves us with:

			pivot		*i*
a	3	2	5	8	6

At this stage the division process is complete. The points to notice are: the pivot is in the correct position, with everything to the left less than it and everything to the right not; the left batch is from position 1 to pivot – 1, and the right batch from pivot + 1 to *n*.

To complete the job we now need to sort the left and right batches. This is done recursively. It involves the following calls:

In C:

```
quicksort(a, 1, pivot-1);
quicksort(a, pivot+1, n);
```

In Ada:

```
quicksort(a, 1, pivot-1);
quicksort(a, pivot+1, n);
```

As far as the Ada version is concerned there is one last job before the code. We need to define the type of a. Typically it could be an array of 100 natural numbers. So, for instance, we might require the following type definition in Ada:

type NATARRAY **is array** (1..100) **of** NATURAL;

We now have all the building blocks in place, and these lead to the code in Fig. 9.1:

In C:

```
void quicksort(int a[], int from, int to)
{
   int i, pivot, new_val;
   if (to>from)
   {
      /* work to do */
      pivot = from;
      /* partition against pivot's value */
      /* less to left, others to right   */
      for (i=from+1; i<=to; i++)
      {
         new_val = a[i];
         if (new_val<a[pivot])
         {
            /* make space for new value to the left of the pivot */
            a[i] = a[pivot+1];
            a[pivot+1] = a[pivot];
            a[pivot] = new_val;
            /* the pivot's position has increased */
            pivot++;
         }
      }
      quicksort(a, from, pivot-1);
      quicksort(a, pivot+1, to);
   }
}
```

In Ada:

```
procedure quicksort (a: in out NATARRAY; from, to: in NATURAL) is
  pivot, new_val: NATURAL;
begin
  if to>from
    then
      -- work to do
      pivot := from;
      -- partition against pivot's value, less to left, others to right
      for i in from+1..to loop
        new_val := a(i);
        if new_val<a(pivot)
          then
            -- make space for new value to the left of the pivot
            a(i) := a(pivot+1);
            a(pivot+1) := a(pivot);
            a(pivot) := new_val;
            -- the pivot's position has increased
            pivot := pivot + 1;
        end if;
      end loop;
```

```
    -- recursively sort left and right batches
    quicksort(a, from, pivot-1);
    quicksort(a, pivot+1, to);
  end if;
end;
```

Figure 9.1 Quicksort procedure

EXERCISES 9.1

1. For each of the following arrays calculate the number of comparisons required for the Quicksort:

   (i) (6, 9, 11, 3, 2, 4, 7)
   (ii) (4, 9, 11, 3, 2, 6, 7)
   (iii) (11, 9, 7, 6, 4, 3, 2)

9.2 Lowest two problem

As a further illustration of the divide and conquer method we will look at a problem which has obvious but rather inefficient solutions and see if we can come up with something more efficient. The problem is this:

- Given an array of n values find, in order, the lowest two values *efficiently*.

To keep life simple we will assume that n is at least 2 and that it is divisible by 2. Let us make sure we understand the problem. Suppose the array holds:

2	4	6	6	3	7

then the result required is 2 followed by 3.

Additionally, we need to be clear about what is required when we have the special case where the lowest number is repeated. For instance, given an array:

3	1	1	4

then the result required is 1 followed by 1.

As is to be expected given the context, we will get to use the divide and conquer approach to come up with a solution. However, we will also use this problem to illustrate how algorithm development can often involve a learning process. In doing so, we will attempt to solve the problem in a number of ways. Some of these will be poor and lead to dead ends, but all will make us ask questions, and cumulatively these will eventually lead us to a successful conclusion.

When confronted with a new problem it is often useful to start by trying an obvious approach. Especially if we have few ideas, we have little to lose by doing this. If it works, we have succeeded; if it does not, we have not wasted much time, and we may even have learnt something useful about the solution.

What is an obvious way to solve this problem? Well, clearly if the data were already sorted the solution would be trivial: just take the first two elements. Unfortunately, we cannot take it for granted that the array is sorted, so if we want to use this approach, we will have to sort the array ourselves. This should not present a problem, since we have already seen how to do just that. However, it does take some effort: a simple sort has complexity $O(n^2)$ and even the best we can do is $O(n \log n)$.

Can we do better? The hunch must be that we can, if only because sorting gives us much more information (the ordering of all the elements) than is required. Or, to put it another way, by sorting we would have, in effect, solved the lowest *n* problem when all we wanted was to solve the lowest two problem. Since, normally, we want to do no more work than asked for, we can probably do better.

The apparent inefficiency of the above approach may make it unsatisfactory, but we do not want to give up. So what do we do now? Well, if we can see no more efficient way of solving the problem as originally stated, it often helps to solve a simpler problem than was asked; again with the hope of learning something along the way. There are two ways the simplification can be made, by focusing on:

1. finding an efficient solution to a simpler problem
2. finding an inefficient solution to the original problem.

For instance, if we want to run a marathon in under three hours, but do not know for the time being how, we might try running a half-marathon in, say, ninety minutes or a full marathon in four hours. Either may be a feasible target. But if it is not, we can try simpler things still. Eventually though, we should be able to find something we can do, and usually, at least as far as algorithms are concerned, doing something is better than doing nothing.

We will adopt this approach here. Clearly, the problem would be simpler if we were asked to find the lowest value, rather than the two lowest. In fact, this is very easy (if for no other reason than that we have already covered it!). We will call the array a and store the lowest value in lowest. The algorithm is shown in Fig. 9.2.

In C:

```
lowest = a[1];
for (i=2; i<=n; i++)
{
   if (a[i]<lowest)
   {
      lowest = a[i];
   }
}
```

In Ada:

```
lowest := a(1);
for i in 2..n loop
  if a(i)<lowest
    then
      lowest := a(i);
  end if;
end loop;
```

Figure 9.2 Program fragment to find the lowest number in an array

This will give us the lowest value for a cost of $n - 1$ comparisons. Of course, to complete the original problem, we still have work to do: we have yet to find the second lowest value. However, it seems likely that the solution to the second part of the problem could involve some similar technique. Moreover, and this is good news, it seems reasonable that finding the second lowest value should be of comparable difficulty to finding the lowest and also use about n comparisons. Thus, we can expect a total of about $2n$ comparisons, which is better than the sorting method tried first.

Where do we go from here? Building on the code above, two approaches seem obvious:

Approach 1: first find the lowest, then find the second lowest

Approach 2: search through the array keeping track of the lowest two found so far

Either way we need to choose names for the lowest two values. We will call the lowest *lowest1* and the second lowest *lowest2*.

Approach 1. To find lowest1, we simply use the code in Fig. 9.2. Then, to find *lowest2* we almost repeat the process. However, we have to be careful not to count the lowest value twice. To do this, we need some way of identifying it, so that in the second run-through it can be discounted. One horribly inefficient way of doing this is to keep track of its position, and to ignore this location on the second run-through. The code for this is shown in Fig. 9.3.

In C:

```
/* find lowest value and its position */
lowest1 = a[1];
position = 1;
for (i=2; i<=n; i++)
{
   if (a[i]<lowest1)
   {
      lowest1 = a[i];
      position = i;
   }
}
/* find second lowest */
if (position!=1)
{
   lowest2 = a[1];
}
else
{
   lowest2 = a[2];
}
for (i=2; i<=n; i++)
{
```

```
    if (i!=position && a[i]<lowest2)
    {
      lowest2 = a[i];
    }
}
```

In Ada:

```
-- find lowest value and its position
lowest1 := a(1);
position := 1;
for i in 2..n loop
  if a(i)<lowest1
    then
      lowest1 := a(i);
      position := i;
  end if;
end loop;
-- find second lowest
if position/=1
   then
      lowest2 := a(1);
   else
      lowest2 := a(2);
end if;
for i in 2..n loop
  if i/=position and a(i)<lowest2
    then
      lowest2 := a(i);
  end if;
end loop;
```

Figure 9.3 Program fragment to find the two lowest numbers

This does the job, in that we find the two lowest values. However, it is inefficient; using almost $3n$ comparisons even though we expected $2n$ to be sufficient. Especially inefficient is the piece of code to find *lowest2*. This is because each *if* makes two comparisons: is i not equal to the position of the lowest; and is the new array value less than *lowest2*. So just this part of the algorithm is taking almost $2n$ comparisons.

We can do better than this by moving the lowest value to the first location after the first run-through. In doing this we cannot simply overwrite what was in the first location already, so we must swap the values (in the code we assume a swap procedure is available). Then, we begin the second run-through at the second value in the array. And now, having moved away the lowest value, we do not need to keep checking for it. This idea is used in the code shown in Fig. 9.4.

In C:

```
/* find lowest value and its position */
lowest1 = a[1];
position = 1;
```

```
for (i=2; i<=n; i++)
{
   if (a[i]<lowest1)
   {
      lowest1 = a[i];
      position = i;
   }
}
/* put lowest1 in the first position */
swap(&a[1], &a[position]);
/* find second lowest */
lowest = a[2]
for (i=3; i<=n; i++)
{
   if (a[i]<lowest2)
   {
      lowest2 = a[i];
   }
}
```

In Ada:

```
-- find lowest value and its position
lowest1 := a(1);
position := 1;
for i in 2..n loop
  if a(i)<lowest1
    then
      lowest1 := a(i);
      position := i;
  end if;
end loop;
-- put lowest1 in the first location
swap(a(1), a(position));
-- find second lowest
lowest2 := a(2);
for i in 3..n loop
  if a(i)<lowest2
    then
      lowest2 := a(i);
  end if;
end loop;
```

Figure 9.4 First improvement to the two lowest numbers in an array program fragment

Notice that this modification has led to code that is clearer and also more efficient. The improved efficiency comes because the revised second stage takes only $n - 2$ comparisons, which is more than twice as quick as before. In total, the revised algorithm uses $2n - 3$ comparisons. Thus, we now have something that looks reasonably efficient. But can we do better?

Approach 2. As already mentioned there is a second approach that could be tried, namely that of continuously keeping track of the lowest two found so far. To do this we can start by setting *lowest1* and *lowest2* to the first two values in the array, making sure that we have them correctly ordered. Then, as we step through the remaining part of the array, the value of each new element, a(*i*), gives rise to three cases.

- Case 1. It is less than *lowest2* and less than *lowest1*, in which case the *lowest2* is changed to the value of *lowest1* and *lowest1* to the new value.
- Case 2. It is less than *lowest2* but not *lowest1*, in which case it replaces *lowest2*.
- Case 3. It is not less than *lowest2* and nothing changes.

Fig. 9.5 shows the three cases.

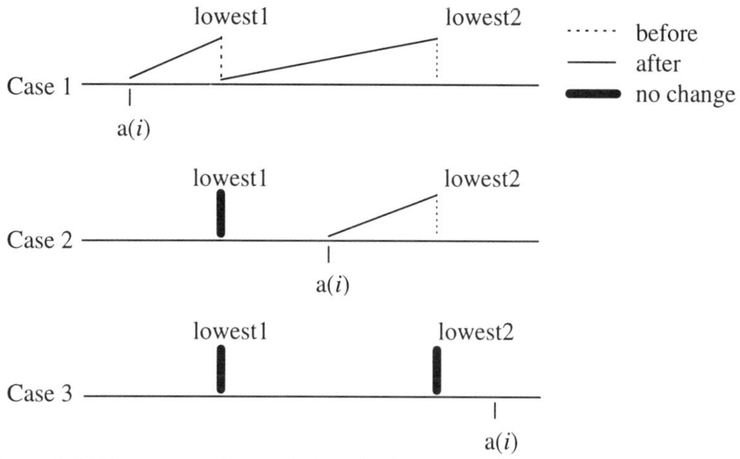

Figure 9.5 Three cases for updating the lowest two

These ideas lead to the code shown in Fig. 9.6.

In C:

```
if (a[1]<a[2])
{
   lowest1 = a[1];
   lowest2 = a[2];
}
else
{
   lowest1 = a[2];
   lowest2 = a[1];
}
for (i=3; i<=n; i++)
{
   if (a[i]<lowest2)
   {
      if (a[i]<lowest1)
      {
         lowest2 = lowest1;
```

```
            lowest1 = a[i];
        }
        else
        {
            lowest2 = a[i];
        }
    }
}
```

In Ada:

```
if a(1)<a(2)
  then
    lowest1 := a(1);
    lowest2 := a(2);
  else
    lowest1 := a(2);
    lowest2 := a(1);
end if;
for i in 3..n loop
  if a(i)<lowest2
    then
      if a(i)<lowest1
        then
          lowest2 := lowest1;
          lowest1 := a(i);
        else
          lowest2 := a(i);
      end if;
  end if;
end loop;
```

Figure 9.6 Second improvement to the two lowest numbers in an array program fragment

The efficiency of this algorithm is more complicated to analyse. Before the loop there is a single conditional. In it, there are at worst two conditionals for each of the $n - 2$ iterations. This gives a total of $2n - 3$, which is the same as before. However, on average we would expect fewer comparisons than that, because if a(i) is not less than *lowest2*, the second conditional is not met. Although better on average, it is the worst case that we are really interested in, so this is not really such a useful improvement. And so, yet again, we ask: can we do better?

It is at this stage that we might want to see what the divide and conquer approach can do for us. We start by looking at the 'divide'. Clearly, there are many ways to divide the array, and we will have to be careful to choose a good one. It does seem reasonable (no more than that, but a useful heuristic nevertheless) that the division should be related to the problem. The problem is concerned with the *two* lowest. Therefore, it seems reasonable to try a division based on two. This leads to a choice: we can divide the array into two parts; we can divide the array into pairs. We look at each of these in turn.

To start with, let us consider a partition into two equal parts each with $n/2$ elements. How could we proceed?

Tempting, but wrong, would be to find the lowest in each half and put these both forward as the two lowest. Certainly, this is quick (finding the lowest in half the array takes $n/2$ comparisons, which gives for the two a total of n). However, it is incorrect. This is because it could be that the two lowest values are both in the same half.

Also tempting would be to sort each half, from which the lowest two could be selected directly and then merging these two pairs in such a way as to get the two lowest for the whole array. This does at least have the virtue of being correct. However, the sorting is costly. The best we can do for each half, that is $n/2$ elements, is about $(n/2)(\log(n/2))$. But we need to sort twice, once for each half. Therefore, in total we have about $(2n/2)(\log(n/2)$ comparisons to do, which equals $n \log n - n$ (this follows because, for base 2, $\log n/2 = \log n - 1$). Thus, sorting the two halves separately only saves about n operations compared with the original method, which sorted the array as a whole. Moreover, we are still left with the problem of taking the two lowest from each group and finding the two lowest overall. Unfortunately, then, we are left with an algorithm which is less efficient than ones that we already have.

We are left with looking at the other partitioning method: dividing the array into pairs. Certainly the problem would be easier if we knew that each pair was in order (sorted), so doing this is a move in the right direction. At this stage we do not know if this is a good approach, but another useful heuristic is: *unless you have a better idea, move in the right direction.*

So, let us try it. We will call it the sort phase. To sort two elements needs a single conditional. Since there are $n/2$ pairs, this takes a total of $n/2$ operations. What now? Well we need to get off to a good start. We can do this by setting *lowest1* and *lowest2* to the first pair. We then need to compare these lowest values found so far with each successive pair and update them as required. We will call this the merge phase. Now for the good news: the merge leads to only four cases. Suppose the new pair of values being looked at are a(i) and a(i + 1), then the only possible results of the update are shown in Table 9.1.

Table 9.1 Case analysis of the update of the lowest two

Case	*New value of lowest1*	*New value of lowest2*	*Comment*
1	*lowest1*	*lowest2*	no change, a(i) is not less than *lowest2*
2	*lowest1*	a(i)	a(i) is less than *lowest2*, but not *lowest1*
3	a(i)	*lowest1*	a(i) less than both *lowest*, but a(i + 1) less than neither
4	a(i)	a(i + 1)	a(i + 1), and hence a(i), less than both lowest values

This follows because, since we have already sorted the pairs, we know that a(i + 1) is not less than a(i) and, therefore, other combinations are impossible. For instance, if a(i) is more than *lowest2*, so must be a(i + 1); there is no need to check.

Now this is where theory is useful. We have four possible cases, and we know that used carefully each conditional can differentiate between two possible routes. Hence, to cover the four cases we need to ask only two questions. Thus, to deal with all $n/2$ groups this merge phase requires using nearly n comparisons ($2(n/2 - 1)$ to be precise). Of course, the pair sorting phase had a cost of $n/2$ comparisons. Thus, with both phases taken together, the total cost is nearly $3n/2$; an improvement on what has gone before.

We will illustrate the algorithm using the following data:

2	6	7	3	5	6	9	2	4	1

The algorithm deals with the array in pairs, as shown:

a	2	6	7	3	5	6	9	2	4	1

The sort phase sorts each pair, to give:

a	2	6	3	7	5	6	2	9	1	4

lowest1 and *lowest2* are initialised to the first pair of values, giving:

lowest1	2
lowest2	6

For the merge phase each of the remaining pairs is considered in turn and the lowest values updated. To show what is happening, in what follows the current pair is shown with asterisks. Thus, considering the second pair

a	2	6	3*	7*	5	6	2	9	1	4

leads to *lowest2* being changed, to give:

lowest1	2
lowest2	3

Considering the third pair

a	2	6	3	7	5*	6*	2	9	1	4

leads to no change.

Considering the fourth pair

a	2	6	3	7	5	6	2*	9*	1	4

leads to *lowest2* being updated, to give:

lowest1	2
lowest2	2

Finally, using the last pair

a										
	2	6	3	7	5	6	2	9	1*	4*

leads to both lowest values being updated to give the correct answer:

lowest1	1
lowest2	2

The code to implement this is shown in Fig. 9.7. (It will be noted that we have moved from using **for** loops to using the equivalent **while** loops. This is not through choice. It is because the pair-wise moves require an iterative step of two, but in Ada **for** loops do not have the facility to do this.)

In C:

```
/* step through the pairs, sorting each */
i = 1;
while (i<n)
{
   if (a[i]>a[i+1])
   {
      swap(&a[i], &a[i+1]);
   }
   i = i + 2;
}

/* initialise lowest to first pair */
lowest1 = a[1];
lowest2 = a[2];

/* step through the remaining pairs, updating lowest by merging */
i = 3;
while (i<n)
{
   if (a[i]<lowest1)
   {
      if (a[i+1]<lowest1)
      {
         lowest1 = a[i];
         lowest2 = a[i+1];
      }
      else
      {
         lowest2 = lowest1;
         lowest1 = a[i];
```

```
        }
    }
    else
    {
        if (a[i]<lowest2)
        {
            lowest2 = a[i];
        }
    }
    i = i + 2;
}
```

In Ada:

```
-- step through the pairs, sorting each
i := 1;
while i<n loop
  if a(i)>a(i+1)
    then
      swap(a(i), a(i+1));
  end if;
  i := i + 2;
end loop;

-- initialise lowest to first pair
lowest1 := a(1);
lowest2 := a(2);

-- step through remaining pairs, updating lowest by merging
i := 3;
while i<n loop
  if a(i)<lowest1
    then
      if a(i+1)<lowest1
        then
          lowest1 := a(i);
          lowest2 := a(i+1);
        else
          lowest2 := lowest1;
          lowest1 := a(i);
      end if;
    else
      if a(i)<lowest2
        then
          lowest2 := a(i);
      end if;
  end if;
  i := i + 2;
end loop;
```

Figure 9.7 Third improvement to the two lowest numbers in an array program fragment

EXERCISES 9.2

1. Using the final method shown above, calculate the number of comparisons required to find the lowest:

   (i) 3
   (ii) 4
   (iii) 5

   (Assume in each case that the array's length is divisible by the number of lowest values to find.)

Summary

- The divide and conquer method works by breaking the data into pieces, solving the problem for each of them, and then finding the solution to the whole problem by combining these results.
- Divide and conquer differs from the top-down approach because it breaks the data into pieces not the tasks.
- Algorithms described:
  —Quicksort
  —lowest two.

10

GREEDY ALGORITHMS

OBJECTIVES

In this chapter you will learn
- the greedy method
- the difference between a greedy and an heuristic algorithm
- algorithms for the following problems
  —coin change
  —optimal service
  —minimum spanning tree

The greedy method is an approach which is particularly suited to solving optimisation problems; problems in which the minimum number of this or the maximum number of that needs to be found. Where it works it gives very efficient algorithms which are simple to understand.

As their name suggests, greedy algorithms are algorithms which make choices according to what is best at present and without any regard to future consequences. They are like a chess player who, thinking only one move ahead, takes a piece without thinking whether or not it is a gambit. They are like a traveller who makes route choices by selecting at each junction that road which points most closely towards the destination. Or, again, they resemble a person who, preferring sweet things, eats the dessert before the main course. In short, they are tactical rather than strategic in their 'thinking'.

Normally, of course, relying on short-term tactics leads to results that are sub-optimal. Where they lead to results which approximate the real answer, such tactics are called *heuristics*. An heuristic becomes a greedy algorithm when there is something about the problem's formulation which ensures that it gives the optimal answer.

GREEDY METHOD
- At each step choose the best currently available option.
- Ensure this approach is guaranteed to give an optimal solution.

10.1 Coin change problem

Our first example of a greedy algorithm is a solution to the coin change problem. This involves calculating the minimum number of coins required to make up a particular amount of change.

We will work with the coins available in Britain. These have the following values (in pence):

- 1
- 2
- 5
- 10
- 20
- 50
- 100

As an example, consider the problem of making up change to the value of 46 pence. There are many ways to do this (the enumeration of which is the subject of an example in a later chapter), as Fig. 10.1 shows.

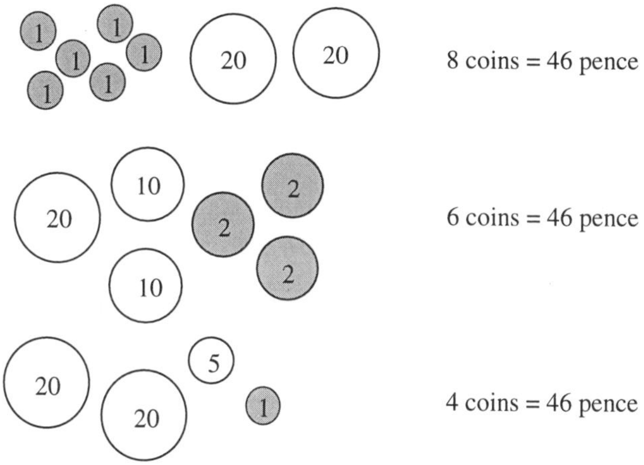

Figure 10.1 Some ways of making up 46 pence of change

Of the three examples given, the first uses 8 coins, the second 6 coins and the third 4 coins. The last example was the best of the three that we looked at, but is it the best that could be found?

Before investigating the greedy route, we should mention that, as always, we could try to solve the problem using the brute strength approach. This would involve listing all possible combinations of coins; checking each to see that it adds up to the right amount; and choosing the best (the one with fewest coins in) of those that do. We can simplify things a bit by realising that, assuming there are no fractional denominations, the maximum number of coins needed to make up n pence is n (that is, n pennies). So we only need to look at change involving up to n coins. Even so, assuming the British example in which there are 7 coins to choose from, this gives 7^n possibilities to look at. Clearly, an astronomical number, and an impractical one to calculate, for anything but the smallest amount of change. We need to be more clever.

The greedy approach involves taking the best route presently available. In terms of coin change this means starting by using the biggest coin that will fit into the change required. So, for instance, with the example of 46 pence, we would start by choosing the 20p coin. This coin is chosen because it is the biggest one that fits; the 50p and 100p (one pound) coin being too large.

What now? Well if we have already chosen a 20p coin then there are 26 pence remaining to find. Faced with this, we do as before: we choose the biggest coin that fits. In this case, that means using a 20p again. We just carry on like this until there is no more money required. Table 10.1 illustrates this process.

Table 10.1 Effect of choosing the largest coin that fits into the remaining amount

Coin chosen (pence).	*Change remaining to find*
	46
20	26
20	6
5	1
1	0

We can see that this process has left us with change made up from 4 coins. The problem now is to show that 4 is the best we can do. In fact we will go further than that, we will show that for any amount of change the greedy method gives an optimal solution using the British coin set.

We start our justification by noting that for any coin set problems can occur if the combined value of a number of lower denomination coins (or one denomination used a number of times) 'leapfrogs' over a higher denomination. (For instance, in a coin set including coins worth 3, 4 and 5 units, the 3 and the 4 'leapfrog' the 5.) See Fig. 10.2.

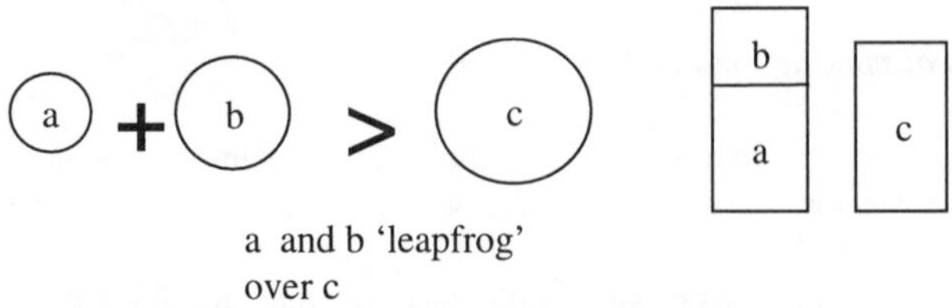

Figure 10.2 The problem of leapfrogging

On the other hand, if the denominations are such that leapfrogging is not possible, nothing can go wrong. This follows because if smaller coins are used even though a more valuable one could have been used instead then, in the absence of leapfrogging, a subset of these lesser valued coins must add up to the larger one; meaning that more coins are being used than is necessary and showing that the non-greedy approach is suboptimal.

Consider now the British coin set specifically. If we look at the sequence of coins formed from 1p, 5p, 10p, 50p and 100p we see that each denomination is a divisor of the succeeding one, and so leapfrogging is impossible. Thus, we know for sure that the greedy algorithm works for them. On the other hand, the 2p and the 20p are not divisors of the 5p and 50p coins, respectively. They allow leapfrogging (for instance, 2 + 2 + 2 leapfrogs 5) and may, therefore, cause problems (see Fig. 10.3).

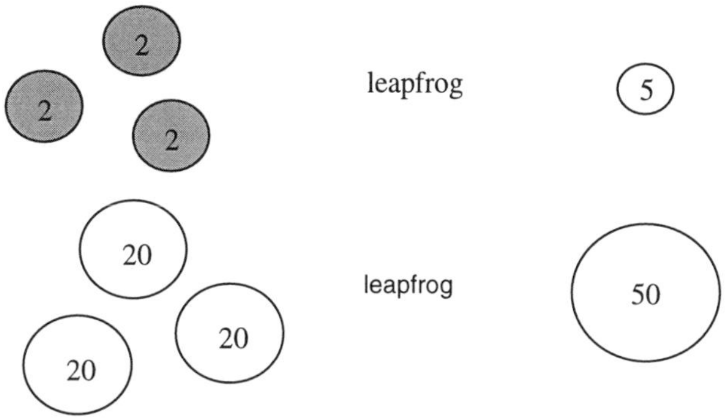

Figure 10.3 Two examples of leapfrogging

Fortunately, though, any leapfrogging situations are covered by other coins: any combination that leapfrogs 5p can be covered in fewer coins by using the 5p and the 1p (2 + 2 + 2 = 5 + 1), and any combination that leapfrogs the 50p is covered by it and the 10p (20 + 20 + 20 = 50 + 10).

Note that the argument above refers to the British coin set and relies on the precise denominations used. There are other coin sets for which optimality is not guaranteed. An example of such a coin set is given in the exercises.

We now need to describe the algorithm in more detail. We call the number of different coins c, and store their denominations in an array value. Since we need to select coins in order of value, we keep the value array sorted, with the lowest values first. We start with the original amount of change to find, n, and with no coins used. Our first choice of coin to investigate is the cth (largest) coin. Then, while there are both coins to choose from and change to find, we see if the present biggest coin can be used. If it is small enough to 'fit', we adjust the amount of change to find accordingly. If is too large, we look to the next largest coin.

We hope that we finish with no change left to find. However, it may be that we end up with a sum to find which is smaller than any of the coins. Clearly, if this happens, we have not satisfactorily answered the problem. We will check for this, returning the answer in a boolean valued variable finished.

This leads to the implementation shown in Fig. 10.4.

At each step of the process either we use a coin, leaving the value of change left to find reduced by at least one, or we do not use it, because it is too big, and go on to look at the next biggest one. Therefore, the maximum number of steps is $n + c$. Of course, we have assumed that the value array is sorted and the effort required to achieve that is at least $O(c \log_2 c)$. However, for any sensible currency, the number of denominations is small, and asymptotically n will predominate. Hence, the algorithm's complexity is $O(n)$.

In C:

```
/* assume value is sorted in ascending order */
to_find = n;
coins = 0;
choice = c;
while (choice>0 && to_find>0)
{
   if (value[choice]<=to_find)
   {
      /* use this coin */
      coins = coins + 1;
      to_find = to_find - value[choice];
   }
   else
   {
      /* try smaller coin */
      choice = choice - 1;
   }
}
finished = (to_find==0);
```

In Ada:

```
-- assume value is sorted in ascending order
to_find := n;
coins := 0;
choice := c;
while choice>0 and to_find>0 loop
  if value(choice)<=to_find
    then
      -- use this coin
      coins := coins + 1;
      to_find := to_find - value(choice);
    else
      -- try smaller coin
      choice := choice - 1;
  end if;
end loop;
finished := (to_find=0);
```

Figure 10.4 Program fragment to find (in a good case) the minimum number of coins to make up some change

EXERCISES 10.1

1. Using the British coin set, calculate the minimum number of coins needed to make change to the following values:

   (i) 9
   (ii) 28
   (iii) 145

2. Improve the efficiency of the algorithm shown by using division.

3. Starting with the British coin set:
   (i) Delete one coin to leave it such that change is not guaranteed.
   (ii) Delete two coins to leave it such that the greedy approach will not work.

4. Before decimalisation in 1971, British coins had the following values:

   - 1d (one penny)
   - 3d
   - 6d
   - 1/- (one shilling)
   - 2/-
   - 2/6 (two shillings and six pence)

   (Note: 12d = 1/-)
   Find a value of change for which the greedy approach does not work for this coin set.

5. Invent another coin set for which the greedy approach will not work.

6. (*Hard*: the technique required is covered in a later chapter.) Write a program which is guaranteed to give the optimal answer for any integer valued coin set.

10.2 Optimal service problem

The optimal service problem involves finding the minimum total waiting time required to serve a group of people in circumstances where they can be served in any order, and where each has a known, fixed service time. Note that in this context a person's waiting time stops increasing once his or her service begins; that is, it does not include the service time.

To illustrate the problem, consider the situation shown in Fig. 10.5 where there are four people, A, B, C and D, and where the numbers indicate the person's service time.

Figure 10.5 Each person has a service time

We start by exploring the problem's behaviour. The obvious (though, as we shall see, non-optimal) way to serve the people is in the order A, B, C, D. This means that A is served immediately and has no waiting time. However, the other three have to wait 3 time units while A is being dealt with, giving a combined waiting time of 9 (3 × 3). When A is finished B's service begins. Of course, the remaining two are again left waiting, this time for the 2 time units that it takes for B to be served, a combined time of 4 (2 × 2), which added to the previous waiting time makes 13. Then C is served, with D waiting another 4 units of time; increasing the total so far to 17. Finally, D is served but, since no one else is waiting, the total waiting time does not increase. Thus, this ordering has led to a total of 17 units of time being spent waiting. We can illustrate this process as in Fig. 10.6.

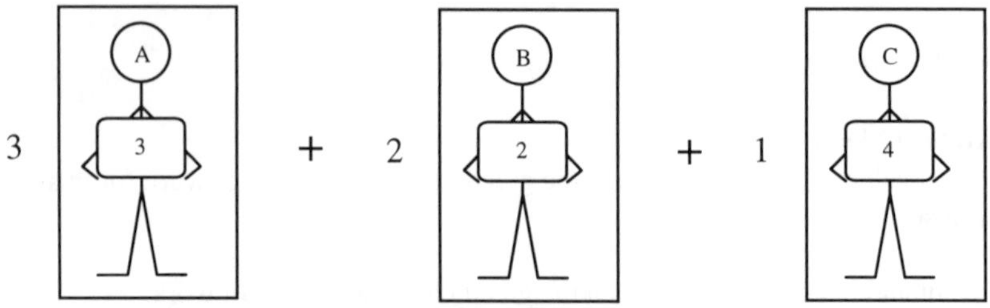

Figure 10.6 Total waiting time is caused by three people waiting as A is served, two while B is served and one while C is served

Before we address the question of how best to control the order in which we serve the people, we need to find a methodical way to calculate the total waiting time. We let n represent the number of people and call the service time of the ith person to be served service_time(i). Then for the first person to be served, the other $n - 1$ people each wait service_time(1). For the service of the second person, $n - 2$ people each wait an additional service_time(2). And so on, until the last person is served, when there is no one waiting. Thus, the total waiting time is given by:

$$(n-1) \times \text{service\_time}(1) + (n-2) \times \text{service\_time}(2) + \ldots$$
$$+ 2 \times \text{service\_time}(1) + 1 \times \text{service\_time}(n-1)$$

We can write this as:

$$\sum_{i=1}^{n-1} (n-i) \times \text{service\_time}(i)$$

To illustrate this process we calculate the total waiting time using a different ordering: D, C, B, A. As shown in Table 10.2, this leads to a total waiting time of 13.

We have now calculated the total waiting time for two different scenarios, and seen that the result is affected by the order in which the people are served. The best result that we have so far is 13. Can we do better? Yes, we can. We are now left with the problem of working out how to do that.

Table 10.2 Total waiting time for the ordering D, C, B, A

Person served	*Service time*	*Number waiting*	*Extra waiting time*	*Total waiting time*
D	1	3	3	3
C	4	2	8	11
B	2	1	2	13
A	3	0	0	13

Clearly one way to solve the problem is to use the brute strength approach. This involves calculating the time required for each ordering, and selecting the shortest. With four people there are 4! (24) orderings. We list these permutations and their service times (calculated using the formula) in Table 10.3.

Table 10.3 Total waiting time for each possible ordering

Order	*Total time*	*Order*	*Total time*
ABCD	17	CABD	20
ABDC	14	CADB	19
ACBD	19	CBAD	19
ACDB	18	CBDA	17
ADBC	13	CDAB	17
ADCB	15	CDBA	16
BACD	16	DABC	11
BADC	13	DACB	13
BCAD	17	DBAC	10
BCDA	15	DBCA	11
BDAC	11	DCAB	14
BDCA	12	DCBA	13

By inspecting the tables we can see that the best we can do is a time of 10, which comes when we serve the people in the order D, B, A, C. (Can you see anything significant about this ordering?) The problem with this method is that it is hopelessly inefficient because, in the general case, there are $n!$ permutations to analyse.

The greedy method suggests a much quicker solution: we serve the people in order of increasing service time. That is, we serve the person with the shortest time first, then the next quickest, and so on until finally we serve the person who is slowest.

We need to justify that this is indeed optimal. To do this is simple. Consider any two people, x and y, whose service times are given by service_time(x) and service_time(y). Suppose x is faster to serve. That is:

service_time(x) <service_time(y)

We argue by contradiction. First, we make the assumption that the optimal route serves y before x. In that case, x waits for service_time(y) while y is being served, contributing service_time(y) to the total waiting time. But we can improve on this by swapping the order in which we serve x and y. If we serve x first, then y waits for service_time(x), increasing the total waiting time by service_time(x). And, since service_time(x) is less than service_time(y), this saves them time. Since nothing else about the system is affected, there is a net reduction to the total waiting time. This contradicts the assumption that we had an optimal ordering. The choice of x and y was arbitrary, therefore it follows that for any pair of people the one with the shortest service time should be served first. And, in turn, applying this improvement to every possible pair, it follows that the optimum approach is to serve the people in order of increasing service time.

The algorithm's implementation is simple. We assume the array of service times is sorted, and implement the summation given in the equation above by using a loop. The code is shown in Fig. 10.7.

In C:

```
/* assumes service times are sorted */
total = 0;
for (i=1; i<n; i++)
{
    total = total + (n-i) * service_time[i];
}
```

In Ada:

```
-- assumes service times are sorted
total := 0;
for i in 1..n-1 loop
  total := total + (n-i) * service_time(i);
end loop;
```

Figure 10.7 Program fragment to find the total waiting time

The code in Fig. 10.7 is very quick, requiring just $n - 1$ additions and $n - 1$ multiplications to come up with the answer. However, we have to be careful. We have assumed that the service times are sorted. With the coin change problem, we said the cost of the sorting there would be insignificant. But, here, because the length of the array to be sorted is the main component of the problem's size, we cannot assume the cost of this is insignificant. The real costs are, therefore, hidden in the assumption, and the algorithm's true complexity comes from the sort. This leaves us with a complexity, at best, of $O(n \log_2 n)$.

EXERCISES 10.2

1. Given three people A, B and C with service times of 5, 2 and 1, respectively, calculate the minimum total waiting time using:

   (i) the brute strength approach
   (ii) the greedy approach

2. (*Hard*) Write a program to solve the problem when there is more than one server.

10.3 Minimum spanning tree

As our final example of how to use the greedy method we will describe an algorithm to solve problems such as this:

- Given a set of towns, and the possibility of building roads that go directly (that is, without any junctions outside of the towns) between some of them, find the length of the shortest road system that can be built which makes it possible to travel between any two towns (Fig. 10.8).

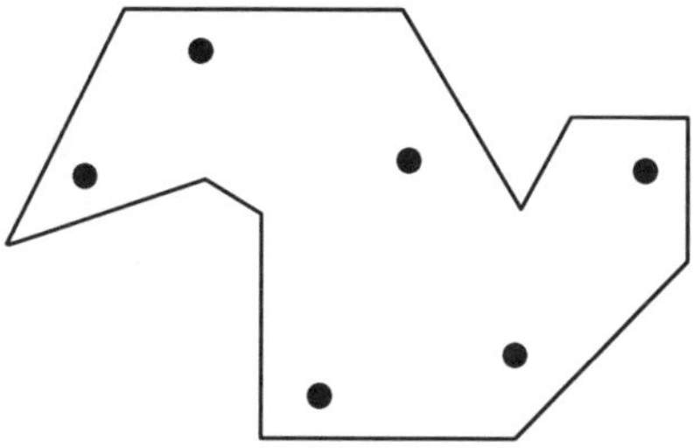

What length of road is needed to connect all the towns on the island?

Figure 10.8 Diagram of an island and its towns

There is, of course, no need to be that specific. The problem generalises to a well known problem in computer science: find the length of the minimum spanning tree of a graph.

Before we go further it is important to ensure that we understand these terms. This is done in the revision box below.

REVISION: GRAPHS

Enough of the terminology of graphs is defined here to understand the problem at hand.

A *graph* is formed from *vertices* (also called *nodes*) and *edges*. An example, with 6 vertices and 6 edges, is illustrated in (A).

In a *weighted graph* each of the edges is given a weight. This can represent anything, for instance distance, time or cost. A weighted graph is shown in (B).

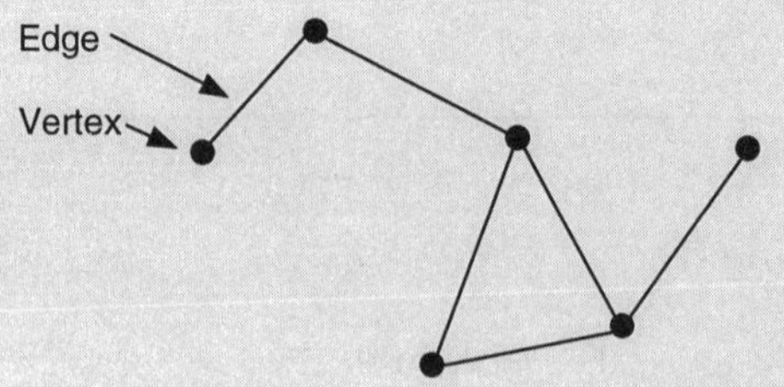

(A)

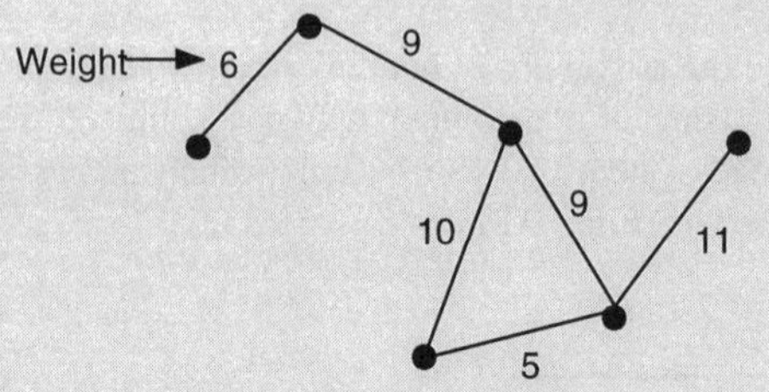

(B)

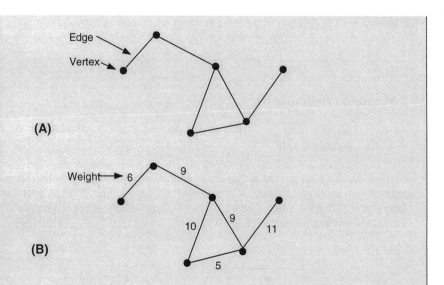

Notice that in both (A) and (B) the edges are *undirected* (that is, two-way, with no sense of direction). This is what we need to model our present problem. However, in different circumstances we might be concerned with directed graphs in which the edges are one-way.

A graph is *connected* if it is possible to get from any vertex to any other vertex. So, for instance, both (A) and (B) are connected, but (C) is not.

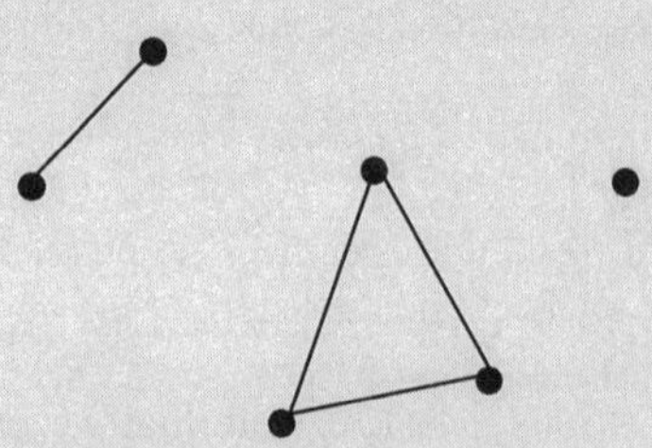

(C)

A *tree* is a connected graph which has no loops (*cycles*). None of the graphs above is a tree, but (D) is.

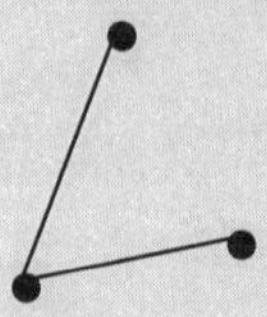

(D)

Finally, a *spanning* tree is a tree which includes every one of a graph's vertices. An example is shown in (E).

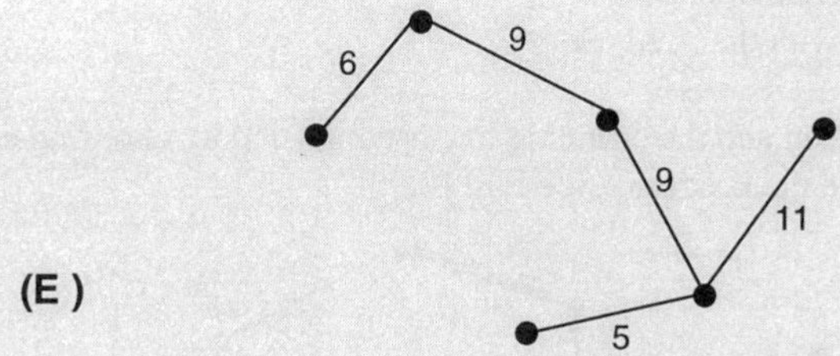

(E) is a tree which spans (B). Moreover, with a total length of 40, it is the best we can find.

Our job here is to find the length of the shortest spanning tree in the general case.

In the simplest case a graph will have a single spanning tree, and all we need to do is detect it and find its length. In some other cases a graph will not have a spanning tree, there being insufficient edges to form one, and the algorithm must be able to detect this. In yet other cases, especially where the graph is dense in the sense that there are many edges, there will be more than one spanning tree, and the length of the shortest one has to be found. This, in turn, reduces to deciding which edges to select.

Before we go any further we note that if a graph has n nodes then any spanning tree must have exactly $n - 1$ edges: any fewer and it cannot be connected; any more and it must have a cycle. This follows because we can form any tree by progressively adding adjacent edges to those already chosen, in which case the first edge puts two nodes into the tree and each remaining edge adds an extra node.

Since we want to minimise distance, wherever possible we will want to choose a short edge rather than a long one. Unfortunately, just selecting the $n - 1$ shortest edges will not necessarily lead to a spanning tree: cycles may be formed and some nodes may be missed. So we will have to be more sophisticated.

Fortunately, we do not have to adapt the naive approach very much to get an algorithm (Kruskal's) which does work. First, we sort the edges. Then, we consider them in order of increasing length, and select them subject to the rule:

- Select an edge provided its inclusion does not form a cycle with those already chosen.

We continue like this until either $n - 1$ edges have been chosen, in which case we have a minimum spanning tree, or until we have run out of edges, but without finding enough edges to form a spanning tree, in which case a spanning tree does not exist. We are obliged to justify these claims.

Suppose we finish having selected $n - 1$ edges. Because of the ways the edges were chosen, there are no cycles. Therefore, we have a single tree connecting all the nodes: a spanning tree.

Next we need to justify that we have in fact found a shortest spanning tree. We show this is true by contradiction. Suppose at one stage of the edge selection process edges a_1, a_2, ..., a_i have been chosen. (We call these the A edges.) Suppose that when further edges are chosen, an edge e is overlooked even though:

- e is the shortest of those remaining
- e does not form a cycle with the A edges

Instead, other edges are chosen and the spanning tree is completed by choosing edges $b_{i+1}, \ldots, b_{n-1}$. (We call these the B edges.) See Fig. 10.9.

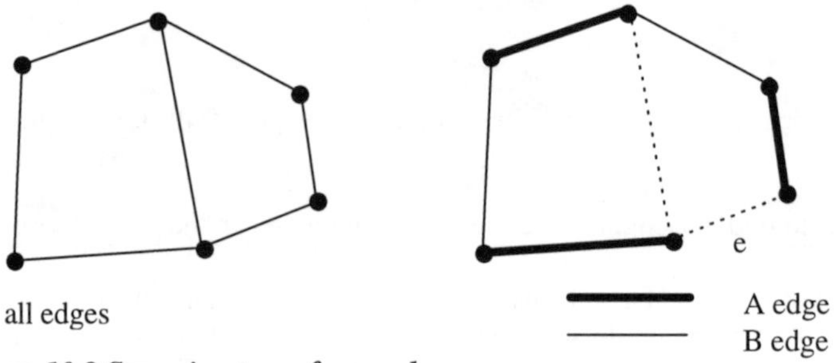

Figure 10.9 Spanning tree of a graph

Now, if we were to add e to the spanning tree formed by the A and B edges, then a cycle must be formed. (This follows because adding any edge to a spanning tree is guaranteed to form a cycle.) The important thing about this cycle is that it is not formed entirely by e and A edges (because the assumption at the start was that this was impossible). Therefore, the cycle must include at least one edge from B. We arbitrarily select one of these edges and call it b. Then, we could produce another spanning tree by including e, but deleting b (it would just unloop the cycle). See Fig. 10.10.

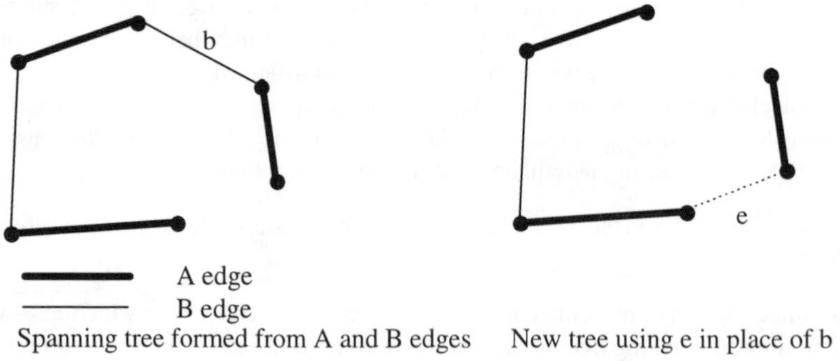

Figure 10.10 Improved spanning tree

But by assumption, each of the B edges is longer than e, so b must be longer than e. Hence, this new tree is shorter than the one we started with. A contradiction. Therefore, the shortest tree should include e.

So we have a method which is guaranteed to give the correct answer, but before we refine the algorithm into code, we will reinforce our understanding of how it works by going through an example. We start with the graph shown in Fig. 10.11.

First, we need to store the edges and sort them into increasing length. We will represent each edge using three values, which give the two end points and the length. So, for instance, (A,B,8) denotes an edge between A and B with a length of 8. This is shown in Table 10.4(a).

Our next job is to sort the edges. This is shown in Table 10.4(b).

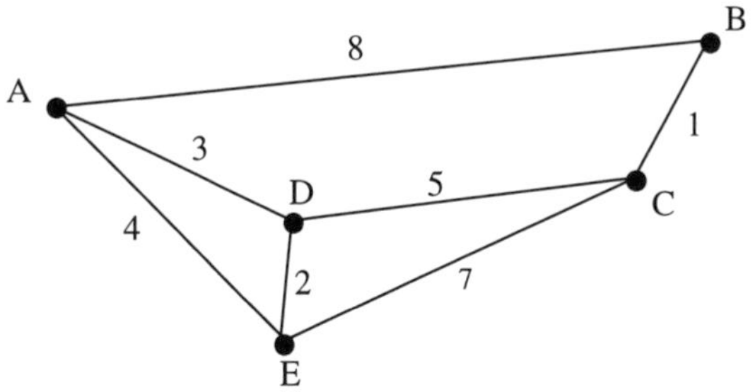

Figure 10.11 Example graph. We need to find the shortest spanning tree

Table 10.4(a) The edges unsorted

Edge	*Length*
(A,B)	8
(A,D)	3
(A,E)	4
(B,C)	1
(C,D)	5
(C,E)	7
(D,E)	2

Table 10.4(b) The edges sorted by length

Edge	*Length*
(B,C)	1
(D,E)	2
(A,D)	3
(A,E)	4
(C,D)	5
(C,E)	7
(A,B)	8

We select the edges in order provided they do not form a cycle with what has gone before. First, we consider the shortest edge, (B,C). Clearly, this cannot form a loop so we select it, giving Fig. 10.12.

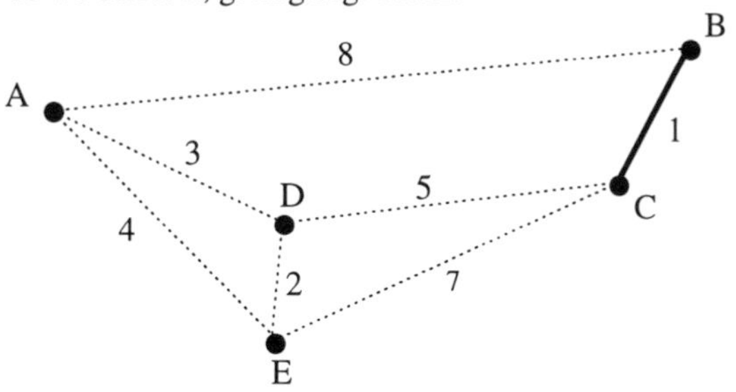

Figure 10.12 The shortest edge is selected

Next we consider (D,E). This does not form a cycle so we select it, to give Fig. 10.13.

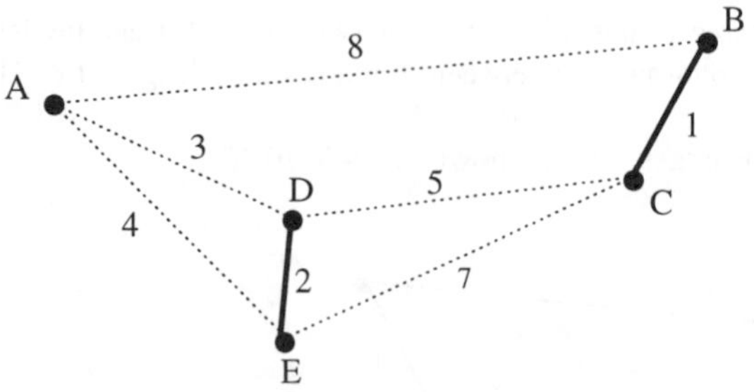

Figure 10.13 The second shortest edge is selected, there being no cycles

Next (A,D). Again no problems (Fig. 10.14).

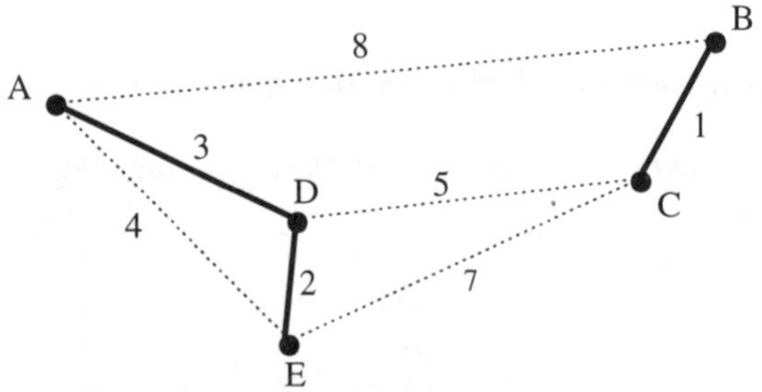

Figure 10.14 The third shortest edge is selected, there being no cycles

The next edge to consider is (A,E). However, this cannot be selected because its inclusion would cause a cycle (ADE) to be formed. Therefore, it is rejected. We go on to look at the next edge, (C,D). It does not cause a cycle, so it is selected (Fig. 10.15).

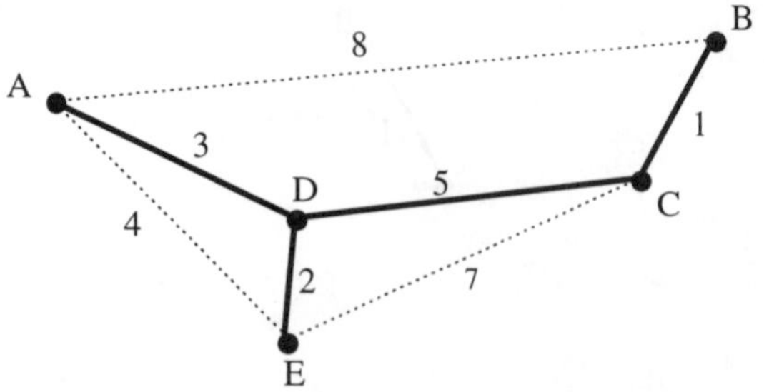

Figure 10.15 The fourth shortest edge is selected, there being no cycles

We now have the four ($n - 1$) edges that we need to form a spanning tree and can stop. Their total length is 11, and we can be sure that this is the best we can do.

So far we have skated over the issue of how to determine whether the addition of a new edge to those already selected will result in a cycle being formed. Cycles may be easy to detect by eye, but that is not an algorithm. Any algorithm must keep track of which nodes are connected, however indirectly. To do this, we can think of groups of connected nodes. That is, groups which have the property that each node can be reached from each other node in the group. Then, if the edge being considered joins two vertices in the same group, it must form a cycle and, consequently, be rejected.

An example is shown in Fig. 10.16. There are two groups and the edge between A and E joins vertices in the same group. Therefore, it forms a cycle and must be rejected.

The process by which the grouping information is kept up to date is not easy to do efficiently. We adopt a simple, but not optimally efficient approach in which for each node we store the number of the connection group to which it belongs. Initially each node is in its own group, giving a connection table that looks like Table 10.5.

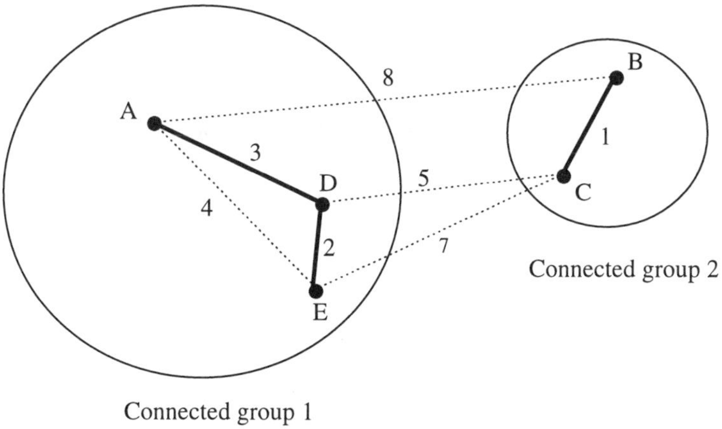

Figure 10.16 Connected groups after three edges have been selected

Table 10.5 The groups initially

Node	*Group*
A	1
B	2
C	3
D	4
E	5

And at the stage shown in Fig. 10.16 the grouping is as shown in Table 10.6.

Table 10.6 The groups after three edges have been selected

Node	Group
A	1
B	2
C	2
D	1
E	1

When an edge is added the groups to which its ends belong are merged. So, if the edge between C and D is added to the partial tree in Fig. 10.16, then all those vertices in group 2 (C's group) are put into group 1 (D's group), and the new group table is shown in Table 10.7.

Table 10.7 The groups after four edges have been selected

Node	Group
A	1
B	1
C	1
D	1
E	1

This process is time consuming, requiring a search through all the vertices each time an edge is added.

One final problem is how to store the edge data. This is most conveniently done by defining an edge type which for each edge holds the end points and the length. This can be done as follows:

In C:

```
typedef struct
   {
      int end1;
      int end2;
      float length;
   } EDGE;
```

In Ada:

```
type EDGE is
   record
      end1: NATURAL;
      end2: NATURAL;
      length: REAL;
   end record;
```

Using this, we can hold the edge information in edges, an array of EDGE. We store the connection group in an array group. The purpose of the remaining variables should be clear from the context.

Putting these ideas together leads to the code in Fig. 10.17.

In C:

```
/* Kruskal's algorithm                                          */
/* Assumes the edges are sorted in order of increasing length */
/* each node is in its own connection group */
```

```
for (i=1; i<=n; i++)
{
   group[i] = i;
}

/* spanning tree length so far */
total_length = 0;

edges_found = 0;
next_edge = 1;

/* Tree has n-1 edges */
while (edges_found<n-1 && next_edge<=number_edges)
{
   /* consider next edge */
   from = edges[next_edge].end1;
   to = edges[next_edge].end2;

   /* ensure no cycle */
   group_from = group[from];
   group_to = group[to];
   if (group_from!=group_to)
   {
      /* no cycle, so can use */
      total_length = total_length + edges[next_edge].length;
      edges_found = edges_found + 1;
      /* update connection groups:                    */
      /* put everything in to's group into from's */
      for (j=1; j<=n; j++)
      {
         if (group[j]==group_to)
         {
            group[j] = group_from;
         }
      }
   }

   /* look at next edge */
   next_edge = next_edge + 1;

}

tree_exists = (edges_found==n-1);
```

In Ada:

```
-- Kruskal's algorithm
-- Assumes the edges are sorted in order of increasing length

-- each node belongs to its own connection group
for i in 1..n loop
   group(i) := i;
end loop;
   -- spanning tree length so far
total_length := 0;
```

```
edges_found := 0;
next_edge := 1;

-- Tree has n-1 edges
while edges_found<n-1 and next_edge<=number_edges loop

  -- consider next edge
  from:= edges(next_edge).end1;
  to:= edges(next_edge).end2;

  -- ensure no cycle
  group_from := group(from);
  group_to := group(to);
  if group_from /= group_to
    then
      -- no cycle, so can use
      total_length := total_length + edges(next_edge).length;
      edges_found := edges_found + 1;
      -- update connection groups: put everything in to's group into from's
      for j in 1..n loop
        if group(j)=group_to
          then
            group(j) := group_from;
        end if;
      end loop;
  end if;
  -- look to next edge
  next_edge := next_edge + 1;

end loop;

tree_exists := (edges_found=n-1);
```

Figure 10.17 Program fragment to implement Kruskal's algorithm

To describe the algorithm's complexity, we let E represent the number of edges and, as everywhere above, n the number of nodes. First, we note that much of the effort required to solve the problem is hidden in the assumption that the edges are sorted. This step has, at best, complexity $O(E \log_2 E)$. As far as the explicit algorithm is concerned we have two constraints: the need to find $n - 1$ edges, which for each edge requires n operations to update the connection groups, so this part of the algorithm has complexity $O(n^2)$; potentially the need to loop through all the edges, requiring $O(E)$ operations. Thus, the complexity of the whole algorithm is determined by the density of the edges. If there are few edges, $E \log_2 E < n^2$ and the connection group update is the predominating factor. If the graph is dense, that is E is close to n^2, then the sort predominates.

EXERCISES 10.3

1. Find a minimum spanning tree and its length for the graphs in Fig. 10.18.

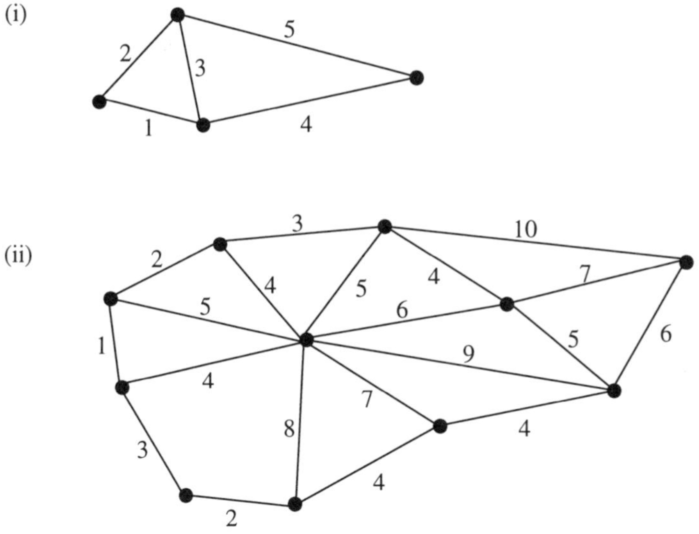

Figure 10.18 Graphs for Question 1

2. Adapt the algorithm so that the minimum spanning tree itself, not just its length, is calculated.

3. Suggest improvements to the subtask of updating the connection group information as edges are added.

Summary

- The greedy method selects the most attractive option at each step.
- Greedy algorithms, as opposed to heuristics, lead to optimal solutions.
- Where greedy algorithms work they are efficient.
- When a greedy algorithm is used a justification must be made that it leads to an optimal answer.
- Algorithms described:

—coin change
—optimal service
—minimum spanning tree.

11

DYNAMIC PROGRAMMING:
ONE DIMENSIONAL PROBLEMS

OBJECTIVES

In this chapter you will learn:

- the dynamic programming method
- how to use dynamic programming
- algorithms for the following problems
  —factorial
  —power
  —vending machine

In Chapter 9 we looked at the divide and conquer approach to solving problems. That method is a top-down approach. It involves partitioning a problem into smaller pieces; solving each of these, which itself often involves breaking them down into still smaller pieces, and then combining these partial solutions to come up with a solution to the whole problem. Dynamic programming also solves smaller problems and combines their results to solve a bigger problem. But, by contrast, it is bottom-up; working from smaller problems to bigger problems. It solves all smaller problems, storing intermediate results, where necessary, to use to help solve bigger problems. It continues building in this way until the original problem can be solved. Where it is applicable, dynamic programming can lead to elegant algorithms that are very efficient.

DYNAMIC PROGRAMMING METHOD
To solve a problem of size n:

- Solve a problem of size 0, and store the result.
- Use this result to solve a problem of size 1, and store the result.
- Use previous results to solve a problem of size 2, and store the result.
  ⋮
- Use previous results to solve a problem of size $n - 1$, and store the result.
- Use previous results to solve the original problem of size n.

The above explanation only tells us what to do with problems whose size is defined by a single number. An example of this type of problem, one which we will look at below, is the calculation of a factorial. Its size is specified by a single number (e.g. 5!, is a problem of size 5). Such problems can be said to be one dimensional. Other problems are more complex, with their 'size' being determined by two or more values. The dynamic programming method generalises to such multi-dimensional problems. These will be discussed in the next chapter. For the rest of this chapter we will be concerned only with one-dimensional problems, and we will illustrate the method by looking at a number of examples of increasing difficulty.

11.1 Factorial problem

To illustrate the differences between the approaches we will look at the problem of working out the factorial of a number.

REVISION
n factorial, written $n!$, is defined as the result of multiplying together all the numbers from 1 to n. So, for instance:
$3! = 1 \times 2 \times 3 = 6$
As a special case, 0! is defined to equal 1.
An alternative, recursive, definition of factorial is:
$0! = 1$
$n! = n \times (n-1)! \qquad \text{for } n > 0$
Factorial is used in many areas, especially in probability theory and statistics.

Using the recursive definition, a solution can be found both by a divide and conquer, top-down approach and by a dynamic programming, bottom-up approach.

To calculate 3! by a divide and conquer approach you would work like this:

$3! = 3 \times 2!$	by the recursive definition
$= 3 \times 2 \times 1!$	"
$= 3 \times 2 \times 1 \times 0!$	"
$= 3 \times 2 \times 1 \times 1$	by definition, the base case
$= 6$	

Using the dynamic programming approach you would work like this:

$0! = 1$	by definition
$1! = 1 \times 0!$	by the recursive definition
$= 1 \times 1$	we know from the above result that 0!=1
$= 1$	
$2! = 2 \times 1!$	by the recursive definition
$= 2 \times 1$	we know from the above result that 1!=1
$= 2$	
$3! = 3 \times 2!$	by the recursive definition
$= 3 \times 2$	we know from the above result that 2!=2
$= 6$	

It is also worth comparing the code. The divide and conquer approach, by working top down, lends itself to recursive programs. Hence, the program fragment in Fig. 11.1.

In C:

```
int factorial(int n)
{
   if (n==0)
   {
      return 1;
   }
   else
   {
      return n * factorial(n-1);
   }
}
```

In Ada:

```
function factorial(n: NATURAL) return NATURAL is
begin
  if n=0
    then
      return 1;
    else
      return n * factorial(n-1);
  end if;
end;
```

Figure 11.1 Code for the factorial function using recursion

The dynamic programming approach, by working bottom up, lends itself to iteration (Fig. 11.2).

In C:

```
factorial = 1;
for (i=1; i<=n; i++)
{
   factorial = i * factorial;
}
```

In Ada:

```
factorial := 1;
for i in 1..n loop
  factorial := i * factorial;
end loop;
```

Figure 11.2 Program fragment to find factorial using iteration

EXERCISES 11.1

The Fibonacci numbers sequence starts with 1 and 1, and continues by forming each succeeding number from the sum of the two preceding values. This process gives:

1, 1, 2, 3, 5, 8, 13 .....

1. Write down the next three Fibonacci numbers.

2. Write code fragments to generate the *n*th Fibonacci number using:

   (i) divide and conquer
   (ii) dynamic programming

3. Calculate the complexity of each approach. Which is better?

11.2 Power problem

In this example we will develop an efficient algorithm to find x to the power n, for $n \geq 0$. Most programming languages provide a way to do this directly. For instance, in Ada we can write x**n. However, finding a solution ourselves is useful because it clearly shows the power of dynamic programming.

REVISION

x to the power n, which is written x^n, means 1 multiplied by x, n times. So for instance:

$x^2 = 1 \times x \times x$, and

$x^3 = 1 \times x \times x \times x$

A special case is x^0 which is defined to equal 1.

The indices rule states that, provided the base, the 'bottom bit', is the same, then the multiple of two numbers can be found by adding their indices. For instance,

$$\begin{aligned} 2^2 \times 2^3 &= 2^{(2+3)} \\ &= 2^5 \end{aligned}$$

To check this, we will do it longhand:

$$\begin{aligned} 2^2 \times 2^3 &= (2 \times 2) \times (2 \times 2 \times 2) \\ &= 4 \times 8 \\ &= 32 \\ &= 2^5 \end{aligned}$$

A similar rule applies for division, in which case the indices are subtracted.

Letting xn represent x^n, the definition leads directly to the iterative solution shown in Fig. 11.3.

In C:	In Ada:

`xn = 1.0;`
`for (i=1; i<=n; i++)`
`{`
`   xn = x * xn;`
`}`
	`xn := 1.0;`
	`for i in 1..n loop`
	`  xn := x * xn;`
	`end loop;`

Figure 11.3 Program fragment to find x^n using iteration

This solution requires n operations, giving a complexity of $O(n)$. It does the job but, as always, we want to know, is there a faster way?

We would be able to make faster progress if each iteration did more than just multiply by x. We can do just that at each iteration by squaring what we have already found. As can be seen in Fig. 11.4 the size of the jump increases at each step, and covers ground much more quickly.

Multiplying by x at each iteration gives:

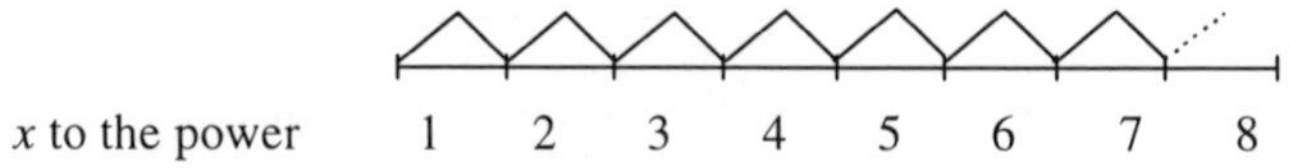

Squaring at each iteration gives:

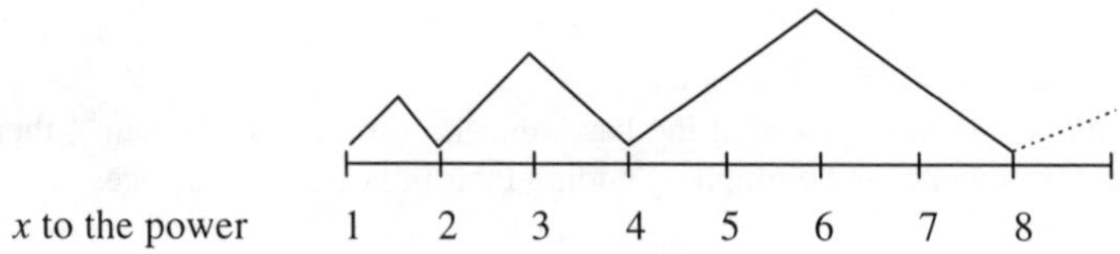

Figure 11.4 x^n can be calculated incrementally or, better, by using lengthening 'jumps'

Using the indices rule (see revision box on previous page) it follows that:

$x^n = x^{n/2} \times x^{n/2}$ for n an even number
$x^n = x^{n/2} \times x^{(n/2)+1}$ for n an odd number

For instance, $x^4 = x^2 \times x^2$ and $x^5 = x^2 \times x^3$. This suggests a divide and conquer approach. We can solve a problem by dividing it into pieces approximately half the original size, solving these, and conquering the original problem by multiplying these parts. This seems efficient because, by multiplying the parts together, we move from a solution to a problem of size $n/2$ (we assume $n/2$ is an integer, that is, n is even, but the principle still holds for n odd) to one of size n in just one step. This compares with the $n/2$ iterations required by the iterative solution to get the same result. So, for instance, the above rule allows us to calculate x^{10} in just one step ($x^5 \times x^5$) once the value of x^5 is known, rather than the five steps required by the direct iterative method. This can be implemented as in Fig. 11.5.

In C:

```
float xn(float x, int n)
{
   if (n==0)
   {
      return 1.0;
   }
   else
   {
      if (n==1)
      {
         return x;
      }
      else
      {
         return xn(x,n/2)  *  xn(x,(n+1)/2);
      }
   }
}
```

In Ada:

```
function xn (x: REAL; n:NATURAL) return REAL is
begin
  if n=0
    then
      return 1.0;
    elsif n=1
      then
        return x;
      else
        return xn(x, n/2) * xn(x, (n+1)/2);
  end if;
end;
```

Figure 11.5 Code for the x^n function using recursion

REVISION: INTEGER DIVISION
Care needs to be taken with the operator / . Both Ada and C interpret / as integer division; returning the integer part of the arithmetic result. For instance, 4/2 evaluates to 2, and 5/2 evaluates to 2.

Unfortunately, this algorithm is not at all efficient. This can be seen by looking at how the recursive calls are made. See Fig. 11.6.

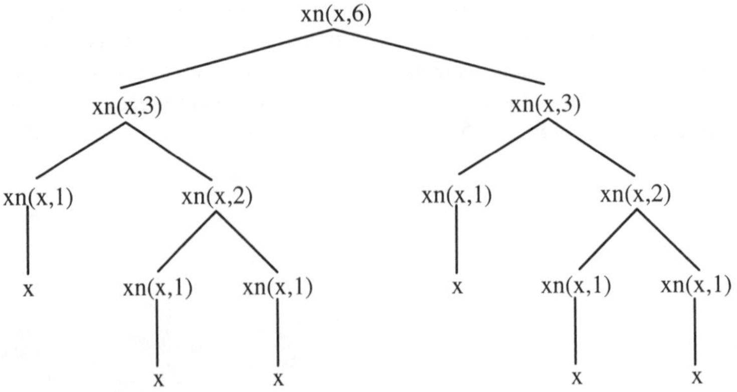

Figure 11.6 Function calls to find x^6 recursively, note the repeated work

The break up of the problem stops only when n is one. This gives n leaves, all of which are the same, xn(x,1). This means, in effect, having to calculate x to the power 1, that is x, n times. Then, working up the tree, each higher node requires an additional multiplication. So, higher powers require a total of $n - 1$ multiplications (that is, 5 in the above tree, for $n = 6$), which is almost the same as the iterative solution. In fact, this algorithm is slower than the iterative approach, because the recursion has its own overheads.

The reason for the above approach's inefficiency is that work is being repeated. x^1 is found 6 times, x^2 twice and x^3 twice. Obviously, an efficient algorithm would avoid doing this, and this is where dynamic programming fits in.

A direct dynamic programming approach is essentially the same as the first approach. It works out all the smaller powers but, in addition, stores the intermediate values as it goes along. With the intermediate values stored in an array, xstore, this leads to the code in Fig. 11.7:

In C:

```
xstore[0] = 1.0;
for (i=1; i<=n; i++)
{
   xstore[i] = x*xstore[i-1];
}
```

In Ada:

```
xstore(0) := 1.0;
for i in 1..n loop
  xstore(i) := x*xstore(i-1);
end loop;
```

Figure 11.7 Program fragment to find x^n using dynamic programming inefficiently

We can be more efficient than this if, once again, we can get more out of the multiply operation. This time we will make efficient use of the squaring technique shown earlier and, therefore, we will not repeat work. The approach we adopt is a variant on the full dynamic programming approach: we will only work out as many intermediate calculations as we need.

We start at x^1, and store this value; square it to calculate x^2, and store this value; then x^4, and so on. We continue doing this until we have passed *n*. We now hold enough intermediate information to get the final answer. To get this, we work backwards, using whatever intermediate results are needed to build up the final solution. So, for instance, to calculate 2^7, we do the intermediate calculations shown in Fig. 11.8.

	1	2	3	4
xstore	2	4	16	256
Stores 2 to the power	1	2	4	8

Figure 11.8 Intermediate calculations to find x^7

This is as far as we go in making intermediate calculations. At this stage we have up to 2^8, which is more than we need. We cannot get the answer to 2^7 from the table directly. The closest we can get without going too far is 2^4, but this leaves us with three (7 – 4) powers to find. Again, this cannot be found directly from the table, the best we can do is to use 2^2. We are left with one power (3 – 2) to find. This can be obtained directly from the table. In effect, what we have done is to make use of the fact that:

$$x^7 = x^4 \times x^2 \times x^1$$

The algorithm can be coded as in Fig. 11.9.

In C:

```
/* store intermediate results */
xstore[1] = x;
i = 1;
power = 1;
while (power<n)
{
   i = i + 1;
   power = 2 * power;
   xstore[i] = xstore[i-1] * xstore[i-1];
}

/* work backwards to get the answer */
used = 0;
result = 1;
while (used<n)
{
   if (used+power<=n)
   {
      result = result * xstore[i];
      used = used + power;
   }
```

```
    power = power / 2;
    i = i - 1;
}
```

In Ada:

```
-- store intermediate results
xstore(1) := x;
i := 1;
power := 1;
while power<n loop
  i := i + 1;
  power := 2 * power;
  xstore(i) := xstore(i-1) * xstore(i-1);
end loop;

-- work backwards to get the answer
used := 0;
result := 1;
while used<n loop
  if used+power<=n
    then
      result := result * xstore(i);
      used := used + power;
  end if;
  power := power / 2;
  i := i - 1;
end loop;
```

Figure 11.9 Program fragment to find x^n using dynamic programming efficiently

EXERCISES 11.2

1. The above algorithm can be improved: there is no need to store the intermediate values. Write a program fragment to show how this can be done. (*Hint*: convert n to binary.)

11.3 Vending machine problem

We will consider a simple vending machine which accepts only 1 penny, 2 pence and 5 pence coins. The problem is to find how many ways there are of inputting coins to a total value of n pence.

Before looking for a general algorithm to solve this problem, let us make sure we understand what we are trying to do. We will do this by working through some simple examples by hand and exhaustively listing all possible ways to input a particular total value of n pence.

For a total of 1 there is only one way to make this sum, simply a single 1 penny.

For a total of 2 we have a choice, either two 1s, or one 2. This gives 2 possible ways.

For a total of 3 the following coin inputs into the vending machine are possible:

1 1 1
2 1
1 2

Do you see a pattern developing? So far the number of possibilities has in each case been equal to n. However, in general this is not the case. The next example will show this.

For a total of 4 the following inputs are possible:

1 1 1 1
2 1 1
1 2 1
1 1 2
2 2

That gives a total of 5 possible ways of inputting the coins.

For 5 the following combinations of inputs are possible:

1 1 1 1 1
2 1 1 1
1 2 1 1
1 1 2 1
1 1 1 2
2 2 1
2 1 2
1 2 2
5

So there is a total of 9 possible ways.

EXERCISES 11.3

1. Calculate the number of ways of inputting the following totals:
   (i) 6
   (ii) 7
2. (i) Construct a table using these results together with those for 1 to 5 shown in the text.
   (ii) Describe the pattern these results show.
3. Use the pattern described in Q.2 to calculate the number of ways of inputting a total of 10 pence. (Do not attempt to list all the possibilities exhaustively. It will take too long.)

We will now search for an algorithm to solve this problem. Let us begin by defining ways(n) to be the number of ways of inputting the coins to make a total of n pence. Once n is more than 5, although we have many choices as to the order in which the coins are input, one thing is sure: the first coin input must be a 1, a 2 or a 5 pence coin. Suppose it is a 1 penny coin, then we have still to input a total of $n - 1$ pence, and the number of ways to do this is given by ways($n - 1$). Alternatively, the first coin input could be 2 pence, leaving us with a total of $n - 2$ pence still to input, and the number of ways to do this is given by ways($n - 2$). Or, again, the first coin input could be a 5 pence, leaving us with a total of $n - 5$ pence still to input, and the number of ways to do this is given by ways($n - 5$). Since we can follow the 1, the 2 or the 5 pence route to start with, and these give different combinations, the total number of ways of inputting n pence is the total for $n - 1$ plus the total for $n - 2$ plus the total for $n - 5$. Thus, we get the recurrence relationship:

$$\text{ways}(n) = \text{ways}(n-1) + \text{ways}(n-2) + \text{ways}(n-5) \qquad \text{for } n > 5$$

(Notice the similarity between this and the Fibonacci sequence, covered in Ex. 11.1.) This is illustrated in Fig.11.10.

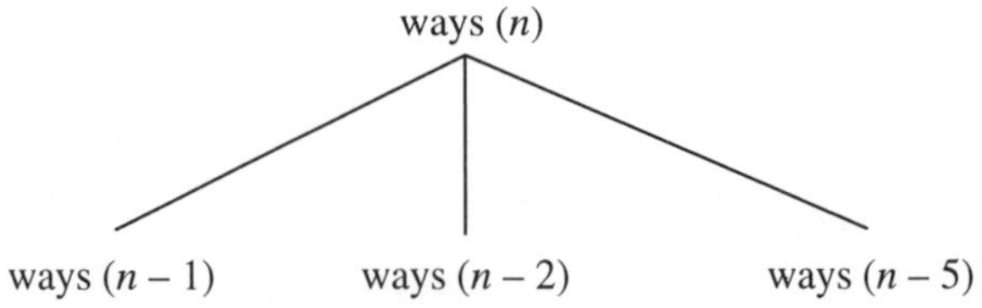

Figure 11.10 Recursive calls generated by the use of a 1p, a 2p or a 5p

There is still the problem of how to get started. That is, what to do for n less than or equal to 5. This is not a problem, because we have already worked these numbers out explicitly:

ways(1) = 1
ways(2) = 2
ways(3) = 3
ways(4) = 5
ways(5) = 9

To see how we can use these rules, we will consider the number of ways to make 6 pence. Working top down we could progress as in Fig. 11.11 (note, to clarify what is happening ways has been omitted from each node). Here, a move diagonally down to the left represents the use of a 1 penny coin, a move directly downwards a 2 pence coin, and a move diagonally down and to the right a 5 pence coin. A sequence of moves ending at a 0 represents a possible way to input 6 pence. Therefore, the number of the leaves of the tree gives the number of ways. In this case, 15, as expected. However, this approach is very inefficient. Why?

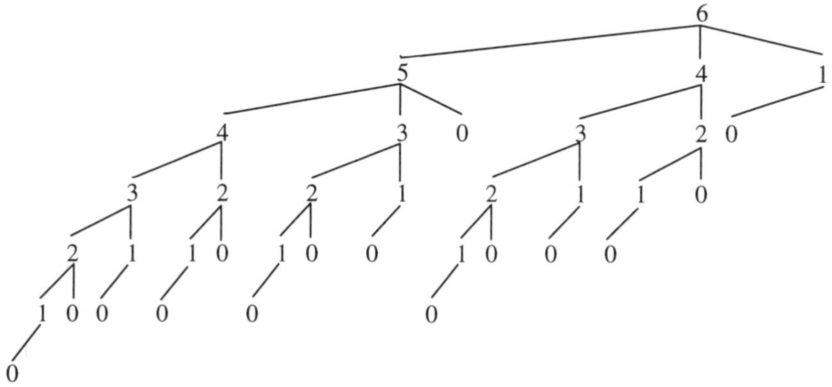

Figure 11.11 Values passed to a recursive function to find the number of ways, note the repeated work

The problem with the above approach is that, once again, much work is repeated. For instance, in calculating ways(6), ways(4) occurs in two places in the tree and, therefore, has to be calculated twice. Indeed, as an approximation, whenever n is increased by 1, the number of leaves trebles, giving a complexity of $O(3^n)$. Clearly, a more efficient algorithm could be found by ensuring that having worked out a result, we stored it and used it for future occasions. This is what we will do next.

The dynamic programming approach is opposite to the above: it works bottom up. To see how this works, we will calculate ways(7). We already know how many ways there are to input coins to the value of from 1 to 5 pence. Our first step is to calculate ways(6). To do this we use the recurrence relation:

$$\begin{aligned} \text{ways}(6) &= \text{ways}(5) + \text{ways}(4) + \text{ways}(1) \\ &= 9 + 5 + 1 \\ &= 15 \end{aligned}$$

Then, using this intermediate result, we calculate ways(7):

$$\begin{aligned} \text{ways}(7) &= \text{ways}(6) + \text{ways}(5) + \text{ways}(2) \\ &= 15 + 9 + 2 \\ &= 26 \end{aligned}$$

Notice that we steadily build up to the answer, with each step taking only two calculations.

In the general case, this process is repeated until n is reached, giving the algorithm in Fig. 11.12.

In C:

```
ways[1] = 1;
ways[2] = 2;
ways[3] = 3;
ways[4] = 5;
ways[5] = 9;
for (i=6; i<=n; i++)
{
   ways[i] = ways[i-1] + ways[i-2] + ways[i-5];
}
```

In Ada:

```
ways(1) := 1;
ways(2) := 2;
ways(3) := 3;
ways(4) := 5;
ways(5) := 9;
for i in 6..n loop
  ways(i) := ways(i-1) + ways(i-2) + ways(i-5);
end loop;
```

Figure 11.12 Program fragment to find the number of ways using dynamic programming

This algorithm is very efficient. The main work is being done by the plus inside the loop. This operation is met twice in each of the $n - 5$ steps as we work from ways(6) to ways(n), giving an algorithm of complexity $O(n)$. (We are making a simplification here. We assume that the effort required by the addition operation is constant. That is, the 'cost' of addition does not increase as ways increases. So, for instance, it is assumed that 15 + 9 takes the same time to calculate as 12 345 + 6789.)

Summary

- Dynamic programming:
  —is a bottom-up approach
  —solves all smaller problems
  —stores intermediate results
  —solves bigger problems using the stored results for smaller problems.
- Dynamic programming can give efficient programs, even leading to algorithms of complexity $O(n)$ where other methods would lead to algorithms of complexity $O(2^n)$.
- Algorithms described:
  —factorial
  —power
  —vending machine.

12

DYNAMIC PROGRAMMING: MULTI-DIMENSIONAL PROBLEMS

OBJECTIVES

In this chapter you will learn

- the dynamic programming method for multi-dimensional problems
- how to use multi-dimensional dynamic programming
- algorithms for the following problems
  - —routes
  - —0–1 knapsack
  - —shortest path

In Chapter 11 we looked at the dynamic programming method applied to one-dimensional problems. We saw there that dynamic programming can produce elegant, efficient algorithms, even when other methods lead to very inefficient ones. In this chapter we extend that work by looking at problems which are multi-dimensional. By this we mean problems which require more than one number to specify their size. That is, problems that can get 'bigger' in more than one way. For instance, and this is a problem which we will look at later in the chapter (actually, we will look at a rather less politically correct version of it), consider the investment decisions of a company. Suppose the company is constrained by the amount of capital it has to invest, a figure which cannot be increased however good the available investment opportunities are, and a number of possible projects in which to invest the money. Furthermore, suppose the cost of each of these projects is known with certainty in advance, as is the profit from each of them. The problem for the company is to choose that portfolio of projects which maximises its total profits subject to the constraint of the limited amount of capital it has to invest. Clearly, this problem can become bigger and harder to solve in two ways: there may be more projects to choose from; there may be more money to invest. If either increases, the problem's size increases, and it becomes harder to solve. (At the limit, a company with no money to invest or no projects to invest in has, at least from the algorithmic point of view, no problem to solve.) There are two variables, so the problem can be said to be two-dimensional.

The general procedure for multi-dimensional dynamic programming is similar to the one-dimensional case: solve all smaller problems and use these results to solve bigger problems, but now we will work in two, or more, dimensions. In effect, this means completing a table of intermediate results.

DYNAMIC PROGRAMMING METHOD: TWO DIMENSIONS

To solve a problem of size $m \times n$:

1. Create a table with m rows and n columns.
2. For row 1 (problems of size 1 in the first dimension), solve for the first column (problems of size 1 in the second dimension) and store the result;
   use this result to solve for the second column, and store this result;
   ⋮
   use these results to solve for the nth column.
3. Go through the same process for row 2, using results from row 1 where necessary.
   ⋮
4. Go through the same process for row m, using results from previous rows where necessary.

The process where, for instance, a new value depends on two previously calculated results is shown in Fig. 12.1.

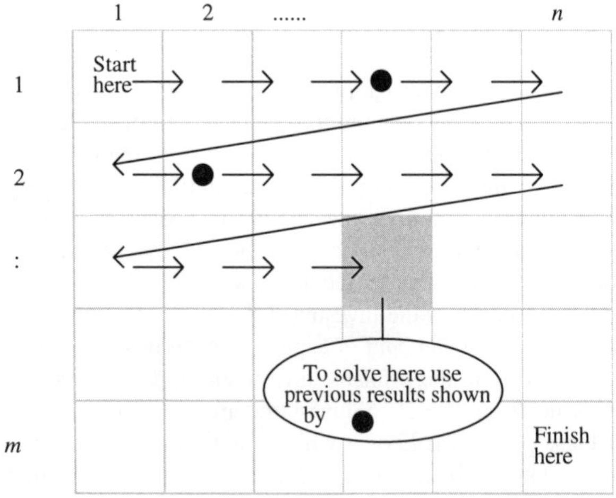

Figure 12.1 The two-dimensional dynamic programming approach

We will now look at three examples of how to use multi-dimensional dynamic programming.

12.1 Routes problem

The first problem we are going to study is the routes problem. This involves a rectangular grid on which it is only possible to move rightwards and downwards; moves to the left and upwards are not allowed. A route involves moving from the top left to the bottom right of the grid. Two routes are said to be different if they differ by at least one edge. That is, they are considered different even if they have some, but not all, edges in common. The problem is to calculate the number of different routes from the top left corner to the bottom right corner.

For instance, given a two by two grid, forming a square with sides of length one, there are two routes as shown in Fig. 12.2.

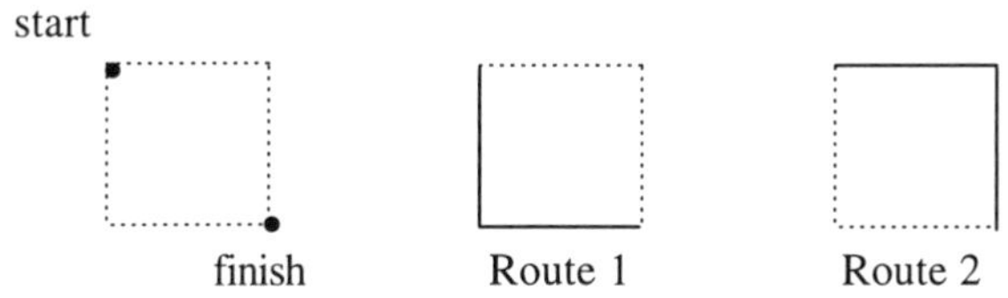

Figure 12.2 A 2 × 2 grid gives two routes

Given a three by three grid there are six routes as shown in Fig. 12.3.

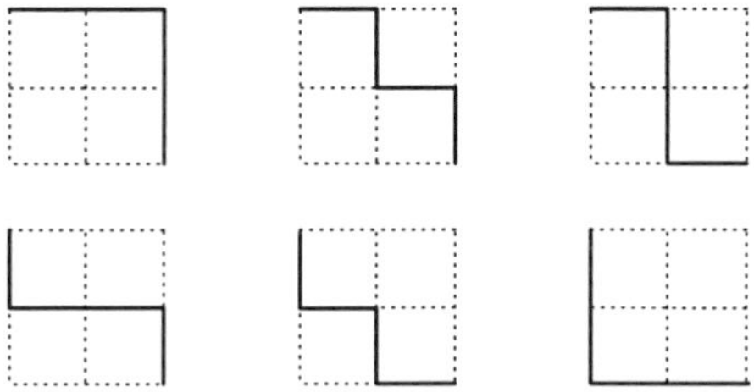

Figure 12.3 A 3 × 3 grid gives six routes

At this stage it is difficult to see a pattern from which we can begin to design an algorithm. We need some help. Dynamic programming will give us that. As usual, we will solve all smaller problems. In this case that means calculating the number of ways of getting from the start to every node in the grid between it and the finish point. (These intermediate nodes represent the smaller problems.) The nodes on the top row can only be reached in one way since backtracking is not allowed, because leftwards and upwards moves are illegal. The same can be said for the nodes on the left-hand side. We can show this in Fig. 12.4 .

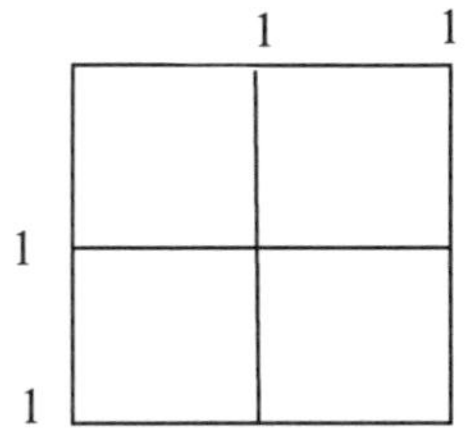

Figure 12.4 There is only one way of getting to nodes on the top row and on the left column

Consider the node which is diagonally down one from the start. This can be reached either from above, which as the diagram shows can itself be reached in one way, or from the left, which can also be reached in one way. This makes a total of two ways, as is shown in Fig. 12.5.

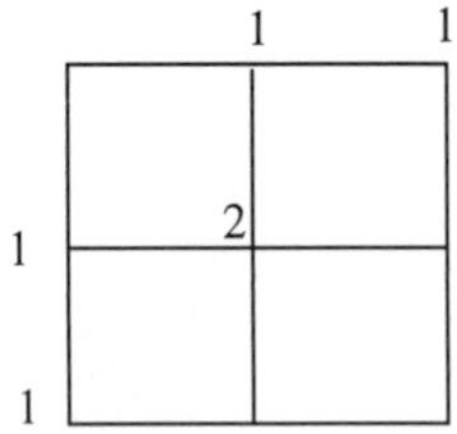

Figure 12.5 The inner node is reachable in two ways

A pattern is now becoming clear: the number of ways to reach a node is the sum of the number of ways of getting to the node above and the number of ways of getting to the node to the left. Hence, the required answer can be found by continuing with the process of adding the number above to the number to the left until the destination is reached. This is shown in Fig. 12.6.

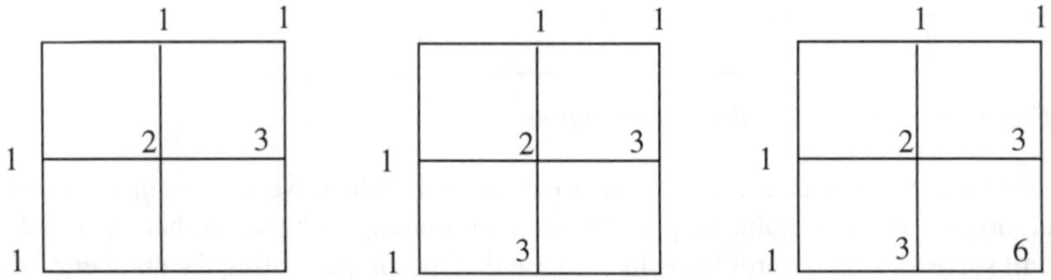

Figure 12.6 Completing the table

We will let m be the number of rows and n the number of columns. Then if ways(i,j) represents the number of routes from the start to row i/column j, then the above process can be written algebraically as:

ways(1, i) = 1
ways(i, 1) = 1
ways(i, j) = ways(i – 1, j) + ways(i, j – 1) for $i > 1$ and $j > 1$

This leads to the code in Fig. 12.7.

The main body of work in this algorithm is being done in the nested loop, where the table is being completed. At each iteration one addition is carried out. So, the complexity is $O(m.n)$.

In C:

```
/* set up top and sides */
for (i=1; i<=n; i++)
{
   ways[1][i] = 1;
}
for (i=1; i<=m; i++)
{
   ways[i][1] = 1;
}

/* fill in the rest of the table */
for (i=2; i<=m; i++)
{
   for (j=2; j<=n; j++)
   {
      ways[i][j] = ways[i-1][j] + ways[i][j-1];
   }
}
```

In Ada:

```
-- set up top and sides
for i in 1..n loop
  ways(1, i) := 1;
end loop;
for i in 1..m loop
  ways(i, 1) := 1;
end loop;
-- fill in the rest of the table
for i in 2..m loop
  for j in 2..n loop
    ways(i, j) := ways(i-1, j) + ways(i, j-1);
  end loop;
end loop;
```

Figure 12.7 Program fragment to calculate the number of ways using dynamic programming

EXERCISES 12.1

1. Find the number of routes for grids of the following sizes:

   (i) 2×3
   (ii) 4×4
   (iii) 5×5

2. (i) Write a recursive program to calculate the number of routes.
   (ii) How does its complexity compare with the approach shown?

3. Use a mathematical approach to find a linear time algorithm to solve this problem.

12.2 0–1 knapsack problem

The 0–1 knapsack problem is really just a rephrasing of the investment decision problem seen at the beginning of the chapter. This time the context is that of a burglar breaking into a house. The burglar will carry away the haul in a knapsack which can hold only a limited weight of booty. This constraint weight must be a natural number. The haul will be chosen from the items in the house, each of which has a known 'profit' and weight (again, a natural number). Not unreasonably, an item cannot be selected more than once, hence the '0–1' in the problem's name; that is, an item is either ignored (0) or selected (1). (In terms of the investment problem seen earlier, the size of the knapsack is equivalent in its effect to the capital constraint, and the items in the house are equivalent to the projects which can be invested in.) Before looking at the dynamic programming solution we will consider two alternative approaches.

To illustrate the different approaches, we will explore the problem by looking at a simple example where the weight limit for the knapsack is 4 and there are 4 items, with profits/weights as shown in Table 12.1, from which to choose.

Table 12.1 The weight and profit of each of 4 example items

	A	*B*	*C*	*D*
Weight	2	3	4	1
Profit	5	6	7	2

12.2.1 Brute strength approach

As always, there is the possibility of adopting a brute strength approach. In the present context, this will mean listing all the possible combinations of items, each 'portfolio' (assuming burglars and capitalists use the same language) that can be stolen. Each portfolio must be checked to ensure that it does not weigh more than can be carried away and, if the total weight is allowed, its value compared with that of the best portfolio found so far. If it is better, that value can be updated. This process is continued until all possible portfolios are analysed. Since every possibility is explored, this approach is guaranteed to give the correct answer.

In terms of the example, enumerating all the portfolios gives the results in Table 12.2. By inspection we can see that the best profit available is 8, and that this is attained by stealing items B and D. Although we have an answer, it is clearly very time-consuming to find. When a portfolio is formed an item is either in it or not in it, so each additional item doubles the number of possible portfolios. Thus, if there are n

items to chose from, there are 2^n possible portfolios. For a typical house with hundreds of different items to select from, our burglar is likely to feel uncomfortable carrying out such a lengthy analysis. (In comparison any possible prison sentence incurred for committing the burglary will be very short!) A faster approach is, therefore, required.

Table 12.2 Calculating the maximum profit by enumerating all possibilities

Selection	*Total weight*	*Allowed by weight*	*Profit*
none	0	YES	0
A	2	YES	5
B	3	YES	6
C	4	YES	7
D	1	YES	2
A,B	5	NO	-
A,C	6	NO	-
A,D	3	YES	7
B,C	7	NO	-
B,D	4	YES	8
C,D	5	NO	-
A,B,C	9	NO	-
A,B,D	6	NO	-
A,C,D	7	NO	-
B,C,D	8	NO	-
A,B,C,D	10	NO	-

12.2.2 Greedy approaches

A greedy approach could be tried. This would work by choosing at each step the 'best' item available and for which there is space, and continuing like that until there are no more items which fit into the remaining space. What is 'best' can be decided in a number of different ways.

The easiest is to choose the most valuable remaining item which can still be carried in the available space. Using the data from Table 12.1, this means selecting item C first (it is the most valuable item), for a profit of 7. However, it takes up all the space leaving no room to select any more items. Thus, the burglar is left with a non-optimal solution.

Alternatively, the best could be chosen by selecting the item which gives the best value for its size (highest profit/weight ratio). In this case: A would be chosen (profit/weight = 2.5), for a profit of 5; then B would be tried (ratio = 2), but there is not enough space left for it, so it cannot be selected; then D would be tried (ratio = 2), it does fit so it can be selected, giving a profit of 2; then C, but again this is too big to fit. This gives a total profit of 7, which is again sub-optimal.

For this problem, then, greedy approaches although quick, and usually giving good estimates of the best available, are not guaranteed to give the best portfolio.

12.2.3 Dynamic programming approach

In dynamic programming we start by solving the simplest of problems. For this problem it must be a house in which there is nothing to steal and in which the burglar's knapsack has zero capacity. Clearly, this situation gives rise to a total profit of 0. Then, even if the knapsack's capacity is expanded step by step to the total weight constraint (4) available, with nothing to steal, the maximum total profit remains at 0. This is shown in the Table 12.3. The top row gives the weight constraint. The first column gives what items are available to be stolen. The other entries show what profits are available.

Table 12.3 For each weight the profit available with no items available to select

Items available/Weight	*0*	*1*	*2*	*3*	*4*
0	0	0	0	0	0

We can extend this by seeing what happens when one item (A) becomes available. Since this weighs 2, it cannot be used unless the knapsack has at least that capacity. Once the knapsack is big enough to hold A, its profit of 5 is available to the burglar. Unfortunately, from the burglar's point of view, however big the knapsack becomes, with just this one item to choose from it is impossible to improve on the profit from this item (remember in the 0–1 knapsack problem an item cannot be stolen twice), and A's contribution is as big as the total profit can become (Table 12.4).

Table 12.4 For each weight the profit available with one item available to select

Items available / Weight	*0*	*1*	*2*	*3*	*4*
0	0	0	0	0	0
1	0	0	5	5	5

As we increase the number of items available and expand the size of the weight constraint there is more choice. This cannot make the burglar worse off. So, with two items (A and B) available, at the very worst the burglar can, simply by ignoring B, do exactly as well was done with just A. However, by choosing B, it may be possible to do better. This time, once the size constraint is at least 3, item B can be chosen. This gives a profit of 6. Although there is now insufficient space to choose A as well, this is an improvement on what A offered. Thus, B should be chosen. The profits from this are shown in Table 12.5.

Table 12.5 For each weight the profit available with two items to select

Items available / Weight	*0*	*1*	*2*	*3*	*4*
0	0	0	0	0	0
1	0	0	5	5	5
2	0	0	5	6	6

With three items (A, B and C) to choose from, there is yet more choice. Again, we cannot do worse than we did with only two items to select from. So, the bottom row of Table 12.5 is the worse we can do. C weighs 4, so it cannot be chosen until the weight constraint is at least that, so the table up to then is the same as with two items. At 4, though, C can be chosen and, since its profit of 7 is better than what we have got so far, it should be chosen. This gives Table 12.6.

Table 12.6 For each weight the profit available with three items to select

Items available / Weight	*0*	*1*	*2*	*3*	*4*
0	0	0	0	0	0
1	0	0	5	5	5
2	0	0	5	6	6
3	0	0	5	6	7

Now for the final step, we consider the case where all 4 items (A, B, C and D) are available. As before, the previous final row (row 3) of the table is the lower limit on the total profit that can be achieved; we may be able to do better, but we cannot do worse. With item D additionally available (weight 1, profit 2), it can be chosen once the weight constraint is 1. Since the previous best profit for this weight was 0, it should certainly be chosen (Table 12.7).

Table 12.7 For each weight the profit available with four items available to select

Items available / Weight	*0*	*1*	*2*	*3*	*4*
0	0	0	0	0	0
1	0	0	5	5	5
2	0	0	5	6	6
3	0	0	5	6	7
4	0	2			

With a weight constraint of 2, there is a choice to make: either select D or be satisfied with what has gone before, which was a profit of 5 without choosing D. If D is chosen, it will give us a profit of 2 directly. But then, since its weight is only 1, there is some weight, 1 (2–1), left over, and we might be able to profit from this. Now for the key point:

we do not need to calculate the best we can do with the remaining weight and the remaining items; we can find this directly from the table of previous results.

The best we can do with the remaining 3 items (A, B and C) and a weight of 1 is given by row 3/column 1 of Table 12.7. That is, a profit of 0. So, if we choose D, the total profit is 2 (2 + 0). Since this is worse than could be done before, the choice should not be made. This leaves the table as shown in Table 12.8.

Table 12.8 Completing the table: 4 items, weight available is 2

Items available/Weight	*0*	*1*	*2*	*3*	*4*
0	0	0	0	0	0
1	0	0	5	5	5
2	0	0	5	6	6
3	0	0	5	6	7
4	0	2	5		

A similar effect occurs when the weight constraint is increased to 3. It is not worth selecting D, and the best profit remains as 6. See Table 12.9.

Table 12.9 Completing the table: 4 items, weight available is 3

Items available / Weight	*0*	*1*	*2*	*3*	*4*
0	0	0	0	0	0
1	0	0	5	5	5
2	0	0	5	6	6
3	0	0	5	6	7
4	0	2	5	6	

Things are rather more interesting when the weight is increased to 4. If D is not chosen, the profit remains as it was for this size but with three items to choose from, at 7 (see row 3/ column 4 in Table 12.9). If D is chosen, then this gives an immediate profit of 2, and leaves us with a weight entitlement of 3 to fill. The best we can do with this and the remaining 3 items is 6, as given in row 3/column 3 of the table. Hence, our total profit is 8 (2 + 6). Thus, D should be chosen, because it increases the profit. The final table is shown in Table 12.10.

Table 12.10 Completing the table: 4 items, weight available is 4

Items available/Weight	*0*	*1*	*2*	*3*	*4*
0	0	0	0	0	0
1	0	0	5	5	5
2	0	0	5	6	6
3	0	0	5	6	7
4	0	2	5	6	8

By describing each step the explanation has been detailed, and this may make this approach seem very complex. However, once the process is understood, following it is simple and rapid: progressively complete the table of best profits found so far by using the following operation:

Fill the next square with the best of:

> the profit above, or
>
> if there is enough space for this item,
> its profit plus the profit for the remaining weight using the remaining items.

The algorithm can be explained algebraically as follows. If w(i) represents the weight of item i, p(i) represents the profit from item i, and profit(i,j) represents the best profit that can be gained by selecting only from the first i items and using up a weight of no more than j, then, either do not choose i, for a profit of profit($i-1$, j) or, if there is space (that is, $j \geq$ w(i)) choose i, for a profit of p(i) + profit($i-1, j-$ w(i)).

Then, since we choose whichever option maximises the profit:

$$\text{profit}(i,j) = \max(\text{profit}(i-1, j), \text{p}(i) + \text{profit}(i-1, j - \text{w}(i)))$$

We will let n represent the number of items to choose from and c represent the weight constraint, and for the other variables we will use the same variable names as above. Then, the algorithm can be implemented as in Fig. 12.8, where max is a function which returns the higher of two values.

In C:

```
/* Initialise first row */
for (i=0; i<=c; i++)
{
   profit[0][i] = 0;
}
/* fill in the table */
for (i=1; i<=n; i++)

{
   for (j=0; j<=c; j++)
   {
      if (j>=w[i])
      {
         profit[i][j] =
            max( profit[i-1][j],
                 p[i] + profit[i-1][j-w[i]] );
      }
      else
      {
         profit[i][j] = profit[i-1][j];
      }
   }
}
```

In Ada:

```
-- Initialise first row
for i in 0..c loop
  profit(0, i) := 0;
end loop;

-- Fill in the table
for i in 1..n loop
  for j in 0..c loop
    if j>=w(i)
      then
        profit(i, j) :=
           max( profit(i-1, j),
              p(i) + profit(i-1, j-w(i)) );
      else
        profit(i, j) := profit(i-1, j);
    end if;
  end loop;
end loop;
```

Figure 12.8 Program fragment solving the 0–1 knapsack problem

To calculate the complexity of this operation, we need to focus on where most of the algorithm's costs are being incurred. Clearly, this is inside the nested loop. The update to profit occurs at most nc times. Which, assuming the cost of each operation is independent of the value of the variables held, gives a complexity of $O(nc)$. This is a vast improvement on the brute strength algorithm. For instance, even for a house with just 20 items to choose from and a knapsack with a capacity of 50, the dynamic programming algorithm is approximately 1000 times faster. (The brute strength approach requires 2^{20} portfolios, approximately 1 000 000, to be analysed; whereas dynamic programming requires the filling of a 20×50 table, that is the evaluation of 1000 entries.)

EXERCISES 12.2

1. Using:
   (i) the brute strength approach
   (ii) the greedy approach
   (iii) dynamic programming

   and given the following items, with weights and profits as shown, find the maximum total profit that can be gained when the weight is constrained to be no more than 6.

Item	1	2	3	4	5
Weight	2	4	3	3	5
Profit	1	6	4	4	7

2. The problem can be redefined slightly to allow for items to be chosen any number of times, but again subject to a total weight constraint. This is called the knapsack problem.

   (i) Solve the knapsack problem for the above data
   (ii) Describe an algorithm to solve the knapsack problem

12.3 Shortest path problem

We will now explore the shortest path problem. In this we are given a set of cities (more formally, vertices or nodes in a graph) and a set of roads of known length between some of them (weighted directed edges). The problem is to complete a table showing the shortest distance between any two cities.

Perhaps we should not be considering the shortest path in this chapter, because strictly speaking it is a one-dimensional problem, in that a single number, the number of cities, specifies its size. However, as we shall find when we come to see how the road information is stored, the problem is inherently two-dimensional.

To illustrate the problem we will consider the situation indicated by the 'map' in Fig. 12.9.

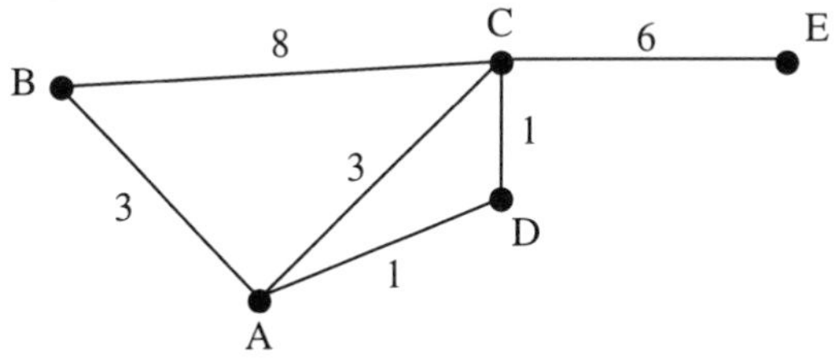

Figure 12.9 Example 'map'

There are five cities, A to E. As indicated by the lines, some have roads between them. To simplify things we have used an example in which all roads are two-way, and have indicated them by a single line, rather than two directed arcs. However, the following algorithms would work even if the roads were one-way. Next to each line (road) is a number which is the 'distance' between the cities at the ends of it. In the example given, the single number indicates that the 'distance' is the same in either direction (but this need not be so, and again our algorithms would work if it were not the case).

Until now we have put distance inside quotation marks because we do not want to interpret it strictly as physical distance (Euclidean distance), measured in miles or kilometres for example. Indeed, notice that if this were the interpretation the above 'map' would be impossible: look at the triangle formed by A, C and D, which does not add up. We want to be more flexible than we would be if we used just physical distances, and so we will use a more generalised metric. For instance, we may want to find the shortest travel time between cities. In this case, the physical distance is only part of the problem, the speed of the roads must also be considered. In this case 'distance' could represent travel time. Now the triangle given by A, C and D is perfectly possible, indicating that the road between A and C is comparatively slow, while those between A and D and D and C are comparatively fast.

We will store the distance data in a two-dimensional array. We will call this d (Fig. 12.10).

	A	B	C	D	E
A	0	3	3	1	∞
B	3	0	8	∞	∞
C	3	8	0	1	6
D	1	∞	1	0	∞
E	∞	∞	6	∞	0

Figure 12.10 Distances between the 'cities'

Note that d(A,B), shown in row A/column B, gives the distance along the road from A to B. Although not the case here, d(B,A), the distance from B to A, could be different. Where there is no direct road between two places the distance between them is given as∞, infinity, which in our algorithms will be approximated by using a suitably large number (larger than any possible route, but not so large as to cause an overflow when added to). The shortest path between two places may involve a number of steps, each going through intermediate cities. For instance, although there is no direct route between D and E, an indirect route of length 7 can be found by going via C (Fig. 12.11).

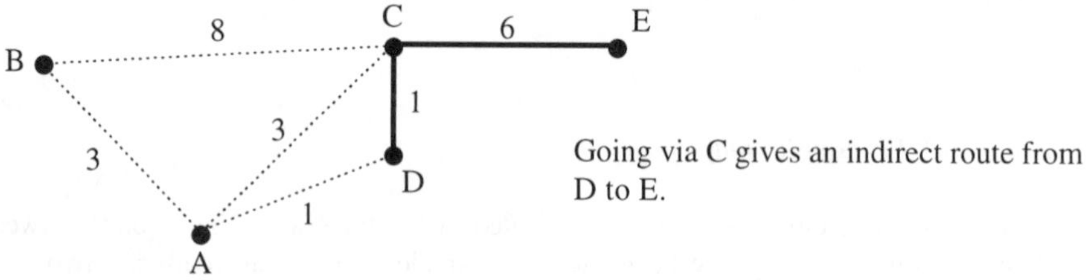

Figure 12.11 Where there is no direct route a shortest path must go via an intermediate city

Even where there is a direct route between two cities, there may be a shorter indirect one. In our example this is the case between A and C. The direct road has length 3, the indirect route going via D has length 2.

Potentially, the shortest route between any two places could go via many other cities Fig. 12.12). Thus, our solution to the shortest path problem must include paths with any number of steps.

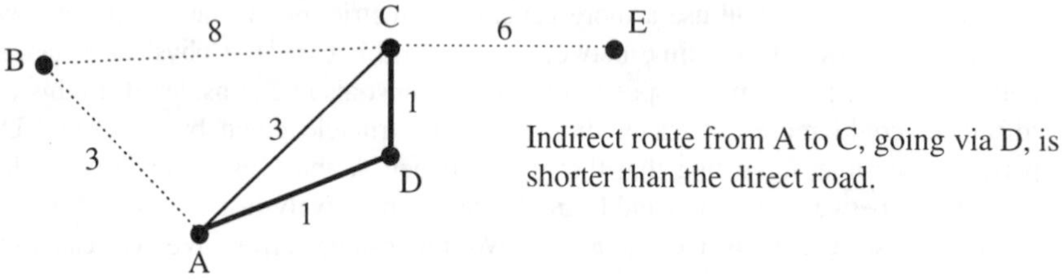

Figure 12.12 Where there is a direct route this may not be a shortest path

We will solve the problem using dynamic programming, but by way of alternative approaches we mention in passing that, as always, a brute strength approach could be tried, in this case by listing all the possible routes between each place and taking the shortest, but this is doomed on the grounds of inefficiency; the greedy approach based on taking the shortest edge at each step, although fast, is not guaranteed to give an optimal result.

Before going any further it is worth describing a couple of insights into the problem's behaviour that will make it considerably easier to solve.

Insight 1. On the shortest route between two places no city appears more than once. This follows from the fact that if one were to appear twice, there would be a loop, and so the route could be made shorter by cutting out the loop. It follows that if there are n cities, there are at most $n - 1$ steps in a route (otherwise a city would appear more than once).

For instance, there is a route with a loop from B to E which goes via C, A, D, and C. This is shown in Fig. 12.13. Clearly, it is inefficient.

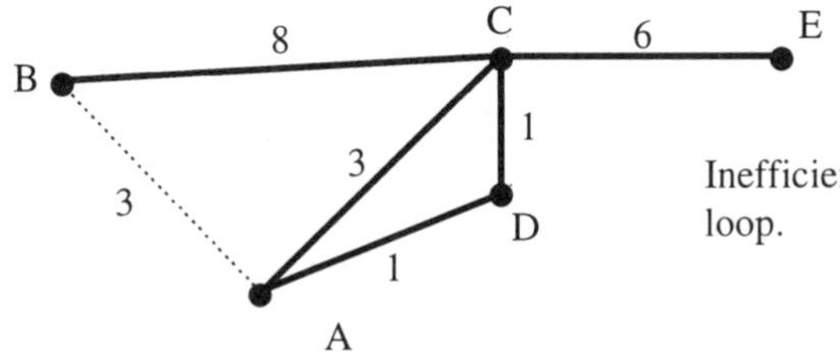

Inefficient route from B to E. It has a loop.

Figure 12.13 No shortest path can include a loop

Insight 2. If the shortest route between two cities, i and j say, goes through another city, k, then that part of this route between i and k must also be the shortest route between i and k, and similarly between k and j. This follows because if this were not the case, we could improve on this 'shortest' route between i and j by taking the shorter routes from i to k or from k to j (Fig. 12.14).

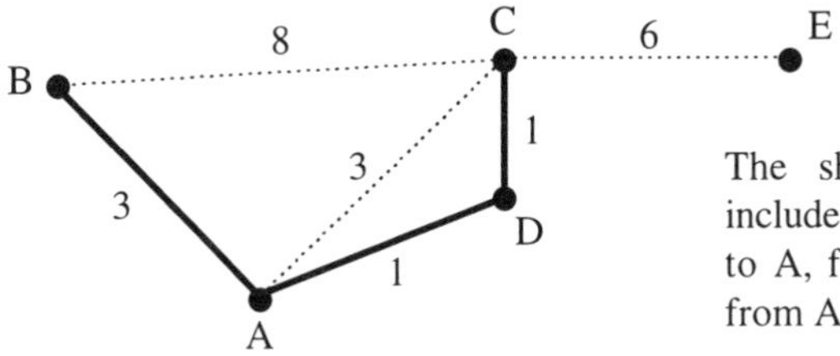

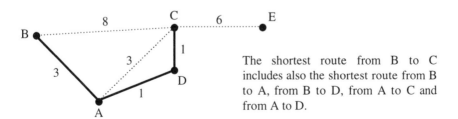

The shortest route from B to C includes also the shortest route from B to A, from B to D, from A to C and from A to D.

Figure 12.14 The shortest path between any two points must also form the shortest path between any intermediate points

We will look at two algorithms to solve this problem: the first is easy to understand (hopefully) but inefficient in terms of both time and space required; the second far cleverer (it was not discovered by the present authors!) but far more efficient in both aspects. In both the algorithms the following variable names will be used:

n the number of cities

d a two-dimensional array showing, where there is a road, the (one-step) distance between each pair of cities, and ∞ otherwise.

12.3.1 All-steps algorithm

We start by looking at what could be called the all-steps algorithm. *Note it is inefficient*, but it gives the correct answer. It uses dynamic programming in an unintelligent but effective way. It works like this.

We have noted that the shortest route between two cities may involve using any number of steps up to $n - 1$. We solve all smaller problems, routes with fewer steps. That is, we find the shortest distance between each pair of cities using paths with only one step (we get that information from d, the distance array) and store this information; then we find the shortest distances using paths with not more than two steps, and store this information; then three, and so on, continuing until we have found the shortest distances for all paths involving not more than $n - 1$ steps. As we go along, we will store the shortest distances found so far in a three-dimensional array, shortest, where:

shortest(step, i, j) represents the shortest distance found between i and j using not more than step steps.

To see how this array is built up, consider the situation where we have completed the array for the first step – 1 number of steps. We now want to extend it to include paths which have up to step steps in them. Consider the distance of the shortest path found from city i to city j. At the present stage we know that the shortest distance found so far, one using not more than step – 1 steps, is already in the table, and is given by:

shortest(step – 1, i, j)

There are now two possibilities. In the first, the shortest distance cannot be reduced even by including a path of step steps. In that case,

shortest(step, i, j) = shortest(step – 1, i, j)

Alternatively, we can improve on this distance by using a path with step steps. How will we know that this is the case? Well, first of all we need to find a path with this number of steps. Secondly, we need to show that it is shorter than what we already have.

For such a path to exist, we must be able to find a city, k, for which there is a path of step – 1 steps from i to k, and a path using just a single step from k to j. This is shown in Fig. 12.15.

We already know the shortest distance from i to k using not more than step – 1 steps, it is given by:

shortest(step – 1, i, k)

and from k to j using exactly one step, it is given by:

d(k,j)

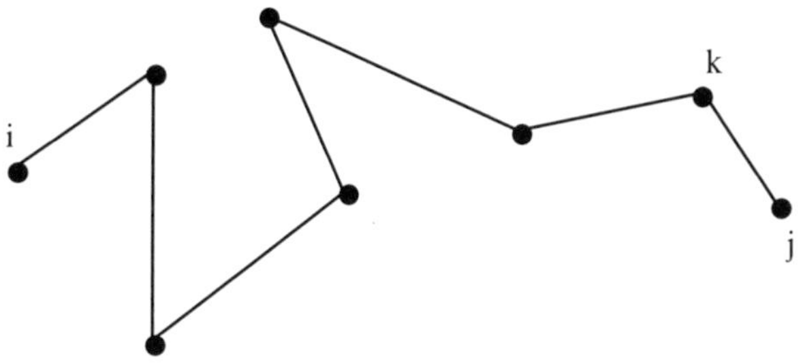

Figure 12.15 The shortest path from i to j may go through k

Therefore, if we use k, the total distance is given by:

shortest(step, i, j) = shortest(step – 1, i, k) + d(k, j)

Clearly, we will only want to use this new route if it gives a shorter route than we already have.

Notice that we do not test to see if there is a road from k to j. In our particular formulation this is taken account of by the distance being 'infinite' if there is not one. But having adopted this approach we must be careful to choose a value for 'infinity' that does not result in the addition causing overflow.

Putting, these ideas together gives the algorithm in Fig. 12.16.

In C:

```
/* Initialize shortest to one-step routes */
for (i=1; i<=n; i++)
{
   for (j=1; j<=n; j++)
   {
     shortest[1][i][j] = d[i][j];
   }
}
/* Complete shortest table for progressively longer routes */
for (step=2; step<n; step++)
{
   for (i=1; i<=n; i++)
   {
      for (j=1; j<=n; j++)
      {
         /* can't do any worse than before */
         shortest[step][i][j] = shortest[step-1][i][j];
         for (k=1; k<=n; k++)
         {
            /* search for an intermediate point */
            if ( shortest[step-1][i][k] + d[k][j] <
                    shortest[step][i][j] )
            {
```

```
                        shortest[step][i][j] =
                           shortest[step-1][i][k] + d[k][j];
                    }
                }
            }
        }
}
```

In Ada:

```
-- Initialise shortest to one-step routes
for i in 1..n loop
  for j in 1..n loop
    shortest(1, i, j) := d(i, j);
  end loop;
end loop;

-- Complete shortest table for progressively longer routes
for step in 2..n-1 loop
  for i in 1..n loop
    for j in 1..n loop
      -- can't do any worse than before
      shortest(step,i, j) := shortest(step-1, i, j);
      for k in 1..n loop
        -- search for a extra intermediate point
        if shortest(step-1, i, k) + d(k, j) < shortest(step, i, j)
          then
            shortest(step, i, j) := shortest(step-1, i, k) + d(k, j);
        end if;
      end loop;
    end loop;
  end loop;
end loop;
```

Figure 12.16 Program fragment to solve the shortest path problem using the all-steps approach

To analyse the algorithm's complexity, we see from the code that the key operation, where we compare the length of a new possible route going via k with the best that we have so far, happens inside loops nested four times over and so, with each loop giving n iterations, the operation occurs n^4 times. We note also that there is a considerable, n^3, space requirement for shortest. Much of this could be avoided: since we use only the previous step's values, it would be simple to update these within one $n \times n$ array as we go along rather than storing them for all steps. Note also that if no changes happen in one step, no more can happen for later steps. So time could be saved if changes were flagged, and the loop exited if none occurred for a whole step.

To illustrate the algorithm's workings we will step through the creation of the shortest path table for the data set seen in Fig. 12.10.

At step 1, shortest is set to the values given in the distance table (Fig. 12.17). In particular, if we focus just on routes from B to E, there is no route using just one step from B to E. This is shown by the infinite distance.

	A	B	C	D	E
A	0	3	3	1	∞
B	3	0	8	∞	∞
C	3	8	0	1	6
D	1	∞	1	0	∞
E	∞	∞	6	∞	0

Figure 12.17 Distances going directly, that is using only one step

At step 2, we get the revised table shown in Fig. 12.18 (changes are indicated by asterisks):

	A	B	C	D	E
A	0	3	2 *	1	9 *
B	3	0	6 *	4 *	14 *
C	2 *	6 *	0	1	6
D	1	4 *	1	0	7 *
E	9 *	14 *	6	7 *	0

Figure 12.18 Distances using at most two steps

As for a route from B to E, there is now one. It uses two steps, and has a length of 14. This is shown in Fig. 12.19.

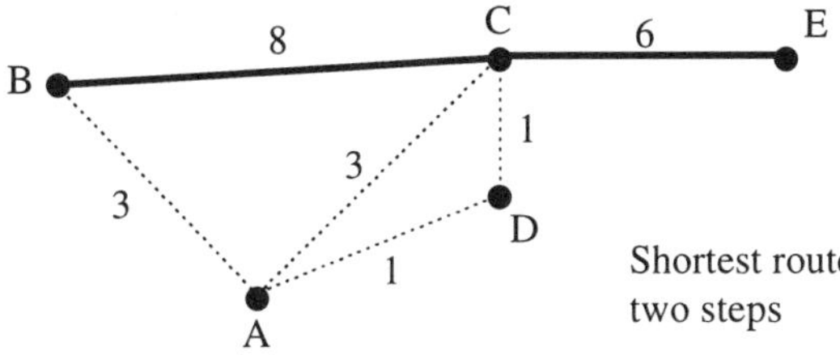

Shortest route from B to E using not more than two steps

Figure 12.19 The best route from B to E using at most two steps

At step 3, we get Fig. 12.20.

	A	B	C	D	E
A	0	3	2	1	8 *
B	3	0	4 *	4	12 *
C	2	4 *	0	1	6
D	1	4	1	0	7
E	8 *	12 *	6	7	0

Figure 12.20 Distances using at most three steps

Focusing again on the path from B to E, with the extra (third) step we can reduce the length of the shortest route to 12. This is shown in Fig. 12.21.

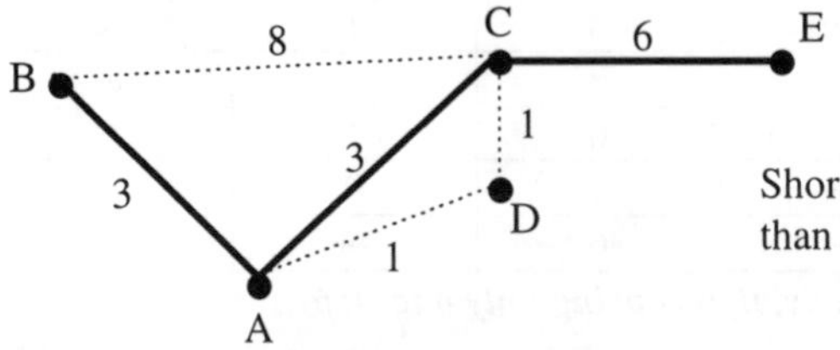

Shortest route from B to E using not more than three steps

Figure 12.21 The best route from B to E using at most three steps

Finally, at step 4 (the number of cities minus one), we get the completed table (Fig. 12.22).

	A	B	C	D	E
A	0	3	2	1	8
B	3	0	4	4	11 *
C	2	4	0	1	6
D	1	4	1	0	7
E	8	11 *	6	8	0

Figure 12.22 Distances using at most four steps

Looking at row 2 (B)/column 5 (E) we get the distance of the shortest path from B to E which is possible using any number of steps. Its length is 11. It is shown in Fig. 12.23.

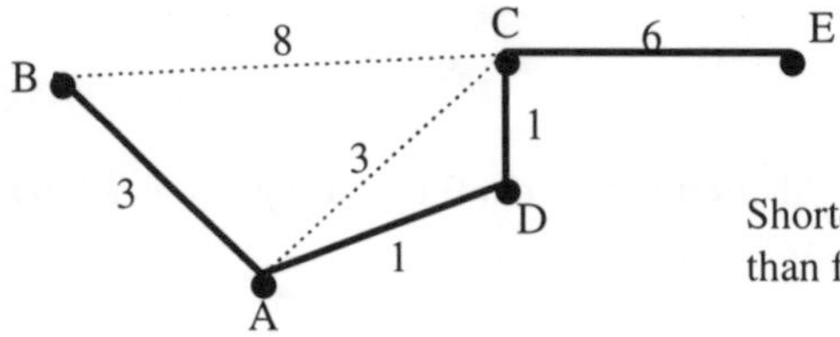

Shortest route from B to E using not more than four steps.

Figure 12.23 The best route from B to E using at most four steps

12.3.2 Warshall's algorithm

To conclude this chapter, we look at a much more efficient algorithm for solving the shortest path problem. It was discovered by Warshall.

The all-steps algorithm shown above has a great weakness: each iteration of the outside loop has very little power. This is because, when looking at new paths, we can only increase the number of steps in a path one at a time. This follows because we must choose an intermediate point, k, to go via which is exactly one step away from j. Thus the outer (steps) loop, which increases the number of steps in a path, must occur $n - 1$ times. In its effect, Warshall's algorithm combines the inner loop, searching for a point to go via, and the outer loop, increasing the number of steps in a path. By eliminating one level of nesting, it reduces the algorithm's complexity to $O(n^3)$. Moreover, it requires much less space, using a single $n \times n$ array to hold the results. It works as follows.

This time shortest is a simple $n \times n$ array which stores the shortest route between each pair of cities found so far; we do not need to store versions for each step, we just update one which shows what we have calculated so far. It is initialised to the original road distances, and at this stage can be thought of as showing the shortest distances between cities going directly, that is via no other places. Progressively we update shortest to see the effect of going via city 1, then city 2 (and this picks up the effect of going via 1), then city 3 (and this picks up the effect of going via 1 and 2), and so on up to n. The beauty of this approach is that not only are we adding to the cities we can go via, but we are also implicitly increasing the number of steps in the routes being investigated.

We need to justify the algorithm's correctness. We get off to a good start by initialising shortest to the original distance values (which, as we noted above, are routes not going via any intermediate points). Then, we progressively consider going via more places. Suppose we have already considered all cities between 1 and k – 1. When we start to consider whether or not to go via k to find a shorter distance between the two cities i and j, say, we already know the following:

shortest(i,k) is the shortest route between i and k going via only places chosen from the cities numbered between 1 and k – 1.

shortest(k,j) is the shortest route between k and j going via only places chosen from the cities numbered between 1 and k – 1.

In fact, we can go further than this, and this is the crucial point:

these values actually represent the shortest route using not just the first k – 1 nodes, but node k as well.

This is because k cannot be an intermediate point on any shortest route of which it is an end point.

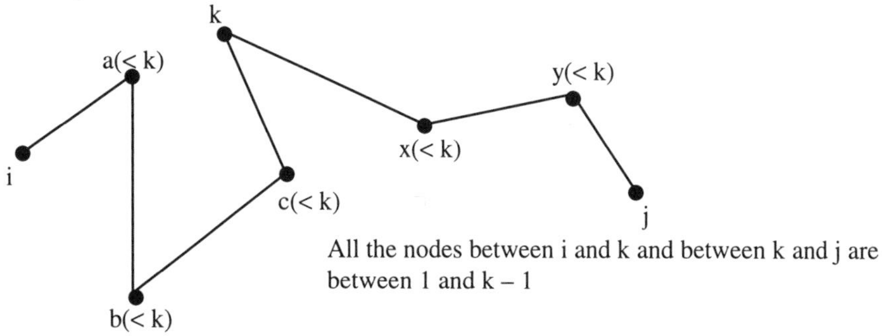
k
a(< k)
y(< k)
x(< k)
i
c(< k)
j
All the nodes between i and k and between k and j are between 1 and k – 1
b(< k)

Figure 12.24 The path from i to j going via k

Now, if we do go via k, the journey is divided into two sub-paths: one from i to k; the other from k to j (Fig. 12.24). This gives a total distance of:

shortest(i,k) + shortest(k,j)

If we do not use k then we cannot do any worse than we did before and we are left with:

shortest(i,j)

Consequently, our decision is based on whether or not

shortest(i,k) + shortest(k,j) < shortest(i,j)

Either way we are sure that we have the shortest path between i and j using only cities numbered between 1 and k as intermediate points. Clearly, if we continue like this for all *n* cities, we finish with the shortest routes possible.

The program can be implemented as shown in Fig. 12.25.

In C:

```
/* initialise shortest */
for (i=1; i<=n; i++)
{
   for (j=1; j<=n; j++)
   {
      shortest[i][j] = d[i][j];
   }
}
/* try going via intermediate points */
for (via=1; via<=n; via++)
{
   for (i=1; i<=n; i++)
   {
      for (j=1; j<=n; j++)
      {
         if ( shortest[i][via] + shortest[via][j] <
                shortest[i][j] )
         {
            /* go via via */
            shortest[i][j] =
               shortest[i][via] + shortest[via][j];
         }
      }
   }
}
```

In Ada:

```
-- initialise shortest
for i in 1..n loop
  for j in 1..n loop
    shortest(i, j) := d(i, j);
```

```
  end loop;
end loop;

-- try going via intermediate points
for via in 1..n loop
  for i in 1..n loop
    for j in 1..n loop
      if shortest(i, via)+shortest(via,j ) < shortest(i, j)
        then
          -- go via via
          shortest(i, j) :=
            shortest(i, via) + shortest(via, j);
      end if;
    end loop;
  end loop;
end loop;
```

Figure 12.25 Program fragment to solve the shortest path problem using Warshall's algorithm

Most of the algorithm's effort is being taken up with making the decision of whether or not to go via the latest point. Since this is inside a loop nested three times over, and since each loop has n iterations, this operation is carried out n^3 times. The remaining costs, those incurred by initialisation, are much lower, requiring n^2 operations. Thus, the overall complexity is $O(n^3)$.

To illustrate how the algorithm works, we will dry-run it to see how it deals with our example data set. To begin with shortest is initialised to the distance table (Fig. 12.26).

	A	B	C	D	E
A	0	3	3	1	∞
B	3	0	8	∞	∞
C	3	8	0	1	6
D	1	∞	1	0	∞
E	∞	∞	6	∞	0

Figure 12.26 Initialisation of shortest

After one iteration of the outer loop we get those improvements that come from taking into account routes that go via the first node, A. With changes shown by an asterisk, we get Fig. 12.27:

	A	B	C	D	E
A	0	3	3	1	∞
B	3	0	6*	4*	∞
C	3	6*	0	1	6
D	1	4*	1	0	∞
E	∞	∞	6	∞	0

Figure 12.27 shortest taking into account routes via A

Again we will focus on the route between B and E. But for these two cities even taking into account paths which go via A (but nowhere else) a route has not been found. This is shown by the infinite distance between them. (Compared to the all-steps method, it does at first sight appear that less progress has been made here. However, remember that one level of nesting has been omitted, so *n* times fewer (5 times fewer in this case) operations have been carried out by this stage.)

At the next iteration we see whatever improvements there may be by including routes which in addition go via B (that is, via A and/or B). In this case, there are no changes.

The next iteration takes into account those routes which can additionally go via C (that is, go via any or all of A, B and C). This time there are changes (Fig. 12.28).

	A	B	C	D	E
A	0	3	3	1	9*
B	3	0	6	4	12*
C	3	6	0	1	6
D	1	4	1	0	7*
E	9*	12*	6	7*	0

Figure 12.28 shortest taking into account routes via A, B and/or C

Now we have a route between B and E, as shown in Fig. 12.29.

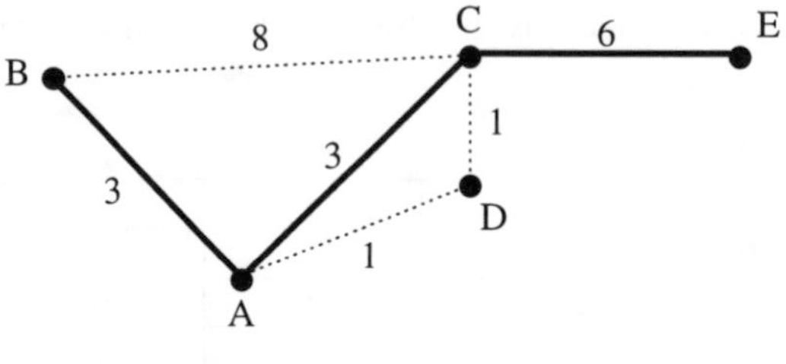

Figure 12.29 Shortest route from B to E going via only cities selected from A, B or C

Next we look at routes which can additionally go via D (that is, via any number of cities chosen from A, B, C and D). This gives Fig. 12.30.

	A	B	C	D	E
A	0	3	2*	1	8*
B	3	0	5*	4	11*
C	2	5	0	1	6
D	1	4	1	0	7
E	8*	11*	6	7	0

Figure 12.30 shortest taking into account routes A, B, C and/or D

We can see that we have a shorter route between B and E, one which goes via D (Fig. 12.31).

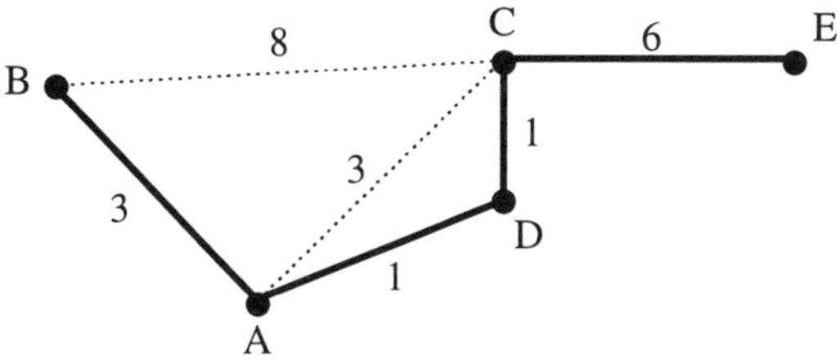

Figure 12.31 Shortest route from B to E going via only cities selected from only A, B, C or D

The final step is to consider routes that go via E. There are none that improve things. Consequently, the table of shortest distance remains unchanged.

Thus, the results are the same as using the all-steps algorithm. However, this time the solution has been found far more efficiently, using only one-fifth of the effort required before.

EXERCISES 12.3

1. Using any approach find the shortest path between each pair of cities for the following maps

(i)

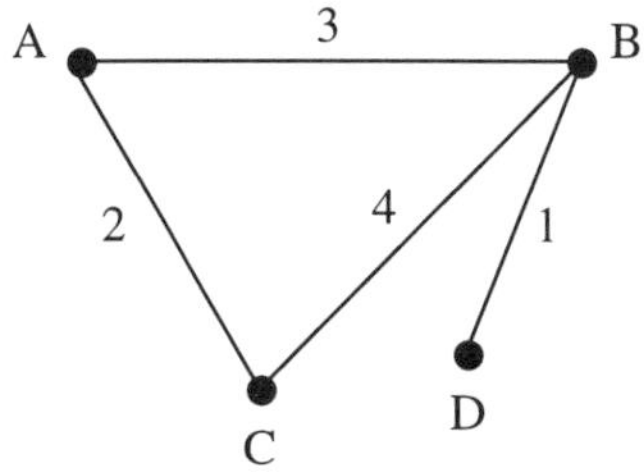

(ii)

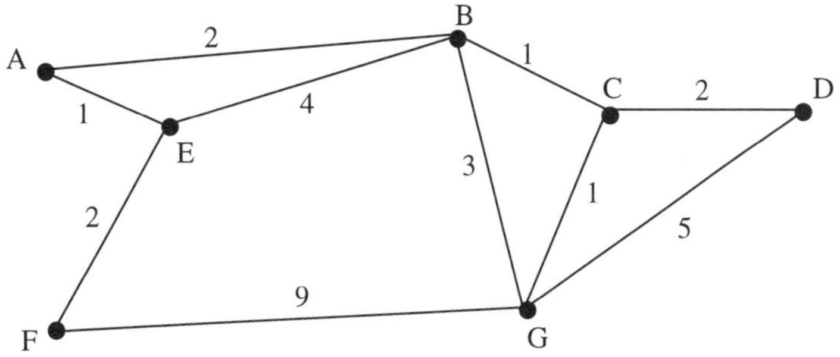

Summary

- Multi-dimensional dynamic programming
  —is a bottom-up approach
  —solves all smaller problems in all dimensions
  —stores intermediate results
  —solves bigger problems using the results stored from smaller problems.
- Algorithms described:
  —routes
  —0–1 knapsack
  —shortest path.

SOLUTIONS TO EXERCISES

Chapter 1

Exercises 1.1

1. This is simply the operation of a function and its inverse on a number:

$$f(x) = (7/12)(x + 3); f^{-1}(x) = \{(3x)/7\}4 - 3$$

Any number of such functions are available, for instance

$$f(x) = 3x^2 - 6; f^{-1}(x) = \sqrt{(x + 6)/3}$$

The presentation of this as a trick is more effective when the operations are disguised, as for instance 'multiply by 4' might be by saying, 'multiply by 8; now divide by 2'.

In order to write an algorithm to do this, the instructions can simply be encoded directly, e.g. as $f(x)$ above. The inverse operations may be embodied in a 'decoding' algorithm.

2. For $x = 13$, we have output 40, 20, 10, 5, 16, 8, 4, 2, 1.
   For $x = 9$, output 28, 14, 7, 22, 11, 34, 17, 52, 26, 13, 40, 20, 10, 5, 16, 8, 4, 2, 1.
   For $x = 1$ there is no output.

The algorithm is, in C:

```
#include <stdio.h>
/* Program hailstone */
void main()
{
  int bounce;
  printf("Enter an integer value\n");
  scanf("%d", &bounce);
    while (bounce > 1)
    {
       if (bounce % 2 == 0)
       {
         bounce = bounce / 2;
       }
       else
       {
         bounce = 3 * bounce + 1;
       }
       printf("Bouncer = %d\n", bounce);
    }
}
```

In Ada:

```
with text_io; use text_io;
procedure hail is
package int_io is new text_io.integer_io(integer);
use int_io;
bounce: integer;
begin
    put("Enter an integer value: ");
    get(bounce);
    while bounce > 1 loop
        if bounce mod 2 = 0 then
            bounce := bounce / 2;
        else
            bounce := 3 * bounce + 1;
        end if;
        put(bounce);
        new_line;
    end loop;
end hail;
```

It is not known whether this algorithm will *always* end with the sequence ...8, 4, 2, 1.

Exercises 1.2

1. These are minimal changes to the detail of the calculation, e.g.

```
if half_price_offer then
   two_cost ←1.5 * price
   new_vol ← 2 * vol
   best_buy ← two_cost  / new_vol
endif

if four_for_three_offer then
   four_cost ← 3 * price
   new_vol ← 4 * vol
   best_buy ← four_cost / new_vol
endif
```

2. The algorithm works identically for any other kinds of goods. Only identifiers might need to be changed, for example 'kilos'.

3. The principle is simple. The quality indicators will need to be accessible to the algorithm, perhaps in a table, and then the final prices weighted by perhaps multiplying by (100/q.i.) to give a 'relative cost' figure.

Exercises 1.3

1. For example, in C:

```
while (valid && go)
{
  printf("To convert sterling to foreign currency, enter S.\n");
  printf("To convert other currencies to sterling, enter R.\n");
  printf("To end the program, enter X\n\n");
  scanf("%c", &money);
  if (money == 'R' || money == 'S')
  {
    getchar();
    printf("Enter Nationality Indicator, as follows:\n");
    printf("Belgium: B; France: F; Germany: D.\n");
    NatInd = getchar();
    printf("Enter the amount of cash:   ");
    scanf("%f", &loot);
    if (money == 'S')
    {
      spend = convert_to(loot, Nat);
    }
    else
    {
      spend = convert_from(loot, Nat);
    }
  }
  else if (money == 'X')
  {
    valid = 0;
  }
  else
  {
    printf("Enter 'R' or 'S' only.\n");
    err_flag3 = 1;
  }
  if (valid && !err_flag3)
  {
    if (err_flag1 || err_flag2)
    {
      printf("Unable to do this conversion: only currencies\n");
      printf("as shown in the initial table are valid.\n");
    }
    else if (money == 'S')
    {
      printf("You get %c%.2f for your money.\n\n",NatInd, spend);
    }
    else
    {
      printf("You get GBP%.2f for your money.\n\n", spend);
    }
  }
  if (valid)
  {
    getchar();
    printf("Again?");
    scanf("%d", &go);
```

```
        getchar();
    }
    if (err_flag1)
        err_flag1 = 0;
    if (err_flag2)
        err_flag2 = 0;
    if (err_flag3)
        err_flag3 = 0;
}
```

In Ada:

```
begin
    while valid = 1 and go = 1 loop
        put("Enter S for sterling-to-foreign, R for foreign-to-sterling;");
        put(" to exit enter X: ");
        get(money);
        if money = 'R' or money = 'S' then
            put("Enter Nationality Indicator, as follows: ");
            new_line;
            put("Belgium: B; France: F; Germany: D.");
            new_line;
            get(NatInd);
            put("Enter amount of cash: ");
            get(loot);
            if money = 'S' then
                spend := convert_to(loot, Nat);
            else
                spend := convert_from(loot, Nat);
            end if;
        elsif money = 'X' then
            valid := 0;
        else
            put("Enter 'R' or 'S' only.");
            new_line;
            err_flag3 := 1;
        end if;
        if valid = 1 and err_flag3 /= 1 then
            if err_flag1 = 1 or err_flag2 = 1 then
                put("Unable to do this conversion; enter B, F or D only: ");
                new_line;
            elsif money = 'S' then
                put("You get ");
                put(NatInd);
                put(spend, fore =>3, aft => 2, exp => 0);
                put(" for your money.");
            else
                put("You get ");
                put("GBP");
                put(spend, fore =>3, aft => 2, exp => 0);
                put(" for your money.");
            end if;
        end if;
```

```
        if valid = 1 then
            new_line;
            put("Again?");
            get(go);
        end if;
        if err_flag1 = 1 then
            err_flag1 := 0;
        end if;
        if err_flag2 = 1 then
            err_flag2 := 0;
        end if;
        if err_flag3 = 1 then
            err_flag3 := 0;
        end if;
    end loop;
end;
```

2. This question is developed at length in Chapter 6. Arrays are frequently useful for data storage, so long as the amount of data to be stored does not increase or decrease very much over time. Problems arise when the quantity of data changes frequently, owing to either the array being too small, or else wastage of space if the array is unnecessarily large. Most languages allow multi-dimensional arrays.

Chapter 2

Exercises 2.1

1.

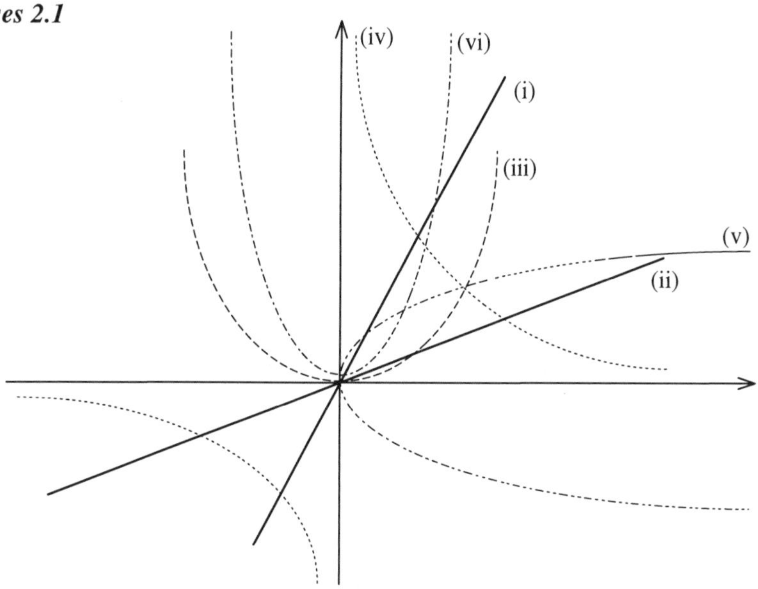

2.

x	−3	−2	−1	0	1	2	3
$f(x)$	−1	n.d.	1	0.5	0.33	0.25	0.20

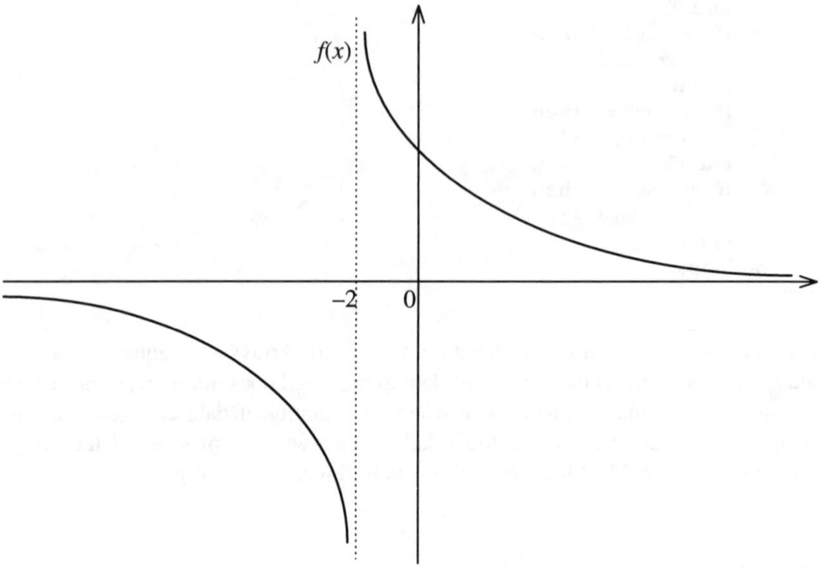

3.

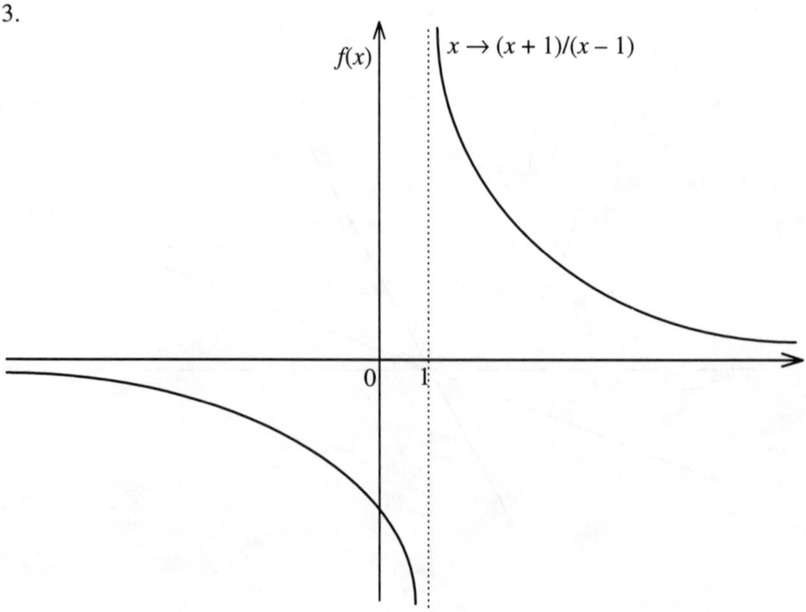

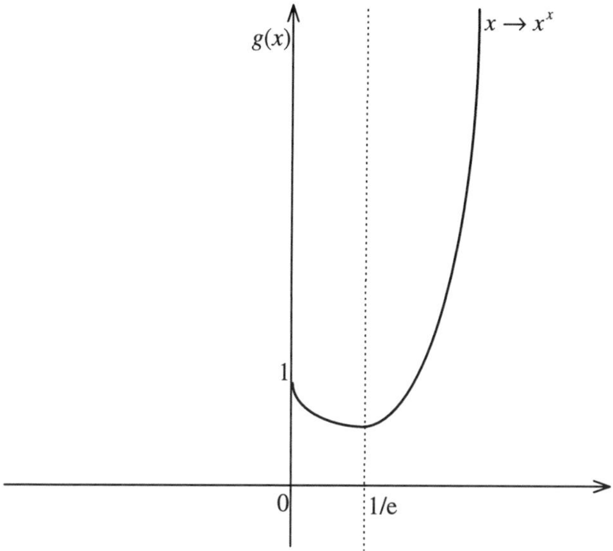

The graph for $x < 0$ is trickier, as all odd non-integral points are complex.

Exercises 2.2

1. Since $\log_a b = c \Leftrightarrow a^c = b$, we have

$$c \times \ln(a) = \ln(b)$$
$$\Rightarrow c = (\ln(b))/(\ln(a))$$

Hence an outline solution is:

Read number (x)
Read logarithmic base (y)
Output ans = $(\ln(x))/\ln(y)$
Stop.

2. (i) 262 144
 (ii) 19 683
 (iii) 27
 (iv) 2.61
 (v) 1
 (vi) 0.000 457
 (vii) Complex: $\sqrt[10]{(-27)}$
 (viii) 1.414
 (ix) 1

3. (i) 0.333
   (ii) 10
   (iii) 5
   (iv) 8
   (v) 1
   (vi) 5
   (vii) 0

Exercises 2.3

1. In C:

```
#include <stdio.h>
#include <math.h>   /* Newton_Raphson iteration for cube roots */
#define eps 0.000000001
float cube_num, cube_root_N, x_g;

float newt (float N, float x_new)
{
   float x_old = N / x_new;
   while (fabs(x_new - x_old) > eps)
   {
      x_old = x_new;
      x_new = ((N / (x_old * x_old)) + (2 * x_old)) / 3.0;
   }
   return x_new;
}
void main()
{
   printf("Enter a number to be cube-rooted: ");
   scanf("%f", &cube_num);
   printf("Enter first guess: ");
   scanf("%f", &x_g);
   if (x_g == 0.0)
   {
      x_g = 0.000001;            /* Avoid division by zero error */
   }
   cube_root_N = newt(cube_num, x_g);
   printf("\nCube root of %.3f is %.5f.\n", cube_num, cube_root_N);
}
```

In Ada:

```
with text_io; use text_io;
procedure NewtRaph is
package int_io is new text_io.integer_io(integer);
package flt_io is new text_io.float_io(float);
use int_io, flt_io;
cube_num, cube_root_N, x_g: float;
eps: constant := 1.0e-9;

function Newt(N: float; x_n: float) return float is
x_old, x_new: float;
```

```
begin
   x_new := x_n;                    -- May not update mode 'in' parameters
   x_old:= N / x_new;
   while abs(x_new - x_old) > eps loop
      x_old := x_new;
      x_new := ((N / x_old ** 2) + 2.0 * x_old) / 3.0;
   end loop;
   return x_new;
end Newt;

begin
     put("Enter a number to be cube-rooted:  ");
     get(cube_num);
     put("Enter first guess: ");
     get(x_g);
     if x_g = 0.0 then
          x_g := 0.000001;            -- Avoid division by zero error
     end if;
     cube_root_N := Newt(cube_num, x_g);
     new_line(2);
     put("Cube root of ");
     put(cube_num, fore => 3, aft =>3, exp => 0);
     put(" is ");
     put(cube_root_N, fore => 3, aft => 5, exp =>0);
end NewtRaph;
```

2. Read number (x)
   Output ans = $(\ln(x))/\ln(2)$
   Stop

Chapter 3

Exercises 3.1

1. (i) Start 4 8 1
   1 8 4
   1 4 8

   (ii) Start 7 7 7 7
   7 7 7 7
   7 7 7 7
   7 7 7 7

   (iii)

Start	2	5	−1	36	5	20	8
	−1	5	2	36	5	20	8
	−1	2	5	36	5	20	8
	−1	2	5	36	5	20	8
	−1	2	5	5	36	20	8
	−1	2	5	5	8	20	36
	−1	2	5	5	8	20	36

Exercises 3.2

1. In C:

```
#include <stdio.h>
#define SORT_MAX  10

void sel_sort( int s1[SORT_MAX] )
{
  int i, j, k, x, temp, ex_cnt, comp_cnt, swap_cnt;
  ex_cnt = 0;
  comp_cnt = 0;
  swap_cnt = 0;
  for (i = 0; i < SORT_MAX - 1; ++i)
  {
    x = i;
    for (j = i + 1; j < SORT_MAX; ++j)
    {
      ++comp_cnt;
      printf("\nComparisons: %d\n", comp_cnt);
      if (s1[j] < s[x])
      {
        x = j;
        ++ex_cnt;
        printf("Exchanges: %d\n", ex_cnt);
      }
    }
    if (x != i)
    {
      temp = s[x];
      s1[x] = s1[i];
      s1[i] = temp;
      ++swap_cnt;
      printf("Swaps: %d\n", swap_cnt);
    }
    printf ("\n\nThe array so far:\n");
    for (k = 0; k < SORT_MAX; ++k)
    {
      printf ("%d ", s1[k]);
    }
  }
  printf("\n\nTotal Comparisons: %d\n", comp_cnt);
  printf("Total Exchanges: %d\n", ex_cnt);
  printf("Total Swaps: %d\n", swap_cnt);
}

void main()
{
  int i;
  int inlist[SORT_MAX];
  void sel_sort ( int s1[SORT_MAX] );
  printf ("Enter %d integers: \n", SORT_MAX);
  for (i = 0; i < SORT_MAX; ++i)
  {
    scanf("%d", &inlist[i]);
```

```
    }
    printf ("\n\nThe array before the sort:\n");
    for (i = 0; i < SORT_MAX; ++i)
    {
        printf ("%d ", inlist[i]);
    }
    printf("\n\n");
    sel_sort(inlist);
    printf ("\n\n\nThe array after the sort:\n");
    for (i = 0; i < SORT_MAX; ++i)
    {
        printf ("%d ", inlist[i]);
    }
    printf("\n\n");
}
```

In Ada:

```
with text_io; use text_io;
procedure select_monitor is

package int_io is new text_io.integer_io(integer);
use int_io;
SORT_MAX: integer := 10;
type sort_type is array (0 .. SORT_MAX-1) of integer;
inlist: sort_type;

procedure sel_sort(s1: in out sort_type) is
x, temp: integer;
ex_cnt, comp_cnt, swap_cnt:integer;
begin
    ex_cnt := 0;
    comp_cnt := 0;
    swap_cnt = 0;
    for i in 0 .. SORT_MAX-2 loop
        x := i;
        for j in i+1 .. SORT_MAX-1 loop
            comp_cnt := comp_cnt + 1;
            new_line;
            put("Comparisons:  ");
            put(comp_cnt);
            new_line;
            if s1(j) < s1(x) then
                x := j;
                ex_cnt := ex_cnt + 1;
                put("Exchanges: ");
                put(ex_cnt);
                new_line;
            end if;
        end loop;
        if x /= i then
            temp := s1(x);
            s1(x) := s1(i);
```

```
                s1(i) := temp;
                swap_cnt = swap_cnt + 1;
                put("Swaps:  ");
                put(swap_cnt);
                new_line;
            end if;
            new_line;
            put("The array so far: ");
            new_line;
            for k in 0 .. SORT_MAX-1 loop
                put(s1(k));
            end loop;
        end loop;
end sel_sort;
begin
        put("Enter ");
        put(SORT_MAX);
        put(" integers:");
        new_line;
        for i in 0 .. SORT_MAX-1 loop
            get(inlist(i));
        end loop;
        put("The array before the sort: ");
        new_line;
        for i in 0 .. SORT_MAX-1 loop
            put(inlist(i));
        end loop;
        new_line(2);
        sel_sort(inlist);
        new_line;
        put("The array after the sort: ");
        new_line;
        for i in 0 ..SORT_MAX-1 loop
            put(inlist(i));
        end loop;
end select_monitor;
```

2. No, because the fact that there was not an exchange on any given pass does not mean that the list is sorted: selection sort moves from left to right, sorting as it goes.

3. No. This would result in unnecessary exchanges of elements which have the same value.

Exercises 3.3

1. This is just a print of the array s1 between the **for** loop statements in sel_sort.

2. This is done in much the same way as for Exercises 3.2 Q.1. For a list comprising six elements in reverse order, there are

	Comparisons	*Exchanges*	*Swaps*
Selection sort	15	9	3
Bubble sort	25	–	15

Selection sort is preferable to the simple version of the bubble sort. Note that each 'Swap' is actually three primitive operations.

Exercises 3.4

1. For a list of 10 elements:

		Comparisons	*Swaps*
Simple bubble sort	*worst*	81	45
	best	81	0
Improved version	*worst*	45	45
	best	45	0
'do–while' version	*worst*	90	45
	best	9	0

2.

	Selection			*'improved' bubble*		*'do–while' bubble*	
	Comps	*Exchs*	*Swaps*	*Comps*	*Swaps*	*Comps*	*Swaps*
(i)	55	13	9	90	23	55	23
(ii)	15	0	0	15	0	5	0
(iii)	21	0	0	21	0	6	0
(iv)	36	20	4	36	36	72	36
(v)	45	5	5	45	5	54	5

3. In C:

```
void bubble(int s1[SORT_LIM])
{
   int i, j, temp, done;
   i = 0;
   do{
        done = 1;
        for (j = 0; j < SORT_LIM-1-i; ++j)
        {
           if (s1[j + 1] < s1[j])
           {
              temp = s1[j];
              s1[j] = s1[j + 1];
              s1[j + 1] = temp;
              done = 0;
           }
        }
        ++i;
     }while (!done);
}
```

In Ada:

```
procedure bubble(s1: in out sort_array) is
temp, done: integer;
i: integer := 0;
begin
      done := 0;
      while done = 0 loop
            done := 1;
            for j in 0 .. LISTSIZE-2-i loop
                  if s1(j+1) < s1(j) then
                        temp := s1(j);
                        s1(j) := s1(j+1);
                        s1(j+1) := temp;
                        done := 0;
                  end if;
            end loop;
            i := i + 1;
      end loop;
end bubble;
```

Chapter 4

Exercises 4.1

1. (i) 4, 5, 6, 7, 8
   (ii) 4, 4.5, 5, 5.5, 6
   (iii) 1, 0.5, 0.333, 0.25, 0.20
   (iv) 4, 2.25, 1.67, 1.375, 1.20
   (v) –1, –0.2, 0, 0.0588, 0.0769
   (vi) –0.20, –0.50, –1, –2, –5
   (vii) 0, 4, 16, 48, 128
   (viii) 1, 4, 27, 256, 3125

Exercises 4.2

2. (i) –4, –9, –14, –19, –24
   (ii) 7, 19, 55, 163, 487
   (iii) 7, 11, 19, 35, 67

3. $f_{n+1} = 2f_n - 2, f_1 = 3$
   $f_n = 2^{n-1} + 2$

4. (i) $f_{n+1} = 5f_n - 6, f_1 = 1$
   (ii) $f_{n+1} = f_n/3 + 2, f_1 = 6$

Exercises 4.3

1. Change while (dupl_interval <= 16 .....)
   to while (dupl_interval <= 24 .....) for 3 days
   while (dupl_interval <= 32 .....) for 4 days, etc.

However, if the other parameters are not changed, the program will simply work as it does for a 48-hour recovery period. See the text, pp. 66–8.

2. max_val limits the size of numbers to those that can be represented accurately in the machine hardware. If the initial value for bugs is too large, a recovery is never effected, unless the kill rate is initially very large, e.g. 2 750 000+ per hour.

Exercises 4.4

1. In C:

```
#include <stdio.h>
#include <math.h>
void main()
{
   int v, v1, v2;
   float s1, s2;
   printf("mph    kph     stop(ft)  stop(m)\n\n");
   v = 5;
   while (v < 105)
   {
      v1 = v;
      s1 = 0.05 * pow(v1, 2) + v1;
      v2 = (v1 * 8)/ 5;
      s2 = 0.006 * pow(v2, 2) + 0.2 * v2 - 1.0;
      printf("%d     %d   %.1f    %.1f\n", v, (v * 8)/5, s1, s2);
      v += 5;
   }
}
```

In Ada:

```
with text_io; use text_io;
procedure stopstab is

package int_io is new text_io.integer_io(integer);
package flt_io is new text_io.float_io(float);
use int_io, flt_io;

s1, s2: float;
v, v1, v2: integer;
begin
    put("              mph        kph        stop(ft)         stop(m)");
    new_line(2);
```

```
    v := 5;
    while v < 105 loop
        v1 := v;
        s1 := 0.05 * float(v1) ** 2 + float(v1);
        v2 := (v1*8)/5;
        s2 := 0.006*float(v2) ** 2 + 0.2 * float(v2) - 1.0;
        set_col(15);
        put(v);
        set_col(32);
        put((v * 8)/ 5);
        set_col(52);
        put(s1, fore => 3, aft => 2, exp => 0);
        set_col(75);
        put(s2, fore => 3, aft => 2, exp => 0);
        new_line;
        v := v + 5;
    end loop;
end stopstab;
```

2. The problem becomes a bit more complicated, though it is still quite tractable so long as the speeds are constant. Assuming the driver behind reacts on seeing the brake lights of the driver in front come on, the front driver will stop in S_B, and the following driver in S_{STOP}. For instance,

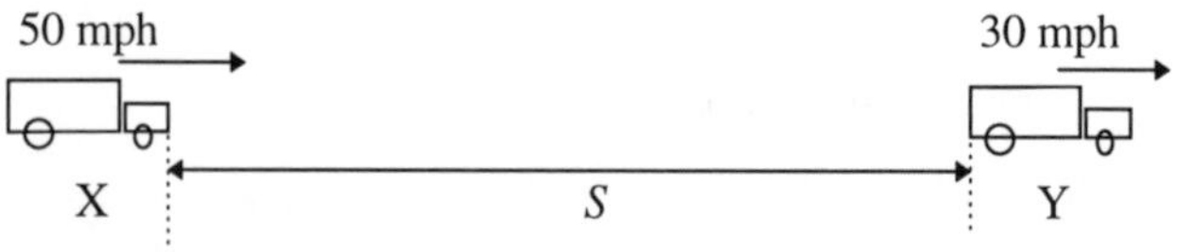

S_B @ 30 mph = 45 feet
S_{STOP} @ 50 mph = 175 feet

Hence if S is less than 130 feet, the vehicles will collide when Y brakes suddenly.

Chapter 5

Exercises 5.1

2. In C:

```
statement                                              cost
#define length n
    /* As required for size of Num_List under consideration */
int Num_Array[length];                                 0
int ex_5_1(int Num_List[])                             0
{
  int i, x = Num_List[0];                              1
```

```
    for (i = 1; i < length; ++i)                 2n
    {
       if (Num_list[i] > x)                      1 /* These ops */
       {                                            /* executed */
             x = Num_list[i];                    1 /* n - 1 times */
       }
    }
    return (x);                                  1
 }
TOTAL:                                           4n
```

In Ada:

```
statement                                                        cost
length: integer := n;        -- As required for size of Num_List under consideration
type Numbers is array (0 .. length - 1) of integer;              0
function EX5_1(Num_List: Numbers) return integer is              0
x: integer := Num_list(0);                                       1
begin
   for i in 1 .. length - 1 loop                                 2n
      if Num_list(i) > x then                                    1    --These ops executed
         x := Num_list(i);                                       1    --n – 1 times
      end if;
   end loop;
   return x;                                                     1
end;
TOTAL:                                                           4n
```

Note that in this case, for the loop [1 .. length – 1] there is one initialisation of i, $n - 1$ increments, and n tests. Hence there are $1 + n - 1 + n = 2n$ operations due to the loop mechanism..

The two statements inside the loop are each executed $n - 1$ times, giving $2(n - 1) = 2n - 2$ operations. There are a further two statements—the assignment and the return—outside the loop.

The total number of operations is thus:

$$1 + n - 1 + n + 2n - 2 + 2 = 4n$$

Exercises 5.2

1. (i) $c = 5$.
   (ii) $c = 3$.
   (iii) $c = 22$.
   (iv) $c = 34$.
   (v) $c = 10$.
   (vi) $c = 13$.
   (vii) $c = 130$.
   (viii) $c = 4$.

2. (i) In practice, we would hope for an expression of the form $T(n) = pn^a + qn^b + rn^c + sn^d + t$, where $d < c < b < a$, and $a \leq 4$. We assume n is a positive integer and a, b, c, d, r, s, t are positive reals.

(ii) As n increases without limit, each of the functions increases linearly: none is bounded above.

Exercises 5.3

1. (i) $O(n)$ $k = 4, p = 0$.
   (ii) $O(n^2)$ $k = 3, p = 0$.
   (iii) $O(n^2)$ $k = 3, p = 13$.
   (iv) $O(n^3)$ $k = 2, p = 4$.
   (v) $O(n^3)$ $k = 5, p = 3$.

Exercises 5.4

1. For bubble sort algorithm (a):

   (i) in the best case, there are $n(n - 1)/2$ comparisons, no exchanges.
   (ii) in the worst case, there are $n(n - 1)/2$ comparisons, $n(n - 1)/2$ exchanges.

For bubble sort algorithm (b):

   (i) in the best case, there are $n - 1$ comparisons, and no exchanges.
   (ii) in the worst case, there are $(n - 1)(n - 1)$ comparisons, and $n(n - 1)/2$ exchanges.

2. Yes: algorithm (a) is twice as fast for comparisons in the best case, and in the worst. For exchanges, it is the same in both cases. Algorithm (b) is $(n - 1)$ times as fast for comparisons in the best case, but the same in the worst case for both comparisons and exchanges.

3. The worst case: selection sort results in $3n^2/4$ operations due to comparisons and exchanges, defining each of these as a unit operation. Bubble sort algorithm (a) gives $(n^2 - n)/2 + (n^2 - n)/2 = n^2 - n$ operations due to similar comparisons and exchanges. Hence selection sort is better (for all $n > 3$).

Bubble sort algorithm (b) gives $(n - 1)(n - 1) + (n^2 - n)/2 = (3n^2 - 5n + 2)/2$ operations due to comparisons and exchanges: selection sort is better (for all $n > 2$).

The best case: selection sort makes $(n^2 - n)/2$ comparisons, no exchanges. Bubble sort algorithm (a) also makes $(n^2 - n)/2$ comparisons, and no exchanges. Bubble sort algorithm (b) makes $n - 1$ comparisons, and no exchanges, and so is $n/2$ times faster.

4. (i) Selection sort makes 55 comparisons, 17 exchanges, and 5 swaps, for a total of 77 such operations. Bubble sort algorithm (a) makes 55 comparisons and 34 exchanges for a total of 89 such operations. Bubble sort algorithm (b) makes 90 comparisons and 34 exchanges, totalling 124 operations. Hence selection sort is best.

(ii) Selection sort makes 28 comparisons, 3 exchanges, and 3 swaps, for a total of 34 such operations. Bubble sort algorithm (a) makes 28 comparisons and 3 exchanges totalling 31 operations, while bubble sort algorithm (b) makes 14 comparisons and 3 exchanges, i.e. 17 operations. Hence in this case bubble sort algorithm (b) is the best of the three.

(iii) Selection sort makes 28 comparisons, 13 exchanges, and 1 swap, for a total of 42 such operations. Bubble sort algorithm (a) makes 28 comparisons and 22 exchanges totalling 50 operations, while bubble sort algorithm (b) makes 56 comparisons and 22 exchanges, i.e. 78 operations. Hence in this case the selection sort algorithm is the best of the three.

5. It may not make a great deal of difference in practice for a list of 10 or 1000 items, as other considerations, especially I/O, will swamp any differences in performance. However, the selection sort will usually be better, and for a random list of 100 000 items, the difference would be a number of minutes for most machines.

6. For both cases, identical items are not switched directly; however, it may be that they are swapped about in the process of sorting, so that identical elements may in fact be swapped. For example, for the selection sort of {7, 5, 5, 1, 3, 9}:

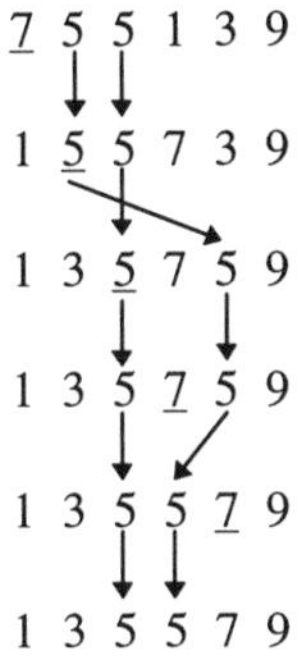

Chapter 6

Exercises 6.1

1. In C:

```
/*  Create an ordered list of integers  */
#include <stdio.h>
#include <stdlib.h>
struct item_type
{
  int item_val;                 /* Record: single integer value */
  struct item_type *next;       /* pointer to next struct item  */
};
typedef struct item_type item;
typedef item *link;             /* link is pointer to struct item */

link insert (int new_val, link p)
{           /* head of list is passed in as formal parameter 'p' */
            /* and manipulated internally */
  link h, st, p1, p2;
  p1 = p;   /* 'p1' is the updated list marker */
  st = malloc(sizeof(item));    /* Allocate a new node */
  st->item_val = new_val;       /* Assign the input value */
  if ((p1 == NULL) || (p1->item_val > st->item_val))
  {         /* If this is is the first item, or the new value...*/
    st->next = p1; /* ...is smaller than the old first item... */
    p1 = st;       /* ...put the new one first. 'h' marks the... */
    h = p1;        /* ...head of the amended list */
  }
  else
  {
    h = p1;      /* Retain 'h' as head of list marker... */
    while ((p1 != NULL) && (p1->item_val < st->item_val))
    {              /* ...and step along until a larger value... */
      p2 = p1;     /* ...than the new one is met... */
      p1 = p1->next;
    }
    st->next = p1;
    p2->next = st;   /* ...link in the new value... */
  }
  return h;          /* ...and pass back the new list head */
}

void display_all (link p)
{
  if(p == NULL)
  {
    printf("Empty list.");
  }
  else
  {
    printf("List is: ");
    while (p != NULL)
    {
```

```
        printf("%5d", p->item_val);
        p = p->next;
      }
   }
}

void main()
{
   int ins_val, i;
   link p, q, head = NULL;      /* 'head' marks the start... */
   display_all(head);
   p = head;      /* ..'p' will be the updated formal head marker */
   for (i = 0; i < 5; ++i)
   {
      printf("Enter an element to add to the list: ");
      scanf("%d", &ins_val);
      q = insert(ins_val, p); /* Insert the new value, get back... */
      p = q;                  /* ...the head of the updated list... */
      display_all(p);         /* ...and print out the updated list */
   }
}
```

In Ada:

```
with text_io; use text_io;
procedure orderedlist is
                                -- Create an ordered list of integers
package int_io is new text_io.integer_io(integer);
use int_io;

type item;
type item_link is access item;
type item is
      record
        item_val: integer;
        next: item_link;
      end record;

subtype link is item_link;
head: link;                     -- 'head' is NULL on declaration
ins_val: integer;

procedure insert(new_elt: in integer; p: in out link) is
p1, p2, st: link;               -- pass in 'p' as formal head of list, pass out updated head
begin
      st := new item'(new_val, NULL);   -- Allocate the new node
      if p = NULL or else p.item_val > st.item_val then
            st.next := p;       -- If this is the first item, or if the new value is smaller
            p := st;            -- than the old first one, make this value the first
      else
            p1 := p.next;
            p2 := p;            -- p2 is one step behind p1
            while p1 /= NULL and then p1.item_val < st.item_val loop
```

```
            p2 := p1;          -- Step along the list until a larger value than...
            p1 := p1.next;     -- ...the current one is met...
         end loop;
         st.next := p1;        -- ...and link in the new value
         p2.next := st;
      end if;
end insert;

procedure display_all(p1: in link) is
p: link:= p1;
begin
   if p = NULL then
      put("List is empty.");
   else
     put("List is: ");
     while p /= NULL loop
         put(p.item_val);
         p := p.next;
     end loop;
   end if;
   new_line;
end display_all;

begin
   display_all(head);
   for i in 1 .. 5 loop
     put("Enter value to insert: ");
     new_line(2);
     get(ins_val);
     insert(ins_val, head);      -- Insert the new value, get back the head of...
     display_all(head);             -- ...the updated list, and print it
  end loop;
end orderedlist;
```

2. Include: in C:

```
link search(int list_val, link p)
{
   if (p == NULL)
   {
     printf("Empty list.\n");
   }
   else
   {
     while ((p->item_val < list_val) && (p->next != NULL))
     {
       p = p->next;
     }
   }
   return p;
}
```

In Ada:

```
function search(list_val: integer; p1:link) return link is
p:link;
begin
   p:= p1;        -- This assignment because mode 'in' variables may not be updated
   if p = NULL then
      put("Empty List.");
      new_line;
   else
         while p.item_val < list_val and then p.next /= NULL loop
            p := p.next;
         end loop;
   end if;
   return p;
end search;
```

3. There are any number of ways of achieving this. One simple possibility is, in C:

```
#include <stdio.h>
#include <stdlib.h>
#include <string.h>
#define STR_LEN 20
          /* String reversal */

struct item
{
  char item_val;             /* Record: single character value */
  struct item *next;         /* pointer to next struct item   */
};
typedef struct item *st_link;   /* link is pointer to struct item */
st_link head = NULL;           /* 'head' is the top-of-stack marker */

void push(char new_elt)
{                         /* Push one character at a time */
  st_link temp;           /* onto the stack */
  temp = malloc(sizeof(struct item));
  temp->item_val = new_elt;
  temp->next = head;
  head = temp;
}

void pop()
{                      /* Pop one character at a time */
  if (head == NULL)
  {
    printf("\nEmpty stack");
  }
  else
  {
    printf("%c ", head->item_val);
    head = head->next;
  }
}
```

```
void main()
{
  int j, i = 0;
  char new_val[STR_LEN], option = 'y';
  while (option == 'y')
  {
    printf("\nEnter string to push onto the stack: \n");
    scanf("%s", new_val);
    while (new_val[i] != '\0')      /* Stack string chars */
    {
      push(new_val[i]);
      ++i;
    }
    for (j = 0; j < i; ++j)
    {
      pop();             /* Output string, character-by-character */
    }
    i = 0;
    printf("\nAgain? (y/n):  ");
    getchar();
    option = getchar();
  }
}
```

In Ada:

```
with text_io; use text_io;
procedure q613 is
package int_io is new text_io.integer_io(integer);
use int_io;
type stack_item;
type st_link is access stack_item;

type stack_item is
    record
        item_val: character;
        next: st_link;
    end record;
head: st_link;
STR_LEN: integer := 20;
subtype letter_type is string(1 .. STR_LEN);
new_val: letter_type;
L1: integer;
option: chracter;

procedure push(top: in out st_link; new_elt: in character) is
begin                                   -- Push one character at a time onto the stack
    top := new stack_item'(new_elt, top);      -- and return updated stack top
end push

procedure pop(top: in out st_link) is
begin
    if top = NULL then
```

```
            put("Empty stack.");
            new_line;
        else
            new_line(2);
            put(top.item_val);
            top := top.next;
        end if;
end pop;

begin
    option := 'y';
    while option = 'y' loop
            put("Enter string to push: ");
            get_line(new_val, L1);
            for i in 1 .. L1 loop
                push(head, new_val(i));
            end loop;
            new_line;
            for j in 1 .. L1 loop
                pop(head);
            end loop;
            new_line(2);
            put("Again?");
            get(option);
            skip_line;
        end loop;
end q613;
```

Chapter 7

Exercises 7.1

1. A malicious programmer could write the following program to swap two numbers:

In C:

```
if (x!=42)
{
   t = x;
}
else
{
   t = y;
}
x = y;
y = t;
```

In Ada:

```
if x/=42
   then
      t := x;
   else
      t := y;
end if;
x := y;
y := t;
```

It works for every *x*, except *x* equal to 42. Even then, if *y* equals 42 as well, it is still correct. So it is actually correct in just over 99 per cent of situations. Though presumably anyone with this degree of malice could get it exactly 99 per cent right if they wanted to. The moral of the story: do not rely entirely on blackbox testing.

Exercises 7.2

1. The code sets *a* to *b*, *b* to *c*, and *c* to *a*. Proof by symbolic execution.

Initial values		a	b	c
In C:	In Ada:	a_0	b_0	c_0
`a = c-a;`	a := c-a;	$c_0 - a_0$	b_0	c_0
`c = c-a;`	c := c-a;	$c_0 - a_0$	b_0	$c_0 - (c_0 - a_0) = a_0$
`a = b-a-c;`	a := b-a-c;	$b_0 - (c_0 - a_0) - a_0$ $= b_0 - c_0$	b_0	a_0
`b = b-a;`	b := b-a;	$b_0 - c_0$	$b_0 - (b_0 - c_0) = c_0$	a_0
`a = a+b;`	a := a+b;	$b_0 - c_0 + c_0 = b_0$	c_0	a_0

Termination is guaranteed because there are no loops.

2. The code sets *a*, *b*, and *c* to 0. Proof by symbolic execution.

Initial values		a	b	c
In C:	In Ada:	a_0	b_0	c_0
`a = c-b;`	a := c-b;	$c_0 - b_0$	b_0	c_0
`b = a+b;`	b := a+b;	$c_0 - b_0$	$c_0 - b_0 + b_0 = c_0$	c_0
`a = c;`	a := c;	c_0	c_0	c_0
`c = c-b;`	c := c-b;	c_0	c_0	$c_0 - c_0 = 0$
`a = b-a;`	a := b-a;	$c_0 - c_0 = 0$	c_0	0
`b = a;`	b := a;	0	0	0

Termination is guaranteed because there are no loops.

Exercises 7.3

1. 4

2. The probable aim of the code is to find the median (middle) value of three numbers. It has a bug.

3. A test case that would show the flaw is $x = 3$, $y = 5$ and $z = 1$. The result from the code would be $t = 1$, which is incorrect, assuming the median is required.

Alternatively, we can detect the error by analysis. The code cannot possibly work because it does not allow for enough possibilities. This follows because there are just four routes through the program; while, to be correct, the code must be capable of dealing correctly with each of the six (3!) permutations of three values that are possible. Since every **if** generates two routes and we need at least as many routes as there are permutations, two **ifs**, generating only four possibilities, are insufficient. At least three comparisons are needed.

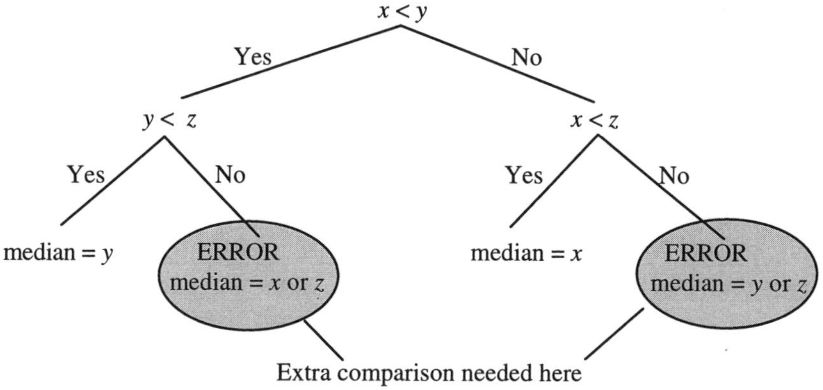

Exercises 7.4

1. 9. A naive approach would try to pair teams off to calculate how many games needed to be played in each round. Unfortunately, with 10 teams it does not work out nicely (it is not a power of 2), and some teams need to be given byes. One possible structure for the cup competition is shown below:

2. No. Since the grid is formed from 25 squares and since each rectangle covers two squares, the invariant is that, however many rectangles are laid and wherever they are laid, there is always an odd number of squares remaining. Given this, total coverage is impossible.

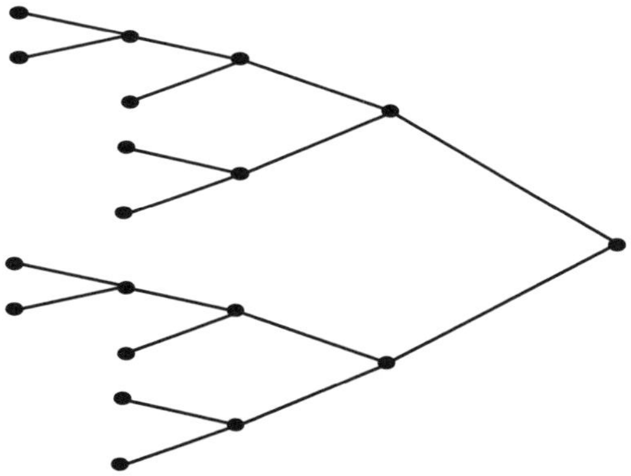

(Usually in computing trees grow downwards. Here we have one that grows sideways!)

A much more elegant solution relies on this fact: each match eliminates one team. The invariant is that the number of matches played plus the number of teams remaining equals the original number of teams. The competition has a winner when all but one of the teams has been eliminated.

3. In C:

```
ordered_so_far = 1;
i=1;
/* A: ordered_so_far = for all j from 1..0,
                                   a(j)≤a(j+1) and i≤n */
while (i<n && ordered_so_far==1)
{
    i = i + 1;
    if (a[i-1]>a[i])
    {
        ordered_so_far = 0;
    }
    /* B: invariant
        ordered_so_far = for all j from 1 to i-1,
                              a(j)≤a(j+1)

        and i≤n */
}
/* C: ordered_so_far = for all j from 1 to n-1, a(j)≤a(j+1) */
ordered = ordered_so_far;
```

In Ada:

```
ordered_so_far := TRUE;
i := 1;
-- A: ordered_so_far = for all j from 1..0, a(j)≤a(j+1) and i≤n
while i<n and ordered_so_far loop
  i := i + 1;
  if a(i-1)>a(i)
    then
      ordered_so_far := FALSE;
  end if;
  -- B: invariant
  -- ordered_so_far = for all j from 1 to i-1, a(j)≤a(j+1)
  -- and i≤n
end loop;
-- C: ordered_so_far = for all j from 1 to n-1, a(j)≤a(j+1)
ordered := ordered_so_far;
```

A specification of ordered is that for all j from 1 to $n - 1$, $a(j) \leq a(j+1)$.

At A, 1..0 is empty so the specification is trivially correct.

At B, from the invariant:

ordered_so_far = (for all j from 1 to $i - 1$, $a(j) \leq a(j+1)$)

$i \leq n$ ①

From the loop condition: ②

$i < n$

ordered_so_far = TRUE ③

From the assignment: ④

$i' = i + 1$

From ③ and ⑤ it follows that $i' \leq n$ ⑤

For the other part of the invariant we need to consider two cases:

Case 1. The **then** is executed. The **if** condition is satisfied, so $a(i' - 1) > a(i')$. But $i' \leq n$, so there is an i which contradicts the specification of ordered. Thus, ordered_so_far′ = FALSE is correct.

Case 2. The **then** is not executed. The **if** condition is not satisfied, so;

$a(i' - 1) \leq a(i')$

From ① and ④ it follows that: ⑥

for all j from 1 to $i - 1$, $a(j) \leq a(j + 1)$ is true

and from ⑤ and ⑥ it follows that

$a(i) \leq a(i + 1)$

Therefore:

for all j from 1 to i, $a(j) \leq a(j + 1)$ is true

Then using ⑤ gives:

for all j from 1 to $i' - 1$, $a(j) \leq a(j + 1)$ is true

Thus, ordered_so_far′ = ordered_so_far = TRUE is correct.

At C, there are two cases:

Case 1. The loop has terminated with ordered_so_far = FALSE, this means a contradiction has been found, and the result is correct.

Case 2. The loop has terminated with ordered_so_far = TRUE and also, therefore, $i = n$. We have from the invariant:

ordered_so_far= for all j from 1 to $i - 1$, $a(j) \leq a(j + 1)$

Hence, substituting for i:

ordered_so_far= for all j from 1 to $n - 1$, $a(j) \leq a(j + 1)$ = TRUE

which is correct.

Termination follows because the loop counter is always incremented and must, therefore, eventually equal i, terminating the loop.

Exercises 7.5

Take it step by step. b's first element is a's last; b's second element is a's last but one; and so on.

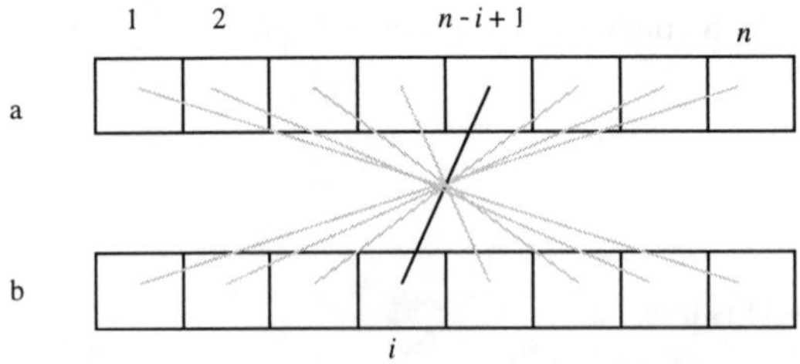

b(i) comes from a($n - i + 1$)

In C:

```
for (i=1; i<=n; i++)
{
   b[i] = a[n-i-1];
}
```

In Ada:

```
for i in 1..n loop
   b(i) := a(n-i+1);
end loop;
```

Chapter 8

Exercises 8.1

1. (i) 7 (choose all of them).
   (ii) 6 (choose the first three)

(iii) 3 (choose the first two)

(iv) 6 (choose them all, the last one more than makes up for the loss from the third).

2. We note that, provided the start point does not change, once we have calculated the profit for a group we do not need to start all over again for the next bigger group. Instead, to get that group's profit, we can just add the extra shop's profit to the figure already found. This insight leads to the following code:

In C:

```
max_profit = 0;
for (start=1; start<=n; start++)
{
   this_profit = 0;
   for (i=start; i<=n; i++)
   {
      this_profit = this_profit + profit[i];
      /* update max if better */
      if (this_profit>max_profit)
      {
         max_profit= this_profit;
      }
   }
}
```

In Ada:

```
max_profit := 0;
for start in 1..n loop
  this_profit := 0;
  for i in start..n loop
    this_profit := this_profit + profit(i);
    -- update max if better
    if this_profit>max_profit
      then
        max_profit := this_profit;
    end if;
  end loop;
end loop;
```

We can see that we have managed to eliminate one of the nested loops, and we now have an $O(n^2)$ algorithm.

3. We can refine the above process still further. We start by noting that, from a given starting point, once the profit from a group of shops becomes negative there is no point in using them: it is always better to start afresh, because by starting later we will not need to take into account the negative contribution of the earlier shops. With this in mind, we start at the beginning and keep track both of the best profit found so far, max_profit, but also of the profit from the present group, this_profit. We move to the

right adding in the profits from additional shops to present_profit, and applying these rules:

- if this_profit becomes more than max_profit we update the maximum
- if this_profit becomes negative we set it to 0 because this group can be ignored.

In C:

```
max_profit = 0;
this_profit = 0;

/* start group at any place */
for (i=1; i<=n; i++)
{
   /* add in new value */
   this_profit = this_profit + profit[i];
   /* if this is better than max update */
   if (this_profit>max_profit)
   {
      max_profit = this_profit;
   }
   else
   {
      if (this_profit<0)
      {
         /* discard and start again */
         this_profit = 0;
      }
   }
}
```

In Ada:

```
max_profit := 0;
this_profit := 0;
-- start group at any place
for i in 1..n loop
  -- add in new value
  this_profit := this_profit + profit(i);
  -- if this is better than max update
  if this_profit>max_profit
    this
      max_profit := this_profit;
    elsif this_profit<0
        then
          -- discard and start again
          this_profit := 0;
  end if;
end loop;
```

Again we have eliminated one of the nested loops and are left with an $O(n)$ algorithm.

Exercises 8.2

1.

Selection	*Option 1*	*Option 2*	*Option 3*	*Option 4*
1	0	0	0	0
2	0	0	0	1
3	0	0	1	0
4	0	0	1	1
5	0	1	0	0
6	0	1	0	1
7	0	1	1	0
8	0	1	1	1
9	1	0	0	0
10	1	0	0	1
11	1	0	1	0
12	1	0	1	1
13	1	1	0	0
14	1	1	0	1
15	1	1	1	0
16	1	1	1	1

2. A starting point for an iterative solution is to see the similarity between selections and binary numbers. For instance, the table above can be thought of as showing the first 16 binary numbers. Given this, it can be seen that what we need to do is to calculate how many possible selections there are (2^n). Then loop through each of the (decimal) numbers from 0 to this minus one and find, in effect, each one's binary representation. We do that by repeatedly dividing by 2 and storing the remainders. This is shown below:

In C:

```
last = pow(2,n) - 1;
for (i=0; i<=last; i++)
{
   value = i;
   for (j=n; j>0; j--)
   {
      /* find binary digits in */
      /* reverse order by */
      /* repeated division by 2 */
      a[j] = (value % 2);
      value = value / 2;
   }
   print_a();
}
```

In Ada:

```
last := 2**n - 1;
for i in 0..last loop
  value := i;
  for j in reverse 1..n loop
    -- find binary digits in reverse order by
    -- repeated division by 2
    a(j) := (value REM 2);
    value := value / 2;
  end loop;
  print_a;
end loop;
```

Exercises 8.3

1. Permutations of four items.

1 2 3 4	3 1 2 4
1 2 4 3	3 1 4 2
1 3 2 4	3 2 1 4
1 3 4 2	3 2 4 1
1 4 2 3	3 4 1 2
1 4 3 2	3 4 2 1
2 1 3 4	4 1 2 3
2 1 4 3	4 1 3 2
2 3 1 4	4 2 1 3
2 3 4 1	4 2 3 1
2 4 1 3	4 3 1 2
2 4 3 1	4 3 2 1

2. Permutations of two items from four.

1 2	3 1
1 3	3 2
1 4	3 4
2 1	4 1
2 3	4 2
2 4	4 3

3. The major change is that we end the recursion when we have made the *m*th choice. In terms of the code, this is:

```
⋮
if option=m
⋮
```

```
⋮
if (option==m)
⋮
```

We also have to alter the print procedure to output only *m* values from the array.

Exercises 8.4

1. 27, 42.

2. There are many different improvements that can be made. Here are just two.

(i) Notice that for each permutation a new one can be generated by reversing the elements. If the distance are symmetrical in the sense that a road from A to B, say, has the same length as one from B to A, then the reversed route must have the same length as the original. Thus, there is no need to consider the reverses, and we double the speed of the algorithm by not doing so.

(ii) We can use the following branch and bound technique. In the algorithm described in the text we completed each route and only then computed its length. Instead of waiting to the end we can calculate a route's length as we go along. That is, as each city is added to the route, we find the length of the route so far. This gives us an advantage, because once the length of this partial route equals or exceeds the length of the shortest completed route found so far we can drop this route, and all permutations based on it.

Chapter 9

Exercises 9.1

1. We use a functional programming style of notation to show what is involved. We let qs s denote the command to Quicksort s. Then:

(1) A Quicksort of (6, 9, 11, 3, 2, 4, 7) involves:

6 comparisons to get qs(3, 2, 4) (6) qs(9, 11, 7)
2+2 comparisons to get qs(2) (3) qs(4) (6) qs(7) (9) qs(11)

All the terms are now base sequences, which require no further comparisons. A total of 10 comparisons are needed.

(ii) A Quicksort of (4, 9, 11, 3, 2, 6, 7) involves:

6 comparisons to get qs(3, 2) (4) qs(9, 11, 6, 7)
1+3 comparisons to get qs(2) (3) qs() (4) qs(6,7) (9) qs(11)
1 comparisons to get qs(2) (3) qs() (4) qs(7) (6) qs() (9) qs(11)

All the terms are now base sequences, which require no further comparisons. A total of 11 comparisons are needed.

(iii) A Quicksort of (11, 9, 7, 6, 4, 3, 2) involves:

6 comparisons to get qs(9,7,6,4,3,2) (11) qs()
5 comparisons to get qs(7,6,4,3,2) (9) qs() (11) qs()
etc.

A total of 21 comparisons (6+5+4+3+2+1) are needed.

Exercises 9.2

1. (i) To find the 3 lowest will mean dividing the array into $n/3$ groups of 3.
First the sort phase. For each group there are 3!, 6, permutations. To differentiate between these will required a decision tree with at least 6 leaves. Since each

conditional doubles the number of leaves, 3 are needed to get the required number of leaves. (In general, we need to find the lowest c for which $2^c \geq$ number of permutations.) So, with $n/3$ groups and each group requiring 3 conditionals, a total of n are required for the sorting phase.

Next the merge phase. The lowest three are initialised to the first group, and then the remaining $n/3 - 1$ groups are merged with this. Counting the number of comparisons required for each merge is more tricky because only some of the permutations are allowed. Here, though, the number of permutations is small enough for us to enumerate. We will call the lowest values l1, l2, l3 (where l1 ≤ l2 ≤l3) and the group to be merged values g1, g2, g3 (where g1 ≤ g2 ≤ g3). Then only the following results are possible from the merge:

```
l1  l2  l3
l1  l2  g1
l1  g1  l2
g1  l1  l2
l1  g1  g2
g1  l1  g2
g1  g2  l1
g1  g2  g3
```

That is, there are 8 allowable permutations. And again, the decision tree theory shows that for each merge 3 conditionals are required. Hence, in total the phase requires $n - 3$ conditionals.

Therefore, the whole process requires $2n - 3$ conditionals.

(ii) To find the 4 lowest will mean dividing the array into n/4 groups of 4.

Each group sort must deal with 4!, 24, permutations, which requires 5 conditionals, for a total of $(5/4)n$.

Each group merge must deal with 16 permutations. (This can be found by enumerating all the possibilities in a similar fashion to that shown above. Alternatively, we note that we can create a group of 4 from each group of 3 listed above in two ways: we can add into the fourth position either l4 or g4. Thus, in general, as the group size increases by 1, the number of group merge permutations doubles.) This requires 4 conditionals per group, for a total of $n - 4$ conditionals.

Therefore, the whole process requires $(9/4)n - 4$ conditionals.

(iii) To find the 5 lowest will mean dividing the array into $n/5$ groups of 5.

Each group sort must deal with 5!, 120, permutations, which requires 7 conditionals, for a total of $(7/5)n$.

Each group merge must deal with 32 permutations, which requires 5 conditionals, for a total of $n - 5$ conditionals.

Therefore, the whole process requires $(12/5)n - 5$ conditionals.

Chapter 10

Exercises 10.1

1. (i) 9p can be made up from 3 coins (5, 2, 2).
   (ii) 28p from 4 coins (20, 5, 2, 1).
   (iii) 121p from 3 coins (100, 20, 1).

2. The algorithm given subtracts the value of each coin as it is used. However, when a coin can be used more than once, this is inefficient; it being quicker to use division to see how many times this coin can be used. Using this approach, the central piece of code becomes:

In C:

```
:
        /* use this coin */
        this = to_find / value[choice];
        coins = coins + this;
        to_find = to_find - this * value[choice];
:
```

In Ada:

```
:
    -- use this coin
    this := to_find / value(choice)
    coins := coins + this;
    to_find := to_find - this*value(choice);
:
```

3. If the 1p coin is deleted, it becomes impossible to make up some values of change (3p, for instance). If the 5 and 10p coins are deleted, the approach becomes sub-optimal. For instance, consider change for 60p. With the two coins missing, the algorithm would give an answer of 6 (a 50p, followed by five 2p), whereas the optimal answer is 3 (three 20p).

4. 4/- (four shillings). The optimal answer is 2 (two 2/-), not 3 as given by the algorithm (2/6, 1/-, 6d).

5. A suitable coin set would include coins to the value of 1, 3 and 4. Then to make change to the value of 6 requires a minimum of 2 coins (3, 3), not 3 (4, 1, 1) as the algorithm would give.

6. Very similar algorithms to this are given in the chapter on Dynamic Programming: multi-dimensional problems. To be brief, we work upwards solving all smaller problems. We keep the same notation as before, with the exception that coins is now an array (coins(i)=5, say, meaning that 5 coins are needed to make up a change of i).

Therefore, the final answer is given in coins(n).

In C:

```
/* Initialise */
coins[0] = 0;
for (i=1; i<=n; i++)
{
   /* signal change not found by n+1 */
   coins[i] = n + 1;
}

/* Build-up table for increasing change values */
for (i=1; i<=n; i++)
{        /* Look at each coin */
   for (j=1; j<=c; j++)
   {
      if (value[j]<=i)
      {
         /* coin fits */
         if (coins[i-value[j]]+1 < coins[i])
         {
            /* use, it's better than present */
            coins[i] = coins[i-value[j]] + 1;
         }
      }
   }
}
finished = (coins[n]<=n);
```

In Ada:

```
-- Initialise
coins(0) := 0;
for i in 1..n loop
  -- signal change not found by n+1
  coins(i) := n + 1;
end loop;

-- Build-up table for increasing change values
for i in 1..n loop
  -- Look at each coin
  for j in 1..c loop
    if value(j)<=i
      then
        -- coin fits
        if coins(i-value(j))+1 < coins(i)
          then
            -- use, it's better than present
            coins(i) := coins(i-value(j)) + 1;
        end if;
    end if;
  end loop;
end loop;
finished := (coins(n)<=n);
```

Exercises 10.2

1. The brute strength approach requires the analysis of 6 (3!) orderings. These and their corresponding total waiting times are given in the table below:

Order	*Time*
ABC	12
ACB	11
BAC	9
BCA	5
CAB	7
CBA	4

The greedy approach sorts the people into order of increasing service time which, in this case, means serving the people in the order C (service time of 1), B (2), A (5). Leading to a total time of: 2(1) + 1(2) = 4

Both approaches give a minimum time of 4.

2. The greedy approach can still be used in the sense that we serve people in increasing order of service time. However, the details of the algorithm must be changed considerably because there is no reason why the servers should keep in step. It is easiest now to use a clock-based modelling technique. We assume now that all times are integer valued.

We call the number of customers *n* and the number of servers *s*, and hold the time at which server *i* finishes serving the current customer in time_next_available(*i*). We keep track of the next person to be served in next. Then, at each 'tick': we update the total waiting time by the number of people still left; see which (if any) servers are available and allocate new people to these.

In C:

```
/* assumes service times are sorted */
/* initialise */
total = 0;
time = 0;
/* allocate initial customers to each server */
server = 1;
next = 1;
while (server<=s && next<=n)
{
   time_next_available[server]= service_time[next];
   server = server + 1;
   next = next + 1;
}

/* update state for each tick */
while (next<=n)
{
   /* update waiting time for last period */
```

```
   total = total + n - next + 1;
   /* increment time                        */
   time = time + 1;
   /* see if any service has finished       */
   server = 1;
   while (server<=s && next<=n)
   {
      if (time==time_next_available[server])
      {
         /* allocate next person to this server */
         time_next_available[server]=
             time + service_time[next];
         next = next + 1;
      }
      server = server + 1;
   }
}
```

In Ada:

```
-- assumes service times are sorted
-- initialise
total := 0;
time := 0;
-- allocate initial customers to each server
server := 1;
next := 1;
while server<=s and next<=n loop
  time_next_available(server) := service_time(next);
  server:= server + 1;
  next := next + 1;
end loop;
-- update state for each tick
while next<=n loop
  -- update waiting time for last period
  total := total + n - next + 1;
  -- increment time
  time := time + 1;
  -- see if any service is finished
  server := 1;
  while server<=s and next<=n loop
    if time=time_next_available(server)
      then
        -- allocate next person to this server
        time_next_available(server):= time + service_time(next);
        next := next + 1;
    end if;
    server := server + 1;
  end loop;
end loop;
```

Exercises 10.3

1.

(i)

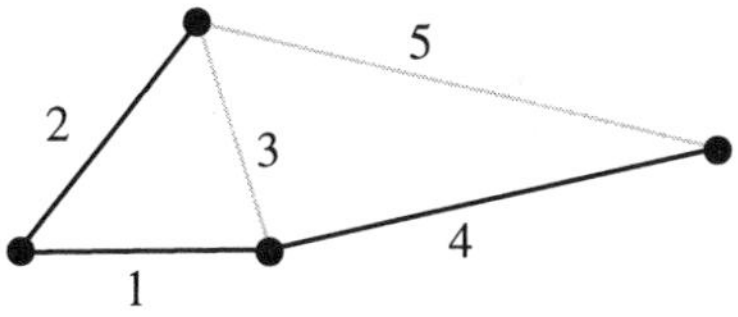

Length = 7

(ii)

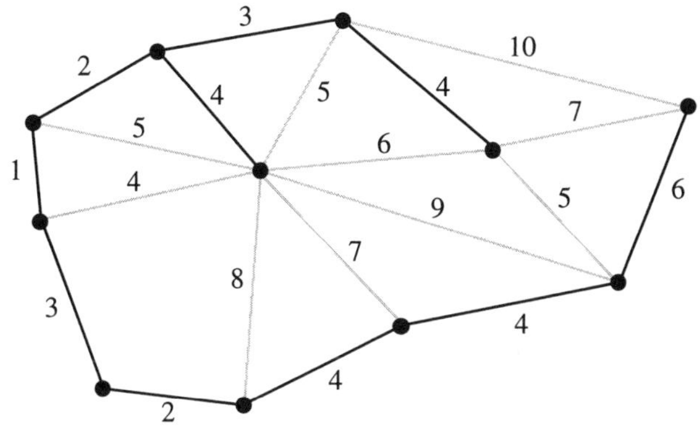

Length = 33

2. To form the minimum spanning tree itself all we need to do is keep track of those edges which have been chosen. We can use a Boolean array, used, to show this. Initially all its values are set to FALSE. Then, once we have decided to select next_edge, we insert the command:

In C:

```
used[next_edge] = 1;
```

In Ada:

```
used(next_edge) := TRUE;
```

3. There are a number of ways of progressing. Given the general approach we adopted in the text, in which we stored the connection group of each node (i.e. the node is the key field) the simplest way to make a substantial improvement to the efficiency of the group update is as follows. We initialise each node's group value to 0, to indicate that no node is in a group. Then the edge selection process, which depends on an edge's end nodes, has four cases:

- *Case 1*. Both nodes are in group 0. Select the edge, and put both nodes in a group labelled by the number of one of these nodes. The other nodes are unaffected, and the cost of this is only 1, compared with the previous algorithm's cost of n.

- *Case 2*. One node is in group 0, one is not. Select the edge, and put the unallocated node in the existing group. Again, the cost is 1, rather than n.
- *Case 3*. Neither node is in group 0, they are in different groups. Select the edge, and change the group membership of all those nodes in one group to the other. This is what the earlier algorithm did, so the cost is n as before.
- *Case 4*. Neither node is in group 0, they are in the same group. Reject.

Then, in the worst case half the edges are selected using Case 1 (that is, both nodes are from group 0) and the remaining edges are selected from Case 3; requiring in total approximately half the operations of the previous method.

A completely different approach would be to treat the connection group as the key field. Then a linked list can be used to hold a group's node membership. When it comes to an update, once the relevant groups have been found the reallocation has unit cost, just the change of a pointer, and this is regardless of the groups' sizes. However, an additional cost now comes from finding to which group a node belongs. To do this efficiently requires more complicated data structures.

Chapter 11

Exercises 11.1

1. 21 (8 + 13), 34 (13 + 21), 55 (21 + 34)

2. The definition leads immediately to the recurrence relationship:

fib(1) = 1
fib(2) = 1
fib(n) = fib(n – 1) + fib(n – 2)

(i) Using divide and conquer and working in a top-down way, with fib as a function, this can be coded as:

In C:

```
int fib(int n)
{
   if (n==1 || n==2)
   {
      return 1;
   }
   else
   {
      return fib(n-1) + fib(n-2);
   }
}
```

In Ada:

```
function fib(n: NATURAL) return NATURAL is
begin
  if n=1 or n=2
    then
      return 1;
    else
      return fib(n-1) + fib(n-2);
  end if;
end;
```

(ii) Alternatively, using dynamic programming and working bottom-up, with fib as an array:

In C:

```
fib[1] = 1;
fib[2] = 1;
for (i=3; i<=n; i++)
{
   fib[i] = fib[i-1] + fib[i-2];
}
```

In Ada:

```
fib(1) := 1;
fib(2) := 1;
for i in 3..n loop
  fib(i) := fib(i-1) + fib(i-2);
end loop;
```

3. The divide and conquer approach leads to a recursive tree.

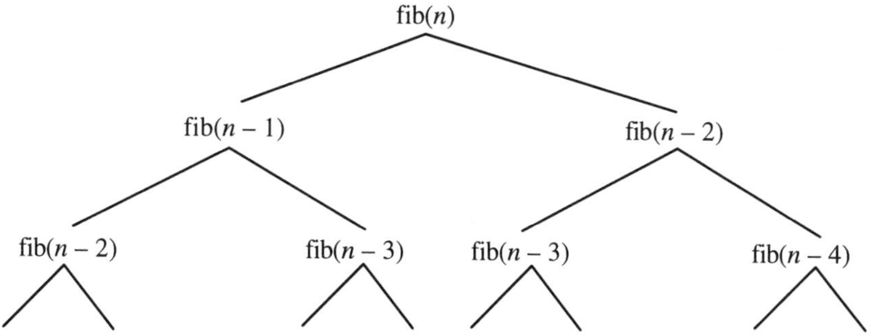

Notice how work is being repeated; for instance, fib(n – 2) is being calculated in 2 places. At each level the tree approximately doubles in size, giving a complexity of $O(2^n)$.

The dynamic programming approach is much more direct, with the work being done in the simple loop, giving a complexity of $O(n)$.

Exercises 11.2

The hint is to convert decimal numbers to binary. Here is a typical approach, converting 11 to binary.

$11 \div 2 = 5$ remainder 1
$5 \div 2 = 2$ remainder 1
$2 \div 2 = 1$ remainder 0
$1 \div 2 = 0$ remainder 1

At each step, divide by two. The remainders give the binary digits (in reverse order). So, reading upwards gives the answer, 1011.

In C:

```
xn = 1.0;
power = n;
xpower = x;
while (power>0)
{
   if (power%2)
   {
      xn = xn * xpower;
   }
   xpower = xpower * xpower;
   power = power / 2;
}
```

In Ada:

```
xn := 1.0;
power := n;
xpower := x;
while power>0 loop
  if power MOD 2 = 1
    then
      xn := xn * xpower;
  end if;
  xpower := xpower * xpower;
  power := power / 2;
end loop;
```

Exercises 11.3

1. (i) For 6 the following combinations are possible:

1 1 1 1 1 1
2 1 1 1 1
1 2 1 1 1
1 1 2 1 1
1 1 1 2 1
1 1 1 1 2
2 2 1 1
2 1 2 1
2 1 1 2
1 2 2 1
1 2 1 2
1 1 2 2
2 2 2
5 1
1 5

So there are 15 possible ways. (To make sure you list all possible combinations it pays to be methodical; if you list them randomly, it is likely that you will miss some. The approach adopted above was to start with the combination using just the 1p coin, then the combinations using one 2p coin and the rest 1p, then using two 2p coins, and so on. And within each category to start with the highest coins on the left and move them to the right..

(ii) For 7 the following combinations are possible

1 1 1 1 1 1 1	1 2 1 1 2
2 1 1 1 1 1	1 1 2 2 1
1 2 1 1 1 1	1 1 2 1 2
1 1 2 1 1 1	1 1 1 2 2
1 1 1 2 1 1	2 2 2 1
1 1 1 1 2 1	2 2 1 2
1 1 1 1 1 2	2 1 2 2
2 2 1 1 1	1 2 2 2
2 1 2 1 1	5 1 1
2 1 1 2 1	1 5 1
2 1 1 1 2	1 1 5
1 2 2 1 1	5 2
1 2 1 2 1	2 5

So there are 26 possible ways.

2.(i)

n	*number of ways*
1	1
2	2
3	3
4	5
5	9
6	15
7	26

(ii) Looking at the number of ways column, we see 3 (2 + 1) and 5 (3 + 2). The pattern that appears to have developed is that each result is the sum of the two previous ones. However, this breaks down once we get to 5; there is one extra option than this pattern would suggest, this comes from using the 5 pence coin. Beyond this, there is a pattern: for each row the number of ways is the sum of the previous two and the one five before. Thus, 9 + 5 + 1 = 15 and 15 + 9 + 2 = 26. We have to be careful and not assume without question that it continues. However, in this case it does. The text explains why.

3. The easiest way to do this is to use the pattern found above and to continue the table:

n	*number of ways*
8	44
9	75
10	128

Chapter 12

Exercises 12.1

1. 3, 20, 70.

2. (i) To get a recursive program, we can adopt a top-down approach based on the recurrence relation derived in the test:

ways(1,n) = 1
ways(m,1) =1
ways(m,n) = ways(m – 1,n) + ways(m,n – 1)   for $m > 1$ and $n > 1$

In C:

```
int ways(int m, int n)
{
    if (m==1 || n==1)
    {
        return 1;
     }
    else
    {
        return ways(m-1,n) + ways(m,n-1);
    }
}
```

In Ada:

```
function ways(m, n: NATURAL) return NATURAL is
begin
  if m=1 or n=1
    then
      return 1;
    else
      return ways(m-1,n) + ways(m,n-1);
  end if;
end;
```

The complexity of this algorithm is $O(2^n)$. It is much less efficient than the dynamic programming approach covered in the text.

3. For this particular problem, dynamic programming does not give the most efficient solution. A mathematical formula giving the answer can be derived, and this can be solved in linear time.

Given an $m \times n$ grid, any route from the top left to the bottom right requires making $m + n - 2$ moves in total, of which $m - 1$ moves must be downwards moves and $n - 1$ moves must be rightwards moves. Provided there are exactly $m - 1$ downward moves, they can be made in any order. The problem becomes, therefore, one of counting the number of combinations in which $m - 1$ like objects can be chosen from a total of $m + n - 2$, where the other $n - 1$ are also identical. There are $(m + n - 2)!$ ways of arranging $m + n - 2$ objects. Any downwards move is indistinguishable from any other downwards move, and the same applies for rightwards moves. Therefore, the number of distinguishable routes is:

$$\frac{(m+n-2)!}{(m-1)!\,(n-1)!}$$

A linear time program can be derived simply from this formula. However, for large problems care must be taken to avoid overflow.

Exercises 12.2

1. (i) Since there are 5 items to choose from there are 2^5, 32, possible portfolios to consider. A methodical way to generate these, and in spirit with the 0–1 of the problem, is to list the digits of the first 32 binary numbers, with a 0 in a column denoting that the item that this column is headed by is not chosen, and a 1 that it is. For each of these, the combined weight of the items used is checked and, if it is in range, the total profit calculated. This is shown in the table below. (In the total profit column, - indicates that a value is not applicable. This is because the portfolio weighs too much given the weight constraint.)

Item 1	*Item 2*	*Item 3*	*Item 4*	*Item 5*	*Total Weight*	*Total Profit*
0	0	0	0	0	0	0
0	0	0	0	1	5	7
0	0	0	1	0	3	4
0	0	0	1	1	8	-
0	0	1	0	0	3	4
0	0	1	0	1	8	-
0	0	1	1	0	6	8
0	0	1	1	1	11	-
0	1	0	0	0	4	6
0	1	0	0	1	9	-

0	1	0	1	0	7	-
0	1	0	1	1	12	-
0	1	1	0	0	7	-
0	1	1	0	1	12	-
0	1	1	1	0	10	-
0	1	1	1	1	15	-
1	0	0	0	0	2	1
1	0	0	0	1	7	-
1	0	0	1	0	5	5
1	0	0	1	1	10	-
1	0	1	0	0	5	5
1	0	1	0	1	10	-
1	0	1	1	0	8	-
1	0	1	1	1	13	-
1	1	0	0	0	6	7
1	1	0	0	1	11	-
1	1	0	1	0	9	-
1	1	0	1	1	14	-
1	1	1	0	0	9	-
1	1	1	0	1	14	-
1	1	1	1	0	12	-
1	1	1	1	1	17	-

By inspection, it can be seen that the maximum profit possible is 8.

(ii) As a first attempt we will postulate a greedy approach based on progressive selecting the most valuable item left which fits in the remaining space. In the present da we start by choosing item 5 for a profit of 7, and which weighs 5 to leave a remainder of Since no item can fit into this space, it cannot be used; leaving the total profit as 7. This sub-optimal; the method being no more than an heuristic.

As a second attempt, we will select on the basis of highest profit/weight ratio. We begi by calculating the ratios:

	1	*2*	*3*	*4*	*5*
Weight	2	4	3	3	5
Profit	1	6	4	4	7
Profit/Weight	0.5	1.5	1.33	1.33	1.4

The relatively most valuable item is 2 with a ratio of 1.5. This is selected to give a profit 6, and leaves a weight of 2 to allocate. Only item one can fit into this, to give an ex profit of 1; making a total of 7. This is sub-optimal.

Notice that the best solution, which is to choose items 3 and 4, uses objects whi individually do not have particularly appealing ratios, but which together fit the availab space better. It is because the greedy approach looks at the performance of individu items, not looking further ahead than the next step, that it misses improved solutions generated by better team-work.

(iii) There are 5 items to choose from and a weight constraint of 6, so, allowing for 0's, the dynamic programming approach involves completing a 6 × 7 table. This is shown below:

Items available/ Weight	*0*	*1*	*2*	*3*	*4*	*5*	*6*
0	0	0	0	0	0	0	0
1	0	0	1	1	1	1	1
2	0	0	1	1	6	6	7
3	0	0	1	4	6	6	7
4	0	0	1	4	6	6	8
5	0	0	1	4	6	7	8

2. (i) Clearly this extra freedom cannot make us worse off. However, in this particular case the maximum profit is still 8.

(ii) At first sight this may appear harder than the 0–1 version because, in being able to choose an object many times over, we have more choice. However, this freedom from keeping track of what has already been used simplifies the problem by reducing the amount of information we have to store. All we need is a one-dimensional array, profit, which stores the maximum profit found so far for each weight value up to the constraint.

We start by initialising the profit array to 0 for each weight up to the maximum constraint. Then, we work through the array position by position. For each starting weight we consider each item in turn and, when one fits in the remaining space, we calculate the combined profit (its own plus the current position's) that its choice would give us. Bearing in mind that using this item will increase the total weight used so far (again, its own plus the current position's), if the combined profit is an improvement for the combined weight, the array is updated.

To see how this works we will work through the above data set. First, we initialise.

Weight	0	1	2	3	4	5	6
	0	0	0	0	0	0	0

Then, we start at a weight of 0 (and a present profit of 0), and see the effect of taking the items. For instance, item 2 weighs 4 and gives a profit of 6, so the profit for weight 4 (0 + 4) is increased to 6 (0 + 6). After considering all the items we have:

Weight	0	1	2	3	4	5	6
Choose from weight 0	0	0	1	4	6	7	0

Next, we start at a weight of 1. Choosing item 5 at a weight of 5 and a profit of 7, giving a profit for weight 6 (1 + 5) of 7 (0 + 7) is the only change.

Weight	0	1	2	3	4	5	6
Choose from weight 1	0	0	1	4	6	7	7

When we start at a weight of 2, there are no changes. This leaves us with:

Weight	0	1	2	3	4	5	6
Choose from weight 2	0	0	1	4	6	7	7

Our last effective starting point is at a weight of 3. Choosing item 3 with a weight of 3 an a profit of 4, gives a profit for weight 6 (3 + 3) of 8 (4 + 4) is the only change.

Weight	0	1	2	3	4	5	6
Choose from weight 3	0	0	1	4	6	7	8

Starting beyond 3 gives no further changes.

Using the same variable names as in the text, the algorithm can be coded as:

In C:

```
/* Initialise profits array*/
for (i=0; i<=c; i++)
{
   profit[i]= 0;
}

/* Complete profits array */
for (i=0; i<=c; i++)
{
   /* starting at i */
   for (j=1; j<=n; j++)
   {
      /* consider item j if it fits */
      if (i+w[j] <= c)
      {
         /* choose j if it improves things */
         if (p[j]+profit[i] > profit[i+w[j]])
         {
             profit[i+w[j]] = p[j] + profit[i];
         }
      }
   }
}
```

In Ada:

```
-- Initialise profits array
for i in 0..c loop
  profit(i) := 0;
end loop;
```

```
-- Complete profits array
for i in 0..c loop
  -- starting at i
  for j in 1..n loop
    -- consider item j if it fits
    if i+w(j) <= c
      then
        -- choose j if it improves things
        if p(j)+profit(i) > profit(i+w(j))
          then
            profit(i+w(j)) := p(j) + profit(i);
        end if;
    end if;
  end loop;
end loop;
```

Exercises 12.3

1. The shortest paths are given by:

(i)

	A	B	C	D
A	0	3	2	4
B	3	0	4	1
C	2	4	0	5
D	4	1	5	0

(ii)

	A	B	C	D	E	F	G
A	0	2	3	5	1	3	4
B	2	0	1	3	3	5	2
C	3	1	0	2	4	6	1
D	5	3	2	0	6	8	3
E	1	3	4	6	0	2	5
F	3	5	6	8	2	0	7
G	4	2	1	3	5	7	0

BIBLIOGRAPHY

Aho, A.V., Hopcraft, J.E. and Ullman, J.D., *Data Structures and Algorithms*, Addison-Wesley, 1983.

Brassard, G., and Bratley, P., *Fundamentals of Algorithmics*, Prentice-Hall, 1996.

Dromey, R. G., *How To Solve It by Computer*, Prentice-Hall, 1982.

Gries, D., *The Science of Programming*, Springer-Verlag, 1981.

Harel, D., *Algorithmics: The Spirit of Computing*, Addison-Wesley, 1992.

Polya, G., *How To Solve It: A new aspect of mathematical method*, Princeton University Press, 1945.

Sedgewick, R., *Algorithms*, Addison-Wesley, 1988.

Sedgewick, R., *Algorithms in C*, Addison-Wesley, 1990.

Standish, T.A., *Data Structures, Algorithms and Software Principles in C*, Addison-Wesley, 1995.

Weiss, M.A., *Data Structures and Algorithm Analysis in Ada*, Benjamin/Cummings, 1993.

INDEX

SOUTH DEVON COLLEGE
LIBRARY